Education, Research, and Practice in Lesbian, Gay, Bisexual, and Transgendered Psychology

PSYCHOLOGICAL PERSPECTIVES ON LESBIAN AND GAY ISSUES

editors

Beverly Greene
Gregory M. Herek

- ◆ 1. Lesbian and Gay Psychology:
  Theory, Research, and Clinical Applications
  Edited by Beverly Greene and Gregory M. Herek

- ◆ 2. AIDS, Identity, and Community:
  The HIV Epidemic and Lesbians and Gay Men
  Edited by Gregory M. Herek and Beverly Greene

- ◆ 3. Ethnic and Cultural Diversity Among
  Lesbians and Gay Men
  Edited by Beverly Greene

- ◆ 4. Stigma and Sexual Orientation: Understanding Prejudice
  Against Lesbians, Gay Men, and Bisexuals
  Edited by Gregory M. Herek

- ◆ 5. Education, Research, and Practice in Lesbian, Gay, Bisexual,
  and Transgendered Psychology: A Resource Manual
  Edited by Beverly Greene and Gladys L. Croom

Education, Research, and Practice in Lesbian, Gay, Bisexual, and Transgendered Psychology

A Resource Manual

editors

Beverly Greene
Gladys L. Croom

Psychological Perspectives on Lesbian and Gay Issues

Volume 5

*Sponsored by the Society for the Psychological Study
of Lesbian and Gay Issues, Division 44 of the
American Psychological Association*

Sage Publications, Inc.
International Educational and Professional Publisher
Thousand Oaks ▪ London ▪ New Delhi

For information:

Sage Publications, Inc.
2455 Teller Road
Thousand Oaks, California 91320
E-mail: order@sagepub.com

Sage Publications Ltd.
6 Bonhill Street
London EC2A 4PU
United Kingdom

Sage Publications India Pvt. Ltd.
M-32 Market
Greater Kailash I
New Delhi 110 048 India

Printed in the United States of America

Library of Congress Cataloging-in-Publication Data
Main entry under title:

Education, research, and practice in lesbian, gay, bisexual, and transgendered psychology: A resource manual/ edited by Beverly Greene and Gladys L. Croom.
     p. cm. —(Psychological perspectives on lesbian and gay issues; v. 5)
     Includes bibliographical references.
     ISBN 0-8039-5382-8 (cloth: acid-free paper)
     ISBN 0-8039-5383-6 (pbk.: acid-free paper)
     1. Gays—Psychology—Study and teaching.
     2. Gays—Psychology—Research. 3. Gays—Mental health services.
     4. Bisexuals—Pyschology—Study and teaching.
     5. Bisexuals—Psychology—Research. 6. Bisexuals—Mental health services. 7. Transexuals—Psychology—Study and teaching.
     8. Transexuals—Psychology—Research. 9. Transexuals—Mental health services. I. Greene, Beverly. II. Croom, Gladys L. III. Series.
     HQ76.25.E38 1999
     305.9′066—dc21   99-6531
     This book is printed on acid-free paper.

00   01   02   03   04   05   06   10   9   8   7   6   5   4   3   2

Acquiring Editor:	Jim Nageotte
Editorial Assistant:	Heidi Van Middlesworth
Production Editor:	Denise Santoyo
Editorial Assistant:	Karen Wiley
Typesetter:	Rose Tylak
Indexer:	Teri Greenberg

Royce W. Scrivner
1939-1997

This volume is dedicated to the memory of Roy Scrivner, a pioneer in lesbian and gay psychology. Roy was a psychologist with a national reputation for advocacy, scholarly work in lesbian and gay psychology, pioneering contributions to lesbian and gay family psychology, and leadership in major psychology organizations. His contributions have had a significant impact on lesbian and gay psychology.

Roy received his doctorate in counseling psychology from the University of Texas at Austin in 1974. He went to work at the Dallas Administration Medical Center in 1975 and was in private practice in Dallas since 1980.

Professionally, Roy founded the APA Division of Family Psychology's Committee on Lesbian and Gay Family Issues and served as chair of that committee for several terms. He was also active in many other forums of professional psychology, including service to Division 44. In 1997, Roy received the Carolyn Attneave Award from the Family Psychology Division for his outstanding contributions to diversity issues in family psychology. He was president of the Texas Psychological Association in 1992 and was quite possibly the first openly gay president of a state psychological association in the United States. Roy established the Texas Psychological Foundation's Lesbian and Gay Research Award in 1986 and was the recipient of the 1987 Distinguished Psychologist Award given by the Dallas Psychological Association. In 1992, Roy was instrumental in writing the brief filed by the Texas Psychological Association, supporting the repeal of the law prohibiting same-sex sexual relations. Roy's writings, his amicus briefs, and his testimony as an expert witness represent other significant contributions to the discipline and to the betterment of the lives of lesbians and gay men. Those who knew him regard his passing as the loss of a warm, sensitive, and supportive friend. This volume is dedicated to him in remembrance of his life and work. He will be greatly missed.

Contents

Preface | ix

1. Beyond Heterosexism and Across the
   Cultural Divide: Developing an Inclusive
   Lesbian, Gay, and Bisexual Psychology:
   A Look to the Future | 1

   BEVERLY GREENE

2. Teaching Lesbian, Gay, and
   Bisexual Psychology: Contemporary Strategies | 46

   CHRISTINE BROWNING
   CRAIG KAIN

3. Including Sexual Orientation in
   Life Span Developmental Psychology | 59

   DOUGLAS C. KIMMEL

4. Confronting Heterosexism in
   the Teaching of Psychology | 74

   JANE M. SIMONI

5. Lesbian, Gay, and Bisexual Lives:
   Basic Issues in Psychotherapy Training and Practice | 91

   KRISTIN A. HANCOCK

6. Including Transgender Issues in Lesbian, Gay,
   and Bisexual Psychology: Implications
   for Clinical Practice and Training | 131

   KATHY A. GAINOR

7. Bisexuality in Perspective:
   A Review of Theory and Research | 161

   RONALD C. FOX

8. Lesbians, Gays, and Family Psychology:
   Resources for Teaching and Practice | 207

   ROBERT-JAY GREEN

9. Lesbian, Gay, and Bisexual Adolescent Development:
   Dancing With Your Feet Tied Together | 226

   JOYCE HUNTER
   GERALD P. MALLON

10. Therapeutic Responses to Sexual Orientation:
    Psychology's Evolution | 244

    DOUGLAS C. HALDEMAN

11. Lesbian, Gay, and Bisexual People of Color:
    A Challenge to Representative Sampling
    in Empirical Research | 263

    GLADYS L. CROOM

12. The Lesbian and Gay Workplace:
    An Employee's Guide to Advancing Equity | 282

    SUSAN GORE

    Appendix I: American Psychological Association
    Policy Statements on Lesbian, Gay, and
    Bisexual Concerns | 303

    Appendix II: Lesbian, Gay, and Bisexual Concerns
    at the American Psychological Association | 315

    CLINTON W. ANDERSON

    Index | 319

    About the Editors | 338

    About the Contributors | 340

Preface

This volume is the fifth in the annual series, Psychological Perspectives on Lesbian, Gay, and Bisexual Issues, sponsored by the Society for the Psychological Study of Lesbian, Gay, and Bisexual Issues (Division 44 of APA). This volume is devoted to providing a basic collection of resources for educators, practitioners, and researchers in Lesbian, Gay, Bisexual, and Transgendered (LGBT) Psychology.

Academic psychologists have been challenged to make psychology curriculums more inclusive. This often involves revising course material and content such that the full spectrum of sexual orientation identity, development, and life dilemmas are represented in undergraduate and graduate courses. Similarly, individuals responsible for training in other mental health disciplines, mental health agencies, and other venues that deliver psychological services to LGBT individuals have been appropriately challenged to make training competent practitioners a priority. Many practitioners who have had no training in LGBT psychology find themselves confronted with clients they feel ill-equipped to address. They often have the desire to develop clinical competencies in this area but may be at a loss to determine how to do so or where to begin. This volume is intended to serve as a basic resource with information on salient LGBT issues and to provide the reader with a range of references and other resources to explore each topic in greater depth.

In Chapter 1, I provide an overview of the conflated aspects of heterosexism and other forms of social oppression and their effects on diverse, and often invisible populations of LGB men and women. This discussion emphasizes the challenge that future LGBT psychology faces in exploring the complex and varied meanings of sexual orientation across the parameters of ethnicity, socioeconomic class, gender, age, and patterned discrimination. In Chapter 2, Christine Browning and Craig Kain provide an excellent overview of the issues that should be considered when developing or teaching an LGB psychology course as well as a wealth of print and media resources, teaching exercises and strategies. While the LGB psychology course is an important component of a curriculum, it is equally important to integrate LGB issues into the spectrum of all psychology courses. Douglas Kimmel discusses in Chapter 3 the ethnocentric and heterocentric focus of developmental psychology courses taught in American universities as reflections of mainstream North American values. His chapter provides insights, questions, and guidelines for teaching life span developmental psychology in ways that reflect the realistic spectrum of sexual orientation. In Chapter 4, Jane Simoni examines heterosexist bias in psychology as it is reflected in psychology textbooks. She presents the results of a survey of current psychology textbooks and evaluates the level of adequacy of coverage of LGB issues. Her chapter also considers the degree to which relevant material is integrated into the topic or treated in a segregated fashion. Her findings describe varied forms of heterosexist content found in the texts surveyed. She also provides suggestions for psychology instructors for avoiding heterosexist bias in their teaching.

Psychologists and other mental health professionals who deliver psychological services to LGB men and women, as well as those who train clinicians will find Chapters 5 through 9 of particular interest. Kristin Hancock's Chapter 5 is a concise but rich review of the breadth of basic issues that should be considered in psychotherapy with LGB men and women. This chapter will be particularly helpful to clinicians who are unfamiliar with affirmative approaches to the treatment of LGB clients. Kathy Gainor's Chapter 6 focuses on descriptions of transgender issues in training and practice in the context of gender construction in Western society. She reviews definitions of transgenderism and its variations, common dilemmas faced by transgendered individuals, and considerations in psychotherapy with the diverse members of this group. Similarly, Ron Fox, in Chapter 7, discusses the development of more recent affirmative approaches to conceptualizing bisexual sexual orientation as a distinct rather than transitional sexual orientation.

In Chapter 8, Robert-Jay Green provides the reader with resources for working with lesbians and gay men in couples and families. His discussion includes treatment planning guidelines for practitioners as well as materials to create training modules for clinical supervision and teaching LGB family therapy courses and workshops. Lesbian and gay youth represent another group of LGB persons who are confronted with unique challenges and unique clinical needs. In Chapter 9, Joyce Hunter and Gerald Mallon view coming out and adolescent development as parallel processes and discuss developmental issues confronting LGB youth. They include case examples from their clinical work with LGB youth, most of whom are also members of ethnic minority groups.

Psychology has come a long way since pathology models dominated the landscape of organized psychology and clinical practice. Conversion therapy, aimed at changing lesbian and gay sexual orientation to heterosexual orientation was once deemed the most appropriate choice of therapy for lesbians and gay men. Douglas Haldeman, in Chapter 10, chronicles organized mental health's passage from conversion models to affirmative approaches. His discussion is specifically helpful to clinicians who are treating LGB people who express the desire to change their sexual orientation or are otherwise distressed and troubled by it.

The under representation of diverse groups of LGB individuals in empirical research has been a continuing problem in LGB psychology. Gladys Croom, in Chapter 11, reviews many of the challenges to conducting empirical research with adequate representation of LGB men and women of color. She discusses the implications of those omissions on research and on practice, to the extent that our research efforts inform practice, and offers strategies aimed at increasing the representation of these groups in research samples.

The heightened visibility of LGB people in the American mainstream has prompted changes in the workplace. Susan Gore highlights strategies designed to promote workplace equity and presents the results of a survey on LGBT workplace issues in Chapter 12.

The American Psychological Association maintains the LGB Concerns Office as a part of its Public Interest Directorate. Clinton Anderson, LGB Concerns Officer, provides us with APA's policy statements on LGB issues as well as resources available through that office.

My term as coeditor of this series ends with this volume. I would like to express my appreciation to those who were instrumental in the completion of this volume as well as individuals who have supported my work in this series. Among them, special thanks to Dorith Brodbar of the New School for Social Research in New York City; my research assistant

Dawnette Jones; Linda Onorato and Joan Wirth of the Psychology Department of St. John's University. I thank the contributors to this volume for their rich contributions, and as always, Sage Publications. I am particularly grateful to Rev. David M. O'Connell, President of the Catholic University of America, and to Dr. Jeffrey Fagen, Chair, Department of Psychology, of St. John's University for their ongoing and generous support of my research in ways that made my participation in this series possible. Finally, I thank my coeditor Gladys Croom for her enthusiastic and timely support as well as her distinct and substantive contributions to the shape and content of this volume.

—BEVERLY GREENE

1

Beyond Heterosexism and Across the Cultural Divide

Developing an Inclusive Lesbian, Gay, and
Bisexual Psychology: A Look to the Future

BEVERLY GREENE

Lesbian, gay, and bisexual (LGB) psychology has come a long way since Evelyn Hooker's (1957) pioneering research contradicting the pathology models of homosexuality in mental health. We have witnessed the development of national organizations devoted to the advocacy of fair treatment for LGB people and the development of areas of study within virtually every academic discipline. In psychology, efforts are dedicated toward developing greater scientific and clinical understanding of the lives of lesbians and gay men and the broader meanings of sexual orientation. We have also witnessed more recently, the appropriate inclusion of bisexual men and women in the scope of this field of study and in the focus of our concerns for social justice. There has been a veritable explosion of psychological literature that not only explores nontraditional sexual orientations but does so from affirmative perspectives. Despite tenacious, ongoing resistance, this

AUTHOR'S NOTE: This chapter was presented as a Division 44 Golden Anniversary of Divisions Invited Address at the 105th Annual Meeting of the American Psychological Association, Chicago, 1997. It is an abridged version of Greene, B., *Beyond Heterosexism and Across the Cultural Divide: Analyzing Societal Privilege and Disadvantage in Psychotherapy*, unpublished manuscript.

collective work has been instrumental in making public policy changes. These changes in public policy have affected long-standing practices that have previously affected the lives of lesbians, gay men, and bisexual men and women in ways that were, and often continue to be, unequivocally damaging.

This is a far cry from the period when conversion therapy represented the normative and neither the exceptional nor controversial view of how nontraditional sexual orientations should be responded to by mental health professionals. Douglas Haldeman chronicles this long struggle in Chapter 10 in this volume. Despite many significant advances in this discipline in the past several decades, the next century confronts us with many new challenges in the need to explore the more complex nuances and varied meanings of sexual orientation as well as the many ways it is interrelated to other aspects of human identity. It is also necessary to conduct similar explorations of heterosexism and its connection to other forms of social oppression.

Conflated Aspects of Heterosexism

Heterosexism is not a singular or isolated experience or event. As such, heterosexism cannot be disconnected from the broader context of an individual's development or existence any more than sexism, for example, can be understood apart from the context of a woman's ethnicity, socioeconomic class, religion, or other significant aspects of her life. I explore a range of aspects of the lives of lesbians and gay men that are conflated by the presence of other identities that transform the experience of heterosexism. The consequence of the invisibility of these individuals in the education and training of clinicians and researchers in mental health are explored as well as the differentials of privilege and disadvantage that give particular meaning to human differences in the United States.

An exclusive focus on heterosexism as the primary locus of oppression for all lesbians and gay men presumes that it is experienced in the same way for all group members and that it has the same meaning and consequences for them. The core of this assumption is common in the psychological literature as well as in practice. In American psychology, human identity is often understood as something that consists of parts that are completely separate from one another. Identity is rarely viewed as an integrated whole in which one component can only be understood in relation to and in the context of others. It is assumed that if you split up the parts of an entity and study those parts in isolation you will arrive at a more accurate or, at least, neater description of the reality. Although such practices make it easier to operationalize the study of complex human behaviors, the results of this practice do not necessarily yield a more accurate understanding of behavior or identity. Essed (1996) argues that many varied actual and potential identities come together in every individual and that those multiple identities allow us to be flexible in our dealings with different people and in different situations. Social domination, however, requires that we take physical and psychological characteristics of people, that in reality exist on a continuum, and treat them as if they are dichotomous. Wachtel (1996) explains this as a mechanism needed to create a category of people who are "not me" or "other" and into whom we can project our own unwanted psychic content, behavior, desires, impulses, and feelings. Siegel (1995) observes that fear is an essential ingredient in the maintenance of the distortion and projection described by Wachtel (1996). In Siegel's (1995) analysis,

> Fear is the glue that maintains existing biases . . . When people are categorized as *we* or *they,* fear becomes part of the process of projecting onto those whom we see as unlike ourselves all of the attributes that we would like to deny in ourselves. *We* are the good self. *They* are the bad self. All players must be maintained in that position and must deny that this is going on. Socially unacceptable traits can thus remain invisible to the self while we stereotype those whom *we* call *they* or *other* and imbue *them* with negative traits. (p. 297)

The unwanted psychic content, feelings, and behaviors that are projected onto members of societally disadvantaged groups are in fact common to all human beings. Despite the common pool of human emotion and desire that by definition all human beings share, when the projection process that Wachtel (1996) and Siegel (1995) describe takes place, the exploitation or exclusion of members of disparaged groups from mainstream life is often perceived as if it is not only justified but may even be seen as mandatory. The latter may often be deemed necessary either to protect members of disparaged groups from themselves or to protect "superior" (privileged) group members from them.

An example of the exclusions previously mentioned are found in feminist psychology. Despite worthy attempts to document gender subordination, feminist psychology has been appropriately assailed for its tendency, historically, to put forth an analysis of women's issues that has been created and articulated primarily by privileged, well-educated, predominantly heterosexual, white middle- and upper-class women. Those perspectives certainly are valid for those who articulate them, however, they cannot be automatically generalized to all women. Such an analysis fails to reflect the wide range of diversity among women. In doing so, this analysis cannot seriously consider the interlocking and complex nature of racial, class, heterosexist, and gender oppression for women of color, older women, lesbians, bisexual women, religious women, poor women, and women with disabilities (Hall & Greene, 1996). In attempts to address these inequities, studies about gender have been challenged to better discern how sexual orientation, ethnicity, other forms of social status, and discrimination transform the meaning or affects the salience of gender oppression for a wider range of women.

Just as feminist psychology has not represented the diverse range of women's concerns, lesbian, gay, and bisexual psychology has often failed to reflect the full spectrum of diversity among lesbians and gay men in an integrated fashion. Doing this leaves us with an incomplete view of the range of challenges that confront this group as whole. We are left without a solid appreciation for how other salient identities transform or color the meaning and experience of heterosexism, or of what it means to be a lesbian, gay man, or bisexual man or woman in a wider range of contexts. Without some discussion of social and cultural context, we are left with a limited view of what is involved in sexual orientation identity development or even whether or not in certain cultures or contexts there is an equivalent to the traditional Western concept. Another consequence of such omissions is that when doing clinical work with diverse populations of lesbians and gay men, practitioners are left ill-equipped to address their clinical needs in ways that are culturally literate and competent.

Psychological Resilience and Vulnerability in Socially Disadvantaged Groups

Just as we have witnessed a significant growth in the psychological literature exploring LGB sexual orientations from affirmative perspectives, there has been a parallel increase in the study of the role of gender, age, socioeconomic class, ethnicity, and membership in other societally disadvantaged groups from affirmative perspectives as well. These perspectives also examine the effects of membership in these groups on the psychological development and coping mechanisms of their members, on the development of psychological theories and paradigms explaining and interpreting human behavior, and on the application of those theoretical paradigms in the practice of psychotherapy and psychological assessment.

Discussion of the relevant effects of membership in institutionally disadvantaged and marginalized groups on the development of what historically has been deemed individual psychopathology and vulnerability have gained increasing prominence. More recently, those discussions have begun to acknowledge that just as social adversity contributes to psychological vulnerability, it can also facilitate the development of psychological resilience and exceptional coping strategies as well, albeit never without a price.

Despite overwhelming social adversity and ill treatment that make them psychologically more vulnerable than heterosexual men and women, lesbians and gay men as a group are not the harbingers of psychopathology that American mental health has historically depicted them to be. Given that they must routinely negotiate a hostile social climate, we might expect to see greater ranges of pathology among lesbians and gay men than their heterosexual counterparts. One might expect similar findings in other groups of disadvantaged people, where they are similarly absent. I suggest that this is no accident. Rather, it is a reflection of a special kind of resilience that may be found among many members of marginalized groups.

Jones (1997) explores the concept of resilience in his review of David Hadju's (1996) biography of the late musical impresario Billy Strayhorn. For more than 30 years Strayhorn was a key collaborator in the work of famed composer Duke Ellington and a major contributor to American jazz music in his own right. His arrangements and compositions bear the indisputable mark of musical genius that was evident early on in what some might consider a potentially difficult and troubled life. Jones (1997), in considering the elements of resilience in Strayhorn's life, observes that "resilience is elusive, difficult to predict and foster . . . it is a complex interaction of individual, constitutional, personality, developmental, and situational variables that like the images one views through a kaleidoscope, contains intricate individual constellations and subtle colorings that change with every shift in ones viewpoint" (p. 10).

Jones (1997) attempts to grapple with the ostensible paradox of musician Strayhorn's phenomenal musical talent, creativity, and a prevalence of satisfying adult relationships and admirers, in the context of his identity as an African American gay man who was relatively open about being gay in the social context of the 1940s. Hadju (1996) observes that Strayhorn's relative openness about his sexual orientation was considered extremely rare and potentially dangerous in a social context that was far more overtly and viciously racist and heterosexist than today's climate. In addition to a disadvantageous social climate, Strayhorn had troubled personal beginnings that left him vulnerable to severe psychological difficulties, some of which he did not successfully overcome.

Born physically frail, a victim of rickets early in life, Billy Strayhorn was often the object of his father's abuse and torment. James Strayhorn experienced persistent difficulty finding and keeping jobs, in part due to the racism that diminished opportunities for black men of that era, and in part due to his own progressive alcoholism. Billy was not legally named until he was nearly 5 years old. Jones (1997) attributed this lapse to both the family's disorganization and to Strayhorn's mother's desire to keep Billy her "baby" for as long as possible, perhaps owing to the death of two children before Billy to childhood illnesses. Prone to depression as an adult, Strayhorn died in 1967 when he was just 51 years old. Although esophageal cancer was the official cause of his death, his chronic alcohol consumption and constant cigarette smoking played a significant role in his premature demise.

For all practical purposes Strayhorn faced the challenge of serious family dysfunction and double layers of societal discrimination from his life's earliest days. He was also described as someone who would not have been conventionally regarded as a popular child. Nonetheless he managed to create and surround himself with what Jones (1997) describes as loyal friends with shared interests, a broader community who saw him as their child prodigy and who ignored differences between Billy and the other children who were his peers, and, as an adult, insulated communities of some of the most talented artists of that period in our history. The precise nature and scope of his family history, his relationship to many communities, and the complexity of his ties to them are beyond the scope of this chapter. The reader is referred to Hadju's (1996) book for a more comprehensive analysis of them. This discussion focuses on the nature of certain components of his life that allowed him, as an African American gay man with troubled personal beginnings, to fortuitously fashion a future from a life that was at risk from its inception. It speaks to the importance of considering the complex nature of understanding someone who has multiple identities, some of which are privileged and others which are disadvantaged. This understanding also involves integrating the personal familial history and the history of other relationships that develop in the aforementioned context.

Jones (1997) describes a phenomenon that seems most prevalent when individuals like Strayhorn, who have societal and personal challenges (and in his case the resource of his talent) maintain a sense of psychological integrity. He describes it as the ability to maintain a kind of psychological independence in which challenged individuals appear to be able to "mentally remove themselves from destructive people and situations" (p. 10). A severe form of this removal is characterized by the defensive operation of dissociation which can be used adaptively to escape the acute phases of a seriously traumatic event. However, another form of psychological independence can also be characterized by an attitude that allows a person to structure their life so as to "ward off the malevolently controlling intentions of others" (Jones, 1997, p. 10). Jones (1997) tells us that this form of psychological independence is nurtured in resilient individuals by loving and effective caregivers. Such caregivers need not be parents or biological relations. However, they are people whose entrance at critical developmental junctures in the course of the resilient individual's life has powerful remedial effects when they occur. In addition to nurturing individuals present at critical junctures, there is also a fortuitous presence of societal opportunities that the individual may use to further develop and strengthen a sense of personal adequacy and effectiveness. The presence and timing of these societal opportunities are often outside of the individual's control. Resilience is further enhanced by another element in a blend of personality traits which Jones (1997) sees as characteristic of resilient people, their capacity to evoke affirming reactions from others. In this context, whenever resilient individuals get an affirming response from someone, it reinforces their preexisting appealing personality style and strengthens their capacity for "independent self-construction" (Jones, 1997, p. 10).

Jones uses this paradigm to explain the resilience of African Americans in ways that are applicable to the lives of lesbians, gay men, other people of color, poor people, people who are physically challenged, and other societally disadvantaged individuals. He observes that a detached, independent, construction of a serviceable reality characterizes the resilience of members of abused groups. For example, because of American racial apartheid, African Americans were forced to live and often work in worlds that were wholly separate from white Americans, and were legally denied many opportunities that were built into the structure of American society. Hence, they were denied advantages and opportunities that were routinely given only to white Americans. While living in segregated worlds blocked many opportunities for upward mobility in the mainstream of America, this resulting "structural isolation" (Jones, 1979, in Jones, 1997, p. 10) fostered the development of distinctive communities in these segregated black communities. A similar kind of structural isolation defined the distinct, often invisible secret subcultures of lesbian and gay communities. Structurally, they bear a striking similarity to the segregated communities inhabited by many other people of color, people with physical challenges as well as other groups rejected by the mainstream.

Despite some of the inequities of segregated communities, they often permit the development of alternative self-images that evolve and even challenge the negative stereotypes and images of victims of discrimination (e.g., African Americans, lesbians, and gay men). Negative stereotypes of members of disparaged groups often represent fictional creations or exaggerations the dominant culture designed to justify the exploitation, exclusion, and oppression of members of disadvantaged groups. Jones (1997) points out that in these segregated communities, African Americans, for example, were socialized to mentally challenge white versions of truth, particularly when those versions of the truth applied to them. This heightened level of suspiciousness observed in African Americans in their encounters with white Americans has served as an effective coping strategy in their adaptive need to be vigilant about the realistic and often likely potential for exploitation, insult, or injury in such encounters. For African Americans this was and continues to be an adaptive mechanism as they cannot conceal their ethnicity and have little choice about being required to negotiate whatever responses they elicit in members of the dominant culture. An important component in the mental health of individuals from societally disadvantaged groups is their ability to rely on their own experiences of themselves and others like them to create self-generated definitions of both themselves, their origins, and to explain their current circumstances. Passively accepting the labels of those who have an obvious stake in defining them by their worst exceptions and believing the worst of them is not a given for members of disadvantaged groups, despite the fact that some group members may do so (internalized racism, homophobia, etc.). The process of independent self-construction allows healthy individuals to materialize the invisible presence of social privilege and correctly understand that their subordinate social position is not the simple result of cultural deficiency, poor or inadequate values, individual or group defect, or mother nature, as they have been told. Rather, social privilege can be recognized as a function of interlocking social systems of selective discrimination and selective patterned advantage that has been deliberately designed to maintain the balance of social power. That balance is reflected in and maintained by the privileging of certain characteristics or identities and the devaluing of others and the different opportunities and rights accorded or denied to individuals on the basis of those identities.

The legacies of discrimination for African Americans and for lesbians and gay men are not exactly the same, neither in their origins, in the comparison of visible and invisible stigmas, nor in many other ways. Despite this, individuals who are members of either or both groups share the need to negotiate societal discrimination. An analysis of the successful methods that members of either group utilize to cope psychologically is illustrative of the concept of psychological independence and its role in maintaining psychological integrity when the environment is ubiquitously hostile. Furthermore, the successful coping strategies employed by one group in negotiating discrimination may be applicable to the dilemmas other groups face. It may also be useful in therapies with individuals who belong to more than one disparaged group. Their development of successful strategies in negotiating one devalued identity may be an important source of resilience in the negotiation of other devalued identities. Overall, the inclusion of these issues, individuals with multiple identities who face societal disadvantage and their study is relevant to a more comprehensive understanding of the effects of societal discrimination on its victims.

Jones (1997) argues articulately that people who move within carefully constructed, at times segregated communities, that facilitate the development of self-constructed psychological realities, can develop a high level of resilience. Pinderhughes (1989) observes that individuals who belong to groups associated with power and privilege may be so used to negotiating reality from a position of power that they are ill-prepared to cope with adversity or situations where they are not powerful. Resilience in disadvantaged individuals can enable them to transform adverse circumstances and even thrive despite them. However, Jones (1997) warns that people who are forced to endure "patterned injustice . . . unwarranted and protracted personal hardship . . . and ongoing oppression" (p. 13), as members of ethnic and sexual minorities and other victims of abuse are often required to do, are exposed to chronic stressors and challenges that are always a threat to their carefully constructed psychological equilibrium. Mental health theoreticians and practitioners must understand that tangible psychological and physical energies and efforts are required to maintain that equilibrium and that an emotional and sometimes physical price (expressed in health problems) is always paid for survival, even among those who thrive. It is therefore important to resist the temptation of using the existence of survivors as a means of either minimizing the negative effects of the oppressive circumstances they are forced to endure, to blame those who fail to endure them, or to suggest that the social system must be working fairly if some of the disadvantaged group's members manage to overcome the barriers and succeed. It is important to understand the nature of vulnerability and resilience in at-risk populations if we are to use the therapy process in optimal ways and if we are to appreciate the complexity of their development as well as the complexity of their current circumstances.

The degree to which racist, sexist, heterosexist, and other forms of biased thinking is embedded in theoretical paradigms and research in mental health, and their subsequent effects on training and practice has become an appropriate focus of attention in the psychological literature. In this context, relevant questions have been raised albeit separately, about the cumulative effects of negative stereotypes about members of distinct oppressed groups and about lesbians and gay men on the thinking of practitioners, research scientists, and theoreticians. The subsequent role of such thinking in perpetuating rather than exposing those negative stereotypes for the distortions that they really represent has also gained greater prominence. Rarely however, do these inquiries analyze the complexity of these issues when a person is a member of more than one of these groups. In this context the process of psychological assessment and treatment must begin to explicitly incorporate an understanding of the interactive effects of these combined phenomena and their effects on research and the delivery of psychological services.

Lesbians and gay men of color, members of white ethnic groups, people with disabilities, who reside in rural parts of the United States or for that matter outside the country altogether, who are poor or homeless, who are old, transgendered or transsexual individuals (see Gainor, Chapter 6 in this volume), and many other lesbians and gay men who are members of more than one group, do not generally see themselves fully integrated in the face of American psychology. Moreover, they do not see themselves integrated in the face of American lesbian and gay psychology either. Failing to understand the more complex nature of the life experiences of such individuals not only limits our understanding of sexual orientation, but limits our understanding of other aspects of human identity as well as the phenomenon of heterosexism. Heterosexism, classism, racism, sexism, and other forms of oppression are embedded in the theories of psychology as an academic discipline and are reflected in practice. This systematic oppression is also reflected in the silent agreement to ignore the blatant omission of many diverse groups in the content of our discourse (Wachtel, 1996).

Gender, Sexism, and Heterosexism: Making the Connection

In *Engendered Lives,* Ellyn Kaschak (1992) writes that the consensual reality of Western culture holds that gender is a given, contained in or identical with the sex of the newborn and that gender and gender-linked attributes are viewed as natural rather than as socially and psychologically constructed. She observes that it is paradoxical that all children must be taught that which is supposed to be natural, and those who do not learn their lessons well are viewed as unnatural (p. 39).

Kaschak's analysis draws our attention to an important but frequently overlooked question. If specific gendered behaviors are natural outgrowths of biological sex and if heterosexual sexual orientation is natural for everyone, why would it be necessary to so assiduously teach that which is supposed to be innate and natural? Furthermore, why would some behavior that is deemed unnatural require such strong prohibitions and stigmatizing to prevent its occurrence? It would seem that natural behavior would just naturally evolve. It is precisely because traditional gender roles, which include heterosexual sexual orientation as the normative sexual orientation, are not ubiquitously natural or normative that they do not naturally evolve in everyone. A natural evolution is not allowed to take place. Gender roles are culturally embedded. As such, a culture's gender roles are socially constructed, assigned, agreed on, and changed over time. It is precisely because of these factors that such roles require enforcing rather than simply allowing them to naturally evolve. In fact, lesbian and gay sexual orientations evolve in individuals in spite of explicit prohibitions, opposition, and punitive responses to them.

Kaschak (1992) observes that it is particularly shameful for people who do not fit neatly into a gender category. This is reflected in the shame and embarrassment that people feel when their gender is mistaken or cannot be quickly discerned. It is as if they have done something wrong, are "queer" or peculiar, or as if something is seriously wrong with them. She adds that when methods of enforcing traditional gender roles and categories fail, or as a result of the damage caused by them, the person in question may be deemed ill and in need of psychotherapy. This insistence on viewing gender as dichotomous and fixed and the sexist practices that tend to accompany such thinking are interrelated with heterosexism.

Heterosexist thinking leads to a range of inaccurate assumptions that are commonly held about gay men and lesbians. These beliefs are held by many people and are based on gendered ideas about what men and women are supposed to be, and on what constitutes normal behavior for them. One of the most commonly accepted of these false beliefs is that to be gay or lesbian is to want to be a member of the other sex (Bohan, 1996; Kite & Deaux, 1987), presumably the most damning evidence of one's defect. Men are expected to be sexually attracted to women only and women sexually attracted to men only. Sexual attraction to the other sex and satisfaction with one's biological sex is believed to be an explicit and essential component of being a normal man or woman. In that context, reproductive sexuality is presumed to be the only form that is psychologically healthy and morally correct. Another fallacious assumption that connects heterosexism and gender dichotomies is that there is a direct connection between sexual orientation and a person's conformity or failure to conform to traditional gender stereotypes of roles and physical appearance (Bohan, 1996; Kite & Deaux, 1987). The erroneous conclusion drawn from this assumption is that men and women who do not conform to traditional gender role stereotypes must be gay or lesbian (Ames, 1996; Bohan, 1996; Kirk & Madsen, 1996). Kirk and Madsen (1996) suggest that one of the seven myths that heterosexual Americans believe about LGB people is that all lesbians and gay men can be easily identified by their outward appearance, that they look like members of the other gender. An equally mistaken assumption is that individuals who conform to traditional gender stereotypes must be heterosexual. These assumptions suggest that to understand the meaning and the reality of being a lesbian or gay man requires a careful exploration and understanding of the importance of cultural gender roles, the nature of the culture's traditional gender role stereotypes, the relative fluidity or rigidity of those roles, their range, rewards for conformity, and punishments for failure to conform (Greene, 1996, 1997).

At this juncture we are left with a series of questions. If we did not socially construct gender in dichotomous and fixed terms, if there were no assigned gender roles or gender attributes, would the concept of sexual orientation exist? If so, would it be relevant? If deemed relevant, what would it encompass and how would it be defined? Perhaps a more important question is whether or not anyone would care. The very existence of people with nontraditional sexual orientations challenges traditional assumptions about gender roles and in turn challenges the male privileges that adherence to traditional gender roles are used to rationalize and perpetuate (Ames, 1996).

Omissions of Diversity in Lesbian and Gay Psychology

Age

There are many lesbians and gay men who are not reflected in contemporary and media images of lesbian and gay communities. In a youth-oriented culture, the lives of older lesbians and gay men do not come under great scrutiny; their underrepresentation in the psychological literature is another indicator of their invisibility. When older people are the focus of such inquiries, the inquiries are usually about the negative aspects of age, such as dependency, decline, deterioration, and disability (Hall & Greene, 1996; Schaie, 1993). Older people are perceived as if they are always in need of care, rather than as the important caregivers that they often are in many cultures (Schaie, 1993). Gatz and Cotten (1994) write that the aged should be included in discussions of nondominant, oppressed groups, as age represents one of the most basic cues by which people are assigned a particular status in the social hierarchy. Negative stereotyping based on age is used to discriminate against people in systematic ways (Gatz & Cotten, 1994). Unlike ethnicity and other variables, the aged represent a group with permeable group boundaries to which if we live long enough we will all eventually belong. Unlike people with disabilities, a group to which potentially any of us *could* belong, or specific ethnic groups to whom we cannot belong unless we are born into them, all human beings go from not belonging to this group to belonging to it (Gatz & Cotten, 1994). As the aged come from all social groups, the degree of their disadvantage due to ageism may vary across the group.

Aging has different meanings across ethnic groups and different implications for men versus women. Ehrenberg (1996) reports that older gay men may be more vulnerable to isolation than older lesbians. Owing to the longer life span of women, lesbians may be more likely to have surviving mates and peers and are less biased (than gay men) against older partners. Older gay men were observed to be more concerned about physical appearance than older lesbians, perhaps owing to the preference for younger partners among older gay men (Ehrenberg, 1996).

Within many subgroups of people of color, older family members are considered elders who are valued for their life's accumulated wisdom and are accorded respect. In some Asian and East Indian cultural groups, adult children are expected to consult and in some instances conform to the wishes of their parents regarding career choices, when and who to marry, and in ways that Western cultures generally do not formally expect. The status of elders in different cultures differs depending on gender as well. In Western or mainstream American cultures, older people are often viewed as if they are no longer as useful as younger people. This perception of older people is confounded if they are no longer producing capital.

Other questions for future research revolve around the invisibility of older lesbians and gay men in a culture where youth and youthful attractiveness are privileged. Older people, like people with disabilities, are frequently regarded as if they are asexual. There may be the assumption that older people do not miss or desire the presence of a romantic partner or companion, are not interested in a date, or do not care about being sexually active. Young, single lesbians and gay men may often find friends matchmaking for them. Older lesbians and gay men may not evoke the same assistance at a time when they may require more help making connections to people. Ehrenberg (1996) reports that finding a partner is an issue for both older lesbians and older gay men. The ab-

sexual relationships in a similar manner. It may be a mistake to presume that the desire for nonmonogamy in bisexual men and women is a direct function of their bisexuality. Clinically it is more appropriate to focus on their capacity to experience sexual attraction more broadly rather than on exaggerations or distortions of their actual sexual behavior. The same logic is not used to define heterosexual sexual orientations or behavior but it has been used to negatively depict lesbian and gay sexual orientations. Members of the latter groups are treated as if their lives are defined by distorted depictions of their sexual activity. Lesbians and gay men appropriately protest and reject these reductionistic and distorted characterizations when they are applied to them; however, they may have no problem in applying them to bisexual men and women. Fox provides a more comprehensive discussion of bisexuality in Chapter 7 of this volume. Ultimately, bisexuality represents an enduring pattern that constitutes a legitimate sexual orientation for many people (Rosenblum & Travis, 1996).

Class Privilege, Class Oppression, and Heterosexism

Rarely do we pose questions regarding the effect of socioeconomic class on the development of lesbian and gay identity. We know that class status and income affects variables like physical health, life span, quality of primary education and access to higher education, likelihood of arrest, likelihood of imprisonment if arrested, and the general quality of life of all people. Yet class is ignored in the equations that seek to examine the lives of lesbians and gay men despite the fact that income may have many direct effects on the circumstances that permit, facilitate, or prevent someone from being out. It can similarly affect their ability to purchase books, magazines, and other cultural commodities of lesbian and gay subcultures, as well as the kinds of venues that are available to them for meeting other lesbians and gay men. Fine and Asch (1988) write that class and race influence not only access to decent housing and schooling but access to cultural and recreational opportunities as well. In their work on disability and its effects on women, they observe that class may similarly alleviate or exacerbate the impact of a disability in ways that are not predictable. It would make sense that class status also affects developing identity. We know that gender and race are important variables affecting job status and income, hence, the realities and effects of class would be gender and ethnically coded for lesbians and gay men, as they are for their heterosexual counterparts. Wyche (1996) observes that despite what we know about the salience of class as an important factor in peoples lives, it is omitted in analyses of how it affects the treatment process as well as the class beliefs and behaviors of the therapist in that process.

American culture takes a dim view of poor people. Newitz and Wray (1997) write that Americans love to hate the poor and that to be labeled poor does not generally elicit sympathy. Instead, being poor may elicit hostility and disgust from others and trigger a sense of shame in one's self. Economic impoverishment is often associated with negative character traits such as having inadequate or the wrong values, ineptitude, laziness, or outright stupidity (Newitz & Wray, 1997; O'Hare, 1986). Poor people are also thought of as refusing to work, living in female-headed households, living in inner-city ghettos, and living off welfare (O'Hare, 1986). Even if it were not for these direct negative characterizations, our feeings about the poor are reflected in our definitions of lower- and middle-class values and behaviors, and of the word "class" itself. The *Merriam-Webster Collegiate Dictionary* (1996) defines "class" as high social rank, elegance, high quality, and a rating based on grade or quality. Wyche (1996) tells us that when we say that someone has "no class" we do not mean this literally. But what do we mean? We mean that they have lower- or working-class values and are behaving like poor or working-class people. The demeaning implication is that to have lower-class values is the same as having "no class" at all. Consistent with *Webster's* definition, being lower class is to lack elegance, to have no or low quality, or to be of low social rank. Middle-class values are generally deemed to include the presence of upwardly mobile aspirations, valuing an education, possessing the ability to delay gratification, and a willingness to save and work hard. By defining middle-class values in this manner, the implication is that people who are middle class acquired that status because they have the correct values and good moral character. This fails to address in any significant way, the critical role of class oppression reflected in differential access to opportunities, such as education, at one time, trade union membership, as well as many jobs or careers that were closed to out LGB people, individuals with disabilities, ethnic minority group members, women, and others. These forms of advancement serve as gateways to middle-class status. These gateways are not equally distributed nor are they distributed reliably on the basis of merit in this society. Poor people are blamed for their circumstances with the assumption that they did not work hard enough or take advantage of available opportunities and are exhorted to feel ashamed of themselves and their circumstances. The pervasive and incorrect assumption is that sufficient opportunities are equally available to everyone. Blaming the poor for their plight serves to further obscure the reality of class oppression in this society.

Rothenberg (1988) writes that she grew up with an obliviousness to her race but an acute awareness of her gender and her Jewish, upper middle-class standing. She recalls being aware that her family was much better off than most people and that she felt sorry for those who were not as well off. Still, she acknowledges believing with absolute certainty that poor people must deserve to be poor because they either failed "to work hard enough, study hard enough, or save enough" (Rothenberg, 1988, p. 38).

Hartigan (1997) asserts that there is an assumed equation between whiteness and economic social privilege that leaves Americans with blackness as the most prevalent image of and association to poverty. African Americans are disproportionately poorer than white Americans (Wyche, 1996), and it is commonly believed that most poor people are black and that most black people are poor (O'Hare, 1986). The invisibility of poverty among white Americans obscures the reality that the vast majority of America's poor are white. This leads to a range of other problematic assumptions. Poverty and many of the stigmata related to it are not merely associated with being African American, but some African Americans come to regard it as if economic hardship is a part of their ethnic identity. As a result, many people who are members of ethnic minority groups and who are middle class frequently experience having their struggles with racism, sexism, and homophobia minimized or negated. Members of these groups may be treated as if having middle- or upper-class status diminishes or negates their ethnic identity, minimizes their struggles with racism and other forms of oppression, and calls their ethnic loyalty into question (Ferguson & King, 1997). Ferguson and King (1997) observe a tendency, in some of their African American female clients, to resist shedding nonfunctional or derogatory identities that may lead to class transformation. There may be a fear that the "better life" will not only invalidate their continuing struggles in the eyes of other group members (as well as their own) but will negate valued aspects of their ethnic identity as well.

There is a perception among many people that most gays (Gates uses the term "gay" throughout his essay to refer to lesbians as well as gay men) are well educated, socially mobile, and financially comfortable if not well off (Gates, 1993). The assumption that most lesbians and gay men are white and that those who are people of color acquired their sexual orientation by assimilating into or identifying with the dominant culture has been observed among many people of color (Chan, 1992; Greene, 1994, 1997). These perceptions reflect both heterosexist and racist beliefs and connect them to one another.

Although many surveys suggest that gay respondents have higher than average educational and income levels, these surveys are rarely done outside major urban areas and may only reflect the responses of younger lesbians and gay men who not only self-identify as lesbian or gay, have the discretionary income to be present in social venues, colleges or universities, or other places where such questionnaires are distributed and are willing to take the time to respond to a questionnaire, but are also willing to identify themselves on a questionnaire itself. It is possible that many lesbians and gay men who are not well educated, who are older, and who are poor might be more secretive and perhaps less likely to be out. As such they might also be less likely to identify themselves, take part in, or even be approached about participating in research. Hence, they remain invisible to us (Bradford, Ryan, & Rothblum, 1994; Gonsiorek, 1991). Their invisibility shapes and perhaps even distorts what we presume to know about lesbians and gay men and socioeconomic class issues among this group. There is a connection between the need to racialize America's poor and the perception that most gays are affluent and well educated.

To discern the connection between the coloring of poverty and the notion that gays are affluent, we must first ask why there is a need to render America's white poor invisible. How does it affect the lives of lesbians and gay men, and how can it transform the varied meaning and experience of lesbian and gay identities? Gates (1993) offers that African Americans perceive most gays as affluent, white, and therefore endowed with greater class and skin color privilege than African Americans. This makes it difficult for many African Americans to see how lesbians and gay men are oppressed. It is as if the presence of class privilege eradicates the often severe consequences of heterosexism. Further, this attitude allows many heterosexual African Americans to minimize the dangerousness of hostile attitudes and physical attacks that are a result of pervasive heterosexism and homophobia, while denying the existence of their own heterosexual privilege. Such thinking contributes to preexisting resentful attitudes toward lesbians and gay men and prompts what Gates (1993) denotes a "blacklash" or a view that being lesbian or gay is a chosen identity and a mere inconvenience, whereas being black is to "inherit a legacy of hardship and inequity" (p. 42). African Americans and members of groups of other people of color often perceive a comparison between heterosexism and racism as oppressions, as one that trivializes their history of racial oppression. Gates (1993) warns however that the temptation to make these kinds of comparisons should be resisted because there are no simple comparisons.

Hartigan (1997) and Newitz and Wray (1997) write that poor whites in West Virginia and the Midwest are characterized as "hillbillies" and are stereotyped as "lazy, licentious, sexually promiscuous, prone to violent and indecorous behavior, alcoholic, and stupid." Different names are used to characterize "white trash" that vary depending on the region of the country, but the negative depictions are consistent. Similar characterizations and negative stereotypes are used in America's racist lexicon to define the traits of African Americans racially. These stereotypes of African Americans are used to draw clear distinctions between black and white behavior and potential in a racially polarized society and in a social hierarchy designed to justify white skin privilege. When these negative stereotypes, usually reserved for African Americans, are observed in white Americans, they "disrupt understandings of what it means to be white," and serve as "ruptures of conventions that maintain whiteness as a normative identity" (Hartigan, 1997, p. 46). Racial identity and class identity in this context become conflated and overlap rather than appearing clear and distinct (Hartigan, 1997, p. 47).

The conflation of race and class identity is an important phenomenon to understand when we attempt to discern the interlocking nature of societal oppressions that include heterosexism. Lesbian and gay sexual orientations challenge traditional definitions of gender, the presumed natural order of male superiority, the gender roles and hierarchies that are based on that presumption, as well as how normal sexual attraction is defined. In doing this, the rationale for male gender privileges based on the presumed natural origins of traditional gender roles is undermined. Similarly, the presence of poor whites who are characterized by all of the negative characteristics usually reserved for African Americans or other people of color blurs the boundaries of race-based human distinctions. Socially constructed distinctions and distortions based on race/ethnicity exist to create a rationale for white skin privilege that denies it as a structured advantage but, rather, frames it as deserved and fair. If poor white people are more visible their very existence contradicts and undermines rationales for white skin privilege based on contrived racial and racist distinctions.

In *Queer White Trash* (1997), Jillian Sandell examines the work of Dorothy Allison in an attempt to explore what she considers the difficulty that Americans in both the LGB as well as heterosexual communities have in discussing class privilege and class oppression. Sandell writes that it is easier among LGB people to focus discussions on sexuality and on heterosexism rather than social class and class oppression. She offers an analysis for Allison's embrace of the term "white trash" as an attempt to make class-based discrimination in the United States visible as well as to expose the structural rather than volitional sources of class oppression (Sandell, 1997, p. 215). Allison (1994) writes:

> I have known I was a lesbian since I was a teenager and have spent a good twenty years making peace with the effects of incest and physical abuse. . . . but what may be the central fact of my life is that I was born in 1949 in Greenville, SC, the bastard daughter of a white woman from a desperately poor family, just a month past 15 when she had me . . . that fact, the inescapable impact of being born in a condition of poverty that this society finds shameful, contemptible, and somehow deserved has had dominion over me to such an extent that I have spent my life trying to overcome or deny it. I have learned with great difficulty that the vast majority of people believe that poverty is a voluntary condition and that the poor are different, less than fully human, or at least less sensitive to hopelessness, despair and suffering. (pp. 14-15)

Allison, author of *Bastard Out of Carolina* (1992), observes that her status as a lesbian and her class status "fall outside of the normative moral orders of both the middle class and the queer community" (Sandell, 1997, p. 216). Like many individuals with multiple identities who experience multiple stigma, Allison (1994) observes that she selectively dropped different aspects of her identity in order to blend in with whatever community she was with at any given time. However, she recounts her sense of alienation as the price she pays for the need to compartmentalize any aspect her identity. Allison (1994) recollects,

My people . . . were the *they* everyone talks about, the ungrateful poor . . . By the time I understood that I was queer, the habit of hiding was deeply set in me, so deeply that it was not a choice but an instinct. Hide to survive, I thought. (pp. 13-14)

Allison (1994) goes on to describe the effects of growing up feeling shamed, learning early on to hide, and describing her lack of appropriate entitlement, reflected in her reluctance to pursue jobs, grants, awards, or other things that her lovers and friends felt she deserved and could easily acquire if only she asked.

Entitlement is a matter of feeling like *we*, not *they* . . . you think you have a right to say things, a place in the world . . . you have a sense of entitlement, of your own importance that I do not have . . . I have never been able to make clear the degree of my fear, the extent to which I feel myself denied, not only that I am queer in a world that hates queers, but I was born poor in a world that despises the poor . . . the need to make my world believable to people who have never experienced it is why I write fiction . . . I know that some things must be felt to be understood, that despair can never be adequately analyzed, it must be lived. (Allison, 1994, p. 14)

Sandell (1997) writes that reviewers of Allison's work tend to occlude certain aspects of her identity reflected in their responses to her writings. Some reviewers focus on her self-proclaimed identity as white trash and ignore issues of gender and sexuality in her stories. Others who concentrate on her essays and short stories focus on her gender and sexuality and neglect race and class issues. In this manner, they further exemplify the need to dichotomize identities as if only one can be important. What is deemed important may be the identity the observer most identifies or feels most comfortable with, or the one that presents the least discomfort.

Sandell (1997) warns that Allison's work reminds us that no single element of identity, be it class, race, gender, or sexual orientation, can truly be understood except in relation to the others. Allison's perspective on her life and stories explores how her willingness to examine her ethnic, class, and sexual selves have contributed to a greater understanding of how poverty shapes and constructs people's lives. When individuals are forced to separate those selves from one another they always experience a sense of alienation.

Ethnicity, Cultural Distinctiveness, and Sexual Orientation: Connecting Racism and Heterosexism

Most of the empirical and clinical research on or with lesbians and gay men is still conducted with overwhelmingly white, middle-class, young, able-bodied participants, most often among urban, college student, or well-educated populations. Those studies conducted with samples recruited in bars are biased toward people who have physical access to bars and clubs (often those who live in urban as opposed to rural communities), consume alcohol, and have sufficient disposable income to spend in those venues (Gonsiorek, 1991). Aside from failing to include representative samples of people of color, most studies fail to mention the ethnicity of their participants as a variable at all. When ethnicity is mentioned at all, if very few participants are people of color, that fact is mentioned; however, its implications on the validity or limited generalizability of the study findings rarely rates any discussion.

Newitz and Wray (1997) argue that whiteness is a socially constructed identity that serves as an unraced center of a racialized world. Its meaning also varies across the lines of sexual orientation, ethnicity, gender, age, and class, and these constructs vary according to the politics of a geographic region. Although having white skin is a part of a dominant cultural identity, it would be a mistake to assume that it is a monolithic experience or that ethnicity is irrelevant to the identities of all white people. Fygetakis (1997) states that not all white Americans are Anglo-Saxon Protestants, nor do they all espouse those values. Just as much of the current body of lesbian and gay psychological research does not generalize to lesbians or gay men of color, it cannot be assumed to generalize in the same ways to all white lesbians and gay men.

Fygetakis (1997) suggests that subjects who comprise most of the subject pools in LGB research consist of those who are out and as such are most likely identified with the dominant culture. She adds that white subjects who are also members of ethnic groups that are less tolerant of lesbian and gay sexual orientations are less likely to be out and therefore less visible. Catholic Italian Americans, particularly those living in concentrated Italian, Portuguese, and Armenian communities; lesbians and gay men who are Russian, Serbian, Byzantine Orthodox, or Orthodox Jewish are examples of groups of white people in which lesbian and gay members constitute hidden and often very closeted populations (Fygetakis, 1997). The factors applied in understanding the role of cultural traditions in lesbians and gay men of color must be similarly understood for white lesbians and gay men whose ethnic identity is very different from the dominant culture, particularly when religion is a part of that ethnic identification (Greene, 1997; Fygetakis, 1997).

Studies whose focus is on ethnicity, race, gender, religion, the presence of disabilities, socioeconomic class, and other topics rarely if ever acknowledges that all of their group's members are not heterosexual. If anything, the heterosexuality of participants is either presumed or the question about sexual orientation is never asked. Questions about sexual orientation may be deemed particularly irrelevant if the focus of the research is not sexuality per se. We know that sexual orientation is an active component in the development of human identity and as such may transform aspects of individual identity and behavior, whether the focus of study is on sexual behavior or not. When the focus of the research is on ethnicity for example, members of that group are treated as if they experience their ethnicity in the same way. Marginalized members of an ethnic group, lesbian and gay members for example, may experience their ethnicity differently than those who are heterosexual. However, questions about differences and similarities in those experiences may not even arise if no thought is given to the inclusion of sexual orientation as yet another salient variable that cannot be presumed. If the degree to which socioeconomic class, gender, age, sexual orientation, and other variables transforms or "codes" the experience of ethnicity is not explored, the complex interaction between sexual orientation and other major aspects of identity development will remain unexplored as well. As a result, the realistic social tasks and stressors that are a component of gay and lesbian identity formation for people with multiple identities are not well understood or studied either. The vicissitudes of racism, cultural similarities, and differences in same-gender couples and the effect of these variables on their relationships will be harder to discern as well. The narrow focus on heterosexual couples found in the literature on ethnic minority clients, and the equally narrow focus on predominantly white couples in the gay and lesbian literature reflects the lack of attention given to these issues.

The aforementioned trends may not only reflect but may in fact reinforce the invisibility of lesbians and gay men of color, distinctions between members of white ethnic groups, and lesbians and gay men who share membership in other disadvantaged or stigmatized groups. It can also facilitate the tendency for families and communities of people of color, as well as some white ethnic and religious groups to deny the existence of their lesbian, gay, and bisexual members (Greene, 1997). Fygetakis (1997) chronicles the invisibility of Greek lesbians among Greeks. "Not only are we invisible in the Greek community, but we also keep ourselves invisible to each other" (p. 155). She adds that "invisibility continues even in language" (p.171). In a limited study with 10 Greek lesbian participants, Fygetakis (1997) asked if any of the women interviewed knew of Greek words that described their sexual orientation. None could name any. She writes that the only Greek words that she is aware of that describe lesbian or gay sexual orientations are derogatory words for gay men. She advises that Greek American lesbians are being culturally consistent when they remain closeted in Greek communities, viewing the prospect of coming out in those communities as too risky and difficult, but who are out, active, and visible in the lesbian and gay communities.

The invisibility of Greek lesbians and gay men stands in stark contrast to the myth of tolerance and receptivity of Greek culture to lesbian and gay sexual orientation. If anything, quite the opposite has been observed (Fygetakis, 1997). Using Western models of acceptance of lesbian and gay sexual orientation that include being out to family and ethnic community as the yardstick for mental health is ill-advised. The specifics of the culture and competing demands on its lesbian and gay members must be taken into account.

Yaakov Levado (1993) is a closeted gay rabbi and writes about his life in anonymity. Levado holds the privilege of white skin, maleness, and within his culture and religion the respected status of a rabbi. However, he is not simply Jewish; he is an Orthodox Jew (hence more visible) in a culture where Christian identity is presumed among people with white skin and is privileged; he is a gay man in a heterosexist world and a Jew in an anti-Semitic world. Despite the ways that he holds societal privilege, he understands the way that being out would collapse the complexity of his multiple identities into the one that others most despise. He writes of this painful dilemma,

> I am closeted and write in anonymity ... Were I to come out ... the controversy would collapse my life, my commitments, my identity as a teacher of Torah into my gayness ... Still, the secrecy of my shadowy existence of the closet are morally repugnant and emotionally draining ... I cannot forever remain in darkness. (p. 60)

Dworkin (1997) writes about the special challenges of being a Jew in a society that presumes Christian-ness, and being lesbian in a society that presumes heterosexuality. The result is a constant need to come out, not only as a lesbian but also as a Jew. She offers,

> Claiming both identities means, among other things, grappling with persuading the heterosexual community that a lesbian identity is more complicated than sexual behavior and simultaneously persuading the lesbian community that a Jewish identity is more complex than mere religious affiliation. . . . invisibility offers some protection and security in a hostile, insecure world, and there are certainly historical reasons for remaining invisible as a lesbian and as a Jew. (Dworkin, 1997, pp. 65-66)

Lesbians and gay men of color represent other groups with multiple identities who lack both white skin privileges as well as heterosexual privileges. They may have other salient identities as well. Chan (1989, 1992, 1997), Espin (1987, 1995), Gock (1985), Greene (1994, 1996, 1997), Greene and Boyd-Franklin (1996), Mays, Cochran, and Rhue (1993), Morales (1990, 1992), Potgieter (1997), Smith (1997), Tafoya (1997), Tremble, Schneider, and Appathurai (1989), Trujillo (1991), Weinrich and Williams (1991), and Williams (1986) provide extensive discussions and research on mental health issues confronting African American, Latino, Mexican, Chicana, Asian American, black South African, and Native American lesbians and gay men. As a detailed discussion of each group is beyond the scope of this chapter, their significant observations and the challenges LGB people of color confront are briefly summarized. Members of these groups face the challenge of integrating more than one major identity that is disparaged and results in societal disadvantage. The presence of multiple oppressions can contribute to the development of special coping strategies and resilience just as their "patterned injustice" can provide challenges that can undermine healthy development.

Many lesbians and gay men of color are taught to challenge the dominant culture's negative ethnic depictions of them and often receive positive cultural mirroring during the course of their development. The psychological independence that Jones (1997) describes is developed in many lesbians and gay men of color before they are aware of their sexual orientation, to combat the pervasive racism they are routinely challenged by. That ability for independent self-construction and a previously developed sense of psychological independence in one aspect of a person's life may be useful in helping them to develop an affirmative response to other identities such as their lesbian or gay sexual orientation. However, lesbian and gay sexual orientations may also represent yet another source of stress, anxiety, and feeling marginalized. Clearly, in dysfunctional families of origin or those where negative ethnic stereotypes are reinforced rather than negated, individuals are likely to be at greater psychological risk.

Lesbians and gay men of color tend to come from cultures with strong ties to families of origin with the involvement of more extended than nuclear family arrangements in complex networks of interdependence and support. While lesbians and gay men of color may be supported by families and ethnic peers in challenging the validity of negative ethnic stereotypes, family and ethnic group members are often the very same source of negative stereotypes about lesbians and gay men. Because family and community are important buffers against racism and sources of tangible support, the homophobia in these communities often leaves lesbians and gay men of color feeling more vulnerable and less likely to be out in the same ways as their white counterparts. As such they may be less visible within their communities as well as outside them. This contributes to the tendency of people of color to deny the existence of lesbian and gay members. A common theme in this denial is the suggestion that lesbian and gay sexual orientations are a "white man's disease" or a "Western sickness," acquired as a result of too much assimilation into the dominant culture. It is also viewed among many people of color as incompatible with the identities of people of color. There is also the belief that lesbian and gay sexual orientation is volitional and represents a poor lifestyle choice rather than an integrated aspect of a person's identity. In some cases, clients may be made to feel as if they are supposed to choose one identity over the other. Although coming out is anxiety provoking for most lesbians and gay men, for lesbians and gay men of color, they may not presume the acceptance or welcome into the dominant lesbian and gay community without continuing confrontations with racism. Hence, alienating themselves from their family and ethnic community may carry a different kind of risk than for their white counterparts. Generally, their position between what seems to be two contradictory worlds can leave members of these groups at risk for feelings of isolation, alienation, and estrangement and therefore at risk for greater psychological vulnerability. Another important factor in work with lesbian and gay men of color is the history of the group's ethnic oppression and its impact on social status and available resources and opportunities, as well as a sense of who can be trusted and who cannot.

Sexual orientation must be contextualized if we are to develop accurate and more comprehensive understandings of it. Cultural values and rituals, sex-role socialization, family expectations and obligations, and religions (the more orthodox, the more challenging) are factors that must be considered if we attempt to understand the meaning of sexual orientation and identity development among lesbians and gay men of color as well as members of white ethnic groups. The presence of other variables such as age, disability, class, and so forth transform these issues and warrant further consideration as well.

These and other exclusions can allow the LGB communities to avoid examining the sexism, ethnocentrism, classism, and other oppressive attitudes that exist within their own ranks by focusing instead solely on their own oppression.

Abilism: LGB People With Disabilities

Another invisible minority of LGB people are those who have disabilities. Research on LGB people who have disabilities are conspicuously absent from the LGB literature. This omission can suggest that sexual orientation is the master identity, that heterosexism is the primary locus of oppression, that there are no lesbians or gay men who have disabilities, which we know is not so, or that the presence of a disability does not have a salient impact on the identity or life of LGB people. Fine and Asch (1988) observe that in research on disability, sexual orientation, gender, race, and class seem to be regarded as similarly irrelevant suggesting that having a disability overshadows all other dimensions of social experience. They suggest that disability (as opposed to the mere presence of physical challenges), like gender, sexual orientation, ethnicity, and so forth is a social construct. Solomon (1993) writes that it is the interaction between the presence of physical challenges or biological impairments and social, environmental, cultural factors, and social prejudice that determines whether or not the disability becomes a handicap. In their reviews of the literature on disabled women, Fine and Asch (1988) found

no data on the numbers of lesbians with disabilities or on their acceptance by nondisabled lesbians as partners, but comments made by many disabled lesbians indicate that within the community of lesbians, the disabled woman is still in search of love. (p. 3)

In their review of published research on women with disabilities, disabled lesbians reported being dismissed, shunned, or relegated to the status of friend and confidante rather than lover, just as heterosexual women with disabilities have been relegated (Fine & Asch, 1988, p. 19). Indeed, when students were interviewed and asked to give their associations to disabled women, their responses included dependent, impaired, crippled, almost lifeless, gray, old, an object of pity, lonely, and ugly (Fine & Asch, 1988). Lesbians are similar victims of the stereotype of being less attractive and less feminine than heterosexual women. Men with disabilities tend to be stereotyped as more feminine than nondisabled men (Asch, 1988). Yet, we have virtually no information about the ways that these identities doubly stigmatize lesbians and gay men with disabilities. Generally, research on disabled women makes it clear that they are not seen as sexual beings. Overall, courses on human sexuality rarely include material on sexual orientation or sexuality relevant to people with disabilities (Linton, 1998). Like men with disabilities, women are less likely to fulfill the gender roles traditionally assigned them. It would be important to develop information on the effect that fulfillment of traditional gender roles or its absence has on the relationships of lesbian and gay men and whether or not there are differences or similarities between that group, heterosexuals, and bisexual men and women. Fine and Asch (1988) question whether or not these variables facilitate greater freedom, particularly for women, in pursuing nontraditional roles such as lesbian relationships. Fine and Asch (1988) observe, "The thought of a disabled woman as a lover may engender fears of merger, exaggerates lack of boundaries, and spawn fantasies of endless responsibility, of unremitting and unreciprocated care" (p. 19).

These observations spawn questions and speculations about the dynamics in lesbian and gay couples when a partner with a disability is involved as well as when both partners are similarly challenged. Whether or not they conform to the patterns observed in heterosexual relationships is unknown due in large measure to a paucity of data. Of the studies reviewed, some had lesbian-identified participants, albeit in small numbers. Women with disabilities in the studies reported, recalled being told by a parent or parents that they would never find a man and should focus on acquiring an education or some kind of skill. Other women reported that their parents actually warned them about sexual relationships with men, with the admonishment that it could be dangerous to them. An example of one direct danger was that they would not be attractive enough to keep a man in their lives. As a result, the parent(s) reasoned, they would be used as sexual objects and then abandoned. Of this group, some women reported that they pursued sexual relationships with women out of the fear that they would be abandoned by men. The data presently available are insufficient to tell us about the ways or to what extent the presence of a disability affects the choices a woman makes about intimate relationships with men or women. Although speculations may emerge from such findings, they should be interpreted with great caution. There is no evidence to warrant assuming that women with disabilities who identify as lesbians do so out of fear of relationships with men or because they feel that they are not sufficiently attractive. The paucity of data on lesbians and gay men with disabilities is such that making any generalizations would be questionable at best. Often, we are left with more questions than answers. Lesbians and gay men are often depicted in ways that overly sexualize them. Indeed, folklore and clinical research often focus on the sexuality of lesbians and gay men as if that were all that defines them. What is it like for women and men in these communities who as a function of their disabilities are not even seen as sexual beings?

Access to the lesbian and gay community may be difficult to obtain for lesbians and gay men who depend on family members or others for care and mobility. Unlike other characteristics or attributes that people share with family members, sexual orientation is not generally one of them. Lesbians and gay men must generally move beyond the boundaries of family to meet other lesbians and gay men. Their families may not only disapprove of their sexual orientation but may deny their sexuality altogether. Lesbians and gay men with disabilities, particularly those who depend on family members for mobility and care may encounter obstacles in making contact with the LGB community or with LGB friends. This may be particularly true if their families do not approve of their sexual orientation. Such objections may not prove to be the same kind of obstacle for their heterosexual, and able-bodied lesbian and gay counterparts.

Making social contacts with other lesbians and gay men, particularly when one is outside lesbian- and gay-identified establishments, depends on knowing who might be lesbian or gay and who is not. Asch

(1988) observes that certain physical impairments (visual, articulation, hand movements) interfere with communication cues. There may be a heightened importance of subtle cues, often based on eye contact, that are not available to lesbians or gay men who are blind or have visual impairments. Furthermore, Asch (1988) reviews studies of the behavior of able-bodied people toward people with disabilities. In those studies, able-bodied people avoided social contact with people with disabilities, reflected in their avoiding eye contact, turning away from the person, or generally ignoring their presence. Although this clearly hinders social interaction for people with disabilities, it may be compounded by obstacles lesbians and gay men already encounter in "finding their own." This is another important area for further research. Fine and Asch (1988) suggest some of the following questions for further inquiry and future research. Do disabled women have less homosexual involvement during adolescence than nondisabled women? Other questions involve exploring the degree to which success or failure in heterosexual relationships during adolescence has any relevance for disabled women who are aware of being lesbian or bisexual. For these women, do parental heterosexual expectations have any effect on their involvement in heterosexual and lesbian activities (Fine & Asch, 1988)?

Despite reports from men and women with disabilities that social factors influence their sexual experiences more profoundly than physiological factors, social factors are rarely discussed in the psychological literature (Linton, 1998). As in other forms of oppression, Davis (1997) observes that "the problem is not the person with disabilities; the problem is the way that normalcy is socially constructed to create the problem of the disabled. Most people have been acculturated to stigmatize those whose bodies or other aspects of their person are deemed aberrant" (p. 9). Linton (1998) argues that people with disabilities need to be contextualized in contexts of human variation; political category; oppressed minority; and cultural group. Scheer (1994) and Linton (1998) observe that people with disabilities share an important commonality with lesbians and gay men. Both groups share the experience of growing up in families with other members who do not share their minority status. Members of both groups learn about what it means to be a member of their minority group outside their families rather than from their families. This sometimes occurs in the proximity of other peers and mentors, but sometimes not. Scheer (1994) suggests that the isolation that results has demonstrative social consequences and may provide an important driving force for a disability culture. Linton (1998) highlights difficulties in the development of group cohesion, culture, and identity formation when there is no consistent intergenerational transmission of culture as is true for lesbians, gay men, and people with disabilities as well (p. 93).

Conducting Inclusive Empirical Research

Gonsiorek (1991) observes that the largest problem in LGB research is in obtaining representative samples. The sampling biases found in the research focusing on lesbian and gay concerns are rarely discussed explicitly either in titles of papers or in statements warning readers of the limited generalizability of their findings. Although there are many realistic obstacles that must be negotiated in obtaining more representative samples in empirical research that should not be minimized, the continued tendency to report the findings of such research as if it generalizes to groups that are not included in samples in representative numbers contributes to the perpetuation of the disturbing trend of invisibility of under represented groups. Conducting research with diverse populations is no easy task and may require rethinking the way we approach subject recruitment, selection, and so forth. It also requires considering why members of some groups are reluctant to participate in research endeavors at all. We recognize that personal examination is an important component to advancing more inclusive practice and treatment, but we must remember that such endeavors must be an active component of research efforts as well.

Nikki Gerrard (1995) offers insights about conducting research with members of disadvantaged groups, primarily her own painful experience as a white feminist researcher attempting to do research on women of color. She urges that feelings elicited in the researcher are important to attend to and can both enrich the process while being respectful of the participant. Gerrard writes that she found herself, despite her good intentions, being treated with suspicion, hostility, anger, and resentment by the women of color she attempted to interview for her research. Despite her pain, she offers us an insight into this experience. She writes that when she was left to feel dismissed, powerless, and hopeless by the women of color she wished to interview, women that she felt she could offer something, she came to an understanding of how these women must feel all the time. She understood the resistance of her research participants to her well-intentioned inquiries and efforts as a manifestation of their resistance to the racism of a white society of which she just happened to be a member. In Chapter 11 of this volume, Croom elaborates on Gerrard's (1995) dilemma and provides strategies for addressing some of the aforementioned methodological challenges.

Silence and Invisibility:
Little Murders and Petty Humiliations

In both the psychology and politics of oppression we acknowledge that those who have the power to define experience also have the power to confer or deny legitimacy to experiences selectively. Exclusive attention to the most explicit, blatant, or outrageous incidents of heterosexism fails to capture the oppressiveness of omission and invisibility for many diverse groups of lesbians, gay men, and bisexual men and women. In his work on the silencing of African American men, Anderson Franklin (1993) refers to the collective effect of these kinds of phenomena as the *invisibility syndrome*. Franklin (1993) writes,

> All black men, if you ask them, can describe the small social slights that accumulate to create what I call invisibility . . . we are not literally invisible . . . that might sometimes be preferable . . . rather, we are seen as potential criminals, or as servants, but not as ourselves . . . You are forced to be aware of the negative reactions you elicit . . . and you are forced to develop ways of psychologically and physically surviving those reactions, which always takes their toll. (pp. 33-34)

Maya Angelou (American Broadcasting Company, 1989) uses Jules Feiffer's words, the little murders, with her own expression, the petty humiliations, to describe what she conceptualizes as the violent and oppressive effect of silencing. The most blatant incidents of oppression, which she calls grand executions, are obvious in their lethality. The petty humiliations, however, have a more insidious, grinding, wearing down effect. They accumulate over time and are just as oppressive and deadly as the grand executions. Boyd-Franklin (1993) refers to the subtle messages that invalidate people on the basis of race, sexual orientation, gender, and other stigmatized characteristics as microaggressions. She warns that the cumulative effect of these events can be psychologically damaging. Therefore the effects of chronic, lifelong stressors associated with invisibility, multiple identities, and complex challenges to the resulting dilemmas that arise for such people must be more carefully addressed in preventive mental health efforts, clinical practice, and in research.

Competing Alliances and Loyalties: Reality or Illusion

The tendency to partition identity into isolated parts and then organize them into hierarchies leads us to assume that we can view the constituents of multiple identities hierarchically as well. The assumption is that different identities or group memberships compete with one another or that one must be considered more important than others across the life span. These assumptions make it more difficult for us to understand more complex experiences as well as the dynamic nature of identity, and the differential importance of different identities across the life span. However, there is a tendency for members of oppressed groups to engage in this practice when they view other oppressed groups, just as do members of the majority. In reality, one aspect of a person's identity may be more salient or prioritized in one setting and less salient or a lower priority in another. One aspect or aspects of an individual's identity may be more salient to them at certain periods of that person's life than others.

Gates (1993) observes that if we judge other prejudices only by the ones that personally apply to us, we will fail to recognize other prejudices *as* prejudices. He observes that all oppressions come with different distinctions and histories and offers the plight of African Americans, Jews, and lesbians and gay men as examples. Stereotypes and distortions of African Americans focus on their presumed inferiority on most desired social characteristics. Conversely, homophobic and anti-Semitic rhetoric bear a striking similarity to one another. Both Jews and lesbians and gay men are regarded as sinister and depicted as small, self-interested groups that stick together and favor their own, as cliquish minorities that command disproportionate world influence (Gates, 1993; Kirk & Madsen, 1996). Kirk and Madsen (1996) also note that what makes lesbians and gay men so suspect is their "conspiratorial invisibility . . . a secret society whose members can be as collusive as spies . . . straights can never be sure whether lesbians and gay men are up to something behind their backs, because they're never entirely sure who might be gay" (p. 410). Certain aspects of homophobia are conflated with racist stereotypes that depict both lesbians and gay men and African Americans as sexually bestial predators, each "ready to pounce on an unwilling victim with little provocation" (Gates, 1993, p. 43). The lesson here is that comparisons between different forms of oppression presume a means of neatly separating and fairly measuring these events; that yardstick does not exist.

Leslie and MacNeill (1995) observe a tendency for members of oppressed groups to cross-blame other oppressed or persecuted communities. They explain that this may be easier on the psyche because it is less daunting than fully acknowledging the potentially overwhelming power of a larger, more powerful, dominant group. Siegel (1995) observes that the best way to avoid being a target of societal discrimination or hostility is to make someone else one.

Summary

Locating Ourselves on the
Spectrum of Oppression and Privilege

We all would tend to agree in principle that human identity consists of multiple identities, and that members of the same group do not necessarily experience the group identity in the same way. This makes the study of human diversity complicated but necessary if we are to develop an inclusive psychology of human behavior and if psychotherapy is to be culturally literate. Despite a sense of intellectual agreement about this among mental health professionals, it frequently fails to make the leap from idea to practice. Although most clinicians agree in principle that exploring and understanding the role of culture, sexual orientation, ethnicity, gender, race, class, age, and other variables is important, they may also acknowledge experiencing great discomfort when confronted with the need to discuss these matters. It is important to consider these and other forms of resistance to acquiring the training needed to competently address cultural realities more broadly and the comfort or discomfort involved in including these realities, routinely in clinical training. For many clinicians the reluctance or avoidance of addressing this material in practice can certainly be attributed to the fact that its inclusion in the formal and routine training of clinical practitioners has been a relatively recent phenomenon. That phenomenon is still not pervasive. Courses on working with culturally diverse and/or disadvantaged populations are still not a routine feature of graduate training. Despite these realities, there are other factors that may contribute to this resistance.

In considering the nexus of multiple identities, cultural differences, and similarities, we are compelled to ask questions that go beyond our understanding of these variables as mere differences or similarities, but speak more directly to their meaning. The need to avoid examining the meaning of differences such as race, ethnicity, class, sexual orientation, and other variables can be attributed at least in part to the discomfort associated with examining the differentials in societal privilege and disadvantage that accompany these human distinctions and give them meaning.

Oliva Espin (1995) defines social privilege as that which provides a person or group with the luxury of not seeing anything that does not have to do directly with them, and the tendency to define whatever it is they do see as if their understanding or interpretation of the phenomenon is the universal truth, or the normative experience. Although social privilege and disadvantage stand at opposite ends of the conceptual continuum, in reality they intersect, crisscross, and interact with one another at every moment. Every person operates at the center of these intersections (Wildman, 1996). Wildman (1996) and Rothenberg (1988) observe that each of us is embedded in a matrix of categories and contexts, where in some contexts we are privileged and in others we may be disadvantaged, each interacting with the other. A form of privilege can moderate a form of disadvantage simultaneously just as membership in a disadvantaged group may negatively moderate a locus of privilege. No person fits into only one static category; rather, each of us exists at the nexus of many groups or categories.

Although privilege and social advantage go hand in hand, they are usually invisible to those who hold them. Ignoring the presence of systems of privilege leads to the denial of disadvantage. That denial silences and renders invisible those who are not privileged and further marginalizes them. Laura Brown (1995) comments on the problematic aspects of this phenomenon in psychotherapy. She asserts that when the existence of social privilege is denied, the client's disadvantage goes unacknowledged and becomes a lie of omission. If heterosexual, white skin, middle class, able-bodied, or other forms of privilege are denied, the disadvantages associated with membership in disadvantaged groups is denied as well.

The experience of oppression and privilege are filtered through the many different lenses and realities that must be incorporated and understood. Hence, universalizing human experience should be carefully scrutinized. It increases disempowerment among those who are invisible, silenced, and therefore marginalized. Universalizing may also serve to avoid the difficult tensions that disrupt the false sense of harmony and security that often exists between members of disadvantaged groups. The result is a failure to give voice to the ways that lesbians and gay men may engage in oppressive behavior toward other lesbians, gay men, bisexual men and women, and transsexual and transgendered men and women both personally and institutionally.

There is the potential for oppressive behavior in anyone who holds societal privilege and the power that accompanies it. Because of that potential, it is important in our work as psychologists to determine the nature of our own multiple identities, where along the spectrum of privilege and disadvantage those identities place us, as the research scientist, therapist, supervisor, or teacher, and in what dimensions. It is important to locate and acknowledge our own locus of social advantage and its impact on our perceptions in our professional work. It is equally important to acknowledge the effect of our own membership in groups that may be marginalized on our view of the client, student, research participant, or supervisee. This process is often anxiety provoking. Although many people may have ability and may work hard, that is not the most salient ingredient in success. Often, social, familial, and political connections with people in positions of power and influence, good timing and sometimes just luck is essential. Most people know this on some level and may even articulate it when they feel they have been treated unfairly. However, if they are confronted with the ways in which their optimal development is or has been enhanced by factors that are not based simply on ability, hard work, or fairness but, rather, have been facilitated by social privilege, they may need to avoid acknowledging that reality. To acknowledge this reality may appear synonymous with minimizing their personal ability and effort. Similarly, many people will minimize the level at which one form of privilege does not necessarily mitigate a locus of disadvantage. The dimension that makes a locus of privilege or disadvantage salient or relevant is often the context. The need to deny the presence of social privilege however, creates major obstacles in implementing diversity and in some settings even in discussing it. However, in research, psychotherapy theory and practice, avoiding the acknowledgment and understanding of the broad and divergent role of societal privilege and disadvantage in people's lives is problematic. It will ultimately result in a failure to deliver optimal services whether in treatment to clients or validity of research findings. Therapists, if they are unable to view themselves and their own position fully, will be unable to view the client and the client's position fully.

The Future

The very act of defining the experiences of all lesbians and gay men by the characteristics of the most privileged and powerful members of that group is an oppressive act. It does not ultimately undermine heterosexism because heterosexism has an interlocking relationship to other forms of oppression (Greene & Sanchez-Hucles, 1997). To the contrary, it facilitates it. It does so by tolerating the invisibility and thus the silencing of people who are not members of the group that is dominant. The silence and absence of a wider range of lesbians, gay men, and bisexual people, often reflected in the failure to speak about them or their needs, and the tendency to represent the needs of the dominant group as if it represents the full spectrum of lesbians and gay men, permit this sinister evasion. It permits majority lesbians and gay men to identify themselves simply as victims of heterosexism and to use that status as a victim to at the very least ignore, and at the worst perpetuate racial, gender, or other social class hierarchies of advantage and disadvantage. It also permits them to avoid a realistic confrontation with their own power and locus of privilege and how they use it.

Racism, sexism, classism, ageism, ableism, and heterosexism are all embedded pervasively in our society and are a part of our socialization. These varied types of societal disadvantage assume both personal and institutional designs. Furthermore, the discriminatory practices that accompany them create a unique range of psychological demands and stressors that victims of disadvantage must learn to manage in addition to the routine range of developmental tasks and life stressors which everyone else faces. Clinical training must include an understanding of the salient factors which must be considered in human development in the context of discriminatory systems and institutions, and in ways that are sensitive to the complex psychological and cultural realities of disadvantaged group members. In the context of heterosexism, its varied incarnations and the different ways that it is experienced must be explored and better understood for a wider range of lesbians and gay men. Failing to consider these variables in the delivery of mental health services and in the theoretical perspectives underlying practice may only serve to perpetuate our ignorance and ultimately contribute to rather than mitigate social ills.

The task of unraveling the conundrum of multiple identities in lesbian, gay, and bisexual psychology theory, research, and practice is no simple task, given that heterosexism is not the primary locus of oppression for all lesbians and gay men. In considering the nexus of LGB psychology on all levels, we are compelled to ask questions that go beyond our understanding of societal disadvantage and privilege as if they exist in isolation. The more that we are aware of the diversity of the lives and experiences of LGB men and women, the more cognizant we become of the need to ask how the intensity and effects of forms of disadvantage and privilege vary or interact with other forms of disadvantage and privilege in an individual, particularly in the therapy process. Our inquiry must also include an examination of the ways that LGB psychology itself can be an instrument that facilitates the marginalization of its less visible members. Consequently, we are led to first consider the extent to which current LGB psychology reflects or fails to be inclusive of the diversity of LGB experiences and to address those failures. Ultimately, we are charged with the task of developing paradigms that assist us in better understanding the ongoing, dynamic, and interactive nature of constituents of human identity, in a context in which any single aspect of identity colors, transforms, and informs the meaning of others in reciprocal ways.

Working through the tension that develops when we are inclusive is necessary in order to authentically achieve both a personal and a professional transformation of the discourse of psychology. When we practice authentic inclusiveness, we enhance LGB psychology and our understanding of heterosexism as well as other interlocking forms of oppression (Greene, 1996, 1997). Fully incorporating the study of many differences that occur simultaneously affords us the multiple perspectives needed to provide for an increasingly comprehensive, representative, accurate, and dynamic knowledge base in psychological theory and practice (Greene & Sanchez-Hucles, 1997). Incorporating diverse perspectives and concerns in our paradigms should facilitate an authentic understanding of all human beings. Omitting these diverse perspectives leaves us with a narrow and distorted view of the worlds and realities of LGB men and women. The inclusion of multiple perspectives, however, can transform the discipline of psychology from an instrument of social control to a powerful instrument of advocacy and social change (Greene & Sanchez-Hucles, 1997). In this paradigm we will no longer need to see people as the same in order to treat them with fairness. We can make the important leap from equal treatment, which presumes sameness, to fair treatment that acknowledges and even celebrates the richness of human differences.

It seems appropriate to give Audre Lorde the last words. In *Sister Outsider* (Lorde, 1984), she writes,

> Somewhere on the edge of consciousness there is what I call a mythical norm, which each one of us within our hearts knows "that is not me." In America, this norm is usually defined as white, thin, male, young, heterosexual, Christian, and financially secure. It is with this mythical norm that the trappings of power reside in this society. Those of us who stand outside that power often identify one way in which we are different, and we assume that to be the primary cause of all oppression, forgetting other distortions around difference, some of which we ourselves may be practicing. (p. 116)

References

Allison, D. (1992). *Bastard out of Carolina*. New York: Plume.

Allison, D. (1994). A question of class. In D. Allison (Ed.), *Skin: Talking about sex, class and literature*. New York: Firebrand Books.

American Broadcasting Company. (1989, June 6). [Interview with Maya Angelou and Alice Walker]. *The Oprah Winfrey show* [televised broadcast]. Chicago: Author.

Ames, L. J. (1996). Homo-phobia, homo-ignorance, homo-hate: Heterosexism and AIDS. In E. Rothblum & L. Bond (Eds.), *Preventing heterosexism and homophobia* (pp. 239-256). Thousand Oaks, CA: Sage.

Asch, A. (1988). Disability: Its place in the curriculum. In P. A. Bronstein & K. Quina (Eds.), *Teaching a psychology of people* (pp. 156-167). Washington, DC: American Psychological Association.

Bohan, J. (1996). *Psychology and sexual orientation*. New York: Routledge.

Boyd-Franklin, N. (1993, July/August). Pulling out the arrows. *Family Therapy Networker*, 17(4), 54-56.

Bradford, J., & Ryan, C. (1987). *National lesbian health care survey: Mental health implications for lesbians*. Rockville, MO: National Institute of Mental Health.

Bradford, J., Ryan, C., & Rothblum, E. (1994). National lesbian health care survey: Implications for mental health. *Journal of Consulting and Clinical Psychology, 62*, 228-242.

Brown, L. S. (1995). Antiracism as an ethical norm in feminist therapy practice. In J. Adleman & G. Enguidanos (Eds.), *Racism in the lives of women: Testimony, theory and guides to practice* (pp. 137-148). New York: Harrington Park.

Chan, C. (1989). Issues of identity development among Asian American lesbians and gay men. *Journal of Counseling and Development, 68*(1), 16-20.

Chan, C. (1992). Cultural considerations in counseling Asian American lesbians and gay men. In S. Dworkin & F. Gutierrez (Eds.), *Counseling gay men and lesbians* (pp. 115-124). Alexandria, VA: American Association for Counseling and Development.

Chan, C. (1997). Don't ask, don't tell, don't know: The formation of a homosexual identity and sexual expression among Asian American lesbians. In B. Greene (Ed.), *Ethnic and cultural diversity among lesbians and gay men* (pp. 240ÿ2D248). Thousand Oaks, CA: Sage.

Davis, L. (1997). Constructing normalcy: The Bell curve, the novel and the invention of the disabled body in the nineteenth century. In L. Davis (Ed.), *The disability studies reader* (pp. 9-28). New York: Routledge.

Dworkin, S. (1997). Female, lesbian and Jewish: Complex and invisible. In B. Greene (Ed.), *Ethnic and cultural diversity among lesbians and gay men* (pp. 63-87). Thousand Oaks, CA: Sage.

Ehrenberg, M. (1996). Aging and mental health: Issues in the gay and lesbian community. In C. Alexander (Ed.), *Gay and lesbian mental health: A sourcebook for practitioners* (pp. 189-209). New York: Harrington Park.

Espin, O. (1987). Issues of identity in the psychology of Latina lesbians. In Boston Lesbian Psychologies Collective (Eds.), *Lesbian psychologies: Explorations and challenges* (pp. 35-51). Urbana, IL: University of Illinois Press.

Espin, O. (1995). On knowing you are the unknown: Women of color constructing psychology. In J. Adleman & G. Enguidanos (Eds.), *Racism in the lives of women: Testimony, theory and guides to practice* (pp. 127-136). New York: Harrington Park Press.

Essed, P. (1996). *Diversity: Gender, color & culture.* Amherst: University of Massachusetts Press.

Ferguson, S. A., & King, T. C. (1997). There but for the grace of God: Two black women therapists explore privilege. *Women & Therapy, 20*(1), 5-14.

Fine, M., & Asch, A. (Eds.). (1988). Beyond pedestals. *Women with disabilities: Essays in psychology, culture and politics* (pp. 1-37). Philadelphia: Temple University Press.

Franklin, A. J. (1993, July/August). The invisibility syndrome. *The Family Therapy Networker, 17*(4), 33-39.

Fygetakis, L. (1997). Greek American lesbians: Identity odysseys of honorable good girls. In B. Greene (Ed.), *Ethnic and cultural diversity among lesbians and gay men* (pp. 152-190). Thousand Oaks, CA: Sage.

Gates, H. L., Jr. (1993, May 17). Blacklash. *The New Yorker, 69,* 13, 42-44.

Gatz, M., & Cotton, B. (1994). Age as a dimension of diversity: The experience of being old. In E. J. Trickett, R. J. Watts, & D. Birman (Eds.), *Human diversity: Perspectives on people in context* (pp. 334-355). San Francisco: Jossey-Bass.

Gerrard, N. (1995). Some painful experiences of a white feminist therapist doing research with women of color. In J. Adleman & G. Enguidanos (Eds.), *Racism in the lives of women: Testimony, theory and guides to practice* (pp. 55-63). New York: Harrington Park.

Gock, T. S. (1985, August). *Psychotherapy with Asian Pacific gay men: Psychological issues, treatment approach and therapeutic guidelines.* Paper presented at the annual meeting of the Asian American Psychological Association, Los Angeles.

Gonsiorek, J. (1991). The empirical basis for the demise of the illness model of homosexuality. In J. Gonsiorek & J. Weinrich (Eds.), *Homosexuality: Research implications for public policy* (pp. 115-136). Thousand Oaks, CA: Sage.

Greene, B. (1994). Lesbian women of color. In L. Comas-Diaz & B. Greene (Eds.), *Women of color: Integrating ethnic and gender identities in psychotherapy* (pp. 389-427). New York: Guilford.

Greene, B. (1996). Lesbians and gay men of color: The legacy of ethnosexual mythologies in heterosexism. In E. Rothblum & L. Bond (Eds.), *Preventing heterosexism and homophobia* (pp. 59-70). Thousand Oaks, CA: Sage.

Greene, B. (1997). Ethnic minority lesbians and gay men: Mental health and treatment issues. In B. Greene (Ed.), *Ethnic and cultural diversity among lesbians and gay men* (pp. 216-239). Thousand Oaks, CA: Sage.

Greene, B., & Boyd-Franklin, N. (1996). African American lesbians: Issues in couples therapy. In J. Laird & R. J. Green (Eds.), *Lesbians and gay men in couples and families: A handbook for therapists* (pp. 251-271). San Francisco: Jossey-Bass.

Greene, B., & Sanchez-Hucles, J. (1997). Diversity: Advancing an inclusive feminist psychology. In J. Worell & N. Johnson (Eds.), *Shaping the future of feminist psychology: Education, research and practice* (pp. 173-202). Washington, DC: American Psychological Association.

Hadju, D. (1996). *Lush Life: The biography of Billy Strayhorn.* New York: Farrar, Straus, and Giroux.

Hall, R., & Greene, B. (1996). Sins of omission and commission: Women, psychotherapy and the psychological literature. *Women & Therapy, 18*(1), 5-31.

Hartigan, J. (1997). Name calling: Objectifying "poor whites" and "white trash" in Detroit. In M. Wray & A. Newitz (Eds.), *White trash: Race and class in America* (pp. 41-56). New York: Routledge.

Hooker, E. (1957). The adjustment of the male overt homosexual. *Journal of Projective Techniques, 21,* 18-31.

Jones, F. (1997, March). Eloquent anonymity. [Review of the book *Lush life: A biography of Billy Strayhorn*]. *Readings: A Journal of Reviews and Commentary in Mental Health, 12*(1), 10-14.

Jones, R. (1979). Structural isolation and the genesis of black nationalism in North America. *Colby Librarian Quarterly, 15,* 256-266.

Kaschak, E. (1992). *Engendered lives: A new psychology of women's experience.* New York: Basic Books.

Kirk, M., & Madsen, H. (1996). A field trip to straight America. In K. E. Rosenblum & T-M. C. Travis (Eds.), *The meaning of difference: American constructions of race, class, sex and gender, social class and sexual orientation* (pp. 400-412). New York: McGraw-Hill.

Kite, M., & Deaux, K. (1987). Gender belief systems: Homosexuality and the implicit inversion theory. *Psychology of Women Quarterly, 11,* 83-96.

Levado, Rabbi Yaakov (pseudonym). (1993, September/October). Gayness & God: Wrestlings of an Orthodox rabbi. *Tikkun: A Bimonthly Jewish Critique of Politics, Culture and Society, 8*(5), 54-60.

Leslie, D., & MacNeill, L. (1995). Double positive: Lesbians and race. In J. Adleman & G. Enguidanos (Eds.), *Racism in the lives of women: Theory, testimony and guides to practice* (pp. 161-169). New York: Harrington Park.

Linton, S. (1998). *Claiming disability: Knowledge and identity.* New York: New York University Press.

Lorde, A. (1984). Age, race and class. In A. Lorde (Ed.), *Sister outsider: Essays and speeches.* Freedom, CA: Crossing Press.

Mays, V., Cochran, S., & Rhue, S. (1993). The impact of perceived discrimination on the intimate relationships of black lesbians. *Journal of Homosexuality, 25*(4), 1-14.

Merriam-Webster's collegiate dictionary (10th ed.). (1996). Dallas, TX: Merriam-Webster & Zane Publishing.

Morales, E. (1990). Ethnic minority families and minority gays and lesbians. In F. W. Bozett & M. B. Sussman (Eds.), *Homosexuality & family relationships* (pp. 217-239). New York: Haworth.

Morales, E. (1992). Counseling Latino gays and Latina lesbians. In S. Dworkin & F. Gutierrez (Eds.), *Counseling gay men and lesbians: Journey to the end of the rainbow* (pp. 125-139). Alexandria, VA: American Association for Counseling and Development.

Newitz, A., & Wray, M. (1997). Introduction. In M. Wray & A. Newitz (Eds.), *White trash: Race and class in America* (pp. 1-12). New York: Routledge.

O'Hare, W. (1986, May). 8 myths about the poverty. *American Demographics, 8*(5), 22-25.

Pinderhughes, E. (1989). *Understanding race, ethnicity and power: Keys to efficacy in clinical practice.* New York: Free Press.

Potgieter, C. (1997). From apartheid to Mandela's constitution: Black South African lesbians in the nineties. In B. Greene (Ed.), *Ethnic and cultural diversity among lesbians and gay men* (pp. 88-116). Thousand Oaks, CA: Sage.

Rosenblum, K. E., & Travis, T-M. C. (1996). Experiencing difference: Framework essay. In K. E. Rosenblum & T-M. C. Travis (Eds.), *The meaning of difference* (pp. 137-162). New York: McGraw-Hill.

Rothenberg, P. (1988). Integrating the study of race, gender, and class: Some preliminary observations. *Feminist Teacher, 3*(3), 37-42,

Sandell, J. (1997). Telling stories of "queer white trash": Race, class and sexuality in the work of Dorothy Allison. In M. Wray & A. Newitz (Eds.), *White trash: Race and class in America* (pp. 211-230). New York: Routledge.

Schaie, K. W. (1993, January). Ageist language in psychological research. *American Psychologist, 48*(1), 49-51.

Scheer, J. (1994). Culture and disability: An anthropological point of view. In E. J. Trickett, R. J. Watts, & D. Birman (Eds.), *Human diversity: Perspectives on people in context* (pp. 244-260). San Francisco: Jossey-Bass.

Siegel, R. J. (1995). Overcoming bias through awareness, mutual encouragement, and commitment. In J. Adleman & G. Enguidanos (Eds.), *Racism in the lives of women: Testimony, theory and guides to practice* (pp. 295-301). New York: Haworth.

Smith, A. (1997). Cultural diversity and the coming out process: Implications for clinical practice. In B. Greene (Ed.), *Ethnic and cultural diversity among lesbians and gay men* (pp. 279-300). Thousand Oaks, CA: Sage.

Solomon, S. (1993). Women & physical distinction: A review of the literature and suggestions for intervention. *Women & Therapy, 14*(3/4), 91-103.

Tafoya, T. (1997). Native gay and lesbian issues: The two spirited. In B. Greene (Ed.), *Ethnic and cultural diversity among lesbians and gay men* (pp. 1-10). Thousand Oaks, CA: Sage.

Tremble, B., Schneider, M., & Appathurai, C. (1989). Growing up gay or lesbian in a multicultural context. *Journal of Homosexuality, 17*, 253-267.

Trujillo, C. (Ed.). (1991). *Chicana lesbians: The girls our mothers warned us about.* Berkeley, CA: Third Woman Press.

Wachtel, P. (1996). The inner city and the inner life [Review of the book *The analyst in the inner city: Race, class and culture through a psychoanalytic lens*]. *Tikkun: A Bimonthly Critique of Politics, Culture and Society, 11*(3), 59-61.

Weinrich, J., & Williams, W. L. (1991). Strange customs, familiar lives: Homosexuality in other cultures. In J. Gonsiorek & J. Weinrich (Eds.), *Homosexuality: Research findings for public policy* (pp. 44-59). Newbury Park, CA: Sage.

Wildman, S. (1996). *Privilege revealed: How invisible preference undermines America.* New York: New York University Press.

Williams, W. L. (1986). *The spirit and the flesh: Sexual diversity in American Indian culture.* Boston: Beacon.

Wyche, K. F. (1996). Conceptualizations of social class in African American women: Congruence of client and therapist definitions. *Women & Therapy, 18*(3/4), 35-43.

2

Teaching Lesbian, Gay, and Bisexual Psychology
Contemporary Strategies

CHRISTINE BROWNING
CRAIG KAIN

During the American Psychological Association's (APA) Convention in August 1996, the authors presented a continuing education program sponsored by APA Division 44 (Society for the Psychological Study of Lesbian, Gay, and Bisexual Issues) on "Teaching Lesbian, Gay, and Bisexual Psychology Courses." The following is an overview of issues we think are essential to consider before developing or teaching a class on lesbian, gay, and bisexual psychology (LGB). In most universities and colleges in the United States, courses on sexual orientation diversity are still rare. Typically, a faculty member will choose to offer a course that is apart from the general course offerings. Not only must one persuade an academic department to offer the course, but frequently, the courses are scrutinized by the campus administration and local community. Although there may be many questions to consider when developing any course, there are unique issues related to the specific experience of teaching a course that addresses issues of sexual orientation. We have posed several questions that we have found useful in the preparation for such a course. These questions are intended to stimulate additional questions that may be unique to your academic setting.

The broad categories for instructors to consider in developing a course are course structure and goals, course content, class composition, activities and assignments, student assessment, and instructors' issues and experience.

Structure and Goals

Many of the issues involved in teaching an LGB course arise even before the instructor enters the classroom. Whether to offer an entire course versus several lectures on LGB psychology for example, has the ability to influence decisions regarding syllabus design, learning activities, and how students are evaluated. Similarly, instructors may teach courses for a variety of reasons ranging from simply exposing students to an overview of sexual orientation diversity to the development of clinical competencies needed to work effectively with LGB clients. Goal setting, like decisions regarding the structure of the course, must be carefully considered in the early stages of development. The following are common issues to examine:

Solo Versus Team Teaching

- How will the instructors represent diversity in perspectives (for example, gender, race, ethnicity, and sexual orientation)?
- Will the instructors each bring a particular area of expertise to the team?
- How will the instructors on a team handle their own personal differences of opinion about controversial issues within LGB psychology?
- If teaching alone, how will you avoid being seen as the "spokesperson" for the entire LGB community?

Sexual Orientation of the Instructors

- Will the instructors choose to disclose their sexual orientation? If so, how will this occur?
- Will students view the credibility of the instructors differently based on the instructors' sexual orientation?
- How can heterosexual instructors establish themselves as experts on LGB issues?
- How can LGB instructors overcome student concern about potential bias in the presentation of course material?
- How can LGB instructors overcome student concern about preferential treatment toward LGB students?

Mainstream Versus Free-Standing Class

- How are decisions made about whether a department offers an LGB psychology course and/or integrates LGB issues into a variety of courses?

Course Goals

- Will the course attempt to change student attitudes about (LGB) issues?
- Will the course attempt to increase the students' skills in providing services to the LGB communities?
- Will the course attempt to increase the students' awareness of their own personal biases about LGB people?
- Can a course attempt solely to increase the students' knowledge base about psychology without also including attitude change as a goal and addressing the students' affective reaction to the material?

Course Content

Regardless of whether one has an entire semester or a single class lecture, there are decisions that need to be made regarding course content. Ideally, the decision to include or exclude topics is tied to the goals of the course. Thus, instructors teaching courses that aim at increasing self-awareness may design courses that rely heavily on experiential exercises such as those in Appendix A. Instructors teaching courses in developing clinical competencies may choose to rely more heavily on the scientific literature in LGB psychology.

Due to the development of LGB psychology as a field of scientific study and the subsequent increase in the literature and available resources, instructors will face decisions about what topics to cover in the course. Here are some factors to consider:

General Content

- On what basis are decisions made about the inclusion or exclusion of content depending upon the length and time allotted for the course?
- How are these decisions communicated to students?

Controversial Issues

- How will issues controversial to LGB communities be addressed in the course?

- How will issues related to academic freedom influence the choice of teaching material?

Diversity

- How will issues of race and ethnicity be represented in the course content?
- How will issues of gender differences be acknowledged?
- How will the curriculum fully integrate issues of bisexuality into the course?
- How will issues of sexism, racism, ageism, ableism, and classism be addressed in the course as they relate to LGB identity?
- How will issues related to transgendered and gender identities be incorporated in the course?

Syllabus

- What implicit messages are conveyed to students by issues omitted from the course syllabus?

Class Composition

Although many aspects of an LGB course are within an instructor's control, one important factor is not: the composition of the classroom. Many variables will affect students' receptivity to material presented and to their interactions with each other as well as the instructor. This includes obvious factors such as ethnicity, gender, and the sexual orientation identities of the students. It also includes less obvious factors such as the students' ages or, if they are LGB, the length of time they have been out. For example, some older lesbians in a classroom may see their sexual identity as closely aligned with their feminist identity, whereas younger lesbians may misunderstand this perspective or be unfamiliar with feminism. Thus, differences within the LGB student community may be as salient as the differences that exist between heterosexual students and LGB students. With respect to class composition, the instructor's task is twofold: (1) to create a learning environment and curriculum where a broad range of individual experiences are represented and respected, and (2) to manage classroom conflict so that differences become

assets and do not become divisive. Issues instructors may want to anticipate include:

Student Demographics

- How might the learning environment differ based on whether the class is predominately heterosexual?
- How might the learning environment differ based on whether the class is predominately LGB?
- How might the learning environment differ based on whether the class has students who reflect a variety of sexual orientation identities?
- How might the learning environment differ based on the gender and ethnic composition of the class?
- In what ways might an instructor need to respond to these class variables?

In-Group/Out-Group Dynamics

- How can instructors help students overcome their fears about their lack of knowledge about LGB issues?
- How can instructors help students overcome their fear of offending other students?
- How can instructors help students address concerns about their own sexual orientation identities?
- How can instructors help heterosexual students understand heterosexual privilege without exacerbating any guilt they might feel?

Issues With Lesbian, Gay, and Bisexual Students

- How can instructors address students' lack of knowledge, inexperience, or bias about other groups in the community (i.e., a gay man's lack of knowledge about women's health issues, a lesbian woman's discomfort with gay male sexuality, a white lesbian, gay, or bisexual person's insensitivity to racial/ethnic discrimination)?
- How can instructors make the best use of information and experience that students bring into the classroom?
- How can instructors address students who may attempt to compete with the teacher for the role of expert?
- How will instructors take into consideration the dynamics related to students who are in varying stages of the coming out process?

Activities and Assignments

In structuring a course or class, most instructors will rely on a variety of instructional methods to convey information to students and engage them in the learning process. Activities and assignments provide students with the opportunity to engage in self-reflection and critical thinking about LGB issues in ways that can be experienced ranging from nonthreatening to confrontational. Instructors must carefully weigh the benefits and costs of any classroom activity or assignments and try to anticipate heterosexual as well as LGB student reactions. Even the most innocuous videotape for some students may be highly offensive to others.

It is important to remember that students come from diverse cultures, childhood experiences, and religious beliefs and may be challenged by some of the material presented. It is always advisable to prepare students in advance for the possible feelings that may arise during the course of an activity, exercise, or assignment. Providing students with a safe place to explore feelings is also crucial. Weekly journal entries read only by the instructor often give students the opportunity to share some of their reactions in a less public forum than classroom discussions. Allowing students a choice of assignments from a list of options may also be helpful. Sample assignments are included in Appendix A. Although this is not an exhaustive list, it should still serve to help instructors generate other original activities and assignments of their own. Here are some other issues to consider when creating course activities and assignments:

Video Resources

- How will issues of gender and ethnicity be taken into consideration when selecting video material for class use?
- What challenges are presented when using sexually explicit material that some students might find objectionable?

Assignments

- How will instructors respond to students who voice concerns or refuse to engage in activities and assignments based on their religious beliefs?

- How might instructors need to alter activities and assignments to take into consideration the life experience of LGB students?

Assessment Issues

How a student's performance in a course is evaluated directly relates to the stated goals of the course. If a course is designed solely to provide students with factual information and research about the LGB communities, objective tests may be devised to measure student learning. These methods of evaluation are often beyond question. Either a student knows the material and scores well or lacks knowledge and scores poorly. If course goals include elements of attitude change or consciousness-raising however, subjective elements in assessment may arise. Measuring a student's shift in attitude or increase in clinical competency is often a difficult task. When the subject matter is about LGB issues, the potential charge of instructor bias or subjectivity may be increased. Instructors, whether or not they are LGB, are often transparent with their positive LGB personal feelings and thus must take extra care to devise some means of evaluating students that is beyond repute.

Often, behavioral markers are a better criterion upon which to base evaluations than classroom discussions. The latter are open to interpretation and faulty memory. For example, a student's lack of empathic responses to gay clients in role-play situations or homophobic remarks in written papers may be a measure of poor course performance. Here are some questions instructors may want to consider when deciding how student learning will be assessed:

Grading

- How will instructors grade students who complete the requirements while maintaining negative attitudes toward homosexuality and bisexuality?
- What criteria will the instructor use for evaluating clinical competency?
- How will the instructor address students' concern that grading may be biased based on the student's sexual orientation?

Instructor Issues and Experiences

Students enrolled in an LGB course often find it life-altering. Similarly, instructors inevitably find themselves changed as a consequence of their decision to offer such a course. For some instructors, offering an LGB course marks another step in their personal and professional development. The decision to come out as an LGB man or woman or as a strong supporter of these communities may involve risks and rewards. Some instructors will take great pleasure in offering a course that may not have been available when they were in school. Some simply enjoy serving as positive role models for their students.

Other instructors may have realistic fears about the consequences of teaching LGB courses. In many educational institutions, LGB courses are not recognized as part of a core discipline. They are often offered as elective courses or as a part of a liberal studies program and as such, a low priority. Thus, instructors of these courses may have their academic credibility questioned. In some institutions, department politics may play a part in a faculty member's decision to offer an LGB course. Some faculty members may choose to wait until after they are awarded tenure to propose or teach such courses.

Anticipating the personal impact of teaching an LGB course is crucial. Instructors interested in initiating such courses but concerned about the possibility of negative consequences may benefit from talking to a trusted colleague in their department. Sharing ideas with other psychologists who have already taught courses is often helpful. The Division 44 listserver provides a computer-accessible means of obtaining advice and support about teaching from psychologists around the world. Here are some personal and professional issues for instructors to consider in advance of offering an LGB course:

Interpersonal Issues

- What are the consequences for instructors when disclosing their sexual orientation in the classroom?

- How will instructors handle the potential for dual relationships given a small LGB community on college campuses?
- What are the consequences of being labeled as the expert on LGB issues?
- How will instructors respond to negative or insensitive student comments when they are directed at the instructor personally?
- How might teaching an LGB course result in changes in departmental support?
- How might teaching an LGB course change one's relationships with colleagues?

Conclusion

We have taught both graduate and undergraduate courses in LGB psychology over the past several years. Although the questions we pose might suggest that there are unique difficulties associated with teaching these courses, there are also unique pleasures. Teaching an LGB psychology course presents one with an unusual opportunity to have an impact on the campus environment by legitimizing issues related to sexual orientation identity. Even when students do not elect to take the course, the power of having the course listed in the class schedule is significant. It is an acknowledgment by the educational institution that scholarly interest in this area is legitimate. It infuses the dominant heterosexual academy with the reality of LGB lives. LGB students who take the course often undergo an increase in their level of self-esteem and confidence. It can be a powerful experience for students who for perhaps the first time are taking a class that acknowledges their lives and articulates their issues and concerns. It also may provide a sense of community with other students who are LGB or heterosexual allies. Finally, it provides an opportunity for intelligent discussion about issues that are so often misunderstood and misrepresented in our society.

Lesbian, Gay, and Bisexual Journals

Journal of Gay, Lesbian, and Bisexual Identity, Human Science Press.
Journal of Gay and Lesbian Social Services, Haworth Press.
Journal of Homosexuality, Haworth Press.
Journal of Lesbian and Gay Psychotherapy, Haworth Press.
Journal of Lesbian Studies, Haworth Press.
Lesbian, Gay, and Bisexual Psychology: Theory, Research, and Clinical Applications, Division 44 annual. Sage Publications.

Appendix A:
Examples of Experiential Activities

The following activities were used by the authors or submitted by others who have used these activities in their classrooms. The authors thank faculty members who provided course descriptions that included the following activities and bibliographic references.[1]

1. Coming Out Story

Students of all sexual orientations are asked to write a 1- to 2-page narrative of how they became aware of their own sexual orientation. Students are given an alternative assignment to write about how they became aware of their gender identity if they do not wish to write about their sexual orientation.

2. Comfort Ratings With Trainee, Client, Supervisor
(for use with clinical/counseling graduate students)

Have students fill out the survey below and then answer the following questions: Which group are you most (least) comfortable with as a colleague, as a client, as a supervisor? How does your comfort level relate to the amount of contact you have had with the group? Based on your comfort and/or contact level, with which group do you feel you need the most work in order to increase your sensitivity to the group's concerns and experiences?

		AMOUNT OF CONTACT		
GROUP		LOW	MODERATE	HIGH
Heterosexual man	Trainee	. . . .		
	Client	. . . .		
	Supervisor	. . . .		

---

[1]Janis Bohan, Ph.D., Christine Browning, Ph.D., Beth Cohen, Ph.D., Oliva Espin, Ph.D., Craig Kain, Ph.D., Jan C. Krupper, Ph.D., Christopher Martell, Ph.D., Bianca Cody Murphy, Ph.D., and Charlotte Patterson, Ph.D.

Gay man	Trainee	....
	Client	....
	Supervisor	....
Lesbian woman	Trainee	....
	Client	....
	Supervisor	....
Heterosexual woman	Trainee	....
	Client	....
	Supervisor	....
Bisexual woman	Trainee	....
	Client	....
	Supervisor	....
Bisexual man	Trainee	....
	Client	....
	Supervisor	....

3. Vignettes— Counseling Situations

In small groups, students read vignettes of various situations. Develop discussion questions to analyze the situations in terms of the issues discussed in class (i.e., coming out process, impact of minority racial/ethnic identity development, counseling strategies). The following are some examples of vignettes used with graduate students in clinical or counseling psychology.

- You are a 19-year-old man from a small farming community. For some time now, you have been aware of sexual feelings toward certain attractive men on campus, but it is scary to think about that since you have never told anyone. You do not want to be ashamed of your feelings. You try to distract yourself from these feelings, but it is difficult to do so. You hate yourself for having these feelings, but you cannot help it. You are slowly becoming more and more depressed as you cannot get rid of these feelings. You cannot be yourself around your friends. You are starting to feel sad all the time. You decide to come to the counseling center and talk to a counselor about how to get rid of these feelings.

- You are a college-age lesbian who is very politically active. You are angry at all the prejudice and discrimination in the world. You have lost many of your friends from high school, getting sneers and jeers from strangers as you walk across campus. You dress in clothing that expresses your political opinions. The woman you are involved with is not politically active and just wants to continue her education and get a degree. You fight with her about your participation in campus marches and speaking at rallies. You love her but are slowly realizing that your life seems unfulfilled. You come to the counseling center to talk about the relationship.

- You are bisexual. You are attracted to certain men and women. You are currently dating a member of the opposite sex. You are out to a number of people but not many. Your gay friends want you to say that you are gay and stop dating the opposite sex. They say you are homophobic and do not want to claim your sexual orientation. You have not told your opposite-sex dating partner about your bisexual feelings. You come to the counseling center to explore this situation.

- You are a college-age lesbian, gay, or bisexual person. You feel extremely angry at all the oppression you experience even on your college campus where you expected much more tolerance of your identity. You easily get depressed and during these episodes do not do well in your studies. You are experimenting with alcohol as it makes you, at least initially, feel a lot better. You have a few gay friends with whom you party a lot. You come to the counseling center to try to get your act together.

- You are a female high school senior who is thinking about going to college. You have a passion for softball and want to play the sport in college. Several of your classmates who play high school softball are the targets of heterosexism and gossip at your high school. They are talked about at lunch and in the halls, with rumors that some of the women are "dykes." This really bothers you. You find yourself drawn to these women on the team. You like being around them and find yourself interested in hanging out with them. You are worried about being labeled as lesbian if you join the softball team when you go to college, but you would feel disappointed if you gave up the sport. You have examined your feelings. You have no real desire to date boys but feel pressured to do so from both family and peers. You feel confused. You do not know what to do. You decide to talk with your high school counselor.

Appendix B: Special Issues on Lesbian, Gay, and Bisexual Topics in Psychology and Related Journals

The Counseling Psychologist, 1998, September 26(5), Lesbian, Gay, and Bisexual Affirmative Training.

American Journal of Orthopsychiatry, 1998, August 60(3). Special section: Sexual orientation and family development.

Professional School Counseling, 1998 February 1(13).

Women and Therapy, 1996. 18(2). Special issue: Lesbian therapists and their therapy: From both sides of the couch.

Harvard Educational Review, 1996, Spring 66(2). Special issue: Lesbian, gay, bisexual, transgender in education.

Journal of Vocational Behavior, 1996, April 48(2).

Individual Psychology: Journal of Adlerian Theory, Research, and Practice, 1995, June 51(2). Special issue: Counseling homosexuals and bisexuals.

Career Development Quarterly, 1995, December 44(2).

Developmental Psychology, 1995, January 31(1). Special issue: Sexual orientation and human development.

Gender and Societies, 1994, September 8(3). Special issue: Sexual identities/sexual communities.

Families in Society, 1994, June 75(6). Special issue: HIV/AIDS.

Journal of Consulting and Clinical Psychology, 1994, April 62(2). Special section: Mental health of lesbians and gay men.

Journal of Homosexuality, 1993, 26(2-3). Special issue: Critical essays: Gay and lesbian writers of color.

Journal of Chemical Dependency Treatment, 1992, 5(1). Special issue: Lesbian and gay men: Chemical dependency treatment issues.

Journal of Homosexuality, 1991, 22(3/4). Special issue: Coming out of the classroom closet: Gay and lesbian students, teachers, and curricula.

The Counseling Psychologist, 1991, April 19(2). Special issue.

Journal of Interpersonal Violence, 1990, September 5(3). Special issue: Violence against lesbians and gay men: Issues for research, practice, and policy.

Journal of Homosexuality, 1989, 18(1/2). Special issue: Homosexuality and the family.

Journal of Counseling and Development, 1989, 68(1). Special issue: Gay, lesbian and bisexual issues in counseling.

Women and Therapy, 1988, 8(1/2). Special issue: Lesbianism: Affirming nontraditional roles.

Journal of Homosexuality, 1988, 15(1/2). Special issue: Psychopathology and psychotherapy in homosexuality.

Journal of Homosexuality, 1987, 14(1/2). Special issue: Psychotherapy with homosexual men and women: Integrated identity approaches for clinical practice.

Journal of Homosexuality, 1984, 10(1/2). Special issue: Homophobia: An overview.

Journal of Homosexuality, 1981-82, Winter/Spring, 7(2/3). Special issue: Homosexuality and psychotherapy.

3

Including Sexual Orientation in
Life Span Developmental Psychology

DOUGLAS C. KIMMEL

Teaching life span developmental psychology in Japan during my year as a Fulbright Visiting Professor provided a valuable perspective on the field. It became clear to me that, in a Japanese cultural context, the topic we assume is developmental psychology can also be taught as an empirical description of North American culture in the 20th century. At my main university, Tokyo Women's Christian University, my courses on adolescence and on adulthood and aging were taught as courses in the sociology department. At a second school, Tsuda College, the course on adulthood and aging was taught in the English department because it was taught in English. At the third school, the University of Tokyo, it was taught in the Department of American Studies. In each case, the course focused on central aspects of adult development and old age in the United States. Thus, my "psychology" course in Japan was really a course in Western social science, English, and American studies simultaneously. Now that I have re-

AUTHOR'S NOTE: This chapter includes the ideas of Anthony D'Augelli and Margaret Rosario who helped me conceptualize and identify the relevant topics.

turned to teach in an urban, multiethnic, public university in the United States, this experience changed my perception of the field to a much broader conception of the significance and context of life span developmental psychology.

If we consider life span developmental psychology as essentially a study of North American experiences of infancy, childhood, adolescence, youth, maturity, and old age, we are reminded of the extent to which the field reflects normative cultural values about those experiences. In previous decades, those normative values tended to reflect male viewpoints, and if gender was considered, it was usually in terms of sex differences. In many studies, age-related and gender-related differences were described by a statistical analysis "broken down by age and sex." A gerontological association once sold T-shirts with that same slogan printed above four bar graphs representing young males, old males, young females, and old females. Likewise, ethnic and racial diversity was once considered as racial or ethnic "differences" and was typically an afterthought, since it was thought that all human development should follow the same predictable course.

Today, the normative values are shifting toward viewing human development as a mosaic of diversity. This shift reflects changes in North American culture toward single-parent families, gender equality, and awareness of racial, ethnic, religious, geographic, cohort, socioeconomic, and other contexts. However, when I teach students from many different cultural backgrounds, it is clear that developmental psychology still reflects mainstream North American perspectives.

The reason this chapter on sexual orientation issues is important is because these issues are not represented in the mainstream perspective. Few developmental psychology, life span development, adolescence, or adulthood texts do more than give a politically correct nod toward this issue. In contrast, gender issues and racial and ethnic diversity have become very significant topics. Sexual orientation parallels these topics and provides a way of exploring them in greater depth and richness by comparing and contrasting those issues with sexual orientation issues.

It may also be noted that the study of sexual orientation is firmly within the realm of developmental psychology. There are several examples of developmental theories of sexual orientation in the literature. The most widely recognized is the Freudian idea of developmental arrest as a result of an unresolved Oedipal conflict during childhood; nonetheless, Freud was an early supporter of civil rights for homosexuals (Bem, 1993). Another developmental model is Sullivan's (1953) idea of the lust dynamism emerging and its dynamic interplay with a preadolescent same-sex chumship; Sullivan is widely known to have been homosexual (Allen, 1995). Storms (1981) found that early pubertal maturation during the period of same-sex social intimacy was associated with homoerotic fantasy in college students and hypothesized that contiguous learning may be a factor in sexual orientation. More recently, Bem (1996) synthesized several models and hypothesized that children find erotic those (exotic) people who engage in activity that is gender-related and different from one's own activity. In addition, many theorists have speculated about the role of early childhood experiences, gender nonconformity, early sexual experiences, abuse, and unsatisfactory heterosexual trials in developing a same-gender sexual orientation. Moreover, the developmental effect of sexual orientation is clearly life span in nature, with continuity of sexual orientation, even beyond the years of sexual activity, as the typical pattern (Money, 1988). Finally, bisexual persons may show developmental patterns such as sequential periods of homosexual and heterosexual attractions, and illustrate the need for a multidimensional model of sexual orientation (Fox, 1995).

In developmental fashion, this chapter discusses topics and issues about sexual orientation in infancy and early childhood, middle childhood, early adolescence, late adolescence, adulthood, and aging. One is always torn between using a topical and a chronological view of development. With a topical view, however, sexual orientation may be segregated from other developmental issues in a separate chapter or lecture related to sexuality, or diversity. In a chronological view, it is clear that sexual orientation is a relevant topic in each segment of the life cycle, no matter how defined or divided into developmental periods. This point is critical since, like gender or race, sexual orientation affects the process and content of developmental experience. It is not limited to sexual development, identity, or any other single topic, but it is a multifaceted, culturally determined, contextually sensitive, pervasive influence throughout the life span. This is especially true in Western cultures with strong taboos about sexuality.

Infancy and Early Childhood

Most developmental psychology courses focus on typical developmental sequences. Some attention is given to contextual factors such as socioeconomic class or parents' educational level, drug use, age, and so on. Important variations are often noted, but usually the focus is on pragmatic topics of infant development and child rearing, research methods and empirical findings about development, parent-infant relations, and the importance of early stimulation and learning. It is usually assumed that the child will be similar to the parent in all important ways, including sexual orientation. Recent research about possible genetic influences on sexual orientation raises the possibility that some infants are born with a predisposition to develop a same-gender erotic orientation just as some may be born with the predisposition to become musicians, left handed, or skilled athletes (or all of the above). One way to integrate sexual orientation into this section of the course is to use examples from nontraditional families, to avoid the assumption that everyone's family has one adult male and one adult female in the role of parents, and to include sexual orientation in class or small group discussions. Possible topics include:

- Behavior genetics—Suppose parents can determine the sexual orientation of their fetus? Is this different from being left handed or exceptionally talented in music?
- Gender nonconformity—What to do about "sissy boys" and "tomboys"?
- Social discrimination against children who are "different" in gender-related ways.
- Psychosocial stressors on children of gay or lesbian parents.
- Gender identity issues—How are gender, physical anatomy (male, female, or ambiguous), and a social role integrated during childhood?
- Should children with ambiguous genitals be made to conform to either male or female forms?
- How do family members and siblings deal with gender nonconformity?

Middle Childhood

This section of the course usually focuses on socialization, cognitive and social-cognitive development (including friendship, self-concept, and person-perception), and elementary education issues. If possible, view the videotape, *It's Elementary* (Women's Educational Media, 1998) to see how well children of this age can deal with sexual orientation issues (often much better than some adults) and to see many examples of ways the topic can be an aspect of an ordinary school curriculum. The following discussion questions would be useful for students to consider in college classrooms:

- Schools—What kind of educational information should be provided in K-6 grades?
- Emotional closeness—How do children deal with being intimate with persons of the same gender and the other gender? Does later sexual orientation affect this?
- Where do children who feel "different" find social support for their self-esteem?
- Victimization—Are gender-nonconforming children more likely to be attacked physically and sexually? What can be done to reduce this risk? How does it shape their view of themselves?
- How do antigay ideas and attitudes (homophobia/heterosexism) form, and can they be prevented or reduced?
- Are there racial, ethnic, cultural, socioeconomic, or religious differences or factors in the formation of antigay attitudes? Why?
- Do Sullivan's concepts of chumship and the "lust dynamism" differ for lesbian, gay, bisexual, and heterosexual preadolescents?

Early Adolescence

The central topic of this segment of human development is puberty and the inner and outer effects of hormones, secondary sex characteristics, and genital maturation. Sexual orientation often emerges as a conscious element at this point, and so it is necessary to include it explicitly in developmental courses in at least two ways. First, it is one dimension of social-cultural identity in that, like ethnic, racial, or religious minorities, a lesbian or gay adolescent is growing up in two cultures: (1) the heterosexual dominant culture; and (2) the (perhaps secret) identification with the gay community (Kimmel & Weiner, 1995). The ways in which this plays out differ greatly among gay and lesbian adolescents, but often there is no parental or community support for one's minority identity (and sometimes overt rejection of it); therefore, it is different from other minority adolescents. Similarly, lesbian, gay, and bisexual sexual orientation is invisible to most people, so one often can keep it secret. Some discussion questions on this topic may include the following:

- How do adolescents learn they are gay or lesbian even before they have sexual relations?
- Styles of adaptation—repression, denial, or disclosure.
- Identity issues—How and when to come out.
- Gender role issues—How can one be "normal" and gay or lesbian or bisexual?
- Is sexual orientation a preference (choice) or orientation (discovery)? Does it matter?

The second important topic to discuss is sexuality. Depending on geographic and ethnic characteristics of the college students, sexual experimentation may begin during early adolescence. In some cases, heterosexual intercourse is a rite of passage affirming one's normality. Many males have same-gender sexual contact, and masturbation is widely practiced. Many females have same-gender crushes and may experience a degree of intimacy that is much more intense than with males. The United States society remains sex-phobic, so most of these topics are never discussed openly and a great deal of ignorance and confusion results, with most adolescents learning about sexuality from their friends and the media. Therefore, even college students may benefit from sex education. Generally, lesbian, gay, and bisexual issues can be integrated into this topic smoothly since, in actual practice, penile-vaginal intercourse is the only difference between same-gender and other-gender behavior. The implications of that fact and gender roles in sexual contact are fascinating; however, students rarely consider them. Try these topics:

- Early sexual experimentation—heterosexual and homosexual.
- Gender differences in learning sexual/erotic arousal responses.
- Puberty— What role does it play? Is early puberty likely to lead to homosexual orientation?
- Consequences of heterosexual experimentation for gay and lesbian adolescents.
- Educational information needed—HIV/AIDS, STDs, abuse, victimization.

Late Adolescence

The usual emphasis of this phase of the course is on identity formation. Sexual orientation is an important component of the interpersonal component of identity; it may also involve ideological and even occupational components. The formation of intimate relationships that integrate sexuality also is usually an important topic. Gender differences in this process, and in the link between identity and intimacy, provide a basis for discussing sexual orientation. Some relevant discussion themes include:

- Dating and safe places for same-gender couples to go on dates.
- Integrating homosexuality into the rest of one's life—for example, career choice, college choice.
- Family, friends, siblings—How to tell them and deal with their reaction.
- Dealing with landlords, roommates, employers, and coworkers.

Adulthood

Obviously, this segment of life span development can be an entire course (Kimmel, 1990). In brief, the central topics are working, loving, and family relationships. Regardless of sexual orientation, many adults provide care for aging parents, young children, or both, and maintain domestic living arrangements of various types. Usually, "adults" are what one thinks about in terms of lesbians, bisexuals, and gay men. Therefore, almost any topic may be discussed in terms of sexual orientation issues (sex is one topic, but it is not all there is).

- Deciding whether, when, and how to "come out."
- To "marry" or not; domestic partnerships.
- To have children or not—How, and why?
- Variations—heterosexual marriage with outside homosexual relations; celibacy; long-term gay/lesbian relationships; gay/lesbian lifestyle with no long-term cohabiting relationships; a bisexual lifestyle without marriage; alternating heterosexual and homosexual relationships; and multiple simultaneous relationships (same-gender polygamy/polyandry).
- Reactions to the reality and perception of discrimination.

- Relations with one's biological family and/or aging parents.
- Divorce, custody, and other legal issues.
- Maintaining intergenerational relationships without a biological family.
- Widowhood and possible discrimination from family and in legal matters.

Aging

As sexuality is often seen as the basis for sexual orientation, and old people are seen as "sexless," many are surprised to find lesbian, gay, and bisexual issues in old age. The beginning of old age is ambiguous and many chronologically "old" people are active sexually, physically, emotionally, and intellectually. However, when health issues begin to take precedence in life, a variety of issues emerge that were not as important before. These issues may include:

- Does being lesbian, gay, or bisexual affect the delivery of appropriate health care?
- Finding support and care during times of need.
- Giving care and wisdom to the younger generation.
- Is there ageism within the gay/lesbian community? What are its effects?
- The need for social, social service, and retirement housing opportunities designed by and for the lesbian, gay, and bisexual community.

Conclusion

When teaching life span developmental psychology, it is difficult to find a topic that does not involve gay, lesbian, or bisexual issues. Often, they can put typical human development concerns in perspective. Sometimes, they can enrich the topic of diversity that is so important in teaching psychology today. Most important, they can enlighten issues of gender that often are studied only in a heterosexual framework.

Two important suggestions emerge from this brief review of sexual orientation issues relevant for developmental psychology. First, there are many research questions raised by asking about gay, lesbian, or bisexual people, or those infants and children who will become gay, lesbian, or bisexual. Second, there are important lessons to be learned by examining the success of those developmental psychologists who studied gender issues. In an important sense, sexual orientation is a subdiscipline of gender studies. As the issue of same-gender marriage makes clear, denial of the right to love and to marry persons of the same gender is a manifestation of gender discrimination. One day, developmental psychologists will include those whose gender preference is different from the heterosexual norm as naturally as they today include those whose gender is different from the male norm of earlier psychology.

Basic Bibliography

The following resources are available for classroom use, supplemental reading, or as background for preparing class discussions and lectures. Each has a developmental perspective.

- Garnets and Kimmel (1993). A collection of classic reprints.
- D'Augelli and Patterson (1995). An anthology of chapters summarizing the state of the art.
- Savin-Williams and Cohen (1996). A text consisting of chapters written by the editors and other experts.

A more complete bibliography of life span developmental issues is provided in Appendix A.

Appendix A
Bibliography for Life Span Development
From a Lesbian, Gay, and Bisexual Perspective

Children and Youth

Bailey, J. M., & Zucker, K. J. (1995). Childhood sex-typed behavior and sexual orientation: A conceptual analysis and quantitative review. *Developmental Psychology, 31*, 43-55.

Buhrke, R. A., & Stabb S. D. (1995). Gay, lesbian, and bisexual student needs. In S. D. Stabb, S. M. Harris, & J. E. Talley (Eds.), *Multicultural needs assessment for college and university student populations* (pp. 173-201). Springfield, IL: Charles C Thomas.

D'Augelli, A. R. (1996). Enhancing the development of lesbian, gay, and bisexual youths. In E. D. Rothblum & L. A. Bond (Eds.), *Preventing heterosexism and homophobia* (pp. 124-150). Thousand Oaks, CA: Sage.

D'Augelli, A. R., & Dark, L. J. (1994). Lesbian, gay, and bisexual youths. In L. D. Eron, J. H. Gentry, & P. Schlegel (Eds.), *Reason to hope: A psychosocial perspective on violence and youth* (pp. 177-196). Washington, DC: American Psychological Association.

DeCrescenzo, T. (Ed.). (1994). *Helping gay and lesbian youth: New policies, new programs, new practice.* New York: Haworth.

French, S. A., Story, M., Remafedi, G., Resnick, M. D., & Blum, R. W. (1996). Sexual orientation and prevalence of body dissatisfaction and eating disordered behaviors: A population-based study of adolescents. *International Journal of Eating Disorders, 19,* 119-126.

Grossman, A. H., & Kerner, M. S. (1998). Self-esteem and supportiveness as predictors of emotional distress in gay male and lesbian youth. *Journal of Homosexuality, 35*(2), 25-39.

Herdt, G. (Ed.). (1989). *Gay and lesbian youth.* New York: Harrington Park. [Also *Journal of Homosexuality,* 17 (1, 2, 3, 4)]

Herdt, G., & Boxer, A. (1993). *Children of Horizons: How gay and lesbian teens are leading a new way out of the closet.* Boston: Beacon.

Hershberger, S. L., & D'Augelli, A. R. (1995). The impact of victimization on the mental health and suicidality of lesbian, gay, and bisexual youths. *Developmental Psychology, 31,* 65-74.

Hetrick, E. S., & Martin, A. D. (1988). Developmental issues and their resolution for gay and lesbian adolescents. In E. Coleman (Ed.), *Psychotherapy with homosexual men and women: Integrated identity approaches for clinical practice* (pp. 25-43). New York: Haworth.

Jennings, K. (Ed.). (1994). *Becoming visible: A reader in gay and lesbian history for high school and college students.* Boston: Alyson.

Pilkington, N. W., & D'Augelli, A. R. (1995). Victimization of lesbian, gay, and bisexual youth in community settings. *Journal of Community Psychology, 23,* 34-56.

Rhodes, R .A. (1994). *Coming out in college: The struggle for a queer identity.* Westport, CT: Bergin & Garvey.

Rotheram-Borus, M. J., Rosario, M., Van Rossem, R., Reid, H., & Gillis, R. (1995). Prevalence, course, and predictors of multiple problem behaviors among gay and bisexual male adolescents. *Developmental Psychology, 31,* 75-85.

Rosario, M., Rotheram-Borus, M. J., & Reid, H. (1996). Gay-related stress and its correlates among gay and bisexual male adolescents of predominately Black and Hispanic background. *Journal of Community Psychology, 24,* 136-159.

Savin-Williams, R. C. (1990). *Gay and lesbian youth: Expressions of identity.* New York: Hemisphere.

Savin-Williams, R. C. (1995). Lesbian, gay male, and bisexual adolescents. In A. R. D'Augelli & C. J. Patterson (Eds.), *Lesbian, gay, and bisexual identities over the lifespan: Psychological perspectives* (pp. 165-189). New York: Oxford University Press.

Savin-Williams, R. C. (1996). Self-labeling and disclosure among gay, lesbian, and bisexual youths. In J. Laird & R. J. Green (Eds.), *Lesbians and gays in couples and families: A handbook for therapists* (pp. 153-182). San Francisco: Jossey-Bass.

Schneider M. (1989). Sappho was a right-on adolescent: Growing up lesbian. *Journal of Homosexuality, 17*(1-2), 111-130.

Tremble, B., Schneider, M., & Appathurai, C. (1989). Growing up gay or lesbian in a multicultural context. *Journal of Homosexuality, 17*(3-4), 253-267.

Unks, G. (Ed.). (1995). *The gay teen: Educational practice and theory for lesbian, gay, and bisexual adolescents.* New York: Routledge.

Uribe, V., & Harbeck, K. M. (1991). Addressing the needs of lesbian, gay, and bisexual youth: The origins of Project 10 and school-based intervention. *Journal of Homosexuality, 22*(3-4), 9-28.

Adulthood and Aging

Adams, C. L., & Kimmel, D. C. (1997). Exploring the lives of older African American gay men. In B. Greene (Ed.), *Ethnic and cultural diversity among lesbians and gay men* (pp. 132-151). Thousand Oaks, CA: Sage.

Berger, R. (1995). *Gay and gray: The older homosexual man* (2nd ed.). New York: Haworth.

Boatwright, K. J., Gilbert, M. S., Forrest, L., & Ketzenberger, K. (1996). Impact of identity development upon career trajectory: Listening to the voices of lesbian women. *Journal of Vocational Behavior, 48,* 210-228.

Boxer, A. M. (1997). Gay, lesbian, and bisexual aging into the twenty-first century: An overview and introduction. *Journal of Gay, Lesbian, and Bisexual Identity, 2,* 187-197.

Butler, S. S., & Hope, B. (1999). Health and well-being for late middle-aged and old lesbians in a rural area. *Journal of Gay and Lesbian Social Services, 9*(4), 27-46.

Copper, B. (1988). *Over the hill: Reflections on ageism between women.* Freedom, CA: Crossing Press.

Davis, N. D., Cole, E., & Rothblum, E. D. (1993). *Faces of women and aging.* New York: Haworth. [Also, *Women and Therapy, 14* (1-2)]

Herdt, G., Beeler, J., & Rawls, T. W. (1997). Life course diversity among older lesbians and gay men: A study in Chicago. *Journal of Gay, Lesbian, and Bisexual Identity, 2,* 231-246.

Herdt, G., Hostetler, A. J., & Cohler, B. J. (Eds.). (1997). Coming of age: Gays, lesbians, and bisexuals in the second half of life. *Journal of Gay, Lesbian, and Bisexual Identity, 2,* 187-308 (whole numbers 3/4).

Jacobson, S., & Grossman, A. H. (1996). Older lesbians and gay men: Old myths, new images, and future directions. In R. C. Savin-Williams & K. M. Cohen (Eds.), *The lives of lesbians, gays, and bisexuals: Children to adults* (pp. 345-373). Fort Worth, TX: Harcourt Brace College Publishers.

Kimmel, D. C. (1978/1993). Adult development and aging: A gay perspective. In L. D. Garnets & D. C. Kimmel (Eds.), *Psychological perspectives on lesbian and gay male experiences* (pp. 517-534). New York: Columbia University Press. [Originally in *Journal of Social Issues, 34*(3), 113-130]

Kimmel, D. C., & Sang, B. E. (1995). Lesbians and gay men in midlife. In A. R. D'Augelli & C. J. Patterson (Eds.), *Lesbian, gay, and bisexual identities over the lifespan: Psychological perspectives* (pp. 190-214). New York: Oxford University Press.

Linsk, N. L. (1997). Experience of older gay and bisexual men living with HIV/AIDS. *Journal of Gay, Lesbian, and Bisexual Identity, 2,* 285-308.

Reid, J. D. (1995). Development in late life: Older lesbian and gay lives. In A. R. D'Augelli & C. J. Patterson (Eds.), *Lesbian, gay, and bisexual identities over the lifespan: Psychological perspectives* (pp. 215-240). New York: Oxford University Press.

Sang, B. E. (1993). Existential issues of midlife lesbians. In L. D. Garnets & D. C. Kimmel (Eds.), *Psychological perspectives on lesbian and gay male experiences* (pp. 500-516). New York: Columbia University Press.

Sang, B., Warshow, J., & Smith, A. J. (Eds.). (1991). *Lesbians at midlife: The creative transition.* San Francisco: Spinsters Book Company.

Sharp, C. E. (1997). Lesbianism and later life in an Australian sample: How does development of one affect anticipation of the other? *Journal of Gay, Lesbian, and Bisexual Identity, 2,* 247-263.

Slusher, M. P., Mayer, C. J., & Dunkle, R. E. (1996). Gay and Lesbians Older and Wiser (GLOW): A support group for older gay people. *Gerontologist, 36,* 118-123.

Couple Relationships

Becker, C. S. (1988). *Unbroken ties: Lesbian ex-lovers.* Boston: Alyson.

Berzon, B. (1988). *Permanent partners: Building gay and lesbian relationships that last.* New York: Dutton.

Berzon, B. (1998). *The intimacy dance: A guide to long-term success in gay and lesbian relationships.* New York: Plume.

Blumstein, P., & Schwartz, P. (1983). *American couples: Money, work, sex.* New York: Morrow.

Buxton, A. P. (1991). *The other side of the closet: The coming-out crisis for straight spouses and families.* Santa Monica, CA: IBS Press.

Clunis, D. M., & Green, G. D. (1988). *Lesbian couples.* Seattle: Seal Press.

Curry, H., Clifford, D., & Leonard R. (1996). *A legal guide for lesbian and gay couples.* (9th Ed.) Berkeley, CA: Nolo Press.

Garcia, N., Kennedy, C., Pearlman, S. F., & Perez, J. (1987). The impact of race and culture differences: Challenges to intimacy in lesbian relationships. In Boston Lesbian Psychologies Collective (Ed.), *Lesbian psychologies: Explorations and challenges* (pp. 142-160). Urbana: University of Illinois Press.

Hostetler, A. J., & Cohler, B. J. (1997). Partnership, singlehood, and the lesbian and gay life course: A research agenda. *Journal of Gay, Lesbian, and Bisexual Identity, 2,* 199-230.

Johnson, S. E. (1990). *Staying power: Long term lesbian couples.* Tallahassee, FL: Naiad Press.

Klinkenberg, D., & Rose, S. (1994). Dating scripts of gay men and lesbians. *Journal of Homosexuality, 26*(4), 23-35.

Kurdek, L. A. (Ed.). (1994). Social services for gay and lesbian couples. *Journal of Gay & Lesbian Social Services, 1* (whole no. 2).

Kurdek, L. A. (1994). The nature and correlates of relationship quality in gay, lesbian, and heterosexual cohabiting couples. In B. Greene & G. M. Herek (Eds.), *Lesbian and gay psychology: Theory, research, and clinical applications* (pp. 133-155). Thousand Oaks, CA: Sage.

Kurdek, L. A. (1995a). Developmental changes in relationship quality in gay and lesbian cohabiting couples. *Developmental Psychology, 31,* 86-94.

Kurdek, L. A. (1995b). Lesbian and gay couples. In A. R. D'Augelli & C. J. Patterson (Eds.), *Lesbian, gay, and bisexual identities over the lifespan: Psychological perspectives* (pp. 243-261). New York: Oxford University Press.

Marcus, E. (1992). *The male couple's guide: Finding a man, making a home, building a life.* New York: Harper Perennial.

Martin, A. (1993). *The lesbian and gay parenting handbook: Creating and raising our families.* New York: Harper Perennial.

Mays, V. M., Cochran, S. D., & Rhue, S. (1993). The impact of perceived discrimination on the intimate relationships of Black lesbians. *Journal of Homosexuality, 25*(4), 1-14.

McWhirter, D. P., & Mattison, A. M. (1984). *The male couple: How relationships develop.* Englewood Cliffs, NJ: Prentice Hall.

Murphy, B. C. (1994). Difference and diversity: Gay and lesbian couples. *Journal of Gay & Lesbian Social Services, 1*(2), 5-31.

Nichols, M. (1990). Lesbian relationships: Implications for the study of sexuality and gender. In D. P. McWhirter, S. A. Sanders, & J. M. Reinisch (Eds.), *Homosexuality/ heterosexuality: Concepts of sexual orientation* (pp. 350-364). New York: Oxford University Press.

Peplau, L. A. (1991). Lesbian and gay relationships. In J. C. Gonsiorek & J. D. Weinrich (Eds.), *Homosexuality: Research implications for public policy* (pp. 177-196). Newbury Park, CA: Sage.

Peplau, L. A., & Cochran, S. D. (1990). A relationship perspective on homosexuality. In D. P. McWhirter, S. A. Sanders, & J. M. Reinisch (Eds.), *Homosexuality/heterosexuality: Concepts of sexual orientation* (pp. 321-349). New York: Oxford University Press.

Peplau, L. A., Cochran, S. D., & Mays, V. M. (1997). A national survey of the intimate relationships of African American lesbians and gay men: A look at commitment, satisfaction, sexual behavior, and HIV disease. In B. Greene (Ed.), *Ethnic and cultural diversity among lesbians and gay men* (pp. 11-38). Thousand Oaks, CA: Sage.

Peplau, L. A., Veniegas, R. C., & Campbell, S. M. (1996). Gay and lesbian relationships. In R. C. Savin-Williams & K. M. Cohen (Eds.), *The lives of lesbians, gays, and bisexuals: Children to adults* (pp. 250-273). Fort Worth, TX: Harcourt Brace College Publishers.

Rothblum, E. D., & Brehony, K. A. (Eds.). (1993). *Boston marriages: Romantic but asexual relationships among contemporary lesbians*. Amherst: University of Massachusetts Press.

Rust, P. C. (1996). Monogamy and polyamory: Relationship issues for bisexuals. In B. A. Firestein (Ed.), *Bisexuality: The psychology and politics of an invisible minority* (pp. 127-148). Thousand Oaks, CA: Sage.

Shernoff, M. (Ed.). (1997). Gay widowers: Life after the death of a partner. *Journal of Gay & Lesbian Social Services* 7(whole no. 2).

Stearns, D. C., & Sabini, J. (1997). Dyadic adjustment and community involvement in same-sex couples. *Journal of Gay, Lesbian, and Bisexual Identity, 2,* 265-283.

Vargo, S. (1987). The effects of women's socialization on lesbian couples. In Boston Lesbian Psychologies Collective (Ed.), *Lesbian psychologies: Explorations and challenges* (pp. 161-173). Urbana: University of Illinois Press.

Parenting

Bailey, J. M., Bobrow, D., Wolfe, M., & Mikach, S. (1995). Sexual orientation of adult sons of gay fathers. *Developmental Psychology, 31,* 124-129.

Barrett, R. L., & Robinson, B. E. (1990). *Gay fathers*. Lexington, MA: Lexington Books.

Benkov, L. (1994). *Reinventing the family: The emerging story of lesbian and gay parents*. New York: Crown.

Bozett, F. W. (1987). *Gay and lesbian parents*. New York: Praeger.

Flaks, D. K., Ficher, I., Masterpasqua, F., & Joseph, G. (1995). Lesbians choosing motherhood: A comparative study of lesbian and heterosexual parents and their children. *Developmental Psychology, 31,* 105-114.

Golombok, S., & Tasker, F. (1996). Do parents influence the sexual orientation of their children? Findings from a longitudinal study of lesbian families. *Developmental Psychology, 32,* 3-11.

Green, G. D., & Bozett, F. W. (1991). Lesbian mothers and gay fathers. In J. C. Gonsiorek & J. D. Weinrich (Eds.), *Homosexuality: Research implications for public policy* (pp. 197-214). Newbury Park, CA: Sage.

Patterson, C. J. (1994). Lesbian and gay couples considering parenthood: An agenda for research, service, and advocacy. *Journal of Gay & Lesbian Social Services, 1*(2), 33-55.

Patterson, C. J. (1995). Families of the lesbian baby boom: Parents' division of labor and children's adjustment. *Developmental Psychology, 31,* 115-123.

Patterson, C. J. (1995). Lesbian mothers, gay fathers, and their children. In A. R. D'Augelli & C. J. Patterson (Eds.), *Lesbian, gay, and bisexual identities over the lifespan: Psychological perspectives* (pp. 262-290). New York: Oxford University Press.

Patterson, C. J. (1997). Children of lesbian and gay parents. *Advances in Clinical Child Psychology, 19,* 235-282.

Patterson, C. J., & Redding, R. E. (1996). Lesbian and gay families with children: Implications of social science research for policy. *Journal of Social Issues, 52*(3), 29-50.

Rohrbaugh, J. B. (1992). Lesbian families: Clinical issues and theoretical implications. *Professional Psychology, 23,* 467-473.

Slater, S. (1995). *The lesbian family life cycle.* New York: Free Press.

Tasker, F. L., & Golombok, S. (1997). *Growing up in a lesbian family: Effects on child development.* New York: Guilford.

General

Geasler, M. J., Croteau, J. M., Heineman, C. J., & Edlund, C. J. (1995). A qualitative study of students' expression of change after attending panel presentations by lesbian, gay, and bisexual speakers. *Journal of College Student Development, 36,* 483-492.

D'Augelli, A. R. (1994). Lesbian and gay male development. In B. Greene & G. M. Herek (Eds.), *Lesbian and gay psychology: Theory, research, and clinical applications* (pp. 118-132). Thousand Oaks, CA: Sage.

Garnets, L. D., & Kimmel, D. C. (Eds.). (1993). *Psychological perspectives on lesbian and gay male experiences.* New York: Columbia University Press.

Herek, G. M., & Capitalis, J. P. (1996). "Some of my best friends": Intergroup contact, concealable stigma, and heterosexuals' attitudes toward gay men and lesbians. *Personality and Social Psychology Bulletin, 22,* 412-424.

Rust, P. C. (1996). Finding a sexual identity and community: Therapeutic implications and cultural assumptions in scientific models of coming out. In E. D. Rothblum & L. A. Bond (Eds.), *Preventing heterosexism and homophobia* (pp. 87-123). Thousand Oaks, CA: Sage.

Savin-Williams, R. C., & Cohen, K. M. (Eds.). (1996). *The lives of lesbians, gays, and bisexuals: Children to adults.* Fort Worth, TX: Harcourt Brace College Publishers.

References

Allen, M. S. (1995). Sullivan's closet: A reappraisal of Harry Stack Sullivan's life and his pioneering role in American psychiatry. *Journal of Homosexuality, 29*(1), 1-18.

Bem, D. J. (1996). Exotic becomes erotic: A developmental theory of sexual orientation. *Psychological Review, 103,* 320-335.

Bem, S. L. (1993). *The lenses of gender: Transforming the debate on sexual inequality.* New Haven, CT: Yale University Press.

D'Augelli, A. R., & Patterson, C. J. (Eds.). (1995). *Lesbian, gay, and bisexual identities over the lifespan: Psychological perspectives.* New York: Oxford University Press.

Fox, R. C. (1995). Bisexual identities. In A. R. D'Augelli & C. J. Patterson (Eds.), *Lesbian, gay, and bisexual identities over the lifespan: Psychological perspectives* (pp. 48-86). New York: Oxford University Press.

Garnets, L. D., & Kimmel, D. C. (Eds.). (1993). *Psychological perspectives on lesbian and gay male experiences.* New York: Columbia University Press.

Kimmel, D. C. (1990). *Adulthood and aging: An interdisciplinary, developmental view* (3rd ed.). New York: John Wiley.

Kimmel, D. C., & Weiner, I. B. (1995). *Adolescence: A developmental transition* (2nd ed.). New York: John Wiley.

Money, J. (1988). *Gay, straight, and in between: The sexology of erotic orientation.* New York: Oxford University Press.

Savin-Williams, R. C., & Cohen, K. M. (Eds.) (1996). *The lives of lesbians, gays, and bisexuals: Children to adults.* Fort Worth, TX: Harcourt Brace College Publishers.

Storms, M. D. (1981). A theory of erotic orientation development. *Psychological Review, 88,* 340-353.

Sullivan, H. S. (1953). *The interpersonal theory of psychiatry.* New York: Norton.

Women's Educational Media. (1998). *It's elementary: Talking about gay issues in school* (Educational training version, 37 minutes). [Video distributed by New Day Films.]

4

Confronting Heterosexism in the Teaching of Psychology

JANE M. SIMONI

Psychology is not immune from the biases of its cultural context, including the devaluation of homosexuality. Historically, the profession has pathologized nonheterosexual orientations and failed to cultivate an appreciation of and sensitivity toward diversity in sexual orientation. Part of the instructor's role, then, is to challenge prevailing heterosexist assumptions and provide accurate information about the psychology of lesbians and gay men. This chapter presents a rationale for making the psychology curriculum more inclusive of lesbian and gay male issues. Results are presented from a survey of current psychology textbooks that indicate inadequate coverage and segregated treatment of the topic of homosexuality. Finally, suggestions are provided to instructors for expanding coverage of lesbian and gay male psychological issues and avoiding heterosexist bias.

AUTHOR'S NOTE: This research was supported in part by NCI Training Grant 5 T32 CA09492 and the Aaron Diamond Foundation. The author acknowledges Linda Garnets and Karina Walters for their comments on earlier drafts of this paper.

Reprinted with permission from *Teaching of Psychology* 23/4 (1995) 220-226.

Confronting Heterosexism in the Teaching of Psychology

The science and pedagogy of psychology are not practiced in a cultural vacuum. As Denmark (1994) suggested, "We must realize that psychology is not value free but rather is a creation of the culture and context in which it has developed" (p. 334). One prevailing aspect of the dominant culture of the United States is heterosexism, here defined as the belief that heterosexuality is the only natural and acceptable sexual orientation and the irrational hatred and discrimination directed at those deemed nonheterosexual (Simoni, 1996). In this country, religious institutions have demonized lesbians and gay men (Boswell, 1980), the general populace has largely harbored antigay attitudes (Herek, 1991), and the courts have historically failed to protect the rights of lesbian and gay male individuals (Rivera, 1991).

This prevailing bias has created a psychology of heterosexuality so entrenched in our notions about human behavior that it is "as the water is to fish, wholly nonconscious and relatively unchallenged" (Brooks, 1992, p. 203). Brooks (1992, p. 204) described the heterosexist bias in psychology as based on the following four assumptions: (1) Lesbianism and homosexuality have to be explained, (2) adult sexual orientation is determined by early childhood experience, (3) lesbianism and homosexuality are negative outcomes of childhood socialization, and (4) lesbians are masculine and masculine women are pathological or gay men are effeminate and effeminate men are pathological. Despite the dearth of evidence to support these assumptions and the research since Hooker (1957) that contradicts them (see Garnets & Kimmel, 1993; Gonsiorek & Weinrich, 1991), many psychologists persist in holding these beliefs.

The heterosexist bias in clinical psychology can be traced to the field's psychoanalytic roots. Although many quote Freud (1935/1960) as writing to the mother of a homosexual son that "homosexuality is assuredly no advantage, but it is nothing to be ashamed of, no vice, no degradation, it cannot be classified as an illness . . . ," they often omit the rest of his sentence, " . . . we consider it to be a variation of the sexual function, produced by a certain *arrest of sexual development*" (emphasis added, p. 423). Later psychoanalytic theorists asserted the pathology of homosexuality, continuing to view it as a fixated and immature state (Bieber & Bieber, 1979; Socarides, 1968, 1978). Until 1973, homosexuality was classified as a mental disorder in the American Psychiatric Association's *Diagnostic and Statistical Manual of Mental Disorders* (*DSM;* Kirk & Kutchins, 1992; Morgan & Nerison, 1993).

Identifying, confronting, and defying heterosexism in the field of psychology should be part of the task of an effective instructor. Success in this endeavor requires breaking the customary silence on the topic and challenging its omission from the traditional psychology curriculum. An indication of this omission is that only one article since the inception of the journal *Teaching of Psychology* in 1974 (i.e., McCord & Herzog, 1991) directly addresses the issue of teaching about homosexuality.

In place of a model of homosexuality based on pathology and rooted in heterosexist bias, instructors should present an affirmative perspective based on an appreciation of diversity (L. D. Garnets, personal communication, March, 29, 1995; King, 1988) and rooted in empirical research (see Garnets & Kimmel, 1993; Gonsiorek & Weinrich, 1991; Hooker, 1957). Such a model is supported by the American Psychological Association (APA), which in 1975 adopted the following resolution: "Homosexuality per se implies no impairment in judgment, stability, reliability, or general social and vocational capabilities: Further, the APA urges all mental health professionals to take the lead in removing the stigma of mental illness that has long been associated with homosexual orientations" (Conger, 1975, p. 633). An affirmative model stresses the equivalent status of heterosexuality and homosexuality, with homosexuality seen as a natural variant in human sexuality. Lesbians and gay men are acknowledged to be equal to heterosexuals in their psychological adjustment and in their capacity to love, relate, and contribute to society. Social psychological and developmental models are used to understand lesbian and gay male experience and the process of coping with a marginal status. The increasing acceptance of this model is demonstrated by the growth of the literature incorporating an affirmative approach (see Appendix A) and the courage, creativity, and commitment shown by many psychologists in their teaching and advocacy within the field.

In this chapter, I present a rationale for adopting an affirmative model of homosexuality in the psychology curriculum, a critique of the treatment of homosexuality in psychology textbooks, and some suggestions for avoiding heterosexist bias and incorporating an affirmative model in the pedagogy of psychology.

Rationale for a
More Inclusive Curriculum

Beyond adherence to APA's directive, there are other compelling reasons for psychologists to challenge heterosexism in their classrooms. The fear, ignorance, and prejudice concerning lesbians and gay men on college campuses and the resulting harassment and violence have been well documented (Comstock, 1991; Herek, 1991). Such negative attitudes and harmful behaviors jeopardize the well-being of all in the university community. Instructors contribute to this devaluation of lesbian and gay male students when they ignore or omit them in their teaching. An incomplete curriculum suggests to lesbian and gay male students that they are "deviant, psychologically abnormal, invisible, or, at best, barely tolerated" (Crumpacker & Vander Haegen, 1993, p. 95). Because the issue of homosexuality is rarely considered in high school courses, the college curriculum may be students' first exposure to accurate and unbiased information and their first opportunity to discuss the topic in a structured academic setting (Watter, 1987). Covering this topic is especially important in introductory psychology and survey courses because classes devoted exclusively to homosexuality are rare and quite often not attended by those who might have the most to learn.

Learning to teach what we have been taught to omit about lesbians and gay men is important to heterosexual students as well. Accurate information compels them to confront their prejudice and move beyond their limited world views. They are given the opportunity to recognize the dangerous consequences of complicity in even mild statements or acts of heterosexism (Crumpacker & Vander Haegen, 1993).

Several points raised by Denmark (1994) in her discussion of the need to "engender" psychology in terms of women's issues are relevant to teaching about homosexuality. She indicated that we are compelled to challenge biased perspectives with our students so that they may obtain an accurate view of the world. She reminded us of our duty to make students careful consumers of information so that they can challenge fallacious stereotypes and harmful generalizations. Finally, she advised that challenging the discipline's unfounded assumptions makes psychology a stronger science and profession.

Critique of Psychology Textbooks

Relevant to the discussion of teaching about homosexuality is an examination of how the subject is treated in textbooks often required for psychology courses. Researchers have evaluated the treatment of lesbianism in women's studies textbooks (Zimmerman, 1982) and women's literature anthologies (Hickok, 1982). Others have examined the treatment of homosexuality in introductory psychology textbooks from 1975 to 1979 (McDonald, 1981); college-level health science textbooks (Newton, 1979); and human sexuality textbooks (Whitlock & DiLapi, 1983). A perusal of psychology textbooks before 1988 indicated that the psychology of lesbians and gay men, when considered at all, was often restricted to a reference to the declassification in the third edition of the *DSM* usually followed by a discussion on etiological theories and reparative therapies (King, 1988). Such discussions usually were relegated to chapters on abnormal psychology and psychopathology. Restricting the mention of homosexuality to one section or chapter, usually one related to sexual dysfunction, has been termed *ghettoization* (Whitlock & DiLapi, 1983).

Methodology

Textbook Sample

I reviewed a convenience sample of 24 textbooks published between 1991 and 1995—six textbooks each in the areas of introductory, social, developmental, and abnormal psychology. Although there is no statistical basis for claiming this sample is representative, the striking similarity among recently published textbooks in each area argues for the generalizability of the findings.

Definitions

How authors define terms relating to sexual orientation often reveals their perspective; therefore, the glossary of each textbook was examined for definitions of the terms *lesbian, gay,* and *homosexual.* In addition, because an affirmative approach involves comparable treatment of homosexuality and heterosexuality, I also looked for the terms *heterosexual* and *sexual orientation.*

Quantity of Coverage

To gather data on the quantity of coverage of lesbian and gay male issues, the number of index headings or subheadings for the five terms mentioned earlier (and derivatives thereof, such as *gay male,* or *homosexual orientation*) were tallied. Moreover, the detailed tables of content were scanned for sections likely to include relevant passages. All major passages were probably identified because most indexes were highly comprehensive. Length of each passage in number of pages, or fraction thereof rounded up to one-half page, was determined.

Context and Content of Coverage

To assess the context of the coverage, I noted whether relevant passages were limited to sections on sex or sexuality, in other sections only, or in both types of sections. The general thematic content of the coverage was identified. As the range of topics was somewhat circumscribed, simply listing the topics covered was possible.

Quality of Coverage

As an indicator of the quality of coverage, I devised a measure that combined quantity, context, and content of the coverage. Terms for the categories were based on those used in a review of the treatment of African American women in psychology of women textbooks (Brown, Goodwin, Hall, & Jackson-Lowman, 1985). *Poor* textbooks did not mention homosexuality (exclusion) or restricted its coverage to a focus on sexuality or etiology (segregation). *Fair* textbooks defined at least one term in the glossary or cited one in the index. In addition, a *fair* textbook included one passage on homosexuality that did not focus mainly on its etiology and was not included in a section on sexuality (tokenism). *Good* textbooks met the criteria for *fair* textbooks and also mentioned lesbians

Table 4.1 Coverage of Homosexuality in 24 College Psychology Textbooks

Evaluation Criteria	Textbook Subject Area			
	Introductory	Social	Developmental	Abnormal
Quantity of Coverage				
Index citations (range/M)	0-10/4.8	0-8/2.3	1-10/4.2	1-10/2.9
Pages (range/M)	0-5.5/2.8	0-7.5/1.9	1.5-2.5/2.5	1-8/4.0
Glossary Definitions	*n*	*n*	*n*	*n*
Gay	1	0	1	1
Heterosexual	0	0	1	1
Homosexual	1	0	1	1
Lesbian	1	0	1	4
Sexual orientation	1	0	3	0
Content of Coverage				
Homophobia/prejudice	3	3	4	5
AIDS and gay men	4	3	3	3
DSM declassification	4	0	2	6
Origins of homosexuality	6	1	3	2
Other	2	2	1	6
Relationships	1	3	3	2
Gay families/parenting	2	0	2	2
Prevalence	2	0	2	1
Identity formation/coming out	2	1	2	0
Ethnic minority issues	2	0	0	0
Context of Coverage				
Not in any section	0	2	0	0
In sexuality section(s) only	4	0	1	1
In other section(s) only	0	1	1	0
In both types of sections	2	3	4	5
Quality of Coverage				
Good (integration)	2	3	0	3
Fair (tokenism)	0	0	4	1
Poor (exclusion/segregation)	4	3	2	2

and gay men in contexts such as parenting or relationships. *Good* textbooks often included photos of identifiable lesbians and gay men or used them as examples in contexts that were entirely unrelated to homosexuality (integration).

Results

Definitions

As seen in Table 4.1, the lack of lesbian and gay male coverage began in the glossary, with the vast majority of textbooks excluding definitions for the terms *gay, lesbian,* or *homosexual.* Not a single social psychology textbook glossary defined any of the five terms examined. *Homosexual* and *sexual orientation* were the most frequently defined terms; only one textbook included a definition for *heterosexual.*

The definitions for *homosexuality* and *sexual orientation* varied widely. The most heterosexist versions focused on sexual behavior, referring to a lifestyle, choice, or condition, and failed to comparably define heterosexuality. For example, Bootzin, Acocell, and Alloy (1993) defined homosexuality as "a condition characterized by sexual activity directed toward one's own sex" (p. G-10) and included none of the other terms in their glossary. One of the best definitions of *sexual orientation,* "an enduring sexual attraction toward members of either one's own sex (homosexual orientation) or the other sex (heterosexual orientation)" (p. G-14), appeared in Myers (1992).

Quantity of Coverage

Three textbooks (two social and one introductory) included no index citations for any of the five terms. As seen in Table 1, the mean numbers of index citations for each subject area were fairly comparable. This limited indexing was reflected in the low quantity of material in the textbooks; most referred to lesbian and gay men or their concerns on fewer than three pages. Two textbooks did not mention the topic.

Context of Coverage

Review of textbook sections in which the material related to homosexuality was found revealed mixed results according to subject area. Authors of introductory textbooks were most likely to include this material only in sections related to sexuality. Social and developmental textbook authors distributed the information more evenly throughout the textbook, and authors of abnormal psychology textbooks were least likely to restrict content on homosexuality to a chapter on sexual disorders and dysfunction. When they did, they often changed the chapter titles to something more appropriate (e.g., "Abnormality and Variation in Sexual Behavior," Bootzin et al., 1993) or relegated the discussion to a box (as in Sue, Sue, & Sue, 1994).

Content of Coverage

The most recurring topics were homophobia and prejudice, AIDS and gay men, the declassification of homosexuality as a mental illness in the *DSM,* and the origins of homosexuality. Focus on the origins of homosexuality seems excessive, especially when no allusion to the possible origins of heterosexuality were explored. Especially disturbing was the scant coverage of ethnic minority issues and homosexuality; only 2 of the 24 textbooks mentioned it.

Quality of Coverage

Over half of the textbooks reviewed were rated *poor.* Either they completely excluded any content addressing homosexuality or lesbians and gay men or they completely segregated such content in sections on sexuality. The omission was particularly glaring in sections such as "Attraction: Liking and Loving Others" (Myers, 1993). These textbooks are representative of those described in King's (1988) review and suggest that calls for more inclusive coverage and increasing visibility in the intervening years have gone largely unheeded.

Four textbooks were rated *fair;* they offered only token coverage of homosexuality. Development psychology textbooks were most likely to receive this rating. In one such textbook (Cole & Cole, 1993), there was no mention of the specified terms in the glossary, although under the term *homosexuality* the index included page references for homosexual identity, orientation, behavior, stigma, and stages of development. However, all references were to one two-page box that concerned mainly a four-stage model of coming out. A close scanning of the rest of the text revealed no other references to lesbians and gay men or the issue of homosexuality.

Seven *good* textbooks succeeded in presenting several issues related to homosexuality and integrating this content across diverse sections. For instance, Wade and Tavris (1993) discussed kissing as a learned behavior and an acquired taste. Accompanying photos displayed three kissing couples, one of two Latina women. In considering the diversity of the United States population, Rubin, Peplau, and Salovey (1993) do not limit their discussion to ethnic diversity; they mentioned as well gay men, lesbians, and bisexual women and men. Beside a description of how various couples are seen in marital therapy, Comer's (1992) textbook displays a gay male couple.

Discussion of Textbook Review

This evaluation of 24 college-level textbooks in introductory, social, developmental, and abnormal psychology revealed scant attention to psychological issues related to lesbians and gay men. Although some textbooks are beginning to do a fair job of covering homosexuality, most disturbing was the lack of systematic incorporation of references to lesbians and gay men in contexts unrelated to their sexual orientation.

For example, a textbook may mention homosexuality in relation to sex but then neglect to refer to it at all in sections on commitment, intimacy, parenting, and other aspects of relationships, as if these were exclusively heterosexual domains. Under such generic headings as "attraction," textbook authors almost always referred exclusively to heterosexual attraction. Such misleading and assumptive restriction conveys the notion that, compared to heterosexuality, homosexuality is deviant, less important, and less natural. Even more disturbing is the complete absence of homosexual content in a textbook. This type of omission has been interpreted as an implied antihomosexual statement to the student (Newton, 1979).

Teaching About Homosexuality

The findings indicate that most textbooks offer insufficient coverage of homosexuality for college psychology courses. To complement textbooks, instructors must rely on supplementary materials and activities. In his review of the literature on teaching about homosexuality in sex education courses, Watter (1987) pointed out that many modalities have been suggested (i.e., lectures, role playing, audiovisual materials, and guest speakers) but that a scientific evaluation is needed to determine the most efficacious of strategies for teaching about homosexuality. Although such a task is beyond the scope of this chapter, some suggestions are offered.

Before teaching about homosexuality and the heterosexist biases in psychology, the instructor must deal with his or her own homophobia. The willing instructor should read materials by or about lesbians and gay men, consult with them or those who specialize in this area, and talk with peers who are also attempting to eradicate bias from their classrooms. This exercise is important for the lesbian or gay male instructor as well as the heterosexual one.

Because usually only a small portion of any psychology class can be devoted specifically to homosexuality, appropriate information and messages must be conveyed. Ideas for course content can be selected from the resources and references lists at the end of this article. Topics might include coming out as part of the developmental process; the origins of sexual orientation (not homosexuality only); the intersections of heterosexism, sexism, and racism; the social and historical context of institutionalized heterosexism; lesbians and gay men as a minority group; or the formation and alteration of heterosexist attitudes. These discussions should reflect the demographic diversity of lesbians and gay men and, therefore, should incorporate issues of ethnicity (see Greene, 1994), gender, and aging. Most important, discussion of same-sex relationships and sexuality should not be covered in lectures on psychopathology or deviant sexuality anymore than discussion of heterosexual relationships would be.

Apart from a specific discussion of homosexuality, instructors should use examples of lesbians and gay men in neutral contexts. I have done this successfully with test items such as the following one: "Jose is besieged with grief and insomnia after the sudden death of Mario, his partner of 10 years. Jose's symptoms are indicative of a diagnosis of . . . ?" In considering interpersonal attraction, which textbooks almost always describe only in terms of male-female attraction, Fontaine (1982) describes to her class the situation of Marita and Joan who are attracted to each other and would like to live together after high school but have conflicts because of different class backgrounds. Fontaine then asks the class how the two teenagers might try to resolve these issues within their relationship.

Didactic presentation of information may not be adequate. Experiential as well as cognitive components may be needed to challenge students' assumptions and prejudices. Pedagogies that validate personal experience affirm the feminist injunction that the personal is political, raise students' political consciousness, and decrease their alienation from intellectual material (Crumpacker & Vander Haegen, 1993). One experiential strategy is the presentation of panels of lesbians and gay men who speak openly about themselves and their experiences and field questions from the class. In such panels, women and people of diverse ethnic backgrounds are necessary to prevent dismissal of the issue due to the belief that it is pertinent only to Anglo-American men. A demographically diverse panel will demonstrate the heterogeneity within the lesbian and gay male community and facilitate the discussion of negotiating a double or triple minority status. McCord and Herzog (1991) summarized topics in which undergraduates were most interested (e.g., AIDS, same-sex marriages, child rearing); their list of 13 topics could help to prepare less experienced panelists. In the absence of panelists, other sources such as films, videos, and slides may be more readily available (Russo, 1981). An instructor might also try clever exercises that involve more active participation. One such exercise begins by asking students to identify their "petual orientation" as either cat-lovers or dog-lovers (Weber, 1990; Weinrich, 1987). Other exercises involve having students wear a pin advocating gay pride all day or read a book in public in which the words *gay* or *lesbian* are prominent on the cover.

Finally, lesbian or gay male educators may consider coming out. Lesbians and gay men of color who can afford to come out in their work are particularly needed as role models. Although coming out publicly is not always feasible (Browning, 1987; Harbeck, 1991; Khayatt, 1992) and may depend on one's gender, ethnicity, class, rank, and the climate of the department, visibility can counter negative stereotypes that are only perpetuated by the absence of upstanding lesbians and gay men in influential positions (Lance, 1987).

Consequences of Inclusion

Finally, a word to instructors on what to expect. Students tend to overestimate the attention paid to ordinarily neglected topics. For example, one student complained that a Women's Studies course reader included too many lesbian writers, when, in fact, less than 10% of the readings were by lesbian authors. In addition, content related to homosexuality is generally an emotionally laden issue. Heterosexual students may fear being blamed for societal homophobia, or feel pressured to adopt a pro-gay position; lesbian and gay male students may have great hopes of affirmation coupled with fears that suspected homophobia in others may become apparent (Browning, 1987). They also may take umbrage at having to educate others. Anticipated consequences, however, are often more negative than actual results. In a recent abnormal psychology section comprising almost 400 students, many of my students commented that they liked the "sociocultural approach"; appreciated the attempts to address "more delicate issues"; and found that the "homosexual angles enhanced the presentation of the material and the class as a whole."

Only one student complained about a lesbian and gay male panel presentation by saying it was a "moral issue." Religious protestations against inclusion of content related to lesbians and gay men should be addressed by emphasizing the scientific and psychological nature of the material. The focus should be on recognizing and respecting differences, not pathologizing or demonizing them. The class can be informed that religious tenets have been used historically to justify oppression of other minority groups (e.g., Native Americans and African slaves) and must, therefore, be critically examined from a scientific perspective. Referrals to the growing number of lesbian and gay male religious organizations or assignment of supplementary readings on the issue of religion and homosexuality (e.g., Boswell, 1980; Davidson, 1986; Griffin, Wirth, & Wirth, 1986) may be helpful.

Conclusion

A survey of recent textbooks in the areas of introductory, social, developmental, and abnormal psychology revealed some progress but still generally scant attention to any aspect of the psychological issues related to lesbians and gay men beyond discussion of the *DSM* declassification and etiology. Instructors need to actively seek textbooks that present affirmative views of lesbians and gay men and reward publishers of these textbooks. Even the most inclusive textbooks, however, must be supplemented with lecture material or additional readings. Instructors not confident in their ability should consult with others more knowledgeable as well as begin to educate themselves and challenge their own belief systems. Instructors who learn to teach about the lives of lesbians and gay men will provide a more inclusive pedagogy of psychology for their students and, perhaps, prompt an intellectual awakening for themselves.

Appendix A: Additional Resources

Boston Lesbian Psychologies Collective. (Ed.). (1987). *Lesbian psychologies: Explorations and challenges.* Urbana: University of Illinois Press.

Committee on Lesbian and Gay Concerns. (1990). *A selected bibliography of lesbian and gay concerns in psychology: An affirmative perspective.* Washington, DC: American Psychological Association.

D'Augelli, A. R. (1991). Teaching lesbian and gay development: A pedagogy of the oppressed. In W. G. Tierney (Ed.), *Culture and ideology in higher education* (pp. 214-233). New York: Praeger.

Forrister, D. K. (1992). The integration of lesbian and gay content in direct practice courses. In N. J. Woodman (Ed.), *Lesbian and gay lifestyles: A guide for counseling and education* (pp. 51-65). New York: Irvington.

Garnets, L. D., & Kimmel, D. C. (1991). Lesbian and gay male dimensions in the psychological study of human diversity. In J. D. Goodchilds (Ed.), *Psychological perspectives on human diversity in America* (pp. 137-192). Washington, DC: American Psychological Association.

Greene, B., & Herek, G. M. (Eds.). (1994). *Psychological perspectives on lesbian and gay issues: Vol. 1. Lesbian and gay psychology: Theory, research, and clinical applications.* Thousand Oaks, CA: Sage.

Herek, G. M., Kimmel, D. C., Amaro, H., & Melton, G. B. (1991). Avoiding heterosexist bias in psychological research. *American Psychologist, 46,* 957-963.

Lee, J. A. B. (1992). Teaching content related to lesbian and gay identity formation. In N. J. Woodman (Ed.), *Lesbian and gay lifestyles: A guide for counseling and education* (pp. 1-22). New York: Irvington.

Schieder, E. (1993). Integrating lesbian content. *Women's Studies Quarterly, 21*(3/4), 46-56.

Refer also to APA Division 44, the National Gay and Lesbian Task Force, and lesbian and gay male community and professional organizations.

References

*Aronson, E., Wilson, T. D., & Akert, R. M. (1994). *Social psychology: The heart and the mind.* New York: HarperCollins.

References marked with an asterisk indicate textbooks included in the survey (not all are cited in text).

*Berk, L. E. (1993). *Infants, children, and adolescents*. Needham Heights, MA: Allyn & Bacon.

Bieber, I., & Bieber, T. B. (1979). Male homosexuality. *Canadian Journal of Psychiatry, 24*, 49-421.

*Bigner, J. J. (1994). *Individual and family development*. Englewood Cliffs, NJ: Prentice Hall.

*Bootzin, R. R., Acocell, J. R., & Alloy, L. B. (1993). *Abnormal psychology: Current perspectives* (6th ed.). New York: McGraw-Hill.

Boswell, J. E. (1980). *Christianity, social tolerance, and homosexuality*. Chicago: University of Chicago Press.

*Brehm, S. S., & Kassin, S. M. (1993). *Social psychology* (2nd ed.). Boston: Houghton Mifflin.

Brooks, W. K. (1992). Research and the gay minority: Problems and possibilities. In N. J. Woodman (Ed.), *Lesbian and gay lifestyles: A guide for counseling and education* (pp. 201-215). New York: Irvington.

Brown, A., Goodwin, B. J., Hall, B. A., & Jackson-Lowman, H. (1985). A review of psychology of women textbooks: Focus on the Afro-American woman. *Psychology of Women Quarterly, 9*, 29-38.

Browning, C. (1987, August). *The process of teaching lesbian/gay psychology: Student and educator issues*. Paper presented at the meeting of the American Psychological Association, New York.

*Carlson, N. R., & Carlson, M. (1993). *Psychology: The science of behavior* (4th ed.). Needham Heights, MA: Allyn & Bacon.

*Cole, M., & Cole, S. R. (1993). *The development of children* (2nd ed.). New York: W. H. Freeman.

*Comer, R. J. (1992). *Abnormal psychology*. New York: Freeman.

Comstock, G. D. (1991). *Violence against lesbians and gay men*. New York: Columbia University Press.

Conger, J. J. (1975). Minutes of the annual meeting of the Council of Representatives. *American Psychologist, 30*, 620-651.

*Craig, G. J. (1992). *Human development* (6th ed.). Englewood Cliffs, NJ: Prentice Hall.

Crumpacker, L., & Vander Haegen, E. M. (1993). Pedagogy and prejudice: Strategies for confronting homophobia in the classroom. *Women's Studies Quarterly, 21*(3/4), 94-105.

Davidson, D. (1986). The spiritual dimension of the gay experience. *Christopher Street, 9*, 29-33.

*Deaux, K., Dane, F. C., & Wrightsman, L. S. (1993). *Social psychology in the 1990s* (6th ed.). Belmont, CA: Brooks/Cole.

Denmark, F. L. (1994). Engendering psychology. *American Psychologist, 49*, 329-334.

Fontaine, C. (1982). Teaching the psychology of women: A lesbian-feminist perspective. In M. Cruikshank (Ed.), *Lesbian studies: Present and future* (pp. 70-80). Old Westbury, NY: Feminist Press.

Freud, S. (1960). Letter to the mother of a homosexual son. In E. L. Freud (Ed.) and T. Steven & J. Stern (Trans.), *Letters of Sigmund Freud* (pp. 423-424). New York: Basic Books. (Original letter written in English 1935)

Garnets, L. D., & Kimmel, D. C. (Eds.). (1993). *Psychological perspectives on lesbian and gay male experiences*. New York: Columbia University Press.

Gonsiorek, J. C., & Weinrich, J. D. (1991). *Homosexuality: Research implications for public policy*. Newbury Park, CA: Sage.

Greene, B. (1994). Ethnic-minority lesbians and gay men: Mental health and treatment issues. *Journal of Consulting and Clinical Psychology, 62*, 243-251.

Griffin, C. W., Wirth, M. J., & Wirth, A. G. (1986). *Beyond acceptance: Parents of lesbians and gays talk about their experiences*. Englewood Cliffs, NJ: Prentice Hall.

Harbeck, K. M. (Ed.). (1991). Coming out of the classroom closet: Gay and lesbian students, teachers, and curricula [Special issue]. *Journal of Homosexuality, 22*(3/4).

Herek, G. M. (1991). Stigma, prejudice, and violence against lesbians and gay men. In J. C. Gonsiorek & J. D. Weinrich (Eds.), *Homosexuality: Research implications for public policy* (pp. 60-80). Newbury Park, CA: Sage.

Hickok, K. (1982). Lesbian images in women's literature anthologies. In M. Cruikshank (Ed.), *Lesbian studies: Present and future* (pp. 132-147). Old Westbury, NY: Feminist Press.

*Holmes, D. S. (1994). *Abnormal psychology* (2nd ed.). New York: HarperCollins.

Hooker, E. (1957). The adjustment of the male overt homosexual. *Journal of Projective Techniques, 21*, 18-31.

Khayatt, M. D. (1992). *Lesbian teachers: An invisible presence.* Albany: State University of New York Press.

King, N. (1988). Teaching about lesbians and gays in the psychology curriculum. In P. A. Bronstein & K. Quina (Eds.), *Teaching a psychology of people: Resources for gender and sociocultural awareness* (pp. 168-175). Washington, DC: American Psychological Association.

Kirk, S. A., & Kutchins, H. (1992). *The selling of DSM: The rhetoric of science in psychiatry.* New York: Aldine de Gruyter.

Lance, L. M. (1987). The effects of interaction with gay persons on attitudes toward homosexuality. *Human Relations, 6*, 329-336.

*Lippa, R. A. (1994). *Introduction to social psychology* (2nd ed.). Pacific Grove, CA: Brooks/Cole.

McCord, D. M., & Herzog, H. A. (1991). What undergraduates want to know about homosexuality. *Teaching of Psychology, 18*, 243-244.

McDonald, G. (1981). Misrepresentation, liberalism, and heterosexual bias in introductory psychology textbooks. *Journal of Homosexuality, 6*, 45-59.

Morgan, K. S., & Nerison, R. M. (1993). Homosexuality and psychopolitics: An historical overview. *Psychotherapy, 30*, 133-140.

*Myers, D. G. (1992). *Psychology* (3rd ed.). New York: Worth.

*Myers, D. G. (1993). *Social psychology* (4th ed.). New York: McGraw-Hill.

Newton, D. E. (1979). Representations of homosexuality in health science textbooks. *Journal of Homosexuality, 4*, 247-253.

*Papalia, D. E., & Wendkosolds, S. (1993). *A child's world: Infancy—adolescence* (6th ed.). New York: McGraw-Hill.

*Rathus, S. A. (1993). *Psychology* (5th ed.). New York: Harcourt Brace Jovanovich.

Rivera, R. R. (1991). Sexual orientation and the law. In J. C. Gonsiorek & J. D. Weinrich (Eds.), *Homosexuality: Research implications for public policy* (pp. 81-100). Newbury Park, CA: Sage.

*Rubin, Z., Peplau, L. A., & Salovey, P. (1993). *Psychology.* Boston: Houghton Mifflin.

Russo, V. (1981). *Celluloid closet: Homosexuality in the movies.* New York: Harper & Row.

*Sarason, I. G., & Sarason, B. R. (1993). *Abnormal psychology: The problem of maladaptive behavior* (7th ed.). Englewood Cliffs, NJ: Prentice Hall.

*Sigelman, C. K., & Shaffer, D. R. (1995). *Life-span human development.* Pacific Grove, CA: Brooks/Cole.

Simoni, J. M. (1996). Pathways to prejudice: Predicting heterosexist attitudes with demographics, self-esteem, and contact with lesbians and gay men. *Journal of College Student Development, 37*, 68-78.

*Smith, E. R., & Mackie, D. M. (1995). *Social psychology.* New York: Worth.

Socarides, C. W. (1968). *The overt homosexual.* New York: Grune & Stratton.

Socarides, C. W. (1978). *Homosexuality.* New York: Jason Aronson.

*Sue, D., Sue, D., & Sue, S. (1994). *Understanding abnormal behavior* (4th ed.). Boston: Houghton Mifflin.

*Wade, C., & Tavris, C. (1993). *Psychology* (3rd ed.). New York: HarperCollins.

Watter, D. N. (1987). Teaching about homosexuality: A review of the literature. *Journal of Sex Education and Therapy, 13,* 63-66.

Weber, A. L. (1990). Teaching tips for social psychology. *Contemporary Social Psychology, 14,* 226-228.

Weinrich, J. D. (1987). *Sexual landscapes.* New York: Scribner's.

Whitlock, K., & DiLapi, E. M. (1983). Friendly fire: Homophobia in sex education literature. *Interracial Books for Children Bulletin, 14,* 20-23.

*Wilson, G. T., O'Leary, K. D., & Nathan, P. (1992). *Abnormal psychology* (2nd ed.). Englewood Cliffs, NJ: Prentice Hall.

*Zimbardo, P. G., & Weber, A. L. (1994). *Psychology.* New York: HarperCollins.

Zimmerman, B. (1982). One out of thirty: Lesbianism in women's studies textbooks. In M. Cruikshank (Ed.), *Lesbian studies: Present and future* (pp. 128-131). Old Westbury, NY: Feminist Press.

5

Lesbian, Gay, and Bisexual Lives

Basic Issues in Psychotherapy Training and Practice

KRISTIN A. HANCOCK

Psychology changed its mind about homosexuality almost a quarter of a century ago. After years of challenges from lesbian, gay, and bisexual (LGB) psychologists and an ever-increasing body of psychological research which refuted the notion of homosexuality as mental illness, the American Psychological Association (APA) passed a resolution stating that homosexual orientations in and of themselves did not indicate psychological disturbance (APA, 1975). In this resolution, APA also urged psychologists to work towards removing the stigma of mental illness from homosexual sexual orientations. However, almost a quarter of a century later, we have seen that changes in organized psychology's position with respect to homosexuality and bisexuality do not necessarily result in changes in practice. Garnets, Hancock, Cochran, Goodchilds, and Peplau (1991) and Nystrom (1997) are among studies that have documented biased, inadequate, and inappropriate psychotherapy with LGB clients. A major problem contributing to the continued presence of biased, inadequate, and inappropriate services is the unavailability of adequate education and training about LGB people (Atkins & Townsend, 1996; Buhrke, 1989; Pilkington & Cantor, 1996). The education and training psychotherapists receive about LGB issues has been and, in many programs, continues to be outmoded, inaccurate, and sometimes pathologizing (Ashbrook, 1997; Atkins & Townsend, 1996; Murphy, 1992; Pilkington & Cantor, 1996).

This chapter discusses some of the basic issues which might be considered in psychotherapy training and practice with LGB clients. The general topics proposed are not put forth as the only relevant topics on psychotherapy with these populations. They are suggested as major sources of information which might help the psychotherapist who is not familiar with the life issues of LGB people. The topics can be used to put together an entire course or used selectively as information relevant to teaching other courses (e.g., information about the issues of the families of LGB people might be helpful in constructing a course on family psychotherapy). The topics reviewed may also be useful to practitioners who seek basic information about prospective clients. It is not possible here to comprehensively review the literature in each of the areas described. Rather, my intention is to discuss some of the basic points and therapeutic issues of each.

Sexual Orientation

To provide competent and sensitive services to LGB clients, and those who have questions about their sexual orientation, a psychotherapist must have a basic understanding of both the science and the politics associated with sexual orientation. Despite evidence that sexual orientation exists on a continuum, for most people homosexuality (lesbian and gay sexual orientations) and heterosexuality have been traditionally regarded as separate and dichotomous orientations. Heterosexuality has been considered the normal, healthy outcome of psychosexual development and homosexuality the pathological deviation from that norm. This perspective dominated psychology for almost a century. Much of the research that supported this view has been challenged because of important methodological flaws that seriously undermine its validity (Davison, 1991; Gonsiorek, 1991, 1995; Haldeman, 1991). Furthermore, a large body of methodologically sound, empirical research continues to counter the belief that homosexuality or bisexuality indicate mental illness. Simply put, there is no scientific basis for the belief that LGB sexual orientations represent psychological disturbance. Therefore, psychotherapists should not approach a LGB orientations with this assumption.

There may be times when difficulties are associated with LGB orientations, but these difficulties are commonly a result of the societal stigmatization of these sexual orientations and not the orientations themselves. Here one must be aware of the psychosocial and political factors associated with sexual orientation in our society. Few clients manage to live unaffected by them. Still, psychotherapists are sometimes confronted with clients who are distressed about their lesbian, gay, or bisexual sexual orientation, some of whom wish to change it. In these cases, a psychotherapist should carefully explore the conditions surrounding the client's request and evaluate the degree to which the request is motivated by internalized negative attitudes toward LGB sexual orientations or the negative attitudes of others. A client may need education about current understanding of a LGB sexual orientation and about the extent to which sexual orientation per se can actually be changed. The reader is referred to Chapter 10 in this volume, in which Haldeman provides a comprehensive review of conversion therapies.

In the dichotomous view of sexual orientation, bisexuality was viewed as a transitional phenomenon and not as a valid sexual orientation. Psychotherapists who approach bisexuality as a temporary state deny the complexity of human sexuality and the experience of those individuals whose relationships and sexual attractions are not limited by the biological sex of those they love. Bisexuality may be transitional for a person who may be in the process of coming to terms with a lesbian or gay sexual orientation. On the other hand, a lesbian or gay sexual orientation may also represent a step toward bisexuality. An informative description of the various experiences and transitions associated with bisexuality is given by Klein (1993). Reviews of psychological theory and research relevant to bisexual sexual orientations are reviewed by Fox in Chapter 7.

Psychotherapists must learn to perceive sexual orientation as complex by nature and multidimensional. They must also be capable of tolerating the infinite ways in which human beings manage this aspect of their lives. Recent studies explore sexual orientation as a multidimensional aspect of human nature which includes such variables as sexual attraction, sexual behavior, fantasies, identity, emotional preference, relationship status, and level of comfort with one's own orientation (Coleman, 1990; Klein, Sepekoff, & Wolf, 1985). Furthermore, sexual orientation occurs within the wider context of culture. The significance and characteristics attributed to a LGB sexual orientation by a culture has everything to do with the experiences of a LGB or questioning client. Hence, the psychotherapist must have a working knowledge of the cultural and ethnic values of the LGB person, the ways that those factors shape sexual orientation and vice versa. In ethnic minority clients, these issues become even more complex. The significance and characteristics associated with a LGB sexual orientation by any culture are a function of that culture's views about gender roles, religious beliefs, procreation, the role of the family, and in ethnic minority populations, the degree of acculturation and assimilation to the dominant culture (Greene, 1997). Clients who present issues pertaining to their sexual orientation are best served by a psychotherapist who appreciates these kinds of complicated factors and who takes the time to explore them thoroughly, thoughtfully, and sensitively. For this reason, issues related to sexual orientation and religion, gender, and cultural diversity should be explicitly considered in courses on psychotherapy with LGB clients.

Religion

Religion has so profoundly influenced our society's views of sexuality that its impact is felt by every person in our culture. It is important for psychotherapists working with LGB and questioning clients to understand that these clients have to contend with the difficulties associated with the moral judgments made about their sexual behavior. In the face of such judgments, many LGB and questioning clients also grapple with the role of religion and spirituality in their lives.

Sadly, for LGB and questioning people, many religious denominations have actively involved themselves in the condemnation of homosexuality conceptually and LGB people specifically. The most vigorous opponents to basic human rights for LGB people have been the ultraconservative or fundamentalist religious groups who continue to view homosexuality and bisexuality as sinful and unnatural (Blumenfeld & Raymond, 1988). LGB people have suffered ridicule, harassment, discrimination, and even physical violence at the hands of those who insist that their views are supported by religious teachings. The effect of such hatred can be devastating when it comes from the mouths of family members and others in congregations who have provided one's earliest experience of love and belonging. The continued condemnation of same-sex relationships and sexual behavior by ultraconservative and fundamentalist religious groups leaves many LGB and questioning individuals to defend their loving feelings against accusations of sinfulness and evil. Not every person will have the emotional and psychological stamina to withstand these charges. Those who must defend themselves against such an onslaught often find themselves in the offices of psychotherapists.

The psychotherapist does not need to study theology to work with lesbian, gay, bisexual, or questioning clients; however, they must have a level of respect for the important role of religious belief in the lives of many individuals. Both client and psychotherapist have more than likely been exposed to religion in some way. If the client is LGB or questioning his or her sexual orientation, the teachings of that religion become an important issue and may have a great deal to do with the client's experience of a religion, its beliefs, and its members. It may also have a devastating effect upon the client if such teachings are or were used against that person.

A psychotherapist's religious beliefs are his or her own personal business unless they become part of the treatment in some way. The ways that such beliefs become manifest in psychotherapy range from the subtle forms of nonverbal communication (e.g., a slight look of disapproval or frown) to less subtle forms of scolding or the delivery of a lecture on morality to a client. Invariably, the duty of the psychotherapist is to respect the integrity and dignity of the client (APA, 1992). A psychotherapist who is critical of a client's LGB sexual orientation is not equipped to help that client affirmatively address the self-criticism he or she has internalized from a society filled with prejudice against LGB people. Practitioners who hold religious beliefs that condemn or denigrate LGB relationships should not accept these or questioning clients for treatment.

On occasion, however, psychotherapists find that issues regarding LGB sexual orientations surface unexpectedly in treatment. The practitioner should have already examined his or her own religious beliefs and determine whether or not they reflect a bias against same-sex relationships. This self-examination should take place before the practitioner has ever seen a client. In many situations, consultation will be necessary and, in some, a competent referral should be sought.

A psychotherapist who, for one reason or another, does not respect the value of religion in people's lives may also not be best equipped to handle a gay or lesbian client's religion-based self-condemnation. A therapist should be prepared not merely to help the client discard an attachment to destructive childhood exposure to prejudicial religious beliefs but also to assist in that client's reconciliation of spiritual need and sexual orientation identity. Such work might involve supporting the client in his or her search for new sources of spiritual support in denominations and congregations which are more affirming of LGB people or possibly assisting a client to retain an affiliation with a religious denomination while freely challenging its position on same-sex relationships. A thoughtful discussion of the psychotherapeutic issues related to spirituality in LGB clients is presented by Haldeman (1996).

Clients who have been castigated by fundamentalist attitudes may have suffered severely. This is particularly true if they had an awareness of their LGB feelings early in childhood or adolescence and were exposed to years of antihomosexual rhetoric. It is important to remember that not all fundamentalist congregations or their members are aggressively vicious about homosexuality or bisexuality, but those who represent the worst of them can be quite destructive to LGB people. LGB youth may be cast out from the home for revealing their sexual orientation. A married adult with children might find themselves cut off from family members who do not understand and cannot tolerate their "lifestyle." Unable to attend the church they once attended regularly, these individuals may also find themselves in the midst of a difficult custody battle for their children. In both examples, the harassment and verbal abuse the person would experience would be extreme.

It is common for fundamentalist arguments to equate loving, LGB relationships with repugnant and destructive forms of sexual behavior such as child molestation and bestiality. At their most tolerant, fundamentalist attitudes may liken homosexuality or bisexuality to diseases such as alcoholism (Blumenfeld & Raymond, 1988). At their worst, they may call for the death of those who have same-sex relationships (White, 1994). A client who has been exposed to this kind of treatment from teachers, clergy, congregation members, or his or her own family has been treated abusively. Depending upon the emotional adjustment of the person and the importance of the perpetrator to him or her, such attacks can do a great deal of psychological damage. They can have a profound impact upon self-esteem, identity development, and interpersonal relations. They can also serve to seriously impair the individual's spiritual life.

For a person who has been harassed by fundamentalist abuse, the struggle is often one of a continuing need for approval from those who have condemned him or her. The client must ultimately come to accept that prejudice against homosexuality and bisexuality in its most aggressive forms is an irrational and unyielding force. It is a wall against which reason fails. A client's understanding of the fallacies in the religious arguments and texts used against homosexuality will help to restore self-respect but will be unlikely to change the attitudes of those who hurl moral invectives. The fundamentalist's belief in the Bible as the revealed word of God and in its condemnation of same-sex relations is absolute. There is seldom much of a dialogue possible and therefore little or no hope of gaining acceptance that includes positive regard for the client's sexual orientation. Coming to terms with this fact is a process of individuation for the client which is apt to involve pain, grief, outrage, and acceptance.

The psychotherapist should be aware that many religious denominations have groups which are specifically welcoming of LGB and questioning people and provide a safe and affirming place in which to practice religion. Groups such as Dignity (Catholic), Oasis/Integrity (Episcopal), Lutherans Concerned, American Baptists Concerned, United Church of Christ, and the Metropolitan Community Church welcome LGB members. Local or even national LGB resource lines or community centers may be able to assist practitioners in locating such groups. For LGB individuals who feel a need to belong to and be connected to a community which focuses on spirituality, such groups can provide a haven from the ambivalence and condemnation in more conservative communities.

Gender Issues

Misconceptions regarding gender, gender roles, and sexual orientation must be addressed in the training of psychotherapists and in practice. The first of these is that gender nonconformity is reliably related to a LGB sexual orientation. According to Bem (1993), LGB people are viewed as occupying a place outside the gendered norms of society. Heterosexuality is presumed to be as natural and as inevitable as the difference between the sexes and a major component of the appropriate gender role picture. If a man is attracted to another man, this is inconsistent with what is traditionally considered manly. Moreover, since it is only women who are supposed to be attracted to men, it makes a man who is attracted to another man, seem by these standards to be more like a woman. By definition, such a man becomes the object of particular animosity since men and what they do has been traditionally valued over women and what they do (Bem, 1993; Blumenfeld & Raymond, 1988; Herek, 1993). In fact, the ways in which LGB people are seen as not measuring up to traditional gender role prescriptions form the basis and justification for the prejudice against them (regardless of whether or not these perceptions are true). They have also served as a foundation for the belief that there is something fundamentally wrong with LGB clients and for developing psychotherapeutic strategies to "cure" them.

Golombok and Fivush (1994) have reviewed the literature on gender nonconformity and homosexuality. At this point in time, a connection between gender nonconformity in childhood and a LGB sexual orientation seems possible, even likely. However, this connection does not mean that all or even most LGB adults were gender nonconforming as children. Moreover, gender nonconformity by no means provides a comprehensive explanation for why people become lesbian, gay, or bisexual. No single factor has been identified as a determinant of sexual orientation (Golombok & Fivush, 1994). Thus, the relationship or connection that exists between gender nonconformity and sexual orientation should not be considered reliable or predictive. Psychotherapists should be cautioned against making such assumptions.

Another misconception regarding gender, gender roles, and sexual orientation stems from a basic confusion between sexual orientation and transsexualism. For a more extensive discussion of transgendered identities, transsexuals, and distinctions between these and other groups, see Gainor, Chapter 6 in this volume.

The fact that a person is lesbian, gay, or bisexual does not change the fact that he or she has been raised with the same socializing agents as a person who is heterosexual. Parental influences, schooling, the media, and peers all tend to deliver the same messages about appropriate gender role behavior. Notions of gender are developed at a very early age and have a profound effect upon one's attitudes, behavior, and sense of identity (Basow, 1992; Golombok & Fivush, 1994). It should not be surprising, then, to note that, in many ways, the issues of gay men and bisexual men actually resemble those of heterosexual men more than they resemble the issues of lesbians or bisexual women. Similarly, the issues of lesbians and bisexual women more closely resemble those of heterosexual women than those of gay men or bisexual men. Thus, although LGB people tend to share a disparaged status in our society and are subject to the oppression which accompanies this status, many of the similarities end there. It is therefore important for psychotherapists to avoid making generalizations too readily on the basis of sexual orientation and to understand the significance of gender differences in the lives of LGB clients.[1]

Although there does appear to be greater diversity, flexibility, and fluidity in the presentation of gender roles in the LGB communities than in the heterosexual community (Burch, 1995; Kurdek, 1987; Matteson, 1996), psychotherapists must be cautioned against pathologizing it. When a group of people are perceived to live outside the gendered norms of society, that group may not experience those norms in the same way the mainstream group experiences them. Regardless of the extent to which members of the marginalized group adopt or manifest the gender norms, there lingers a sense of "other-ness" about these norms for masculinity and femininity. Gender roles in the LGB communities may be experienced as ways of being in the world that can be changeable across time and circumstance, for some people (Burch, 1993, 1995; Butler, 1990; Pearlman, 1995), as well as immutable and enduring for others. The challenge this poses for psychotherapists is directly related to their attitudes about men, women, and what is or is not appropriate for each gender. Because our culture is so prescriptive about gender, nonconformity or androgyny can be perceived as subversive and/or unhealthy by the psychotherapist who has accepted these traditional norms. If such a practitioner is presented with gender nonconformity in a client, he or she may find it uncomfortable, annoying, disgusting, or even profoundly unsettling. Sometimes it is difficult for a psychotherapist who has not worked with gender nonconforming people to realize the challenge it may pose to therapists' basic values. It might be particularly difficult for gender conforming male therapists since they themselves have been socialized according to stricter standards with harsher sanctions against nonconformity. Gender nonconformity presents itself in a variety of ways in the lesbian, gay, and bisexual communities from subtle forms of gender-bending to the phenomenon known as "drag." The psychotherapist needs to know himself or herself well enough to know the degree of gender nonconformity he or she can accept and the point beyond which pejorative attitudes take over. Some psychotherapists may be quite comfortable working with gay, lesbian, or bisexual clients who present as appropriately masculine or feminine by societal standards. However, a psychotherapist may at times be working with attitudes toward gender that are strange or unfamiliar to most people in heterosexual society. One may observe an ability to view the gendered world from the outside in and play with the prescriptions and a flexibility and sense of freedom to try on masculinity and femininity like clothes in one's wardrobe. If the therapist cannot accept this, a referral to an accepting colleague is in order.

Multiple Sources of Oppression

For many LGB people, sexual orientation is not the only source or even the primary source of oppression. When a LGB person operates within more than one culture, he or she must negotiate a set of norms, values, and beliefs with regard to LGB sexual orientations for each (cf. Chan, 1992; Gutierrez & Dworkin, 1992; Icard, 1986; Liu & Chan, 1996; Loiacano, 1989; Savin-Williams, 1996). Cultural variation in these norms, values, and beliefs about sexual orientation can be a major source of psychological stress (Gutierrez & Dworkin, 1992; Jones & Hill, 1996; Morales, 1992; Rust, 1996).

A major difficulty is that there is no one group to which the ethnic minority LGB person can necessarily anchor his or her identity and receive full acceptance. A given culture's attitudes towards homosexuality and bisexuality as well as racism within the LGB communities can exacerbate and complicate the process of identity development and be a source of considerable stress in the lives of ethnic minority LGB people (Gonsiorek & Rudolph, 1991; Greene, 1997; Gutierrez & Dworkin, 1992; Jones & Hill, 1996; Morales, 1992; Rust, 1996). Greene (1997) notes that ethnic minority gay men and lesbians exist as minorities within minorities and as such, experience and must manage multiple levels of discrimination.

Ethnic minority LGB individuals may be reluctant to jeopardize their supportive familial and community ties by making their sexual orientation known to others (Chan, 1992; Espin, 1993; Greene, 1997; Morales, 1992; Rust, 1996; Smith, 1997). An ethnic minority LGB person's declaration of an LGB sexual orientation to his or her family may be met with rejection or hostiliy. Although this poses a problem for any LGB person, it is of particular significance in the lives of ethnic minority group members because of the additional significance of the family as a source of love, support, identification, and safety from racism. A number of authors (Chan, 1995; Espin, 1993; Greene, 1997) observe that LGB family members do not necessarily lose their place in the family because of their sexual orientation per se. It is sometimes the direct expression or disclosure of one's LGB sexual orientation or a confrontation with the family about one's sexual orientation which tends to provoke condemnatory responses in family members. If the issue is not raised, the family often ignores, excuses, or tolerates the situation and does not reject the LGB family member. However, the family's "silent tolerance" of the LGB family member should not be mistaken for acceptance of the member's sexual orientation. Rather, it may in fact represent the family's denial of it (Greene, 1997; Jones & Hill, 1996).

Still other ethnic-minority LGB individuals may choose to turn to the LGB community for support. However, here they may experience racism. LGB identified social groups, political organizations, or social services can hinder the full participation of people of color and provide limited, if any, access to leading roles in these places. Biased service at restaurants or bars or discriminatory practices at LGB-owned places of employment occur just as they do in society at large (Jones & Hill, 1996).

The clinical implications of multiple minority status and the ways it can affect the psychotherapeutic relationship are discussed by Greene (1997) and Rust (1996). The basic education and training of practitioners has more than likely not prepared them for working with clients who must contend with oppression stemming from both race and ethnicity, and sexual orientation. Expertise or experience in addressing sexual orientation issues does not guarantee competence or even comprehension of issues associated with ethnic minority issues and vice versa. The reader is referred to Greene (1997) and Chapter 1 in this volume for a discussion of cultural literacy, and its applicability to the prevention of potential errors in the treatment of lesbians and gay men of color.[2]

In addition to the dilemma of multiple minority status and its associated difficulties, psychotherapists must be aware of the fact that there are a number of variables which affect a culture's attitudes toward LGB sexual orientations and that these variables may differ from culture to culture. Greene (1997) suggests that a given culture's attitudes toward sexuality and procreation can affect its attitude toward LGB sexual orientations as can its beliefs about gender roles, religious values, and its relationship to the dominant culture. Degrees to which group members are acculturated and have assimilated into the dominant culture must also be taken into account.

Until recently, there has not been a great deal of information available on ethnic minority LGB people. Fortunately, the unique challenges and concerns of these groups are now being explored by such authors as Chan (1992, 1995), Espin (1993, 1997), Gonzalez and Espin (1996), Greene (1997), Jones and Hill (1996), Liu and Chan (1996), Morales (1992, 1996), Manalasan (1996), Nakajima, Chan, and Lee (1996), Rust (1996), and Trujillo (1991, 1997).

Heterosexism, Internalized Prejudice, and Victimization

Psychotherapists must understand the prejudice and victimization that LGB people face if they are to work competently with these populations. Prejudice against LGB people continues to be a serious and prevalent problem in our society. The National Lesbian and Gay Task Force Policy Institute (1992) reports that gay men and lesbians are subject to harassment and threats of violence, bomb threats, physical assault, police abuse, vandalism, arson, and homicide. Among the most common forms of victimization are harassment, threats of violence, and physical assault (National Gay & Lesbian Task Force Policy Institute, 1992). Verbal harassment is the most common form of victimization. Although recent surveys show an increasing willingness to extend basic civil rights to gay and lesbian people, there remains widespread moral condemnation of homosexuality and a tendency to reject or feel uncomfortable with LGB people among most heterosexual Americans (Herek, 1996).

Psychotherapists should keep in mind that it is impossible to grow up in a culture in which such attitudes are so prevalent and not internalize them to some extent. When they are internalized, they can have a tremendous impact upon self-esteem and cause considerable psychological distress. Gonsiorek and Rudolph (1991) describe psychological disturbances which can range from mild self-doubt when confronted with prejudice to overt self-hatred and self-destructive behavior. Shidlo (1994) concludes that since the internalization of negative attitudes about homosexuality is such an important determinant of psychopathology in LGB individuals, psychotherapy with these populations must include its assessment and treatment. He further suggests that the reduction of internalized negativity can be viewed as an important measure of therapeutic success.

Assessment of internalized prejudice can sometimes be challenging as its manifestations can range from obvious behaviors (e.g., total denial of one's homosexual or bisexual orientation, contempt for other more obvious LGB people, acting upon same-sex feelings without taking responsibility for them, compartmentalization of homoerotic feelings, fear and withdrawal from friends and relatives, and even suicide attempts) to more subtle behaviors (e.g., minimizing contact with LGB people, efforts to "pass" or not be mistaken for a LGB person in manner or appearance). A psychotherapist must also remember when assessing internalized prejudice that some of the behaviors associated with internalized prejudice may also be adaptive and does not necessarily reflect the individual's acceptance of society's negative attitudes. Their adaptive value will depend upon the nature and extent of the actual prejudice in a person's social and occupational contexts and the attitudes associated with the behavior. It might be wise, for instance, not to reveal one's homosexual or bisexual orientation in a context in which one would be physically assaulted because of it.

In addition to the internalization of negative societal attitudes about LGB sexual orientations, LGB people are also confronted with the manifestations of prejudice and discrimination against them in the world. The victimization of LGB people can include murder, physical assault, property damage, verbal abuse (which includes threats of violence), arson/bombings, and police harassment and abuse (Berrill, 1992; Klinger & Stein, 1996). Many LGB individuals experience some form of violence or harassment at some point. It is not unusual for a LGB person to experience such treatment within his or her own family of origin (Berzon, 1992; Brown, 1989; Markowitz, 1995; Strommen, 1990; Weise, 1992). This fact distinguishes prejudice against LGB people from other forms of prejudice, such as racism, in which such harassment or rejection from one's own family is unlikely.

Garnets, Herek, and Levy (1992) describe the unique difficulties for victims of violence against LGB people. Most important, the victim's sexual orientation can become associated with the feeling of vulnerability which is normative in such situations (Garnets et al., 1992; Klinger & Stein, 1996). A victim is apt to attribute the attack to his or her sexual orientation. Negative attitudes which had been previously internalized are thereby exacerbated and attempts to comprehend the meaning of the violence may lead to the conclusion that it was a consequence of (or punishment for) one's LGB sexual orientation. Garnets and her colleagues (1992) note that the consequences of verbal assault can be just as severe as those of physical assault. Not only might victims find it difficult to understand the emotional aftermath of a verbal assault, they may also tend to minimize the feelings they do experience. Because victims are sensitive to the potential for physical assault, they will also tend to restrict their behavior. Psychotherapists must be careful not to prematurely dismiss the client's fears as paranoid or underestimate the realistic potential for such assaults.

The response to victimization is affected by the degree to which survivors have come to terms with their sexual orientation. Individuals who have gone through the process of coming to terms with their sexual orientation and are more comfortable with it will be more likely to have a wider range of resources to assist in coping with this kind of crisis (e.g., social support and friendship networks, resources in the community, and a positive association with being lesbian, gay, or bisexual). However, people who are in the early stages of coming to terms with their sexual orientation or who remain deeply conflicted about it may have far fewer resources to assist them in recovering from victimization. The result is likely to be the attribution of blame to sexual orientation, associated depression, and feelings of helplessness (Garnets et al., 1992; Klinger & Stein, 1996).

The psychotherapist who works with survivors of violence against LGB people must have accurate information regarding LGB identity development, community resources, and the mental health issues of victims. The psychotherapist must also be sensitive to his or her own heterosexist biases.

As described by Herek (1990, 1996), heterosexism involves the denial, denigration, and stigmatization of nonheterosexual behavior, identity, relationship, or community. As an ideological system, heterosexism pervades our culture and its institutions. It also resides within our personal values, attitudes, feelings, and assumptions. For psychotherapists, when heterosexist assumptions form the basis of how LGB clients are assessed and treated, it is problematic. For example, many well-intended psychotherapists might approach LGB clients as if they are no different from clients who are heterosexual. Such an approach denies the stigmatization of LGB orientations and the effects of discrimination on the lives of LGB people. In the absence of information to the contrary, clients who do not specify a sexual orientation will most likely be regarded as heterosexual by practitioners (Glenn & Russell, 1986). When a psychotherapist is aware of a client's LGB sexual orientation, errors in clinical judgment are possible as the differences in heterosexual, lesbian, gay and bisexual experiences are minimized or denied altogether (Winegarten, Cassie, Markowski, Kozlowski, & Yoder, 1994). Garnets, Hancock, Cochran, Goodchilds, and Peplau (1991) describe situations in which gay and lesbian relationships were discounted and discouraged by psychotherapists who also sometimes utilized a heterosexual frame of reference to formulate therapeutic interventions with LGB clients. For example, in one situation described in this study, a lesbian client was told by her therapist to read a book about heterosexual marriage problems because these difficulties were the same as those in her lesbian relationship. This approach does not take stigmatization and its effects upon the lesbian relationship seriously, denies the presence of important differences in same-sex relationships, and generally lacks sensitivity. The inadequacy and often complete lack of education and training in LGB issues reflects the prevalence of the heterosexist tradition in graduate programs in clinical psychology.

LGB people face very real problems in daily life (i.e., housing, employment, personal discrimination, victimization) because of heterosexist prejudice. Additional problems with self-acceptance because of the internalization of these societal attitudes is an important issue in psychotherapy with LGB clients. It is essential that the psychotherapist understands that the prejudice and its associated stigma is the problem, not the sexual orientation of the client. This understanding crosses theoretical perspectives and treatment approaches and should serve as a fundamental principle of psychotherapy with LGB and any other clients exploring the issue of sexual orientation in psychotherapy.

Coming Out

Coming to terms with one's LGB identity ("coming out") is no small task. The challenge for LGB people as they come to terms with their sexual orientation is to develop a positive identity in a psychosocial context that stigmatizes and oppresses them (Gonsiorek, 1995). This challenge imposes additional developmental tasks and psychological challenges. Gonsiorek and Rudolph (1991) review and discuss the stages of coming out and the special developmental tasks associated with this process.

Coming out involves a major shift in an individual's identity, which may often include varying degrees of emotional distress. How well the individual facing such change fares with this process depends on his or her psychological disposition as well as the kind, quality, and extent of interpersonal support available. Psychotherapists should keep in mind that a LGB person does not usually share his or her sexual orientation with his or her family of origin (i.e., they are usually heterosexual). The coming out process often begins in isolation. In this context, there is little modeling or intergenerational support to help negotiate a range of challenges. These challenges include the difficulties of developing positive feelings about the self in the face of societal stigmatization. The psychotherapy office may be the first place where support is sought.

It is also important to note that the development of lesbian, gay, or bisexual self-identification can cease at any point in this process. Cass (1979, 1996) refers to this outcome "identity foreclosure" and points to any number of reasons for it (e.g., negative societal attitudes, negative attitudes of significant others, the extent to which these are internalized, the ability of the individual involved to be self-aware, and the inability to assume responsibility for one's actions).

Psychotherapists must carefully explore the attitudes and feelings of any individual struggling with identifying themselves as lesbian, gay, or bisexual. It is crucial to keep in mind that there is an important difference between *behavior* which may be interpreted as lesbian, gay, or bisexual and *identifying* as lesbian, gay, or bisexual. The toll taken by delayed identity development should also be carefully assessed and explored with the client. The strength and resilience of the client going through the process and the quality of his or her support system are also important factors to evaluate. A person with a more rigid character style is likely to have more difficulty than one who can more readily accommodate intrapsychic change. For those who are religious, coming out represents an identity shift that may conflict with a deep-seated Judeo-Christian tradition. In this context, punishment for coming out can include the loss of one's family and friends. Cass (1996) suggests that psychotherapists meet the client who is struggling with this issue at the appropriate stage of the process. In other words, it is not appropriate to approach clients as though they are lesbian, gay, or bisexual, if they are confused about their behavior and what it means. It is advisable to deal with the specific issues and questions pertaining to the client's particular stage in the process. Psychotherapists should also keep in mind that coming out does not occur apart from other processes and issues in a person's life. A client's ability to negotiate the various challenges in a given stage will be related to the nature of other challenges confronting the client at the same time.

Gonsiorek and Rudolph (1991) report gender differences in coming out: "This process for males appears more abrupt and more likely to be associated with psychiatric symptoms, whereas the process for women appears characterized by greater fluidity and ambiguity" (p. 165). The reasons for the differences are related to gender-role socialization differences. Basow (1992) notes that boys receive more intense socialization pressure to behave in gender-appropriate ways than girls, with more punishment for not doing so. As a result, females have greater gender-role flexibility than males. Another difference has to do with the meaning that is ascribed to homoerotic feelings and behavior. Because women's relationships are generally characterized by greater emotional expressiveness and intimacy, strong feelings or attachments to another woman may not be immediately interpreted as erotic. It is not until the feelings are identified as sexual and sexual behavior occurs that a woman is confronted with identifying herself as lesbian or bisexual (Gramick, 1984). It is this latter aspect of a woman's feelings that she is apt to repress or deny even after other strong emotions have existed for some time. For men, the process tends to be more abrupt, manifesting in sexual behavior without the emotional intimacy that characterizes female relationships. Similarly, men are then apt to repress or deny the significance of this behavior. Fox discusses coming out among bisexual men and women in Chapter 7.

Coming out is also heavily influenced by culture, class, and ethnicity (Alquijay, 1997; Chan, 1995, 1997; Fygetakis, 1997; Greene, 1997; Gonsiorek & Rudolph, 1991; Smith, 1997). Cass (1996) warns psychotherapists against universally applying the notion of LGB identity formation to various racial and ethnic populations in the United States. Members of ethnic minority populations are often faced with complicated and difficult decisions regarding cultural identity and LGB identity. Smith (1997) suggests that coming out is often inappropriately evaluated with norms established upon white research and clinical samples and warns that what may be healthy and adaptive for one group is not necessarily so for the other. Chan (1989) found that Asian gay men report more discrimination regarding their sexual orientation, whereas Asian lesbians report more discrimination for being Asian. Thus, within-group differences are also factors with which to contend in coming out.

Relationships

In some ways, same-sex relationships are similar to those of heterosexuals. Both heterosexual and lesbian and gay couples tend to go through similar stages in their relationships (Clunis & Green, 1988; Kurdek, 1987, 1995; Kurdek & Schmitt, 1986; McWhirter & Mattison, 1984). Conflicts common to heterosexual relationships (e.g., issues regarding money or the way in which a partner's career interferes with the relationship) are also typical in same-sex relationships (Blumenstein & Schwartz, 1983). Characteristics that predict relationship satisfaction and stability are similar for gay, lesbian, and heterosexual couples (Kurdek, 1995).

A number of authors have discussed the impact of gender and gender role socialization in same-sex relationships (Green, Bettinger, & Zacks, 1995; Hancock, 1995; Peplau, Veniegas, & Campbell, 1996; Peplau, 1991). Gender differences seem to manifest most clearly in the area of sexual frequency and exclusivity. Gay male couples appear more sexually active than lesbian or heterosexual couples, and less partner exclusivity is noted (Blumstein & Schwartz, 1983; Kurdek, 1995; Peplau, 1991). Higher income has been associated with personal power in gay male and heterosexual relationships but not in lesbian relationships (Blumstein & Schwartz, 1983). Although differences such as these might lead to the conclusion that gender and gender role socialization are important factors in understanding the nature of gay and lesbian relationships, psychotherapists should also be aware of the ways in which the dynamics of gay and lesbian couples do not reflect gender role norms.

Green, Bettinger, and Zacks (1996) found that, apart from the areas of sexuality and an emphasis upon work, gay men vary considerably from heterosexual men in many ways and suggest that the "relational styles, abilities, and values" of gay men are in fact quite different from those of heterosexual men. They also challenge the notion that the closeness often discussed in lesbian relationships (Burch, 1982, 1986, 1993, 1995; Clunis & Green, 1988; Hancock, 1995; Krestan & Bepko, 1980) reflects pathological fusion. Green and his associates describe lesbians and gay men as being more androgynous and therefore less influenced by gender role programming. This is not to say, however, that gay men and lesbians in couples merely manifest cross-gender attitudes and behaviors. Rather, it is to say that gay men and lesbians draw from both masculine and feminine attitudes and behaviors in their relationships. They create their roles, duties, and responsibilities in relationships without as much of a foundation in traditional gender role socialization as may be experienced by heterosexual couples. For psychotherapists, this means that knowledge and familiarity with gender role socialization is helpful in understanding gay and lesbian relationships. However, information is also needed about the ways in which these norms do not apply to gay and lesbian relationships.

Bisexuality creates additional challenges for psychotherapists working with couples. As noted earlier, sexual orientation has traditionally been approached as a transitional phenomenon rather than as a sexual orientation unto itself. Although, in some instances, this may be accurate, in many cases it is not. The ways in which couples resolve the complexities posed by a partner's bisexuality vary. Sometimes, couples wish to maintain their primary relationship and negotiate relationships with other partners outside the marriage while remaining committed to their primary relationship. Psychotherapists should be prepared to assist the couple in such negotiations. In Chapter 7, Fox offers a more comprehensive discussion of the characteristics associated with the successful negotiation of heterosexual marriages.

There are, of course, stressors and challenges that LGB couples face which heterosexual couples do not face. The social stigmatization of LGB sexual orientations often prevents many LGB couples from being open about their relationships. There is considerably less social and familial support for LGB relationships than for heterosexual relationships (Kurdek, 1988; Kurdek & Schmitt, 1987). The relationships of LGB couples do not enjoy the legal recognition heterosexual marriages are afforded. These difficulties should not be underestimated and can make same-sex relationships significantly more challenging.

Well-intended psychotherapists who believe there are no differences between heterosexual and LGB relationships do not perceive the impact of stigmatization and must be educated about the numerous ways in which it permeates the lives of LGB couples. Brown (1989) describes situations in which families attempt to undermine a LGB relationship or

ways in which heterosexual marriages are afforded attention and privileges where LGB relationships are not and the associated stress upon
members of the couple. Psychotherapists with more traditional, unexamined values about heterosexuality and marriage have been shown to
trivialize, devalue, and demean LGB relationships (Garnets et al., 1991).
Similarly, they have underestimated the significance of same-sex relationships, viewed them as transient or unhealthy, or rely upon inaccurate stereotypes about masculine and feminine roles to inform them
(Peplau et al., 1996).

Families

LGB people have families of origin and create families of their own by
having children and by forming alternative families in the LGB communities. There is much for a psychotherapist to keep in mind when working with LGB individuals about the nature and meaning of families in
their lives.

Family of Origin Issues

Perhaps one of the most difficult and painful areas to explore in psychotherapy with LGB individuals is their families of origin. Families
supply physical and emotional sustenance, connect us with our past,
and provide a context within which we learn about the world, including
the attitudes and mores of our society (Berzon, 1992). Unfortunately,
families' visions do not usually include LGB sexual orientations for family members. The conflicts over the disclosure of one's LGB identity to
one's family of origin often bring an individual into psychotherapy.
Situations in which a family member's LGB sexual orientation is inadvertently revealed or discovered also create family (as well as personal)
crises for which the family, the LGB member, and the psychotherapist
may be ill-prepared. In these situations, the information pertaining to
the sexual orientation of the individual may not have been revealed under the most positive of circumstances. Unlike instances in which sexual
orientation is disclosed voluntarily, here the LGB person may be confronted by a family member (or members) and find him- or herself in a
stressful position. It is often with good reason that LGB individuals anticipate trouble with disclosure to their families of origin (Brown, 1988;

Rust, 1996; Strommen, 1990). According to Strommen (1990), the central issue is the family's notions about same-sex relationships (which usually reflect the societal biases against LGB sexual orientations) and its perceptions and expectations of the LGB family member.

Before a family member's LGB identity is disclosed or discovered, various coping strategies are negotiated between the individual and his or her family. Brown (1988) describes several tactics: (1) distancing, emotionally and/or geographically, from the family of origin; (2) a tacit agreement between the individual and the family that no one will discuss the individual's personal life; and (3) disclosure to one parent or sibling who is supportive, with the understanding that the individual will not tell another or other family members. Brown (1988) reminds psychotherapists that the LGB person living under these arrangements may not present them as a problem for psychotherapy. She notes that the failure to recognize them as stressful and maladaptive can reflect the internalized negative attitudes about homosexuality or bisexuality of the particular family member in question. What the psychotherapist may observe is the toll taken by these unspoken "negotiated settlements" (e.g., problems with self-esteem, relationship difficulties, and disagreements over not being "out" to one's family). For LGB clients of other cultures, the psychotherapist must consider the "settlement" as it relates to the benefits a client receives (e.g., continued sense of community and support within an oppressive dominant culture) in exchange for silence and realize that what may be problematic in one cultural context may not be in another (Smith, 1997).

According to Strommen (1990), when the LGB family member's sexual orientation is disclosed or discovered, the revelation initiates two processes in the family of origin. First, the family struggles for a way to understand the LGB member. This occurs in the context of the family's values and belief system. It is important for the psychotherapist who works with a family to which a member has just "come out" to become familiar with the family's attitudes towards LGB sexual orientations, gender roles, and religion, as each of these is related to how its members will respond (cf. Basow, 1992; Blumenfeld & Raymond, 1988; Greene, 1997; Martin & Hetrick, 1988; MacDonald & Games, 1974). As the family struggles with this "revelation crisis," they also experience a sudden alienation from the LGB member. Previous perceptions of him or her as a sibling, spouse, or child are negated by the new identification. The individual may be experienced as a stranger in the family. Parental reactions can include a sense of guilt and failure regarding the sexual orientation of their child while siblings tend to respond more with anger and confusion (Strommen, 1990). If the disclosure is initiated by the LGB family member, the family may be told in increments, with the emotionally closest members being told first. Usually, this is a sibling, and the individual may adjust the manner in which the disclosure is made based upon the reactions received from the most supportive family member.

More positive scenarios still involve a family's struggle with convention. If the concern for the LGB family member triumphs, the family adapts its attitudes and beliefs to establish a new identity for the LGB member. The psychotherapist should understand that this process, in many cases, does not occur overnight. Families who confront this new information need to grieve the loss of their previous perceptions, expectations, and dreams regarding the LGB member which more than likely have been heterosexual in nature. The family needs time and sometimes assistance in dealing with the loss. There are many instances in which a negative initial response tempers and transforms into a more positive adaptation with time. This may sometimes take years. Families who are more positive in their responses may still require assistance in dealing with the LGB member "in the context of openness" (Brown, 1988). Worth mentioning here is the difficulty these families have in figuring out how to treat this relationship and its members. The negative attitudes against LGB sexual orientation which surface in simple interactions about family occasions (e.g., dinners, weddings, holidays, and reunions) can be more subtle but are nevertheless present and can be a major problem.

Typically, the family lacks models for dealing with same-sex relationships. The same-sex partner of the LGB member is more apt to be treated and referred to as a friend than as a dating or committed partner. Because friendships are socially accepted relationships between members of the same sex, viewing the relationship as a friendship allows the family to avoid the dissonance, anxiety, and other emotional responses to the sexual aspect of the relationship. Same-sex partners of LGB family members are also commonly referred to and treated as "roommates." Relations between the family and its LGB member may become strained as a result of the individual's relationship being perceived in such a manner. Thus, the psychotherapist should be aware of the fact that important issues surface after the disclosure or revelation of LGB sexual orientation to the family. In these cases the practitioner must be prepared to evaluate the various sources of stigmatization within the family as well as in its LGB member.

Lesbian, Gay, and Bisexual Parenting

LGB men and women have always been parents. Until about 20 years ago, this fact was primarily a result of having had children in a heterosexual marriage prior to coming out. LGB people in same-sex relationships had traditionally been regarded as otherwise childless by society and by LGB people themselves. In the 1970s, the courts were increasingly challenged by gay men and lesbians who were fighting to retain custody or visitation rights of their children from former marriages. These parents faced enormous difficulties as the courts reflected the negative attitudes of society toward same-sex relationships (i.e., that exposure to individuals with a LGB orientation would be detrimental to the psychological and emotional development of children). However, after two decades of such cases, resources for these parents have been dramatically increased and the consciousness of the courts has been raised (at least in areas where large numbers of LGB people live) (Ariel & Stearns, 1992; Rubenstein, 1996). In the 1980s, the number of LGB families increased. The subsequent increase in births to women who were out as lesbians has been referred to as a lesbian "baby boom." Options other than heterosexual marriage (e.g., foster parenting, adoption, and artificial insemination) are now widely used. Parenthood is now viewed as a viable choice for LGB people.

It is important for the psychotherapist to understand that there is no evidence to support the notion that having a LGB parent or parents is harmful to a child (Ariel & Stearns, 1992; Patterson, 1992, 1996). Moreover, Patterson (1996) observes that there is no evidence that psychological adjustment among lesbian or gay parents is in any way impaired.

Despite these findings, parenthood does confront the LGB parent(s) with new challenges. From the initial stages of conception, parenthood brings LGB parents into increased contact with a heterosexually oriented society. Interactions with the medical system, issues of child care, interactions with the school system, the child's friends and their (usually heterosexual) parents, and the need to make decisions about when and how to inform others of one's uncommon family structure can prompt the resurfacing of coming out issues in major ways for each family member (Ariel & Stearns, 1992). The lack of legal status afforded gay and lesbian relationships also presents significant problems for LGB parents and their children in situations such as separation, medical emergencies, and death (Ariel & Stearns, 1992; Rubenstein, 1996). Partnership agreements, authorization to consent to medical treatment for a minor, and other legal forms are used to assist the couple in clarifying their roles and responsibilities (Pies, 1988).

LGB parents operate without societal sanction or tradition. There are no role models to balance the heterosexual images of family life. For this reason, the psychotherapist must be sensitive to the ways in which internalized negativity surfaces in the couple. Familial obligations and responsibilities may also isolate LGB parents from their communities. As parents, they may not be as mobile or able to socialize as friends who are not parents. To counter the absence of guidelines for parenting and the isolation that may be associated with LGB parenthood, the psychotherapist might find it useful to acquire LGB community information and materials about parenting groups.

Because of the various options available to LGB persons for becoming parents, they often have to contend with situations, decisions, and negotiations that heterosexuals do not have to face. For example, one common issue for lesbian couples considering parenthood is whether or not to actively involve the male donor in a relationship with the child. Many times, lesbian couples decide that the donor remain anonymous, thereby defining their roles with regard to the child more clearly. This option is available through artificial insemination. Gay men clarify their boundaries for similar reasons through adoption or the use of a surrogate mother (Ariel & Stearns, 1992). Another issue is that the nonbiological parent has no legal rights even though he or she is actively involved in the process from the beginning. Attempts on the part of the nonbiological parent to legally adopt the child still depend on state laws and regulations regarding LGB sexual orientations and the rights of LGB people to adopt children that vary from state to state (Ariel & Stearns, 1992). Yet another concern is what happens if the couple's relationship ends. To what extent does the nonbiological parent participate in the continued parenting of the child? A psychotherapist is in a position to assist couples negotiate these difficult decisions. It is essential that he or she remain aware of how difficult it is to confront these issues without the social support and legal structure available to heterosexual couples. Other parenting concerns might include differences between members of a couple in their desire to parent as well as in their expectations regarding coparenting. Psychotherapists can help with a couple's parenting concerns by working with each member to communicate clearly and negotiate compromises which respect the feelings of both partners and by validating the difficulties and challenges of parenting within a society often hostile and unsupportive of LGB parents.

Alternative Families

Because LGB individuals do not usually share their stigmatized sexual orientation status with their family of origin, it should not be surprising that they tend to derive less support in adulthood from their family origin than their heterosexual counterparts (Laird & Green, 1996). Alternative families (which often include one's primary relationship partner and a close group of friends) provide the love, support, and acceptance which heterosexuals find in families of origin and are sometimes created when an LGB person's own family of origin is hostile, distant, or unsupportive because of the member's sexual orientation. Alternative families also exist in addition to a supportive family of origin. Friendships have been perceived as more important than long-term primary partners by gay men in a study by Kurdek (1988). This contrasts with the tendency in heterosexual relationships to designate the relationship as most important and friends less so (Laird & Green, 1996). Psychotherapists need to recognize and respect the diverse family forms which LGB people have. Alternative families may differ in structure from the "nuclear family" (i.e., husband, wife, and child) and other heterosexual norms with which psychotherapists are more familiar but their importance cannot be underestimated.

Youth

The identity development of LGB youth can be arrested or slowed by factors directly related to societal prejudice against LGB sexual orientation (Cass, 1979; Cohen & Savin-Williams, 1996; Gonsiorek & Rudolph, 1991; Malyon, 1981; Troiden, 1988). This prejudice and discrimination deprives these young people of the socialization structures that their heterosexual counterparts enjoy as they make the difficult and sometimes tumultuous transition between childhood and adulthood. Even worse, it can subject them to emotional, verbal, and physical abuse by those closest to them and strangers alike. Internalized, it can also take a tremendous toll upon the self.

The reconciliation of same-sex attractions with the internalized stigma against these attractions and those who experience them poses a difficult and additional developmental task upon LGB youth (Gonsiorek, 1991). "At a time when most youths are gradually building self-esteem and establishing an identity, some sexual minority adolescents are learning from peers and adults that they are amongst the most hated in society" (Cohen & Savin-Williams, 1996, p. 124). The internalization of societal condemnation can result in an inhibition of sexuality, self-doubts about one's psychological normality, decreased self-esteem, depression, isolation, loneliness, and self-destructive behavior (Cohen & Savin-Williams, 1996; Gonsiorek, 1991, 1995). Coleman and Remafedi (1989) note that "most teenagers describe themselves as heterosexual unless there is compelling evidence to the contrary; and predominantly homosexual adolescents often waffle between heterosexual, homosexual, and bisexual labels" (p. 37). Cohen and Savin-Williams (1996) review defensive strategies used by adolescents to help them cope with the feelings they experience for the same sex. These strategies include rationalization, relegation to insignificance, compartmentalization, withdrawal from situations which may be provocative in order to remain celibate or asexual, denial (which may include engaging in heterosexual dating or sexual behavior), and redirecting energies to other pursuits such as work or school. Suicide risk is also a problem frequently raised in the literature on LGB youth. A review by Gibson (1989) suggests that gay and lesbian youth may be two to three times more likely to make suicide attempts than their heterosexual counterparts. In a survey of 1,900 lesbians from 17 to 24 years of age conducted by the National Lesbian and Gay Health Foundation (1987), 59% were found to be at risk for suicide. Evans and D'Augelli (1996) report substantial levels of emotional distress, substance abuse, depression, and anxiety among LGB youth. It is difficult to address these issues when a LGB youth denies or refuses to admit to same-sex attractions. When these attractions are acknowledged, issues still exist with regard to trust and personal safety. These fears are not groundless.

Heterosexual youth enjoy parental support to one degree or another and parents can call upon their own experiences as they help their adolescent son or daughter navigate this phase of development. However,

LGB youth do not share their sexual orientation status with their parents and must either contend with parental and sibling responses to it if and when it is revealed or discovered or work daily to conceal his or her sexual orientation from the family. Parental responses to the LGB orientation of a child are unpredictable although a positive prior relationship history can indicate a more positive outcome (Cohen & Savin-Williams, 1996). Often, the relationship between the LGB youth (or young adult) and parents suffers initially as both parties struggle to come to terms with the parents' lost vision of their son or daughter. Gonsiorek (1988) states that many youths are "rejected, mistreated, or become the focus of the family's dysfunction" (p. 116) after their sexual orientation is revealed or discovered. LGB youths can suffer physical and verbal abuse from parents and/or be evicted from the home (Savin-Williams & Cohen, 1996). Sometimes, initial difficulties alter with time and understanding. Sometimes, they do not.

Without parental support or mentoring, LGB youth also face another tremendous difficulty: a lack of support from peers. Hunter and Schaecher (1987) found that one fifth of the lesbians and one half of the gay male adolescents had experienced harassment, threats, and/or assault in junior high school or high school because they were perceived to be homosexual. LGB youth are well aware of the peer and societal pressure to conform to a heterosexual standard or suffer the consequences of prejudice. LGB youths lose friends, are ridiculed, ostracized, and physically abused by peers for being different (Savin-Williams & Cohen, 1996). This awareness profoundly affects the way in which the emergent LGB identity is addressed. It may be denied, closely guarded, or disclosed with considerable caution. Many conceal their sexual orientation by attempting to "pass" as heterosexual (e.g., dating the opposite sex, expressing heterosexual interests to friends) during high school and do not reveal their nontraditional sexual orientation for years.

LGB adolescents have few role models. How, then, do these youth find out about what it is like to be lesbian, gay, or bisexual? Paroski (1987) found that most gay male youth were educated about gay lifestyles through sexual encounters (96%), the media (91%), word of mouth (87%), and by going to places frequented by gay men (81%). Lesbian youth acquired such information through TV and the media (88%), word of mouth (81%), and associating with lesbians (50%). Health care providers played only a small role in this process (i.e., 20%) for gay male adolescents and 13% for lesbian adolescents. Between half and three quarters of the participants in Paroski's (1987) study believed common myths about lesbian and gay sexual orientations which include that gay men and lesbians identify with the opposite sex, dislike members of the opposite sex, and lead unhappy and unfulfilled lives. There are far fewer places for bisexual youth to turn for information regarding bisexuality as a viable sexual orientation.

Accurate information about LGB identity development and the problems associated with internalized negative attitudes against LGB sexual orientations must be obtained and used by those psychotherapists who provide services to adolescents. Therapists are urged to explore the psychological and psychosocial problems resulting from societal stigmatization, including alienation from peers, family of origin, homelessness, prostitution, and the abuse of drugs and alcohol (Evans & D'Augelli, 1996; Remafedi, 1987; Savin-Williams & Cohen, 1996; Slater, 1988). Psychotherapists working with adolescents who are questioning their sexual orientation ought not to try to resolve this issue prematurely (Gonsiorek, 1988). A number of authors support the use of group psychotherapy with LGB youth (e.g., Athey, 1993; Gertsel, Feraios, & Herdt, 1989; Lenna, 1992; Uribe, 1991). They suggest combining education and group interaction in a safe environment. Education is particularly important to counter myths and stereotypes that lesbian, gay, and bisexual youth may have internalized. A group also provides a place in which the adolescent can safely interact with other LGB teenagers, develop socialization skills, and combat isolation. Hunter and Mallon discuss issues relevant to the treatment of lesbian and gay adolescents in Chapter 9 of this volume.

Psychotherapy Issues

No training in psychotherapy with LGB clients is complete without attention being paid to the attitudes, behaviors, and concerns of the psychotherapist (Brown, 1987, 1991, 1996; Cabaj, 1988; Dworkin, 1992; Gonsiorek, 1989; Isay, 1991, Stein, 1988). Stein (1988) describes several important concerns for psychotherapists which include the attitudes and beliefs of the psychotherapist toward the view that LGB sexual orientations indicate psychopathology, the psychotherapist's level of familiarity with LGB issues outside the pathological perspective, and the personal characteristics of the psychotherapist which directly influence the conduct of psychotherapy with these clients. In addition, it is also important to distinguish concerns unique to psychotherapists who are heterosexual from those who are lesbian, gay, or bisexual themselves.

One of the most important issues to discuss in the education and training of psychotherapists is one's basic attitudes and beliefs about LGB sexual orientations. If a psychotherapist holds the belief that LGB sexual orientations represent psychopathology, despite the fact that research and current thinking point to the contrary, the client who receives treatment from such a provider may be at risk for increased mental health problems (Stein, 1988). The many problems associated with a client's internalized prejudice will very likely be perpetuated by a psychotherapist who believes that LGB sexual orientations indicate psychopathology. Stein (1988) states that therapeutic neutrality is impossible when treatment is provided from this perspective because it permeates the entire treatment process and mandates the need to change the sexual orientation of the client.

Psychotherapists who hold a dichotomous view of sexual orientation may well trivialize or disregard bisexuality in a client even if lesbian and gay sexual orientations are accepted as valid (Firestein, 1996). The result may be increased confusion, anxiety, and depression on the part of the client and a tendency on the part of the therapist to try to approach the client as either lesbian, gay or heterosexual with attractions which do not fit one or the other considered invalid or inconsequential. Psychotherapists who hold this "either/or" view of human sexuality are not well equipped to assist bisexual clients in establishing a positive identity or to help clients negotiate meaningful resolutions with partners when concurrent lesbian/gay and heterosexual attractions are an issue.

Another major concern is the level of familiarity with LGB concerns on the part of psychotherapists (Buhrke, 1989; Cabaj, 1988; Glenn & Russell, 1986; Murphy, 1991; Stein, 1988). Even if the psychotherapist does not believe that LGB clients are mentally ill, he or she is working against important training deficits unless training and supervised experience in psychotherapy with these populations have been obtained. Unfortunately, this sort of training is rare and usually requires extra effort on the part of the clinician. Lack of information about LGB issues cultivates incompetence and unethical service provision (Brown, 1996). Even in the most well-intended psychotherapists, heterosexism, if unchallenged, marginalizes and minimizes the experiences and relationships of LGB people. It disregards or overlooks the effects of stigma, presumes heterosexuality as normative, and holds it as a standard against which LGB lives are measured. With little or no understanding of what is normative for LGB people, a psychotherapist can underestimate or overestimate the difficulties posed by an individual client's LGB orientation (Garnets et al., 1991). To overcome the deficits in education, training, and supervised experience in LGB issues, Stein (1988) proposes that psychotherapists explore their attitudes about same-sex relationships and specific sexual acts, increase their awareness of the impact of stigmatization, familiarize themselves with the patterns and stages of coming out, and learn about the lifestyles of LGB people. It is also important for the psychotherapist to familiarize him or herself with the LGB community resources available locally and nationally.

As it is impossible to grow up in the United States without acquiring negative stereotypes and feelings about LGB sexual orientations, it is important for a psychotherapist to be willing to look at his or her own attitudes and feelings about them. To deny the presence of antigay/lesbian/bisexual prejudice within oneself is unrealistic even for the most enlightened psychotherapist who is heterosexual, lesbian, gay, or bisexual. Whether they manifest as overt bias and discrimination or more subtly as heterosexism, unexplored negative attitudes and feelings about LGB orientations impede judgment and are generally harmful to the client. Thus, psychotherapists who work with LGB clients must cultivate an awareness of their own heterosexist biases and safeguard treatment through the careful exploration of their reactions to these clients. Being LGB does not by any means exclude a psychotherapist from harmful attitudes or behavior. Of particular concern here are LGB psychotherapists who are struggling with feelings of self-hatred because they themselves have not yet come to terms with their own LGB orientation. Such therapists are more likely to engage in self-destructive behaviors themselves and countertransference acting out in the therapeutic relationship (Brown, 1996). Psychotherapists struggling with coming out themselves should refrain from working with LGB clients until self-acceptance is achieved (Brown, 1989, 1996).

The sexual orientation of the psychotherapist and its disclosure to clients are issues that continue to be debated in the literature (e.g., Coleman, 1989; Isay, 1991; Matteson, 1996; Stein, 1988). Coleman (1989) feels that the psychotherapist's disclosure of his or her sexual orientation can impose an unnecessary burden upon the client, particularly for clients early in the stages of coming out who may be apprehensive that the psychotherapist will pressure them one way or another with regard to sexual orientation. Stein (1988) reasons that, since there is societal pressure for a LGB person to keep sexual orientation a secret, a willingness on the part of the psychotherapist to share his or her sexual orientation might be helpful. It is important to recall that LGB people are particularly vulnerable to the internalization of negative attitudes about them and their sexual orientation. If a LGB psychotherapist denies or refuses to acknowledge his or her sexual orientation to a client, the shame, self-depreciation, and fear of disclosure he or she feels will be conveyed (Isay, 1991). Psychotherapists, for the most part, are assumed to be heterosexual by clients unless the sexual orientation of the therapist has been disclosed (Schwartz, 1989; Stein, 1988) or if referral is made with the therapist's LGB orientation known. Stein (1988) does note that the degree of comfort and acceptance of sexual orientation on the part of the psychotherapist is more important than any client's knowledge of the therapist's sexual orientation. Suggestions regarding disclosure can be found in Gartrell (1984), Perlman (1991), and Schwartz (1989). For psychotherapists who prefer not to disclose their sexual orientation, Coleman (1989) has some helpful suggestions on how to handle direct questions from the client about it.

The gender and gender role attributions of a psychotherapist are also important characteristics to address in practice and in training clinicians to work with LGB clients. Gender roles have traditionally defined masculinity and femininity and have been directly linked to heterosexuality. If the psychotherapist, whether LGB or heterosexual, has incorporated traditional gender roles to a large degree, he or she may become uncomfortable when confronted with a person who is more androgynous. Moreover, the psychotherapist may not be conscious of the ambivalence. It is crucial to keep in mind that sexism and prejudice against LGB sexual orientations are closely aligned. Any discomfort, disapproval, or anxiety that the psychotherapist experiences should be explored in consultation, or the therapist's own therapy, not with the client.

Stein (1988) and Cabaj (1988) both discuss the difficulties that heterosexually oriented psychotherapists may experience when erotic components of the client/therapist relationship surface with someone of the same sex. Although a heterosexual psychotherapist might be prepared for transference of this sort from a client of the other sex, the same psychotherapist may well feel somewhat anxious and uncomfortable when it surfaces in a client who is a member of the same sex as the therapist.

The same thing applies to countertransference reactions. Cabaj (1988) states that positive feelings, particularly those with an erotic component, toward a LGB client of the same sex may frighten and confuse the therapist (Greene, 1997). The reason for an honest and thorough self-examination of one's feelings, values, and beliefs about LGB sexual orientations becomes very clear in such situations. In the case of psychotherapists who are struggling with questions about their own sexual orientation, Brown (1996) and Gonsiorek (1994) both suggest that these providers should not work with LGB clients until their own issues with self-acceptance have been resolved in their own personal psychotherapy. Close supervision in such cases is also particularly important.

When the LGB client is also a member of an ethnic minority group which differs from that of the psychotherapist, additional challenges arise. Greene (1997) describes the manner in which psychotherapist errors in judgment are made when psychotherapists are insensitive to the ways in which ethnic minority clients experience oppression or when psychotherapists overcompensate for feelings of guilt, anger, or discomfort about racism and idealize the client's struggles with racism. She explores the synergistic effects of the psychotherapist's sexual orientation and race/ethnicity upon the client/therapist relationship and advises psychotherapists who work with ethnic minority LGB clients to "have broad familiarity with the general characteristics of their clients' cultures as well as with the special needs and vulnerabilities" of LGB clients (Greene, 1997, p. 228).

A unique issue for LGB psychotherapists involves the provision of services in small communities and the associated boundary issues for psychotherapists. This subject is considered by Brown (1989, 1996), Dworkin (1992), Gartrell (1994), and Gonsiorek (1989). Brown (1989) notes that the traditional model of psychotherapy service provision assumes that the community of the psychotherapist does not overlap with those of the client. Psychotherapists therefore are unprepared for living and working in a world in which one meets one's clients in one's private life. Yet this is precisely what LGB psychotherapists face, even in large metropolitan areas. What surfaces are immediate issues related to boundaries and their ethical management by the psychotherapist. Psychotherapists are ethically required to protect the therapeutic relationship and its boundaries. Unfortunately, ethical guidelines are insufficient in helping the LGB psychotherapist manage these boundaries. LGB psychotherapists have had to struggle with responses to these situations. Brown (1996) differentiates between "dual roles" in which a client is exploited by the psychotherapist to satisfy his or her emotional, financial, sexual, or other needs and "overlapping roles" in which unintentional and inevitable boundary crossings occur in the lives of clients and psychotherapists due to the small size of the community. Although dual roles are clearly unethical, it is the overlapping role situations that often prove to be difficult for LGB psychotherapists. Brown (1996) suggests that psychotherapists who find themselves in these kinds of situations be especially attentive to issues related to boundary violations (e.g., breaches of confidentiality). She also proposes that psychotherapists take the initiative in discussing the possibility of overlapping role situations with clients while making the welfare of the client and the protection of the therapeutic relationship the most important priorities. Gonsiorek (1989) suggests that LGB psychotherapists cultivate "systems of consultation and support to handle the particularly intense and frequent boundary decision which they often face" (p. 119).

To work with LGB clients, psychotherapists must address the gaps in their education, training, and supervised experience regarding these issues. Brown (1996) notes that this is true for LGB as well as heterosexual providers. It is essential that this additional education not only include pertinent information on the areas named in this chapter but that it address the more visceral responses of the practitioner to them. Without doing so, the treatment of one's LGB clients is jeopardized.

Notes

1. Gender differences are particularly important in the areas of coming out, sexuality, and intimate relationships. There are a number of authors who discuss the differences between men and women in these areas (e.g., Basow, 1992; Fox, 1995; Gonsiorek & Rudolph, 1991; Hancock, 1995; Matteson, 1996; Peplau, 1993).

2. Similar psychotherapist difficulties in the treatment of gay and lesbian clients have been noted in a survey of psychotherapists by Garnets, Hancock, Cochran, Goodchilds, and Peplau (1991).

References

Alquijay, M. (1997). The relationships among self-esteem, acculturation, and lesbian identity formation. In B. Greene (Ed.), *Psychological perspectives on lesbian and gay issues:*

Vol. 3. Ethnic and cultural diversity among lesbians and gay men (pp. 249-265). Thousand Oaks, CA: Sage.

American Psychological Association. (1975). Proceedings of the American Psychological Association for the year 1974: Minutes of the annual meeting of the Council of Representatives. *American Psychologist, 30,* 620-651.

American Psychological Association. (1992, December). Ethical principles and code of conduct. *American Psychologist, 47*(12), 1597-1611.

American Psychological Association. (1997). *Resolution on appropriate therapeutic responses to sexual orientation.* Adopted by the American Psychological Association Council of Representatives, August 14, 1997.

Ariel, J., & Stearns, S. (1992). Challenges facing gay and lesbian families. In S. Dworkin & F. Gutierrez (Eds.), *Counseling gay men and lesbians: Journey to the end of the rainbow* (pp. 95-112). Alexandria, VA: American Association for Counseling and Development.

Ashbrook, P. (1997). Training gay, lesbian and bisexual psychotherapists in non-supportive environments. Paper presented at the annual meeting of the American Psychological Association, Chicago.

Athey, K. (1993.) *A proposed group treatment model to provide support and advocacy for gay youth.* Unpublished master's thesis. California State University, Hayward, CA.

Atkins, D., & Townsend, M. (1996). Issues for gay male, lesbian, and bisexual mental health trainees. In R. Cabaj & T. Stein (Eds.), *Textbook of homosexuality and mental health* (pp. 645-655). Washington, DC: American Psychiatric Press.

Basow, S. (1992). *Gender: Stereotypes and roles* (3rd ed.). Pacific Grove, CA: Brooks/Cole.

Bayer, R. (1981). *Homosexuality and American psychiatry: The politics of diagnosis.* Princeton, NJ: Princeton University Press.

Bem, S. (1993). *The lenses of gender.* New Haven, CT: Yale University Press.

Berrill, K. (1992). Anti-gay violence and victimization in the United States: An overview. In G. Herek & K. Berrill (Eds.), *Hate crimes: Confronting violence against lesbians and gay men* (pp. 19-45). Newbury Park, CA: Sage.

Berzon, B. (1992). Telling the family you're gay. In B. Berzon (Ed.), *Positively gay: New approaches to gay and lesbian life* (pp. 67-78). Berkeley, CA: Celestial Arts.

Blumenfeld, W., & Raymond, D. (1988). *Looking at gay and lesbian life.* Boston: Beacon.

Blumenstein, P., & Schwartz, P. (1983). *American couples.* New York: Morrow.

Brown, L. (1989). Lesbians, gay men, and their families: Common clinical issues. *Journal of Gay and Lesbian Psychotherapy, 1*(1), 65-77.

Brown, L. (1991, June). Ethical issues in feminist therapy: Selected topics. *Psychology of Women Quarterly, 15*(2), 323-336.

Brown, L. (1996). Ethical concerns with sexual minority patients. In R. Cabaj & T. Stein (Eds.), *Textbook of homosexuality and mental health* (pp. 897-919). Washington, DC: American Psychiatric Press.

Buhrke, R. (1989). Training issues for counseling psychologists in working with lesbian women and gay men. *Counseling Psychologist, 19*(2), 216-234.

Burch, B. (1982). Psychological merger in lesbian couples: A joint ego psychological and systems approach. *Family Therapy, 9*(3), 201-277.

Burch, B. (1985). Psychotherapy and the dynamics of merger in lesbian couples. In T. Stein & C. Cohen (Eds.), *Contemporary perspectives on psychotherapy with lesbians and gay men* (pp. 57-71). New York: Plenum.

Burch, B. (1993). *On intimate terms: The psychology of difference in lesbian relationships.* Chicago: University of Illinois Press.

Burch, B. (1995). Gender identities, lesbianism, and potential space. In J. Glassgold & S. Iasenza (Eds.), *Lesbians and psychoanalysis: Perspectives in theory and practice* (pp. 287-307). New York: Free Press.

Butler, J. (1990). *Gender trouble: Feminism and the subversion of identity.* New York: Routledge.

Cabaj, R. (1988). Homosexuality and neurosis: Considerations for psychotherapy. *Journal of Homosexuality, 15*(1/2), 13-23.

Cass, V. (1979). Homosexual identity formation: A theoretical model. *Journal of Homosexuality, (4),* 219-235.

Cass, V. (1996). Sexual orientation identity formation: A Western phenomenon. In R. Cabaj & T. Stein (Eds.), *Textbook of homosexuality and mental health* (pp. 227-251). Washington, DC: American Psychiatric Press.

Chan, C. (1992). Asian-American lesbians and gay men. In S. Dworkin & F. Gutierrez (Eds.), *Counseling gay men and lesbians: Journey to the end of the rainbow* (pp. 115-124). Alexandria, VA: American Association for Counseling & Development.

Chan, C. (1995). Issues of sexual identity in an ethnic minority: The case of Chinese American lesbians, gay men, and bisexual people. In A. D'Augelli & C. Patterson (Eds.), *Gay, lesbian and bisexual identities over the lifespan: Psychological perspectives* (pp. 87-101). New York: Oxford University Press.

Chan, C. (1997). Don't ask, don't tell, don't know: The formation of a homosexual identity and sexual expression among Asian American lesbians. In B. Greene (Ed.), *Psychological perspectives on lesbian and gay issues: Vol. 3. Ethnic and cultural diversity among lesbians and gay men* (pp. 240-248). Thousand Oaks, CA: Sage.

Clunis, D., & Green, G. (1988). *Lesbian couples.* Seattle, WA: Seal Press.

Cohen, K., & Savin-Williams, R. (1996). Developmental perspectives on coming out to self and others. In R. Savin-Williams & K. Cohen (Eds.), *The lives of lesbians, gays, and bisexuals: Children to adults* (pp. 113-151). Fort Worth, TX: Harcourt Brace.

Coleman, E. (1989). The married lesbian. *Marriage and Family Review, 14*(3/4), 119-135.

Coleman, E. (1990). Toward an understanding of sexual orientation. In D. McWhirter, S. Sanders, & J. Reinisch (Eds.), *Homosexuality/heterosexuality: Concepts of sexual orientation* (pp. 267-276). New York: Oxford University Press.

Coleman, E., & Remafedi, G. (1989). Lesbian, gay, and bisexual adolescents: A critical challenge to counselors. *Journal of Counseling and Development, 68,* 36-40.

Davison, G. (1991). Constructionism and morality in therapy for homosexuality. In J. Gonsiorek & J. Weinrich (Eds.), *Homosexuality: Research implications for public policy* (pp. 137-148). Newbury Park, CA: Sage.

Dworkin, S. (1992). Some ethical considerations when counseling gay, lesbian, and bisexual clients. In S. Dworkin & F. Gutierrez (Eds.), *Counseling gay men and lesbians: Journey to the end of the rainbow* (pp. 325-334). Alexandria, VA: American Association for Counseling & Development.

Espin, O. (1993). Issues of identity in the psychology of Latina lesbians. In L. Garnets & D. Kimmel (Eds.), *Psychological perspectives on lesbian and gay male experiences* (pp. 348-363). New York: Columbia University Press.

Espin, O. (1997). Crossing borders and boundaries: The life narratives of immigrant lesbians. In B. Greene (Ed.), *Psychological perspectives on lesbian and gay issues: Vol.3. Ethnic and cultural diversity among lesbians and gay men* (pp. 191-215). Thousand Oaks, CA: Sage.

Evans, N., & D'Augelli, A. (1996). Lesbians, gay men, and bisexual people in college. In R. Savin-Williams & K. Cohen (Eds.), *The lives of lesbians, gays, and bisexuals: Children to adults* (pp. 201-226). Fort Worth, TX: Harcourt Brace.

Firestein, B. (1996). Bisexuality as a paradigm shift: Transforming our disciplines. In B. Firestein (Ed.), *Bisexuality: The psychology and politics of an invisible minority* (pp. 263-291). Thousand Oaks, CA: Sage.

Fox, R. (1995). Bisexual identities. In A. D'Augelli & C. Patterson (Eds.), *Lesbian, gay, and bisexual identities over the lifespan: Psychological perspectives* (pp. 48-86). New York: Oxford University Press.

Fygetakis, L. (1997). Greek American lesbians: Identity odysseys of honorable good girls. In B. Greene (Ed.), *Psychological perspectives on lesbian and gay issues: Vol. 3. Ethnic and cultural diversity among lesbians and gay men* (pp. 152-190). Thousand Oaks, CA: Sage.

Garnets, L., Hancock, K., Cochran, S., Goodchilds, J., & Peplau, L. (1991, September). Issues in psychotherapy with lesbians and gay men: A survey of psychologists. *American Psychologist, 46*(9), 964-972.

Garnets, L., Herek, G., & Levy, B. (1992). Violence and victimization of lesbians and gay men: Mental health consequences. In G. Herek & K. Berrill (Eds.), *Hate crimes: Confronting violence against lesbians and gay men* (pp. 207-226). Newbury Park, CA: Sage.

Gartrell, N. (1984). Issues in psychotherapy with lesbian women. In *Work in progress* (no. 10). Wellesley, MA: Wellesley College, Stone Center.

Gartrell, N. (1994). Boundaries in lesbian therapist-client relationships. In B. Greene & G. Herek (Eds.), *Psychological perspectives on lesbian and gay issues: Vol. 1. Lesbian and gay psychology: Theory, research, and clinical applications.* Thousand Oaks, CA: Sage.

Gertsel, C., Feraios, A., & Herdt, G. (1989). Widening circles: An ethnographic profile of a youth group. In G. Herdt (Ed.), *Gay and lesbian youth* (pp. 75-92). New York: Harrington Park.

Gibson, P. (1989). Gay male and lesbian youth suicide. *ADAMHA Report of the Secretary's Task Force on Youth Suicide* (Vol. 3, pp. 110-142; DHHS Publication No. ADM 89-1623). Washington, DC: Government Printing Office.

Glenn, A., & Russell, R. (1986, March). Heterosexual bias among counselor trainees. *Counselor Education and Supervision, 25*(3), 222-229.

Golombok, S., & Fivush, R. (1994). *Gender development.* New York: Cambridge University Press.

Gonsiorek, J. (1988). Mental health issues of gay and lesbian adolescents. *Journal of Adolescent Health Care, 9,* 114-122.

Gonsiorek, J. (1989). Sexual exploitation by psychotherapists: Some observations on male victims and sexual orientation issues. In G. Schoener, J. Milgram, J. Gonsiorek, E. Luepker, & R. Conroe (Eds.), *Psychotherapist's sexual involvement with clients: Intervention and prevention* (pp. 113-119). Minneapolis, MN: Walk-In Counseling Center.

Gonsiorek, J. (1991). The empirical basis for the demise of the illness model of homosexuality. In J. Gonsiorek & J. Weinrich (Eds.), *Homosexuality: Research implications for public policy* (pp. 115-136). Newbury Park, CA: Sage.

Gonsiorek, J. (1995). Gay male identities: Concepts and issues. In A. D'Augelli & C. Patterson (Eds.), *Gay, lesbian and bisexual identities over the lifespan: Psychological perspectives* (pp. 24-47). New York: Oxford University Press.

Gonsiorek, J., & Rudolph, J. (1991). Homosexual identity: Coming out and other developmental events. In J. Gonsiorek & J. Weinrich (Eds.), *Homosexuality: Research implications for public policy* (pp. 161-176). Newbury Park, CA: Sage.

Gonzalez, F., & Espin, O. (1996). Latino men, Latina women, and homosexuality. In R. Cabaj & T. Stein (Eds.), *Textbook of homosexuality and mental health* (pp. 583-601). Washington, DC: American Psychiatric Press.

Gramick, J. (1984). Developing a lesbian identity. In T. Darty & S. Potter (Eds.), *Women identified women* (pp. 31-44). Palo Alto, CA: Mayfield.

Green, R., Bettinger, M., & Zacks, E. (1996). Are lesbian couples fused and gay male couples disengaged? Questioning gender straightjackets. In J. Laird & R. Green (Eds.), *Lesbians and gays in couples and families: A handbook for therapists* (pp. 185-230). San Francisco: Jossey-Bass.

Greene, B. (1997). Ethnic minority lesbians and gay men: Mental health and treatment issues. In B. Greene (Ed.), *Psychological perspectives on lesbian and gay issues: Vol. 3. Ethnic and cultural diversity among lesbians and gay men* (pp. 216-239). Thousand Oaks, CA: Sage.

Gutierrez, F., & Dworkin, S. (1992). Gay, lesbian, and African-American: Managing the integration of identities. In S. Dworkin & F. Gutierrez (Eds.), *Counseling gay men and lesbians: Journey to the end of the rainbow* (pp. 141-156). Alexandria, VA: American Association for Counseling & Development.

Haldeman, D. (1991). Sexual orientation conversion therapy for gay men. In J. Gonsiorek & J. Weinrich (Eds.), *Homosexuality: Research implications for public policy* (pp. 149-160). Newbury Park, CA: Sage.

Haldeman, D. (1996). Spirituality and religion in the lives of lesbians and gay men. In R. Cabaj & T. Stein (Eds.), *Textbook of homosexuality and mental health* (pp. 881-896). Washington, DC: American Psychiatric Press.

Hancock, K. (1995). Psychotherapy with lesbians and gay men. In A. D'Augelli & C. Patterson (Eds.), *Gay, lesbian and bisexual identities over the lifespan: Psychological perspectives* (pp. 398-432). New York: Oxford University Press.

Herek, G. (1990). The context of anti-gay violence: Notes on cultural and psychological heterosexism. *Journal of Interpersonal Violence, 5*(3), 316-333.

Herek, G. (1993). On heterosexual masculinity: Some psychical consequences of the social construction of gender and sexuality. In L. Garnets & D. Kimmel (Eds.), *Psychological perspectives on lesbian and gay male experiences* (pp. 316-330). New York: Columbia University Press.

Herek, G. (1996). Heterosexism and homophobia. In R. Cabaj & T. Stein (Eds.), *Textbook of homosexuality and mental health* (pp. 101-113). Washington, DC: American Psychiatric Press.

Hunter, J., & Scheacher, R. (1987). Stresses on lesbian and gay adolescents in schools. *Social Work in Education, 9*(3), 180-190.

Icard, L. (1986). Black gay men and conflicting social identities: Sexual orientation vs. racial identity. In J. Grinton & M. Valentich (Eds.), *Social work practice in sexual problems* [Special issue, *Journal of Social Work & Human Sexuality, 4*(1/2), 83-93]. New York: Haworth Press.

Isay, R. (1991). The homosexual analyst: Clinical considerations. *The Psychoanalytic Study of the Child, 46,* 199-216.

Jones, B., & Hill, M. (1996). African American lesbians, gay men, and bisexuals. In R. Cabaj & T. Stein (Eds.), *Textbook of homosexuality and mental health* (pp. 549-561). Washington, DC: American Psychiatric Press.

Klein, F. (1993). *The bisexual option.* (2nd ed.). New York: Harrington Park Press.

Klein, F., Sepekoff, B., & Wolf, T. (1985, Spring). Sexual orientation: A multivariate dynamic process. *Journal of Homosexuality, 11*(1/2), 35-49.

Klinger, R., & Stein, T. (1996). Impact of violence, childhood sexual abuse, and domestic violence and abuse on lesbians, bisexuals, and gay men. In R. Cabaj & T. Stein (Eds.), *Textbook of homosexuality and mental health* (pp. 801-818). Washington, DC: American Psychiatric Press.

Krestan, J., & Bepko, C. (1980). The problem of fusion in the lesbian relationship. *Family Process, 19*(3), 277-289.

Kurdek, L. (1987). Sex role self-schema and psychological adjustment in coupled homosexual and heterosexual men and women. *Sex Roles, 17,* 549-562.

Kurdek, L. (1988). Perceived social support in gays and lesbians in cohabitating relationships. *Journal of Personality and Social Psychology, 54,* 504-509.

Kurdek, L. (1995). Lesbian and gay couples. In A. D'Augelli & C. Patterson (Eds.), *Lesbian, gay, and bisexual identities over the lifespan: Psychological perspectives* (pp. 243-261). New York: Oxford University Press.

Kurdek, L., & Schmitt, J. (1986). Early development of relationship quality in heterosexual married, heterosexual co-habiting, gay, and lesbian couples. *Developmental Psychology, 22,* 305-309.

Kurdek, L., & Schmitt, J. (1987). Perceived emotional support from family and friends in members of homosexual, married, and heterosexual co-habiting couples. *Journal of Homosexuality, 14,* 57-68.

Laird, J., & Green, R. (1996). Lesbians and gays in couples and families: Central issues. In J. Laird & R. Green (Eds.), *Lesbians and gays in couples and families* (pp. 1-12). San Francisco: Jossey-Bass.

Lenna, H. (1992). The outsiders: Group work with young homosexuals. In N. Woodman (Ed.), *Lesbian and gay lifestyles: A guide for counseling and education* (pp. 67-85). New York: Irvington.

Liu, P., & Chan, C. (1996). Gay, lesbian and bisexual Asian Americans and their families. In J. Laird & R. Green (Eds.), *Lesbians and gays in couples and families: A handbook for therapists* (pp. 137-152). San Francisco: Jossey-Bass.

Loiacano, D. (1989). Gay identity issues among Black Americans: Racism, homophobia, and the need for validation. *Journal of Counseling & Development, 68,* 21-35.

MacDonald, A., & Games, R. (1974). Some characteristics of those who hold positive and negative attitudes toward homosexuals. *Journal of Homosexuality, 1,* 9-27.

Malyon, A. (1981). The homosexual adolescent: Developmental issues and social bias. *Child Welfare, 60,* 321-330.

Manalasan, M. (1996). Double minorities: Latino, Black, and Asian men who have sex with men. In R. Savin-Williams & K. Cohen (Eds.), *The lives of lesbians, gays, and bisexuals: Children to adults* (pp. 393-415). Fort Worth, TX: Harcourt Brace.

Markowitz, L. (1995). Bisexuality: Challenging our either/or thinking. *In the Family, 1*(1), 6-11, 23.

Martin, A., & Hetrick, E. (1988). The stigmatization of the gay and lesbian adolescent. *Journal of Homosexuality, 15*(1/2), 163-183.

Matteson, D. (1996). Counseling and psychotherapy with bisexual and exploring clients. In B. Firestein (Ed.), *Bisexuality: The psychology and politics of an invisible minority* (pp. 185-213). Thousand Oaks, CA: Sage.

McWhirter, D., & Mattison, A. (1984). *The male couple: How relationships develop.* Englewood Cliffs, NJ: Prentice Hall.

Morales, E. (1992). Counseling Latino gays and Latina lesbians. In S. Dworkin & F. Gutierrez (Eds.), *Counseling gay men and lesbians: Journey to the end of the rainbow* (pp. 125-139). Alexandria, VA: American Association for Counseling & Development.

Morales, E. (1996). Gender roles among Latino gay and bisexual men: Implications for family and couple relationships. In J. Laird & R. Green (Eds.), *Lesbians and gays in couples and families: A handbook for therapists* (pp. 272-297). San Francisco: Jossey-Bass.

Murphy, B. (1991). Educating mental health professionals about gay and lesbian issues. *Journal of Homosexuality, 22*(3/4), 229-246.

Nakajima, G., Chan, Y., & Lee, K. (1996). Mental health issues for gay and lesbian Asian Americans. In R. Cabaj & T. Stein (Eds.), *Textbook of homosexuality and mental health* (pp. 563-582). Washington, DC: American Psychiatric Press.

National Lesbian & Gay Health Foundation. (1987). *National Lesbian Health Care Survey: Mental health implications.* Atlanta, GA: Author.

National Lesbian & Gay Task Force Policy Institute. (1992). *Anti-gay/lesbian violence, victimization and defamation in 1991.* Washington, DC: Author.

Nystrom, N. (1997, February). *Mental health experiences of gay men and lesbians.* Paper presented at the annual meeting of the American Association for the Advancement of Science, Houston, TX.

Paroski, P. (1987). Health care delivery and the concerns of gay and lesbian adolescents. *Journal of Adolescent Health Care, 8,* 188-192.

Patterson, C. (1992). Children of lesbian and gay parents. *Child Development, 63,* 1025-1042.

Patterson, C. (1996). Lesbian and gay parents and their children. In R. Savin-Williams & K. Cohen (Eds.), *The lives of lesbians, gays, and bisexuals: Children to adults* (pp. 274-304). Fort Worth, TX: Harcourt Brace.

Pearlman, S. (1995). Making gender: New interpretations/new narratives. In J. Glassgold & S. Iasenza (Eds.), *Lesbians and psychoanalysis: Revolutions in theory and practice* (pp. 309-325). New York: Free Press.

Peplau, L. (1991). Gay and lesbian relationships. In J. Gonsiorek & J. Weinrich (Eds.), *Homosexuality: Research implications for public policy* (pp. 177-196). Newbury Park, CA: Sage.

Peplau, L. (1993). Lesbian and gay relationships. In L. Garnets & D. Kimmel (Eds.), *Psychological perspectives on lesbian and gay male experiences* (pp. 395-419). New York: Columbia University Press.

Peplau, L., Veniegas, R., & Campbell, S. (1996). Gay and lesbian relationships. In R. Savin-Williams & K. Cohen (Eds.), *The lives of lesbians, gays, and bisexuals: Children to adults* (pp. 250-273). Fort Worth, TX: Harcourt Brace.

Perlman, G. (1991). The question of therapist self-disclosure in the treatment of a gay married man. In C. Silverstein (Ed.), *Gays, lesbians, and their therapists: Studies in psychotherapy* (pp. 201-209). New York: Norton.

Pies, C. (1988). *Considering parenthood.* San Francisco: Spinsters.

Pilkington, N., & Cantor, J. (1996). Perceptions of heterosexual bias in professional psychology programs: A survey of graduate students. *Professional Psychology: Research and Practice, 27*(6), 604-612.

Remafedi, G. (1987). Homosexual youth: A challenge to contemporary society. *Journal of the American Medical Association, 258*(2), 222-225.

Rubenstein, W. (1996). Lesbians, gay men, and the law. In R. Savin-Williams & K. Cohen (Eds.), *The lives of lesbians, gays, and bisexuals: Children to adults* (pp. 331-343). Fort Worth, TX: Harcourt Brace.

Rust, P. (1996). Managing multiple identities: Diversity among bisexual women and men. In B. Firestein (Ed.), *Bisexuality: The psychology and politics of an invisible minority* (pp. 53-83). Thousand Oaks, CA: Sage.

Savin-Williams, R. (1996). Ethnic and sexual minority youth. In R. Savin-Williams & K. Cohen (Eds.), *The lives of lesbians, gays, and bisexuals: Children to adults* (pp. 152-165). Fort Worth, TX: Harcourt Brace.

Savin-Williams, R., & Cohen, K. (1996). Psychosocial outcomes of verbal and physical abuse among gay, lesbian and bisexual youths. In R. Savin-Williams & K. Cohen (Eds.), *The lives of lesbians, gays, and bisexuals: Children to adults* (pp. 181-200). Fort Worth, TX: Harcourt Brace.

Schwartz, R. (1989). When the therapist is gay: Personal and clinical reflections. *Journal of Gay and Lesbian Psychotherapy, 1*(1), 41-51.

Shidlo, A. (1994). Internalized homophobia: Conceptual and emprirical issues in measurement. In B. Greene & G. Herek (Eds.), *Psychological perspectives on lesbian and gay issues: Vol. 1. Lesbian and gay psychology: Theory, research, and clinical applications* (pp. 176-205). Thousand Oaks, CA: Sage Publications.

Slater, B. (1988). Essential issues in working with lesbian and gay male youths. *Professional Psychology: Research and Practice, 19*(2), 226-235.

Smith, A. (1997). Cultural diversity and the coming-out process: Implications for clinical practice. In B. Greene (Ed.), *Psychological perspectives on lesbian and gay issues: Ethnic and cultural diversity among lesbians and gay men* (Vol. 3, pp. 279-300). Thousand Oaks, CA: Sage.

Stein, T. (1988). Theoretical considerations in psychotherapy with gay men and lesbians. *Journal of Homosexuality, 15*(1/2), 75-95.

Strommen, E. (1990). Hidden branches and growing pains: Homosexuality and the family tree. In F. Bozett & M. Sussman (Eds.), *Homosexuality and family relations* (pp. 9-34). New York: Harrington Park Press.

Troiden, R. (1988). *Gay and lesbian identity: A sociological analysis.* New York: General Hall.

Trujillo, C. (1997). Sexual identity and the discontents of difference. In B. Greene (Ed.), *Psychological perspectives on lesbian and gay issues: Vol.3. Ethnic and cultural diversity among lesbians and gay men* (pp. 266-278). Thousand Oaks, CA: Sage.

Trujillo, C. (Ed.). (1991). *Chicana lesbians: The girls our mothers warned us about.* Berkeley, CA: Third Woman Press.

Uribe, V., & Friends of Project 10. (1991). *Project 10 handbook: Addressing lesbian and gay issues in our schools* (3rd ed.). Los Angeles: Friends of Project 10, Inc.

Weise, E. (1992). Introduction. In E. Weise (Ed.), *Closer to home: Bisexuality and feminism* (pp. ix-xv). Seattle: Seal Press.

White, M. (1994). *Stranger at the gate: To be gay and Christian in America.* New York: Plume/Penguin Books.

Winegarten, B., Cassie, N., Markowski, K., Kozlowski, J., & Yoder, J. (1994, August). *Aversive heterosexism: Exploring unconscious bias toward lesbian psychotherapy clients.* Paper presented at the annual meeting of the American Psychological Association, Los Angeles.

6

Including Transgender Issues in
Lesbian, Gay and Bisexual Psychology

Implications for Clinical Practice and Training

KATHY A. GAINOR

This chapter introduces the reader to transgender issues and challenges persistent pathological views of gender nonconformity. I
have attempted to capture the complexity of this topic as well as the intensity of the debate about gender and gender identity while being
nonexhaustive. In order to provide a context for examining transgender issues, the concept of gender construction in Western society is explored. Second, contemporary definitions of transgenderism, and its
variations, are presented. Medical and psychological classifications of
transgenderism are addressed as are parallels between lesbian and
gay sexual orientations and transgenderism. Third, psychological dilemmas frequently experienced by transgendered people are examined. The developmental challenges involved in growing up with a
nonconforming gender identity are also outlined. Fourth, psychotherapeutic considerations with transgendered people are addressed,

AUTHOR'S NOTE: This chapter is an abridged version of Gainor, K. (1998). *Forgotten identities: Transgender issues in clinical training and practice.* Unpublished manuscript.

highlighting the importance of a culturally sensitive approach to psychological practice with this population. Important factors involved in educating clinicians about transgenderism are also addressed.

Introduction

In 1973, the American Psychiatric Association declassified homosexuality as a mental disorder and voted to remove it from its third edition of the *Diagnostic and Statistical Manual of Mental Disorders* (DSM-III; APA, 1968, 1980). However, 24 years later, departures from traditional gender identity remains a psychiatric classification under the diagnostic titles of *transvestic fetishism* and *gender identity disorder* (APA, 1994; Wilson, 1997a, 1997b). Continued designation of gender nonconformity as a mental illness allows us, lead by medical and psychological professionals, to unfairly stigmatize individuals who fail to conform to standard gender roles. As a result of that stigma, gender nonconforming individuals are seen as not deserving of the many basic civil liberties afforded any other citizen.

In 1966, endocrinologist and sexologist Dr. Harry Benjamin published his groundbreaking text, *Transsexual Phenomenon*. Marking a movement toward a humane and sympathetic approach to addressing the distress experienced by many transsexuals, Benjamin was one of the first physicians to conclude that psychoanalytic approaches to transsexualism were inappropriate because transsexuals did not have a mental disorder (Califia, 1997). Although he continued to view transsexuals and other transgendered people as suffering from an incurable endocrinological condition (Tully, 1992), Benjamin (1966) regarded them as deserving no less compassion than individuals struggling with a major illness or disorder.

An examination of the historical response to lesbians and gay men, and transsexuals is replete with examples of discommendation ranging from mild disapproval to overt hostility and violence directed at any nonconforming expressions of gender and sex roles. Despite the prevalence of accurate information to the contrary, beliefs persist among the general public that gay men want to be women, lesbians want to be men, and bisexuals want the best of both worlds. Gender variation sparks a highly personal and emotional response from people that often leads to expressions of hostility and aggression toward gender-nonconforming individuals. Califia (1997) notes, "[t]ranssexuals challenge our ideas of right and wrong, politically correct and politically incorrect, mental health and mental dysfunction" (p. 2).

Perhaps more than gay and lesbian sexual orientations, the existence of transgenderism goes to the root of what it means to be a man or a woman in both the biological and psychosocial/sociological sense. Thus, the transphobia[1] experienced by transgendered people from their families, workplace, and medical, legal, and social services, is a reflection of society's intense fear of losing a fundamental means by which we not only come to understand our sense of self, but also how we come to know our place and purpose in social hierarchies. Sex and gender role expectations inform many people about who they are and what they are suppose to do in the world and in their relationships in very fundamental ways. Without a definitive sense of their roles being defined in absolute ways, many people experience a state of psychological disequilibrium. For some people, questioning gender is akin to contradicting indisputable facts, such as insisting that black is white (Brown & Rounsley, 1996). The mere existence of people who define their gender roles with greater flexibility may be experienced by those who do not have that flexibility as disquieting and even personally disruptive.

Despite our reactions, the reality is that transgenderism and all of its forms has been present throughout history, in a variety of cultures and societies, across a wide spectrum of populations (Feinberg, 1996). Although commonly presented as documenting the existence of gays and lesbians, often by gay historians and anthropologists (Herdt, 1994; Katz, 1976; Roscoe, 1991; Williams, 1986), descriptions of non-Western cultures are filled with examples of transgendered people of varying sexual orientations (Califia, 1997). For example, the Hijra of India were born men or hermaphrodites and assumed parental roles in which they would adopt intersex infants (Herdt, 1994). Polynesian cultures recognized a third sex, whereby biological men are permitted to dress and behave as women would generally behave (Caplan, 1987). The Native American *two-spirit people* are better viewed as a gender role, rather than as a sexual identity (Allen, 1996, in Tafoya, 1997; Califia, 1997). Popular cultural icons, such as singer songwriter k.d. lang, former Chicago Bulls forward Dennis Rodman, and media personality RuPaul, are people who exemplify various expressions of modern Western gender nonconformity. Responses to them range from confusion, humor, and amazement to disapproval and even disgust by various constituencies of our culture (Feinberg, 1996). Thus, the mere existence of a social role for gender-nonconforming and transgendered people within a culture does not mean that they or those roles are socially acceptable (Califia, 1997).

Discrimination against transgendered people is directly linked to homophobia. For example, the current approach to addressing gender-nonconforming children is aimed at preventing homosexuality (Pela, 1997). Termed, "the prehomosexual agenda," by Wilson (1997a, 1997b), there are examples of children as young as 3 years of age being treated for gender identity disorder (GID) often at the insistence of parents who wish to alter a perceived gay or lesbian sexual orientation (Burke, 1996). Zucker (in Pela, 1997) observes that parents want their children to feel better about being a boy or a girl (as defined from an essentialist view) and to be heterosexual because they want their children to have an easier life.

The existence of this diagnostic entity is based on the unproven assumption that there should be no discontinuity between biological sex and gender identity, despite the fact that gender identity is socially contrived. GID also indirectly pathologizes lesbian and gay sexual orientations. Its presence is used in the continued abuse of gay and lesbian children through the use of painful and sometimes aversive therapies such as electroconvulsive shock treatments (Burke, 1996; Pela, 1997). Although some treatment approaches to so-called "effeminate" boys have been relatively benign (i.e., promoting more contact with fathers, socialization with nonaggressive male peers, and participation in non-competitive activities; Zucker & Bradley, 1995), the goal of that treatment is clearly motivated by the stigma of transsexuality and lesbian and gay sexual orientations in our society. In that context, it can be just as damaging to a child's self-concept and self-esteem.

Treatment of gender nonconformity in children is being defended by the following assumptions. First, it is deemed to help reduce social ostracism; however, it treats the victim and not the perpetrators of such ostracism. Second, it is presumed to be treating some form of underlying psychopathology; however, that assumption is based on psychodynamic theories of etiology and are drawn solely from clinical populations. Third, such treatment is assumed to prevent GID in adulthood, despite the absence of any empirical evidence to support this idea (Wilson, 1997a, 1997b).

Despite the parallel struggles against oppression for transgendered people, gay men, lesbians, and, more recently, bisexual men and women, discrimination against transgendered people is prevalent even within the lesbian and gay community. Discrimination against transgendered people within the lesbian and gay community rests on a peculiar irony. It was in fact a group of courageous drag queens, many of whom were also people of color, who spearheaded an uprising in a police bar raid in New York City in 1969. Their decision to fight back against police brutality and terror, and the subsequent 4-day uprising, sparked what is now remembered as the infamous Stonewall Rebellion, traditionally regarded as the beginning of the modern gay rights movement.

As with gays, lesbians, and bisexuals, there is much debate over the prevalence of transgenderism. This is due, in part, to the diversity which exists within the transgender community (e.g., transsexuals, transvestites, intersexed persons) as well as the lack of reliable methods for collecting such data, especially in the United States (Brown & Rounsley, 1996). Many transgendered people remain "closeted," justifiably fearful of being ostracized by family, peers, and coworkers. Nevertheless, it is estimated that transsexuals constitute .01% of the population. By 1988, an estimated 6,000 to 10,000 transsexuals had undergone genital reassignment surgery.

Regardless of actual numbers, increasing attention is being given to transgender issues in employment, social services, and legislation. To date, a number of cities and municipalities provide civil rights protections for transgendered people. Proposition L in San Francisco prevents discrimination of transgendered state employees based upon gender. New York City, Minneapolis, Seattle, and Santa Cruz, California have similar protections, although the latter two cities cover transgendered people under sexual orientation (Green & Brinkin, 1994). On the other hand, the Nixon administration removed certain protections, thus allowing insurance companies to deem genital reassignment surgery as cosmetic or experimental and therefore no longer a reimbursable medical expense. More recently, Jesse Helms campaigned for and won the removal of transgendered people from the Americans with Disabilities Act (Green & Brinkin, 1994). These examples demonstrate how political agendas influence how transgender issues are viewed, thus affecting medical and psychological interventions and changes in those efforts.

Examining the Concepts of Gender and Gender Identity

Currently, our society appears to enjoy greater flexibility in its gender role expectations than it has in the past. Many men have more freedom to pursue traditionally female activities (e.g., nursing, stay-at-home parenting); while a number of women are experiencing even greater acceptance in pursuing traditionally male endeavors (e.g., police officers, corporate executives, professional boxing, and basketball). However, disagreement continues to abound over the normalcy of gender expression that does not conform to traditional gender role standards. Pursuing some other gender activities may be sanctioned by our society, but behaving as or "being" the other gender is still regarded as a psychological disturbance or a medical condition in need of treatment. Hence, while the United States culture has enjoyed many changes in its definitions and flexibility of gender and gender roles, the majority of Americans maintain fairly fixed beliefs about the limits of masculine and feminine behavior (Reid & Whitehead, 1992).

Historically, sex and gender have been defined from an essentialist, binary perspective (Money, 1994) in which sex and gender are equivalent, immutable, and hence biological (i.e., chromosomally and genetically determined). From this perspective, one must be male *or* female; any categories in between are unacknowledged, unacceptable, and deemed socially inappropriate (Reid & Whitehead, 1992). Gender nonconformity is viewed as a disorder or abnormality that requires correction or "cure" by medical or psychological means.

Unlike the existentialist view that equates sex with gender, a social constructionist perspective views sex as distinct from gender. *Sex* is defined as a biological construct. *Gender,* a relatively recent term, is a sociocultural construct referring to the behavioral, psychological, social, and cultural features and characteristics that have become strongly associated with being male and female (Forisha, 1978; Unger, 1979). Often citing the examples from non-Western cultures, several proponents of a social constructionist view of gender (Bornstein, 1994; Kessler & McKenna, 1978) articulate that our ideas of masculinity and femininity are shaped by people and based on ideas about the standards that we want people to conform to, rather than what they are.

Unger (1989) has observed that even the construction of sex as a biological category is problematic because it is confounded by social experiences and expectations. Biological sex is more complex than the dichotomous model implies (Coombs, 1997). Many of the categories used to classify people as male and female (e.g., genitalia, hormones, and secondary sex characteristics) do not actually divide people into two distinct groups. Examples include people who may have both or ambiguous genitalia, women with more facial hair than some men, and individuals who possess male genitalia and female sex characteristics due to a lack of testosterone (Coombs, 1997).

Removing our current binary constructions of sex and gender would create greater movement for gender freedom (Califia, 1997). However, it is this very freedom that so terrifies our society, as it threatens to dismantle the patriarchal system that serves as the model for American society and in which some people thrive. Our current constructions of gender serve to provide society with an external yardstick by which to measure and identify those who are allowed to gain or are denied access to certain gender-based privileges.

Whereas gender is the external, societal identification of what is male or female, *gender identity* refers to the internal, individual identification with maleness and femaleness as well as the processes by which such feelings (and their subsequent roles) are internalized and presented to society (Isreal & Tarver, 1997). As Eyler and Wright (1997) have emphasized, masculinity and femininity may differ markedly by degrees depending on individual and social interpretations. However, in a society that constructs gender along a fairly rigid dichotomy, gender becomes problematic and disruptive to the personal identity of individuals who do not conform to a binary gender construct (Reid & Whitehead, 1992).

It is important to distinguish gender identity from *sexual orientation.* Sexual orientation defines "the sex of the individual to whom one is erotically and emotionally attracted" (Brown & Rounsley, 1996, p. 19). For example, a persistent societal myth that lesbians view themselves as men because of their attraction to other women, is based on the assumption that only men are (or should be) attracted to women. Despite this erroneous belief, lesbians have a clear sense of their gender identity as women who are attracted to other women and do not by definition experience themselves as men or imitations of men. Therefore, gender identity is defined as one's internal sense of being male or female, whereas sexual orientation is defined by the biological sex of the object of one's attraction.

The concept of gender identity does impact on our notion of sexual orientation. As we currently understand it, sexual orientation presumes a fixedness about gender roles and sexual attraction. Without those roles, the construct of sexual orientation changes and may vanish altogether. Gender identity and expressions of gender identity are not synonymous. Romantic attractions between people are based on perceptions of a person's expressed gender identity, what they present themselves to be; this may or may not be synonymous with the person's internal sense of gender (B. Greene, personal communication, February 16, 1998). To the extent that gender and gender roles are socially constructed, then sexual orientation is a social construct as well (Greene, Chapter 1 in this volume; Hancock, Chapter 5 in this volume; Kitzinger, 1987).

When a person's inner sense of gender identity does not match his or her external, biological sex, that experience is defined as *gender dysphoria*. A general term, gender dysphoria refers to the "discomfort characterized by a feeling of incongruity with the physical gender assigned to one at birth" (Isreal & Tarver, 1997, p. 7). Like the diagnosis "ego-dystonic homosexuality" (APA, 1980), medical and mental health professions have tended to define gender dysphoria in the absence of the context of a society that oppresses gender nonconforming people just as it oppresses lesbians and gay men. Therefore it is difficult for gender nonconforming people to avoid experiencing discomfort, torment, and despair about their gender identity, when little support and overt abuse is directed at them.

Gender identity disorder, first listed in the *DSM-III* in 1980[2] (APA, 1980), is the commonly used diagnostic term for more severe forms of gender dysphoria. According to the *DSM-IV* (APA, 1994), gender identity disorder is characterized by a strong and persistent cross-gender identification (not merely a desire for any perceived cultural advantages of being the other sex); persistent discomfort with one's biological sex or sense of inappropriateness in the gender role of that sex; and clinically significant distress or impairment in social, occupational, or other important areas of functioning.

Gender identity disorder is also classified as intersex conditions and accompanying gender dysphoria, transient and stress-related cross-dressing, or a persistent preoccupation with castration or penectomy with a desire for the sex characteristics of the other sex (APA, 1994). Wilson (1997a, 1997b) highlights the conceptual problems with the current diagnostic category for children and adults (reviewed later in this chapter).

In a society with fairly fixed notions of sex and gender, the concepts of gender dysphoria and gender identity disorder are socially constructed to maintain a patriarchal social system. In this system, one sex or gender (i.e., male) is deemed more desirable, powerful, and deserving of social privilege than the "other" sex or gender (i.e., female). The failure to conform to accepted notions of sex, gender, gender identity, and gender roles is deemed pathological, rebellious, or even criminal. Like gay men, lesbians, and bisexual men and women, transgender advocates have recently become more vocal in highlighting the diversity that exists within our society with respect to biological sex and gender expression.

Thus, the current literature and political climate suggests that the concept of gender should be restructured to allow for a better understanding of the experiences of gender-nonconforming people and those with gender dysphoria. The concept of two genders should be reconsidered given the reality of variation and diversity of gender expression throughout history. What is currently considered a gender identity disorder may simply be a variant of normal human sexuality. Instead of expecting people to fit into prescribed identities based on contrived frameworks, we must consider ways of altering those structures to more accurately reflect the realities of human beings.

Understanding Transgender

To understand a topic as complex and emotionally laden as gender identity, it is important to define what is meant by the term transgender. The meaning of transgenderism has changed over the years, adding to its complexity and to the misunderstandings that currently abound.

Defining Transgender

The concept *transgender* is commonly regarded as an umbrella term describing transvestites, transsexuals, transgenderists, androgynists, and intersex people. Contrary to traditional psychiatric diagnostic criteria, when a person identifies as transgender, the term gender dysphoric is no longer appropriate when referring to this individual (Califia, 1997; Isreal & Tarver, 1997). This does not mean, however, that self-identified transgendered people will not continue to experience some feelings of discomfort related to gender identity issues as they further explore their needs and move toward self-identification (Isreal & Tarver, 1997). Such feelings of gender dysphoria would be inescapable given the intensity of transphobia that permeates our society. Thus, the term gender dysphoria is most applicable to individuals who are in the beginning stages of transition and who may yet be unaware that they have a transgender identity (Isreal & Tarver, 1997).

The term *transgenderists* refers more specifically to people who live and work in the other gender continuously (i.e., full-time cross-dressers and nonsurgical transsexuals; Green & Brinkin, 1994). Isreal and Tarver (1997) include in this definition those individuals who live the role part-time as a member of the other gender. Occasionally, transgenderists may self-identify as *bigender*, highlighting their emotional need to maintain certain aspects of both masculinity and femininity. Transgenderists may often be interested in taking hormones and occasionally in having cosmetic surgery and/or castration. They do not, however, wish to have genital reassignment surgery (Green & Brinkin, 1994; Isreal & Tarver, 1997).

Unlike transgenderists, who have received little attention in the professional literature, most medical and psychological practitioners and researchers interested in transgender issues have focused on the transsexual. *Transsexuals* feel an overwhelming desire to permanently fulfill their lives as members of the other gender (Isreal & Tarver, 1997). They frequently experience a profound lack of congruence between mind (gender identity) and body (biological sex) and are most uncomfortable with the gender role that society expects them to play based on their biological sex (Brown & Rounsley, 1996). Transsexuals are subsequently plagued by the most acute effects of gender dysphoria and are most interested in cross-living, sex hormones, and GRS (Brown & Rounsley, 1996; Ramsey, 1996; Isreal & Tarver, 1997). Regardless of their surgical status, transsexuals possess a cross-sex identity (Bolin, 1988; 1992). Preoperative male-to-female (MTF) transsexuals (or *transsexual women*) are born male, yet self-identify as female; preoperative female-to-male (FTM) transsexuals (or *transsexual men*) are born female, but self-identify as male (Brown & Rounsley, 1996; Green & Brinkin, 1994; Isreal & Tarver, 1997).

Transvestites (or *cross-dressers*) dress in other-gender clothing for emotional satisfaction and/or erotic pleasure. Transvestites differ from drag queens, kings, and performance artists who cross-dress for entertainment or for sex-industry purposes and are stereotypically associated with gay and lesbian communities (Isreal & Tarver, 1997). For the transvestite, cross-dressing provides an outlet for exploring feelings and behaviors associated with the other gender while retaining one's biological sex (Isreal & Tarver, 1997). Although most cross-dressers are heterosexual, they can be gay, lesbian, or bisexual (Isreal & Tarver, 1997). Transvestites may have fantasies about being a member of the other sex, but they do not possess a cross-sex identity (Bolin, 1988, 1992) and do not desire to change their sex surgically or otherwise (Brown & Rounsley, 1996; Isreal & Tarver, 1997). Many of these individuals prefer the term cross-dresser rather than the more clinical label of transvestite (Isreal & Tarver, 1997).

Androgynes, or *androgynous persons,* vary in their gender identity. They may present bigender mannerisms and wear gender-neutral clothing. In addition, androgynous people may wish to be identified as both male and female or may even prefer not to be identified as either male and female. While some androgynes may identify in this manner to fulfill their identity needs, others may make a conscious decision to do so as a challenge to social stereotypes (Isreal & Tarver, 1997).

Unlike transgenderists, transsexuals, cross-dressers, and androgynes who typically possess biological attributes of one sex or another, *intersex* (or *hermaphroditic)* individuals have medically established physical or hormonal attributes of both the male and female sexes, whether full or partial (Brown & Rounsley, 1996; Green & Brinkin, 1994; Isreal & Tarver, 1997). Often detectable at birth, the child is almost always assigned a gender at that time (i.e., male or female) solely on the basis of physical appearance (Isreal & Tarver, 1997). The assignment may also be based on the meaning attached to that child's physical appearance by medical doctors and parents. In cases where the "assigned" gender or the surgically "corrected" genitalia do not match the child's gender identity, the individual is likely to experience gender dysphoria (Pela, 1997) and in some cases seek GRS like the transsexual (Brown & Rounsley, 1996). Even when the assigned gender and gender identity do match, surgical intervention often interferes with sexual stimulation and satisfaction later in the individual's life (Califia, 1997; Pela, 1997). Some, but not all, intersex people may present as androgynous or self-identify as transgendered.

Identification as a transgendered person or a member of a transgender subgroup is the sole right and responsibility of individuals exploring their gender identity issues. Therefore, clinicians and consumers must avoid hastily labeling them. The fact that most such individuals do not fall neatly into one category or another underscores the need for caution in this area (Isreal & Tarver, 1997).

Classifying Transgender

Regardless of the specific subgroup, transgenderism has been traditionally viewed by medical and psychological professionals as a disorder, a significant departure from the accepted and approved norms of
sex and gender warranting diagnosis and treatment. Therefore, the preponderance of medical and psychological literature on transgenders
(e.g., Benjamin, 1966; Doctor, 1988; Roberto, 1983; Schott, 1995; Tully,
1992) has focused on diagnosis, etiology, and treatment with the majority devoted to transsexuals and cross-dressers. Many practitioners who
work with transsexuals, for example, have traditionally advocated two
primary approaches to treatment. One involves the use of physical or
psychological techniques for removing the transsexual's presumed
pathological wishes and desires. Another, in more appropriate cases, to
facilitate a change of sex by medical means. Both approaches profess to
seek harmony in a discordant situation, however, they also seek to ensure that identity, social status, and biology all "match," thus preserving
the binary structure of gender (Ekins & King, 1995; Isreal & Tarver, 1997).

Explanations regarding the cause of transgenderism have ranged
from the psychological (e.g., crises during the individuation-separation
phase of development; Doctor, 1988) to the biological (e.g., errors in nature; Money, 1994; Tully, 1992). Such explanations provide support for
continued classification of transgendered people as mentally disordered
(Green & Blanchard, 1995; Meyer, 1997). Empirical studies offered as
support for these theories are typically based on clinical and psychiatric
populations with no control groups consisting of transgendered people
who are not receiving medical or psychiatric treatment. As such, these
studies have basic methodological flaws. Hence, despite their claims,
these theories are not supported by reliable empirical research. Further,
these theories and their relevant research perpetuate myths and stereotypes of transgendered people (e.g., having overbearing mothers or being effeminate children; Wilson & Hammond, 1996).

Wilson (1997a) examines how conflicting, ambiguous, sexist, and
prejudicial language used in the *DSM-IV* legitimizes an intolerance of
gender diversity in our society. For example, transvestites (renamed,
"transvestic fetishism," in the *DSM-III-R*; APA, 1984) are clinically classified as cross-dressing heterosexual males (see *DSM-IV* for full definition; APA, 1994). From this definition, one could conclude that all
cross-dressers are heterosexual, thus ignoring the existence of gay, les-

bian, or heterosexual female cross-dressers (cf. Bullough & Bullough, 1997). On the other hand, this definition could lead one to conclude that cross-dressing is pathological in heterosexual men but that it is not in gay men, lesbians, and heterosexual women. This conclusion implies that in a society where men have more power and privilege than women, biological men who emulate women are presumed to be mentally disordered or defective as men, whereas biological women who emulate men are not considered equally defective (Wilson, 1997a). The latter defect is more tolerable by society because women emulating men are seen as identifying with the more socially desirable and powerful figure.

Wilson and Hammond (1996) note that the criteria for cross-dressing and GID contradicts *DSM*'s own definition of mental disorder that excludes deviant behavior or individual-societal conflicts from the diagnosis of mental disorder. Therefore, well-adjusted transgendered individuals can receive a psychiatric diagnosis by virtue of the extent or pervasiveness of their cross-gender wishes, interests, or activities. Thus, one may deviate from or conflict with societal expectations, to a certain degree and not receive a diagnostic label. However, if one's behavior crosses an arbitrary line, one can receive a diagnosis (Wilson & Hammond, 1996).

The notion of "distress or impairment" in the *DSM-IV* criteria lies at the heart of this issue. This definition ignores, or at least leaves ambiguous, whether or not an individual's distress is inherent to their gender identity struggles or is imposed by societal pressures to conform to arbitrary gender role expectations (Wilson & Hammond, 1996). Further, a "clinical significance" criterion, added to the diagnostic criteria for all sexual and gender identity disorders (APA, 1997; Wilson, 1997b), leaves the diagnosis of the transgendered person to vary with the tolerance level of the clinician rather than with reliable clinical criteria. Tolerant clinicians may infer that any presenting impairment in the transgendered client is the result of societal intolerance and prejudice. The intolerant clinician may assume that an individual with cross-gender identity or expression is inherently impaired regardless of his or her level of happiness and well-being (Wilson, 1997a). That is, depending on the subjective assumptions of the diagnostician regarding "normal" sex and gender roles and the distress that accompanies one's experience with societal prejudice, gender-nonconforming children and adults may or may not receive diagnoses of transvestic fetishism or gender identity disorder (Wilson, 1997a, 1997b). Such ambiguity contributes to this problem and provides an over-inclusive system that allows for the re-classification of lesbian and gay sexual orientations as a mental disorder in need of preventive treatment in gender-nonconforming children (Wilson, 1997a, 1997b).

As discussed in the introduction, the sociopolitical histories of transgenderism and homosexuality have much in common. Transgenderism and homosexuality are deeply linked politically, because they are viewed by society as linked. As such, they are treated as different aspects of a similar deviance by the dominant patriarchal, heterosexual community (Coombs, 1997). Wilson (1997b) highlights parallels between past characterizations of homosexuality and current characterizations of gender identity and transgenderism by the psychiatric community, particularly noting that the theories that unsuccessfully justified the pathologizing of sexual orientation and those that continue to classify gender orientation are remarkably similar. Coombs (1997) outlines how discussions concerning whether gay and lesbian same-sex marriages should be legalized in our society have implications for those same-sex marriages (i.e., ones in which one partner has undergone GRS or other forms of gender transition), which are indirectly related.

The eventual removal of homosexuality from the *DSM* was influenced by the recognition of experienced distress and impairment that many gays, lesbians, and bisexuals experience especially in the early stages of their coming out process. However, this recognition has yet to be applied to transgendered people (Wilson, 1997b). It is certainly possible (and quite likely) that transgendered people commonly go through an ego-dystonic phase in response to stigma similar to that of gays and lesbians (Wilson, 1997b). The distress and impairment seen by the diagnostician may represent an early part of the coming out process as denial gives way to self-acceptance (Wilson & Hammond, 1996).

Although the history and issues of gays men, lesbians, and bisexuals and those of transgendered people are similar, there are also important differences. For example, coming out as gay, lesbian, or bisexual does not challenge society's basic notions about human nature in the same way that coming out as transgendered does. Although both entail revealing a long-held and deeply personal secret, the transgendered person's revelation includes that he or she is of another gender and in the case of transsexuals, seeking to change his or her gender role and body (Brown & Rounsley, 1996).

In addition, coming out as gay, lesbian, or bisexual typically involves a revelation to others of one's inner feelings and desires. Although the reactions of others can be severe, the gay, lesbian, or bisexual person's outward appearance, sex, and social roles typically remain the same. Coming out as transgendered, by contrast, involves not only the revelation of one's inner life but also, especially in the case of transsexuals, the revelation of the dramatic process of outer appearance and social role change (Brown & Rounsley, 1996).

Psychological Issues
Facing Transgendered People

People who do not conform to societal expectations of biological sex and/or gender experience profound oppression and hostility (ranging from great reluctance to harassment and abuse) from those who do conform. For example, transsexuals often face intense negative reactions by family and friends (Ramsey, 1996). Spouses can react adversely with custody battles that add further pain and turmoil for the transsexual. One transsexual woman, testifying at the San Francisco Human Rights Commission public hearing held in 1994, described being slammed up against a wall and having her pants pulled down by a shopkeeper who wanted to see what a transsexual woman looked like (Green & Brinkin, 1994).

Oppression of transgendered people also takes the form of pressure to conform to societal expectations for a heterosexual sexual orientation. For example, many gay and lesbian MTF and FTM transsexuals report being refused treatment by gender clinics until they self-identify as and profess to maintain a heterosexual sexual orientation (Green & Brinkin, 1994).

While there appears to be some progress in alleviating that oppression and hostility, transgendered people continue to experience discrimination in areas such as employment, housing, medical treatment (e.g., hospitals, substance abuse treatment centers), social services (e.g., rape crisis centers, homeless and battered women's shelters), sport competition, and military eligibility (Green, 1994; Green & Brinkin, 1994; Kirk & Rothblatt, 1995; Swartz, 1997). It is therefore, no wonder that many transgendered people experience intense feelings of low self-esteem.

Growing Up Transgendered

Identifying as transgendered possesses unique feelings and experiences that vary with the lifestage developmental period (i.e., childhood, adolescence, or adult) of the individual. Brown and Rounsley (1996) and Ramsey (1996) provide excellent descriptions of the experiences and conflicts characteristic of transsexuals during their childhood, adolescent, and adult years that may be applied to other transgendered people. Although briefly summarized here, readers are referred to these texts for more detailed descriptions.

Transsexual children characteristically reveal their gender choice and dysphoria by their actions (i.e., playmates, games, clothes, and toys) rather than by words (Ramsey, 1996). They often use cross-gender play as a way to temporarily transform themselves into an entity that more closely resembles their own internal identity and to help them achieve a sense of wholeness, a rarity in their daily lives (Brown & Rounsley, 1996). As these children enter elementary school, their verbal interactions become progressively more revealing and may, if the environment is safe, begin to share that they feel different from other children (Ramsey, 1996).

Like most children, transsexual children want to please their parents. However, they experience intense conflict between the desire to please parents and live up to the gender role they are expected to play and the wish to feel good about themselves (Brown & Rounsley, 1996). The underlying message they most often receive is "Don't be you." Dinno (1997), a young transsexual female, describes the kinds of subtle and overt messages transgendered children may receive from the adults in their lives.

> At the age of four or five I asked my mother why that lady had a beard on her face. I was told, "That was probably a transsexual." These were explained to be men who wanted to be women and lived shitty lives because they had to endure years of living as women while having men's bodies before they were allowed to become women . . . At the age of eight I sat down to watch "Evening Magazine" on CBS with my grandfather. The intro mentioned something about a little girl born a few decades ago who was now the father of an all-American family. The TV was immediately shut off. . . . At the age of 16 I "learned" that transsexuals were unhappy people who almost always ended up with their lives in ruins after they had surgery. This was from a high-school health teacher who had a decidedly odd adoration of the male high school football athlete ideal. . . . How, I ask, are young transgender people supposed to develop a coherent understanding with this level of information? (pp. 205-206)

A cloud of secrecy adds to the pain and confusion of the intersex child. Although these children are burdened with feelings of conflict and shame, they often do not know why. Cheryl Chase, founder of ISNA, describes the traumatic experience faced by many intersex children whose birth is treated as a medical emergency in need of surgical and hormonal intervention.

> The parents are so traumatized and shamed that they will not reveal their ordeal to anyone, including the child as he/she comes of age. The child is left genitally and emotionally mutilated, isolated, and without access to information about what has happened to them. The burden of pain and shame is so great that virtually all intersexuals stay deep in the closet throughout their lives. (C. Chase as quoted in Feinberg, 1997, p. 104)

Transgendered children thus learn to cope with growing up in a gender-inflexible society by pretending to be as they are expected to be. They often become little expert actors, chameleons, and imposters (Brown & Rounsley, 1996). Transgendered children frequently daydream to escape from their dark cloud of confusion. They are not only taunted, teased, and often bullied by other children but by adults as well. They can also become victims of verbal, physical, and even sexual abuse.

With the emergence of secondary sex characteristics, the transsexual adolescent experiences a profound sense of loss. During this period, they often feel that they must give up all hope of becoming the other gender. Feelings of betrayal, shame, despair, and anger about developing the wrong adult body are common responses. Therefore, they frequently have a strong negative body image and may even dissociate from their bodies (Brown & Rounsley, 1996). For the intersex youth, puberty may mark the awakening of hormones that do not coincide with their medically assigned gender, thus causing severe gender dysphoria. Those who reach adolescence without being told about their intersexuality may experience additional feelings of isolation. This sense of isolation is compounded by the absence of any information to help them understand their feelings.

Ostracized by their peers, transgendered adolescents feel isolated and often desperate. Parental pressure to conform often increases and further intensifies their sense of alienation. They experience conflict about dating as they desire to be around members of the other sex to fulfill their needs for association and identification. Despite this need, they also experience confusion about their sexual orientation and identify as gay, lesbian, or bisexual before having a sense of being transgendered (Brown & Rounsley, 1996). Still legally and financially dependent on parents and guardians, the typical transsexual youth has no resources and little control over their gender transition. Economic hardships are compounded by the restrictions of parenting figures on what can and will be done to the young person's mind and body (Dinno, 1997). Without sufficient supports, transgender-identified and gender-questioning youth are at a high risk for suicide, self-mutilation, alcohol and drug abuse, and school drop-out. Such youngsters may experience ostracization and abuse by their families. This rejection by those closest to them may lead to running away from home and often joining the ranks of the homeless (Brown & Rounsley, 1996; Ramsey, 1996).

The adult transsexual may be more adept at keeping their gender dysphoria under wraps. They cope by playing a role, but this role playing has a price. The need to hide their feelings can lead to stress-related medical conditions like ulcers, migraines, eating disorders, and anxiety attacks. They may feel as if they are not only betraying themselves but their loved ones as well. In an adaptive response, many transsexuals may postpone pursuing the GRS until a significant milestone or change in their current life circumstances (e.g., adult children leaving home or death of a spouse). At this point, intense feelings of urgency and hypervigilence may be the predominant emotion for the adult transsexual.

Lamborn (1997), an adult transsexual female, who waited until her son graduated from college before pursuing GRS, equates this sense of urgency with a feeling of time lost.

> My sessions with the therapist were, in the beginning, always tearful. Here I was, late middle-aged and only now coming to terms with my own feelings. I cried with grief over the fact that I had not begun my transition much earlier in life. I mourned the lost years I had spent in my hated male gender role. I wanted to proceed with my transition as quickly as possible in order to make up for the years that I had lost. It took many months of therapy for me to shake this feeling of lost time. (p. 21)

Transgendered People of Color

In addition to the developmental transitions that all transgendered people face, transgendered people of color must also cope with the realities of racial discrimination and prejudice as well as the rejection of their ethnic communities. Transphobia and racism, along with classism and sexism, become daily obstacles to overcome. Many also face demands from their culture to choose and divide identities across race and gender lines.

Little information is available regarding transgendered people of color. Most of the research on gender nonconforming people of color consists of cross-cultural and anthropological studies of transsexuals and cross-dressers in countries like Japan, the Phillipines, Brazil, and Mexico. Only one published study explored psychiatric psychopathology in five black, self-identified FTM transsexuals requesting GRS (Lothstein & Roback, 1984). The authors indicated that each of the participants displayed severe psychopathology with severe gender identity pathology. They erroneously concluded that the low incidence of transsexualism in black women (as defined by their clinic's statistics) is attributed to the matriarchal family structure of black families. In this schema, according to Lothstein & Roback (1984), black women may have a healthy integration of aggression into their feminine identity (Lothstein & Roback, 1984).

There are several problems with this study and its conclusions. The authors base their opinions on a largely distorted interpretation of the gender role flexibility observed in African American families. Those distortions are captured in the matriarchal theories. They have historically been used either as an example of or the reason for pathology in African American families. This fallacious concept alleges that females and not males are dominant in African American families and suggests that this arrangement is counter to what traditional mental health has viewed as normal in families. Lothstein and Roback (1984) take this concept of matriarchies in African American families to a further extreme by using it to support their, at best, premature conclusion of a low incidence of transsexualism among African American females. Their sample consisted of merely five biological females, four of whom demonstrated severe psychopathology. It is inappropriate to make such sweeping generalizations based on observations of such a small, restricted sample, particularly when it is connected to a historically distorted concept of African American family structures and functioning, as well as an ethnocentric view of what healthy family structures should be.

Counseling and Psychotherapy
With Transgendered Clients

Transgendered people seek psychological services for reasons that are directly related to their gender identity as well as for psychological and routine life problems unrelated to their gender identity. In this manner they are no different from clients who do not identify as transgendered. Even in the case of the transsexual seeking GRS who is required by the Standards of Care for Gender Dysphoric Persons (Walker, 1990) to undergo psychotherapy as a prerequisite to medical intervention, the process of counseling or psychotherapy may address issues unrelated to gender identity or transformation.

Traditional psychotherapeutic approaches have historically focused on curing transgendered people of their presumed pathology. Such cures have involved long-term, intensive psychotherapy and sometimes aversive techniques designed specifically to eliminate the transgendered identity. For example, Lothstein asserts that mental health professionals should initially attempt to change the wishes of a person who wants to transition to the other gender. In Lothstein's view, support for wishes to transition should be provided only if attempts to change have failed; to do otherwise is deemed unethical and premature. Lothstein's position is synonymous with unenlightened and unethical attempts to alter the sexual orientation of lesbians, gay men, and bisexual men and women as a matter of course. The reader is referred to Haldeman, Chapter 10 in this volume, for a more extensive discussion of the American Psychological Association's policy and stance toward conversion therapies.

Traditional approaches to psychotherapy with transgendered people have often been ineffective because they pathologize that which is not inherently pathological. Research shows that attempts to repair something that is not broken are doomed to fail. For this reason, clinicians must avoid the temptation to attribute all presenting concerns transgendered clients bring to therapy as if they are directly related to their gender nonconformity. Transgendered clients can benefit from psychotherapy as treatment for mental disorders unrelated to their gender identity as well as a means of psychological support for coping with the trauma imposed by intolerant family members and society.

Whether the focus of therapy is on the process of gender reassignment, a mental disorder unrelated to a client's transgendered identity or gender dysphoria (e.g., major depression, general anxiety, posttraumatic stress), or ordinary problems of life (e.g., career choice, retirement), the clinician must take a culturally sensitive approach to working with transgendered clients. The culturally sensitive clinician considers the relevance of culture for each individual client by recognizing the importance of culture and behavior, entertaining more than one interpretation of their client's observed behavior, having some knowledge of how culture influences behavior, and collecting relevant data to test their cultural hypotheses (Lopez et al., 1989).

Transgendered clients can be effectively served by individual supportive counseling or psychotherapy (Isreal & Tarver, 1997). Support groups and group therapy can be helpful in breaking through the feelings of guilt, shame, and isolation and to provide validation for the transgendered person's emotions and experiences (Brown & Rounsley, 1996; Isreal & Tarver, 1997). Actually, the clinician's theoretical orientation and therapeutic approach is not as important as his or her level of knowledge, understanding, flexibility, open-mindedness, and comfort level regarding transgender issues and gender nonconformity (Brown & Rounsley, 1996).

As with all clients, the clinician should explore not only the transgendered client's presenting concern but also psychological stressors, coping and defense mechanisms, family history and dynamics, social support network, relationship and sexual history (including sexual orientation issues), any history of emotional, physical, and/or sexual abuse, possible substance abuse or other addictive behaviors, motivation for seeking therapy at the present time, and goals and expectations (Brown & Rounsley, 1996). Transgendered clients can present with a number of distressing feelings and issues that include fear, anger, guilt, shame, and poor self-esteem (Brown & Rounsley, 1996). Common mental health issues presented by transgendered people include adjustment difficulties (e.g., divorce, death of a loved one, physical disability), anxiety, and posttraumatic stress symptoms (e.g., assault, childhood abuse; Brown & Rounsley, 1996; Isreal & Tarver, 1997). Depression, which can result from hormonal treatments, is frequently a major concern. During the initial assessment, clinicians should be careful to distinguish difficulties related to transgenderism or gender nonconformity and those related to more severe psychopathology, such as schizophrenia, dissociative identity disorders, confused sexual orientation, body dysmorphic disorders, borderline personality disorder, obsessive-compulsive disorder, and malingering (Brown & Rounsley, 1996; Isreal & Tarver, 1997). For example, a person with body dysmorphic disorder (APA, 1994) believes that his or her physical body is inexplicably altered perhaps with features of the other gender. However, there is no objective physical change in the person's body and the person expresses no desire to be the other gender (Isreal & Tarver, 1997). In addition, it should be noted that unresolved transgenderism and the stress related to it (e.g., ongoing abuse by intolerant family members) can result in severe clinical depression or other mental illness (Brown & Rounsley, 1996).

As previously discussed, it is important to distinguish between intrinsic distress of true gender dysphoria or gender identity disorder and the experienced distress associated with having a nonconforming gender identity. Over the years, mental health professionals have recognized the distinction between emotional distress or mental impairment caused by societal disadvantage or oppression and distress that was believed to be inherent in nontraditional sexual orientations themselves. Although this distinction remains unresolved in the diagnostic literature concerning transgenderism (Wilson, 1997b), clinicians are not prevented from making such a distinction in their work with these clients. This distinction not only determines the appropriate treatment plan but also affects how the client will adapt to his or her unique situation. For example, when a transgendered person is a victim of job discrimination, the therapeutic work can focus on addressing the discrimination directly or it can focus solely on how the person can conform to expected standards (either by remaining in the assigned sex and expected gender role or by changing sex). Articulating the distinction between inherent and experienced distress and impairment and assisting clients in understanding this distinction is particularly important in working with children who may be prematurely diagnosed as having gender identity disorder without having expressed any desire to be the opposite gender.

Therapists must acknowledge and assist transgendered clients in working through the problems associated with societal intolerance, discrimination, violence, undeserved shame, and denial of personal freedoms that most people take for granted (Wilson, 1997b). We would not expect African Americans or any other people of color to have race reassignment surgery based on the rationale that it would make their lives easier. Such a rationale places the burden to change on the victim of discrimination rather than the perpetrators. Therapy with members of oppressed groups, be it by race, sexual orientation, sex, or gender expression, must first correctly identify unfair treatment, oppressive behavior, and both its perpetrators and victims. Next, it must address the pathology of the oppressive behavior rather than exclusively focusing on the victim's response to that oppression or on blaming the victim for it (Greene, 1998). Finally, assisting the victim in using previously acquired adaptive strategies and developing new ones to address their dilemma must be an integral part of the therapeutic work (Greene, 1994, 1997).

As previously discussed, it is important for clinicians to fully understand the difference between gender identity and sexual orientation. This is relevant whether one is working with a self-identified transgendered client, a gay, lesbian, or bisexual client, or a heterosexual client. In addition to understanding themselves as transgendered, clients also come to understand the nature of the objects of their sexual attractions, be they men, women, both men and women, or other transgendered people. In some cases, clients may alter their sexual orientation (e.g., from heterosexual to gay or lesbian; Coleman & Bockting, 1988).

It is also important to have an understanding about the process of GRS in order to provide support and to correct misunderstandings that the client may have. Readers may consult Isreal and Tarver (1997), Kirk and Rothblatt (1995), and Ramsey (1996) for detailed descriptions of the process of medical interventions available to transgendered people. Isreal and Tarver (1997) caution clinicians not to expect transgenderists and androgynous people to conform to transsexual models of transgenderism. The end result of psychotherapy with these clients should be directed toward integrating their actual gender-identity needs and not simply on GRS. In addition, intersex youth should not be subjected to testing or research beyond what is required for medical intervention, particularly since children cannot speak for themselves but must rely on a parent's informed consent (Califia, 1997; Isreal & Tarver, 1997).

Central to the therapeutic process is the establishment of a trusting, working alliance between client and therapist. The therapist must demonstrate an unconditional respect for the client as a worthwhile person, who has the right to define and freely express their own gender identity. Clients must be able to trust the therapist as well as the therapeutic process in order to develop trust in themselves and their feelings (Brown & Rounsley, 1996). Clinicians should therefore refer to transgendered clients by their chosen names and appropriate pronouns (Isreal & Tarver, 1997). In clinical reports, therapists should avoid including pathologic references. That is, therapists should document the diagnosis and treatment of only that which is disordered and diseased remembering that a transgender identity is not in and of itself pathological (Isreal & Tarver, 1997).

The establishment and maintenance of a trusting therapeutic relationship can be difficult to achieve when working with transgendered clients. Understandably, they may be distrustful of an establishment that has perpetuated negative stereotypes and misinformation about transgendered people. The requirement for transsexuals who desire GRS to undergo psychotherapy places the therapist in the role as gatekeeper. This presents an ethical dilemma for the therapist whose philosophy is to treat clients in an open-minded and nonjudgmental manner (Anderson, 1997). Transsexual clients who are in the initial stages of their gender transition may view the counselor as an obstacle to their goal and therefore present with the necessary and "correct" attitude that they believe will result in obtaining the consent letter needed for hormonal treatments and surgery to proceed (Pollack, 1997).

The therapist, however, is more than simply a gatekeeper to the GRS process (Anderson, 1997; Isreal & Tarver, 1997; Vitale, 1997). He or she is also in the position of healer. These two roles are inherently contradictory in relation to each other. Anderson (1997) recommends that this conflict be resolved by having two mental health professionals involved in a case. One professional would provide the therapeutic relationship for counseling, supporting, and interpreting unconscious material and educating and encouraging the transsexual client to explore all the possibilities that promote growth and change in the desired direction. The evaluator, furnished with records of the process and outcome of treatment, would evaluate the client and make a recommendation or withhold endorsement for surgery (Anderson, 1997).

Throughout the therapeutic process, clinicians must be cognizant of their own views and values concerning sex, gender, and sexual orientation. Therapists must be vigilant in acknowledging bigender and other gender-related biases that may be manifested as countertransference problems in the therapeutic work. Countertransference issues may emerge for even the most culturally sensitive and skilled therapists. Unlike experiences such as grief or depression, many therapists have no prior firsthand experience with gender dysphoria (Vitale, 1997). This makes the process of developing and maintaining empathy for transgendered clients difficult. The therapist may not have a similar or comparable personal experience from which to draw, hence imagining the persistent, intense anxiety caused by gender dysphoria may be difficult, if not impossible, for most therapists (Vitale, 1997).

Further, working with transgendered clients may challenge a clinician's own sense of gender security, triggering feelings that range from subjective mild to intense discomfort to overt hostility (Ramsey, 1996). Influenced by the same society that ostracizes transgendered people, therapists may discover in themselves an unexpected gut-level disgust for people who do not conform to traditional expectations of gender expression. As Califia (1997) heeds,

> [a] fear of transsexuals [and other transgenders] is directly traceable to a fear of your own opposite sex self, . . . in order to be complete, women need to be able to reach into the black box called "maleness" and take out anything there that they find useful. And until men are able to face, love, learn from, and incorporate the feminine, we will be enemies. It's worth it to spend time (a lot of time) thinking about how your fear of transsexuality manifests itself, and how your fear of stepping outside the boundaries of "appropriate" gender conducts limits your life [and those of our clients]. (p. 117)

It is important, therefore, for clinicians who work with transgendered clients to maintain professional contacts with colleagues with whom they can consult about dilemmas that arise with these clients.

Therapists who identify as transgendered themselves also need to guard against over-identifying with the client. Therapists who overidentify with clients may have the unwarranted expectations that the transgendered client will report feelings and experiences identical to that of the therapist. In addition, transgendered therapists must be alert to the issues that arise when any therapist treats members of groups that the therapist belongs (e.g., boundaries). Hence, transgendered and nontransgendered clinicians alike must be confident and secure in their own gender identity to avoid feeling threatened by those who do not conform to traditional expectations of gender roles and gender identity.

Training Considerations

Clinicians who work with transgendered people must be properly and adequately trained to address the unique issues and concerns of this population. Therapists without such training should have access to alternative resources to refer those clients. Vitale (1997) recommends the development of a clear definition of "qualified" gender therapists. A good gender specialist should be a licensed mental health professional who has sufficient training and supervision regarding psychotherapeutic work with transgenderism. The specialist in this area must also have a readiness to accept cross-dressing and sex or gender incongruity as a psychologically unchangeable, congenitally attributed, natural phenomenon. It is essential that the therapist have no personal investment in the direction the client undertakes in pursuit of his or her true self and no organizational restrictions (aside from the Standards of Care) that prevent the therapist from providing individualized care (Vitale, 1997). Isreal and Tarver (1997) recommend that the training curriculum goals for gender specialists include a familiarity with suicide and crisis intervention, basic skills in diagnosing psychopathology, an awareness of critical gender-oriented consumer needs, knowledge and skills in safer sex interventions, and a basic understanding of gender and sexual identity concerns. Overall, gender therapists should have or develop the necessary skills for managing the often adversarial roles they may find themselves in when delivering services to transgendered patients (Anderson, 1997; Isreal & Tarver, 1997; Vitale, 1997).

Transgender issues should be included in the training of all mental health practitioners and researchers. Transgendered people are not only potential clients for many therapists who may not be gender specialists, they are also potential research participants. Gender research may yield different results and interpretations when designed to account for more than two genders. In addition, people who are not transgendered but who are the lovers, family, friends, and coworkers of those who are may also seek psychological services related to the interactions and relationships to the transgendered person in their lives. Thus, material relevant to transgendered people should be included in subject-specific courses like cultural diversity, psychology of gender, psychology of women, psychology of men, and human sexuality. These concerns should also be integrated into foundational courses like theories and practice of counseling and psychotherapy, research methods, and ethics.

Conclusions

In general, sexual orientation and gender identity are controversial topics in society. Mental health is no exception to this controversy. The very existence of transgendered or gender-nonconforming individuals challenges the core of our social, psychological, and even political structures by forcing us to examine our preconceived notions of sex, gender, gender roles, gender identity, and sexual orientation. Transgendered children, adolescents, and adults face unfair treatment and oppressive behaviors by intolerant people who support essentialist, binary views of gender expression. Therapists working with transgendered clients should be knowledgeable about the experiences, issues, and concerns of this population.

Further, as debates about transgenderism and the inevitable backlash continue, it is vital that clinicians take a culturally sensitive approach to working with transgendered people. This process should begin with clinicians challenging their own biases about sex and gender. In order to work effectively and ethically with this diverse population, therapists need to be cognizant of their own bias about gender conformity and what it means to be a man, a woman, neither, or both.

This chapter represents a preliminary exploration of many complex and often highly controversial issues associated with gender nonconformity. In the interest of presenting an overview, many important areas (e.g., distinctions between MTF and FTM transsexuals, lesbians who identify as butch or femme) were not explored. Readers are encouraged to review the growing literature on transgenderism.

Notes

1. Refers to an irrational fear of, aversion to, or discrimination against transgenderism and transgendered people (Brown & Rounsley, 1996, p. 71).
2. Ironically after the removal of homosexuality in the same edition.

References

References marked with asterisks are highly recommended.

American Psychiatric Association. (1968). *Diagnostic and statistical manual of mental disorders* (2nd ed.). Washington, DC: Author.

American Psychiatric Association. (1980). *Diagnostic and statistical manual of mental disorders* (3rd ed.). Washington, DC: Author.

American Psychiatric Association. (1984). *Diagnostic and statistical manual of mental disorders* (3rd ed. rev.). Washington, DC: Author.

American Psychiatric Association. (1994). *Diagnostic and statistical manual of mental disorders* (4th ed.). Washington, DC: Author.

Anderson, B. F. (1997). Ethical implications for psychotherapy with individuals seeking gender reassignment. In G. E. Isreal & D. E. Tarver, II (Eds.), *Transgender care: Recommended guidelines, practical information, and personal accounts* (pp. 185-189). Philadelphia: Temple University Press.

Benjamin, H. (1966). *Transsexual phenomenon.* New York: Julian.

Bolin, A. (1988). *In search of Eve: Transsexual rites of passage.* South Hadley, MA: Bergin & Garvey.

Bolin, A. (1992). Coming of age among transsexuals. In T. L. Whitehead & B. V. Reid (Eds.), *Gender constructs and social issues* (pp. 13-39). Chicago: University of Illinois Press.

*Bornstein, K. (1994). *Gender outlaws: On men, women, and the rest of us.* New York: Routledge.

*Brown, M., & Rounsley, C. A. (1996). *True selves: Understanding transsexualism—for families, friends, coworkers, and helping professionals.* San Francisco: Jossey-Bass.

Bullock, B., & Bullock, B. (1997). Are transvestites necessarily heterosexual? *Archives of Sexual Behavior, 26,* 1-12.

*Burke, P. (1996). *Gender shock: Exploding the myths of male and female.* New York: Anchor.

*Califia, P. (1997). *Sex changes: The politics of transgenderism.* San Francisco: Cleis.

Caplan, P. (Ed.). (1977). *The cultural construction of sexuality.* London: Tavistock.

Coleman, E., & Bockting, W. O. (1988). "Heterosexual" prior to sex reassignment—"homosexual" afterwards: A case study of a female-to-male transsexual. *Journal of Psychology and Human Sexuality, 1,* 69-82.

Coombs, M. (1997). Transgenderism and sexual orientation: More than a marriage of convenience. *National Journal of Sexual Orientation Law* [On-line], *3*(1). Available: http://sunsite.unc.edu/gaylaw/issue5/coombs.html

Dinno, A. B. (1997). From the perspective of a young transsexual. In G. E. Isreal & D. E. Tarver II (Eds.), *Transgender care: Recommended guidelines, practical information, and personal accounts* (pp. 203-207). Philadelphia: Temple University Press.

Doctor, R. F. (1988). *Transvestites and transsexuals: Toward a theory of cross-gender behavior.* New York: Plenum.

Ekins, R., & King, D. (Eds.). (1995). *Blending genders: Social aspects of cross-dressing and sex-changing.* New York: Routledge.

Eyler, A. E., & Wright, K. (1997). Gender identification and sexual orientation among genetic females with gender-blended self-perception in childhood and adolescence. *International Journal of Transgenderism* [on-line] *1*(1), Available: http://www.symposion.com/ijt/ijtc0102.htm

*Feinberg, L. (1996). *Transgender warriors: Making history from Joan of Arc to Dennis Rodman.* Boston: Beacon.

Forisha, B. L. (1978). *Sex roles and personal awareness.* Morristown, NJ: General Learning.

Gergen, K. J. (1985a). Social constructionist inquiry: Context and implications. In K. J. Gergen & K. E. Davis (Eds.), *The social construction of the person* (pp. 3-18). New York: Springer-Verlag.

Gergen, K. J. (1985b). The social constructionist movement in modern psychology. *American Psychologist, 40,* 266-275.

Green, J., & Brinkin, L. (1994, September). *Investigation into discrimination against transgendered people.* San Francisco: San Francisco Human Rights Commission.

Green, R. (1994). Transsexualism and the law. *Bulletin of the American Academy of Psychiatry and the Law, 22,* 511-517.

Green, R., & Blanchard, R. (1995). Gender identity disorders. In H. I. Kaplan & B. J. Sadock (Eds.), *Comprehensive textbook of psychiatry/VI* (6th ed., Vol. 1, pp. 1347-1360). Philadelphia: Williams & Wilkins.

Greene, B. (1994). Ethnic minority lesbians and gay men: Mental health and treatment issues. *Journal of Consulting and Clinical Psychology, 62,* 243-251.

Greene, B. (1997). Psychotherapy with African American women: Integrating feminist and psychodynamic models. *Journal of Smith College School of Social Work: Theoretical, Research, Practice, and Educational Perspectives for Understanding and Working With African American Clients, 67,* 299-322.

Greene, B. (1998). Sexual orientation. In M. Hersen & A. Bellack (Eds.), *Comprehensive clinical psychology: Volume 10. Sociocultural and individual differences.* Oxford, UK: Elsevier Science Ltd.

Herdt, G. (Ed.). (1994). *Third sex, third gender: Beyond sexual dimorphism in culture and history.* New York: Zone.

*Isreal, G. E., & Tarver II, D. E. (Eds.). (1997). *Transgender care: Recommended guidelines, practical information, and personal accounts.* Philadelphia: Temple University Press.

Katz, J. (1976). *Gay American history: Lesbians and gay men in the U.S.A.* New York: Thomas Y. Crowell.

Kessler, S., & McKenna, W. (1978). *Gender: An ethnomethodological approach.* New York: John Wiley.

Kirk, S., & Rothblatt, M. (1995). *Medical, legal, & workplace issues for the transsexual.* Watertown, MA: Together Lifeworks.

Kitzinger, C. (1987). *The social construction of lesbianism.* London: Sage.

Lamborn, H. (1997). A midlife transition. In G. E. Isreal & D. E. Tarver II (Eds.), *Transgender care: Recommended guidelines, practical information, and personal accounts* (pp. 211-214). Philadelphia: Temple University Press.

Lopez, S. R., Grover, K. P., Holland, D., Johnson, M. J., Kain, C. D., Kanel, K., Mellins, C. A., & Rhyne, M. C. (1989). Development of culturally sensitive psychotherapists. *Professional Psychology: Research and Practice, 20,* 369-376.

Lothstein, L. M. (1983). *Female-to-male transsexualism: Historical, clinical and theoretical issues.* Boston: Routledge & Kegan Paul.

Lothstein, L. M., & Roback, H. (1984). Black female transsexuals and schizophrenia: A serendipitous finding? *Archives of Sexual Behavior, 13,* 371-386.

Meyers, J. K. (1995). Paraphilias. In H. I. Kaplan, & B. J. Sadock (Eds.), *Comprehensive textbook of psychiatry/VI* (6th ed., Vol. 1, pp. 1334-1347). Philadelphia: Williams & Wilkins.

Money, J. (1994). *Sex errors of the body and related syndromes.* Baltimore: Paul H. Brooke.

Pela, R. L. (1997, November 11). The gender blend: Separated at birth. *The Advocate,* pp. 51-52, 54-59.

Pollack, R. (1997). What is to be done? A commentary on the recommended guidelines. In G. E. Isreal, & D. E. Tarver II (Eds.) , *Transgender care: Recommended guidelines, practical information, and personal accounts* (pp. 229-235). Philadelphia: Temple University Press.

Ramsey, G. (1996). *Transsexuals: Candid answers to private questions.* Freedom, CA: Crossing.

Reid, B. V., & Whitehead, T. L. (1992). Introduction. In T. L. Whitehead & B. V. Reid (Eds.), *Gender constructs and social issues* (pp. 1-9). Chicago: University of Illinois Press.

Roberto, L. G. (1983). Issues in diagnosis and treatment of transsexualism. *Archives of Sexual Behavior, 12,* 445-473.

Roscoe, W. (1991). *Living the spirit: A gay American Indian anthology.* New York: St. Martin's.

Schott, R. L. (1995). The childhood and family dynamics of transvestites. *Archives of Sexual Behavior, 24*, 309-327.

Swartz, L. H. (1997). Updated look at legal responses to transsexualism: Especially three cases in U.K., U.S. and New Zealand. *International Journal of Transsexualism* [On-line], *1*(2), Available: http://www.symposion.ijt/ijt0201.htm

Tafoya, T. (1997). Native gay and lesbian issues: The two-spirited. In B. Greene (Ed.), *Psychological perspectives on lesbian and gay issues: Vol. 3. Ethnic and cultural diversity among lesbians and gay men* (pp. 1-10). Thousand Oaks, CA: Sage.

Tully, B. (1992). *Accounting for transsexualism and transhomosexuality.* London: Whiting & Birch.

Unger, R. (1979). Toward a redefinition of sex and gender. *American Psychologist, 34*, 1085-1094.

Unger, R. (1989). Imperfect reflections of reality: Psychology constructs gender. In R. T. Hare-Mustin & J. Marecek (Eds.), *Making a difference: Psychology and the construct of gender.* New Haven, CT: Yale University Press.

Vitale, A. (1997). The therapist versus the client: How the conflict started and some thoughts on how to resolve it. In G. E. Isreal & D. E. Tarver II (Eds.), *Transgender care: Recommended guidelines, practical information, and personal accounts* (pp. 251-255). Philadelphia: Temple University Press.

Walker, P. A. (Ed.). (1990). *Standards of care: The hormonal and surgical sex reassignment of gender dysphoric persons* (Rev. ed.). Palo Alto, CA: Harry Benjamin International Gender Dysphoria Association.

Williams, W. (1986). *The spirit and the flesh: Sexual diversity in American Indian culture.* Boston: Beacon.

Wilson, K. K. (1997a, July). *Gender as illness: Issues of psychiatric classification.* Paper presented at the 6th Annual ICTLEP Transgender Law and Employment Policy Conference, Houston, TX [On-line]. Available: http://www.transgender.org/tg/gic/icitext.html

Wilson, K. K. (1997b). *The disparate classification of gender and sexual orientation in American psychiatry.* [On-line]. Available: http://www.priory.com/psych/disparat.htm

Wilson, K. K., & Hammond, B. E. (1996, March). *Myth, stereotype, and cross-gender identity in the DSM-IV.* Paper presented at the National Conference of the Association for Women in Psychology, Portland, OR [On-line]. Available: http://www.abmall.com/gic/awptext.html

Zucker, K., & Bradley, S. (1995). *Gender identity disorder and psychosexual problems in children and adolescents.* New York: Guilford.

7

Bisexuality in Perspective

A Review of Theory and Research

RONALD C. FOX

A more affirmative approach toward bisexuality has come about in psychology and the social sciences as a result of changes in how the concept of bisexuality has been defined in psychological theory, clinical practice, and research. Two factors have contributed significantly to a greater acknowledgment of bisexuality as a valid sexual orientation and sexual identity: the elimination of homosexuality as a clinical diagnostic category, and a critical reexamination of the dichotomous model of sexual orientation. The rejection of the illness model of homosexuality in psychiatry and psychology encouraged the development of lesbian and gay identity theory and the articulation of a multidi-

AUTHOR'S NOTE: Portions of this chapter are adapted or exerpted from Fox, R. C. (1995). Bisexual identities. In A. R. D'Augelli & C. J. Patterson (Eds.), *Lesbian, gay, and bisexual identities across the lifespan: Psychological approaches* (pp. 48-86). New York: Oxford University Press. Used with permission. © 1995, Oxford University Press. Portions are also excerpted or adapted from Fox, R. C. (1996). Bisexuality: An examination of theory and research. In R. P. Cabaj & T. S. Stein (Eds.), *Homosexuality and mental health: A comprehensive review* (pp. 159-184). Washington, DC: American Psychiatric Press. Used with permission. © 1996, American Psychiatric Press.

This current chapter has been published in B. Firestein (Ed.). (1996). *Bisexuality: The psychology and politics of an invisible minority* (pp. 3-50). Thousand Oaks, CA: Sage.

mensional model of sexual orientation has led to the development of theory and research on bisexuality and bisexual identities.

Bisexuality has existed as a concept and descriptive term in the psychological literature since the process of psychosexual development was first conceptualized. For example, bisexuality has been used as a theoretical construct to explain aspects of evolutionary theory, psychosexual development, psychopathology, masculinity and femininity, and homosexuality. Furthermore, evidence from historical and cross-cultural research clearly indicates that bisexuality, defined as sexual attractions toward or sexual behavior with persons of both genders, has existed throughout history in diverse cultures around the world. This chapter examines the emergence of affirmative approaches to bisexuality as a sexual orientation and sexual identity by reviewing the ways in which the concept of bisexuality has been used in several related areas: psychoanalytic theory, lesbian and gay identity theory, sexual orientation theory, historical and cross-cultural inquiry, research on sexuality, and finally, theory and research on bisexuality and bisexual identities.

Bisexuality in Psychoanalytic Theory

The concept of bisexuality first appeared in psychoanalytic theory as a way of explaining the development of homosexuality in terms of evolutionary theory (Ellis, 1905/1942; Freud, 1905/1960; Krafft-Ebing, 1886/1965; Weininger, 1903/1908). Psychoanalytic theorists believed that the human species evolved from a primitive hermaphroditic state to the gender-differentiated physical form of today, and that individual physiological and psychological development parallels this evolutionary process (Ritvo, 1990; Sulloway, 1979). Like his contemporaries, Freud (1925/1963) found the theory of bisexuality helpful in accounting for homosexuality, which he saw as an indication of arrested psychosexual development. At the same time, he believed that everyone has some homosexual feelings:

> The most important of these perversions, homosexuality . . . can be traced back to the constitutional bisexuality of all human beings. . . . Psychoanalysis enables us to point to some trace or other of a homosexual object-choice in everyone. (pp. 71-72)

Stekel (1922/1946) believed that bisexuality is normative during childhood and that adult sexual orientation results from repression that occurs during the developmental process:

> All persons originally are bisexual in their predisposition. There is no exception to this rule. Normal persons show a distinct bisexual period up to the age of puberty. The heterosexual then represses his homosexuality. . . . If the heterosexuality is repressed, homosexuality comes to the forefront. (p. 39)

Most psychoanalysts saw the theory of bisexuality as essential for understanding psychosexual development (Stekel, 1922/1946), masculinity and femininity (Stoller, 1972), psychopathology (Khan, 1974; Kubie, 1974), and homosexuality (Alexander, 1933; Limentani, 1976). Some psychoanalysts disagreed, however, arguing that individual responses to family influences are more relevant in understanding these subjects (Bieber et al., 1962; Rado, 1940).

Havelock Ellis (1905/1942) saw bisexuals as a distinct category of individuals who are attracted to persons of both genders, and he concluded that "there would thus seem to be a broad and simple grouping of all sexually functioning persons into three comprehensive divisions: the heterosexual, the bisexual, and the homosexual" (pp. 87-88). Freud (1937/1963) later also used the term *bisexual* to describe persons with both homosexual and heterosexual attractions and behavior:

> It is well known that at all times there have been, as there still are, human beings who can take as their sexual objects persons of either sex without the one trend interfering with the other. We call these people bisexual and accept the fact of their existence without wondering much at it. . . . But we have come to know that all human beings are bisexual in this sense and that their libido is distributed between objects of both sexes, either in a manifest or a latent form. (pp. 261-262)

Others viewed sexual orientation in strictly dichotomous terms and rejected the term *bisexual* as a descriptive category referring to individuals with both homosexual and heterosexual attractions or behavior. For example, Bergler (1956) believed that those who consider themselves bisexual are denying a homosexual orientation:

> Bisexuality—a state that has no existence beyond the word itself—is an out-and-out fraud. . . . The theory claims that a man can be—alternatively or con-

comitantly—homo and heterosexual. . . . Nobody can dance at two different weddings at the same time. These so-called bisexuals are really homosexuals with an occasional heterosexual excuse. (pp. 80-81)

This point of view lent support to the belief that the diagnostic category *homosexuality* was appropriate for individuals with *any* same-gender sexual attractions or behavior. Furthermore, the goal of psychoanalytic psychotherapy was an exclusively heterosexual orientation, which was seen as more easily attainable by individuals with some heterosexual attractions or behavior (Bieber et al., 1962; Hatterer, 1970; Socarides, 1978).

The illness model of homosexuality, however, was not universally accepted in the psychiatric community (Bayer, 1981). Prominent authors in the field (Green, 1972; Hoffman, 1968; Hooker, 1956, 1965; Marmor, 1965, 1972; Szasz, 1965, 1970; G. Weinberg, 1972) challenged the illness model on the basis of evidence from surveys of sexual behavior, cross-cultural research on homosexuality, and the identification of biases inherent in research and clinical assessment and treatment based on the illness model. The 1973 American Psychiatric Association decision to remove homosexuality as a diagnostic category signaled a move away from the illness model and toward a more affirmative approach to homosexuality.

Bisexuality in Lesbian and Gay Identity Theory

An affirmative approach to understanding the development of lesbian and gay identities first appeared in several studies of gay men and lesbians living in urban communities (Cronin, 1974; Dank, 1971; de Monteflores & Schultz, 1978; Gagnon & Simon, 1968; Hooker, 1965; Saghir & Robins, 1973). Researchers found that the expression *coming out* was used to signify acknowledging one's homosexual attractions, contacting and participating in the lesbian and gay community, and identifying oneself to other people as being gay or lesbian. The articulation of detailed models of lesbian and gay identity development followed the elimination of homosexuality as a diagnostic category (Cass, 1979, 1983/1984; Coleman, 1981/1982b; Troiden, 1988). The first stage of the coming out process is the individual's awareness of homosexual attractions. This is followed by same-gender sexual experiences and relationships, self-identification as gay or lesbian, and disclosure of one's sexual orientation to others. The developmental process culminates in participation in the lesbian and gay community, exclusively same-gender sexual relationships, and an integrated lesbian or gay identity. The term *coming out* is used to refer to the entire developmental process, including but not limited to disclosing one's sexual orientation to others.

Cass (1984) followed up her theoretical formulation with a study designed to assess the validity of her developmental stages. Although she found evidence for the general order of milestone events, she also found that some individuals did not follow the exact sequence she had proposed, and others moved through more than one stage at the same time. These findings are in accord with similar variations found in research on lesbian identity development (Chapman & Brannock, 1987; Sophie, 1985/1986) and support the perspective that stage theories give a general rather than an exact outline of events involved in the coming out process (Coleman, 1981/1982b; Troiden, 1988).

As with other developmental models, explanations were offered for deviations from the typical sequence of events. For example, Cass (1979) saw bisexual self-identification as an example of identity foreclosure, delaying or preventing the formation of a positive homosexual identity. From this point of view, persistent heterosexual attractions or behavior are only transitional phenomena some individuals experience as they move toward exclusively same-gender sexual attractions and behavior and permanent lesbian and gay identities. In contrast, Coleman (1981/1982b) suggested that the developmental stages that he articulated for the coming out process might also apply to bisexuals. Troiden (1988) also saw bisexuality as a valid sexual orientation. He believed, however, that the general lack of recognition given to bisexuality and the lack of a supportive community of similar others makes it difficult for an individual to sustain a bisexual identity. Cass (1990) has suggested more recently that homosexual, heterosexual, and bisexual identities form along distinct developmental pathways, the components of which are both similar and different. She emphasized that although sexual identities may be long lasting, they are not necessarily fixed. An individual might minimize the relevance of experiences that imply a different sexual identity in order to maintain an already established homosexual, heterosexual, or bisexual identity, or might question this identity, potentially initiating the development of an alternative sexual identity.

166 I EDUCATION, RESEARCH, AND PRACTICE

In summary, the emergence of lesbian and gay identity theory represented an important shift in emphasis in developmental theory, away from the concern with etiology and psychopathology characteristic of the illness model and toward articulation of the factors involved in the formation of positive gay and lesbian identities. There has been an equally important shift within lesbian and gay identity theory regarding bisexuality. Although sexual orientation was initially viewed in dichotomous terms, and bisexuality was seen as a transitional phenomenon, a more inclusive perspective has developed, in which bisexuality is regarded as a distinct sexual orientation and identity.

Bisexuality and Sexual Orientation Theory

The theoretical and research literature on gay and lesbian identities emerged after psychiatry and psychology moved to consider homosexuality from a more affirmative point of view. The predominance of a dichotomous view of sexual orientation, however, constrained the development of a comparable theoretical and research literature on bisexuality and bisexual identities. Examination and critique of the dichotomous model led to the development of a multidimensional approach to sexual orientation that allows for more accurate representation of the complexity of sexual orientation and acknowledgment of bisexuality as a sexual orientation and sexual identity.

Kinsey and his associates (Kinsey, Pomeroy, & Martin, 1948; Kinsey, Pomeroy, Martin, & Gebhard, 1952) were among the first to depart from traditional thinking about sexual orientation in their emphasis on the inadequacy of a dichotomous model for describing the diversity of human sexual experience (Kinsey et al., 1948):

> Males do not represent two discrete populations, heterosexual and homosexual. The world is not divided into sheep and goats. Not all things are black nor all things white. It is a fundamental of taxonomy that nature rarely deals with discrete categories. Only the human mind invents categories and tries to force facts into separated pigeon-holes. The living world is a continuum in each and every one of its aspects. The sooner we learn this concerning human sexual behavior the sooner we shall reach a sound understanding of the realities of sex. (p. 639)

They were aware that the term *bisexual* had been used to refer to individuals with both heterosexual and homosexual attractions or behavior. They believed, however, that the use of three categories (heterosexual, bisexual, and homosexual) rather than two categories (heterosexual and homosexual) failed to represent the continuum of human sexual behavior as accurately as the 7-point scale that they had developed.

Other authors viewed heterosexuality and homosexuality as independent aspects of sexual orientation, which they saw as the individual's physical and affectional preferences for persons of the same and/or other biological sex (Shively & De Cecco, 1977; Storms, 1980). Sexual orientation was seen as one of four components of sexual identity, along with biological sex, gender identity, and social sex role (Shively & De Cecco, 1977). The research literature has articulated various criteria for defining sexual orientation, including sexual behavior, affectional attachments (close relationships), erotic fantasies, arousal, erotic preference, and self-identification as bisexual, heterosexual, or homosexual (Shively, Jones, & De Cecco, 1983/1984).

The Klein Sexual Orientation Grid (KSOG) is a comprehensive instrument developed for assessing sexual orientation (Klein, 1990; Klein, Sepekoff, & Wolf, 1985). The KSOG includes scales for emotional preference, social preference, heterosexual-bisexual-homosexual lifestyle, and self-identification, as well as scales for sexual attractions, fantasies, and behavior. Individuals are asked to rate themselves on a 7-point heterosexual-bisexual-homosexual scale for each variable for past, present, and ideal time frames, yielding a total of 21 self-ratings. This multidimensional approach integrates bisexuality as a valid and useful category and describes more accurately factors that are involved in an individual's sexual orientation over time.

Another instrument was designed to facilitate clinical interviews in which the presenting issues include sexual orientation concerns. The Assessment of Sexual Orientation (Coleman, 1987) asks the client to indicate current relationship status, sexual orientation self-identification, desired future identification, and level of comfort with present orientation. A series of circles is also marked, in terms of both "up to the present" and "ideal" time frames, to indicate physical identity, actual and fantasized gender identity, sex-role identity, as well as sexual, fantasy, and emotional aspects of sexual orientation.

In summary, a multidimensional model of sexual orientation has evolved out of the need to more accurately represent the diverse factors involved in the development and expression of human sexuality. This approach takes into consideration emotional and social preferences, lifestyle, and self-identification as well as sexual attraction, fantasy, and behavior, and changes in these factors of sexual orientation over time. This has led to the development of more comprehensive tools for assessing sexual orientation and a wider acknowledgment of bisexuality as a distinct sexual orientation and identity. Furthermore, the application of a multidimensional view of sexual orientation has been essential in contemporary research on bisexual identity development, in research on HIV/AIDS, and in research on sexual identity and sexual behavior cross-culturally and in diverse ethnic minority populations.

Bisexuality in Historical and Cross-Cultural Inquiry

Homosexuality and bisexuality have been the focus of considerable interest and discussion for historians, classical scholars, and anthropologists as well as for psychologists and sociologists. There is extensive information about homosexual behavior and relationships in classical Greece and Rome (Cantarella, 1992; Dover, 1978; Downing, 1989; Eglinton, 1964; Sergent, 1984) and premodern Europe (Bailey, 1975; Boswell, 1980; Gerard & Hekma, 1989). There is also extensive cross-cultural data on homosexuality and bisexuality in the anthropological literature (Adam, 1985; Blackwood, 1985; Carrier, 1980; Churchill, 1967; Davenport, 1977; Ford & Beach, 1951; Herdt, 1990; Mead, 1961; Opler, 1965).

In many cultures, some individuals with homosexual behavior also exhibit heterosexual behavior, either concurrently or at different life stages. Furthermore, historians, classical scholars, and anthropologists have provided detailed descriptions of how bisexuality has been integrated into such cultures. Nevertheless, dichotomous thinking about sexuality and sexual orientation has had a strong influence in these fields, and bisexuality has not generally been seen as a relevant descriptive category for addressing the relationship between homosexuality and heterosexuality in cultures in which it exists. Rather, the discussion of homosexuality and bisexuality has been framed primarily in terms of several categories of homosexual behavior articulated most clearly in the anthropological literature (Adam, 1985; Blackwood, 1985; Greenberg, 1988; Herdt, 1990; Murray, 1992). These categories are based on factors such as age (homosexual relationships between individuals of different ages), gender role variance (individuals adopting the gender-role of the other biological sex, and in some cases taking on a special social role such as Shaman), and egalitarian relationships (not based on age, gender role, or specialized social role).

In some cultures, for example, individuals of different ages form homosexual relationships that are limited in duration for the younger partner to a specified period in adolescence. The younger individual is then expected to marry and initiate heterosexual relations and, in some societies, to have a homosexual relationship with a younger person. Classical scholars have described examples of such relationships in ancient Greece and Rome (Cantarella, 1992; Dover, 1978; Eglinton, 1964; Sergent, 1986). Anthropologists have described similar initiatory relationships between men among the Azande, Mossi, and Siwa in Africa (Adam, 1985), as well as in Melanesia (Adam, 1985; Davenport, 1977; Herdt, 1984), Australia (Adam, 1985), China (Hinsch, 1990; Ruan, 1991), and Japan (Ihara, 1972; Watanabe & Iwata, 1989), and between women in Lesotho in Southern Africa and in Carriacou in the Caribbean (Blackwood, 1985).

In other cultures, some women and men give up the gender role typical of their original biological sex in favor of that characteristic of the other biological sex. Examples include Native American Two-Spirit people (Blackwood, 1984, 1985; Roscoe, 1987, 1988; Whitehead, 1981; Williams, 1992), Siberian Chukchee and Koryak shamans (Greenberg, 1988), the Indian Hijra (Nanda, 1985), and the Tahitian Mahu (Blackwood, 1985; Greenberg, 1988). The gender role transformation may be partial or complete and either temporary or permanent. While it is more usual for such individuals to limit their sexual behavior to partners of the same biological sex, in some societies they may have relationships with persons of the other biological sex, as in Madagascar, Samoa, Celebes, and the Marquesas Islands, as well as among the Chukchee (Callender & Kochems, 1985) and the Koryak and Yokaghir (Murray, 1992). Homosexual behavior may also be structured according to active and passive roles. This is typical of Mediterranean and Latin American cultures, where bisexuality is normative for a great part of the male population. The active partner typically has sexual relations with both women and men, and is not considered homosexual. The receptive partner has sexual relations exclusively or primarily with other men and is considered homosexual (Carrier, 1985; Parker, 1991).

In some cultures, egalitarian same-sex relationships are more typical than relationships based on age differences, gender-role, or occupational specialization. For example, homosexual relationships between adolescents are common in many cultures until the age of heterosexual marriage. Egalitarian relationships also occur between adult men among the Azande (Adam, 1985) and Hottentot in Africa (Greenberg, 1988) as well as the Akuna, Asmat, and Santa Cruz Islanders in Melanesia (Murray, 1992). Similar relationships are described between women in the Near East, China, and Australia (Blackwood, 1985) as well as in Africa among the Nyakyusa (Adam, 1985), Nandi and Akan (Greenberg, 1988), and the Azande, Nupe, Hausa, and !Kung (Blackwood, 1985). Murray (1992) sees modern Western gay and lesbian relationships as a type of egalitarian homosexuality that is taking place in a separate subculture, in which individuals have a sense of being a distinct kind of person. Contemporary lesbian and gay relationships are not typically bound by gender roles and the sexual behavior of the partners is likely to be exclusively homosexual.

The historical and anthropological literatures provide clear evidence of the existence and integration of bisexual behavior in diverse cultures around the world. The authors of an early cross-cultural survey of sexual behavior note the challenge that this presents to traditional dichotomous thinking about sexuality:

> When it is realized that 100 percent of the males in certain societies engage in homosexual as well as heterosexual alliances, and when it is understood that many men and women in our own society are equally capable of relations with partners of the same or opposite sex, . . . then it should be clear that one cannot classify homosexual and heterosexual tendencies as being mutually exclusive or even opposed to each other. (Ford & Beach, 1951, p. 242)

Mead (1975) also saw bisexuality as normal, remarking that "even a superficial look at other societies and some groups in our own society should be enough to convince us that a very large number of human beings—probably a majority—are bisexual in their potential capacity for love" (p. 29). She believed that social attitudes about sex and love constrain the expression of bisexual attractions in terms of sexual behavior.

The integration of bisexuality into a particular culture is exemplified by the coexistence of heterosexual and homosexual behavior in East Bay, a Melanesian society (Davenport, 1965):

> Not all [men] become exclusively heterosexual at marriage. There is no doubt that some do, but most do not. . . . In other words, this is a society that quite frankly expects and accepts some bisexual behavior in most men, although there is nothing odd or deviant about an exclusively heterosexual male. (pp. 201-202)

Concurrent homosexual and heterosexual behavior also characterizes another Melanesian society (Herdt, 1984):

> The Sambian male . . . has the opportunity for direct experience of both homo-sexual and heterosexual relations and the opportunity to compare and evalu-ate them. Shared communications about the relative qualities of all sexual activities are an ordinary part of male discourse. . . . The self-esteem of bisexu-als in Melanesia is relatively high and their bisexuality ego-syntonic. Neither they nor their fellows are out to lobby for or against their bisexuality. Bisexuals bear no stigma. (p. 59)

Bisexual behavior has also been examined in research on Mexico (Car-rier, 1985) and Brazil (Parker, 1991) and in a survey of bisexuality in both Western and non-Western societies (Tielman, Carballo, & Hendriks, 1991a), including Australia (M. Ross, 1991a), India (Kumar, 1991), Indo-nesia (Oetomo, 1991), Latin America (Parker & Tawil, 1991), Mexico (Garcìa, Valdespino, Izazola, Palacios, & Sepulveda, 1991), the Nether-lands (Sandfort, 1991), New Zealand (Chetwynd, 1991), Sub-Saharan Africa (Aina, 1991), Thailand (Sittitrai, Brown, & Virulrak, 1991), the United Kingdom (Boulton & Coxon, 1991), and the United States (Doll, Peterson, Magaña, & Carrier, 1991).

In summary, the preponderance of historical and anthropological evi-dence points to the existence of bisexual attractions and behavior in many cultures. Bisexuality has been and remains normative in many cul-tures in which homosexual behavior exists. As anthropologist Gilbert Herdt (1991) has noted:

> Homosexuality cannot . . . be disengaged from the study of heterosexuality . . . since both forms of sexual action occur in the same ongoing social field of in-stitutions, roles and symbols which take as their objects male and female expe-rience. (p. 209)

This position articulates the emerging awareness in historical, classical, and cross-cultural research of the necessity to take care in applying dichotomous sexual orientation categories cross-culturally and to Western ethnic minority populations. This reconsideration of Western sexual orientation and sexual identity constructs also parallels the earlier reexamination in psychiatry and psychology of the illness model of homosexuality and the dichotomous view of sexual orientation. The result has been a greater understanding of the range of sexual behavior and relationships that have existed historically and cross-culturally as well as a more affirmative approach toward bisexuality and bisexual issues.

Bisexuality in Sexuality Research in the United States

Survey research on human sexuality has included inquiry into both homosexual and heterosexual attractions and behavior. General survey research and studies focused specifically on homosexuality have consistently included individuals with both heterosexual and homosexual attractions and behavior in addition to individuals with exclusively homosexual and exclusively heterosexual attractions and behavior. In much of this research, data from respondents with both homosexual and heterosexual attractions and behavior have typically been grouped with data from individuals with exclusively homosexual attractions and behavior since bisexuality was not considered a distinct sexual orientation category. In some research, however, bisexual and homosexual respondents have been differentiated on the basis of sexual attractions and behavior, and in some cases, on the basis of self-identification as well, and responses from these groups have been compared.

Bisexuality in General Surveys of Sexual Behavior

One of the most striking findings of the research conducted by Kinsey and his associates (Kinsey et al., 1948; Kinsey et al., 1952) was the substantial proportion of respondents whose sexual experience included some homosexual behavior. The data revealed that 46% of the men and 28% of the women had at least one homosexual experience in their lives and that 37% of the men and 13% of the women had a same-gender sexual experience since adolescence. For a period of 3 years between the

ages of 16 and 55, about 30% of the men reported at least incidental homosexual contact, 25% reported more than incidental homosexual contact,
and 10% had more or less exclusively homosexual experiences. About 8%
of the men had exclusively homosexual experiences after puberty,
whereas about 4% of the men and 1% to 3% of the women reported only
same-gender experiences throughout their lives. On the basis on these
figures, about 42% of the men and 25% to 27% of the women had both homosexual and heterosexual experiences at some time in their lives.

Several subsequent general population surveys, using statistically
representative samples, have also gathered data on respondents' homosexual and heterosexual behavior and have attempted to estimate the incidence of homosexual behavior in the United States. The findings of
such large-scale studies have indicated lower proportions of homosexual behavior than suggested by the results of the original research of Kinsey and his associates. For example, in the 1970 Kinsey Institute
sponsored National Opinion Research Corporation (NORC) survey,
20.3% of male respondents reported at least one same-gender sexual experience in their lives (Fay, Turner, Klassen, & Gagnon, 1989; Rogers &
Turner, 1991). The Janus study, using a nonrepresentative sample, found
that 22% of women and 17% of men respondents had at least one same-
gender sexual experience in their lives (Janus & Janus, 1993). Similarly, in
the 1994 National Health and Social Life Survey (NHSLS), 9.1% of the
men and 4.3% of the women reported at least one homosexual experience since puberty (Laumann, Gagnon, Michael, & Michaels, 1994). In
the National Survey of Sexual Attitudes and Lifestyles, a general population survey conducted in the United Kingdom, 6.1% of the men and
3.4% of the women indicated that they had at least one same-gender sexual experience in their lives (Wellings, Wadsworth, & Johnson, 1994). In
a French general population survey, Les Comportements Sexuals en
France, 4.1% of the men and 2.6% of the women reported at least one homosexual experience in their lives (ACSF Investigators, 1992; Spira, Bajos, & le Groupe ACSF, 1993).

In the NHSLS survey, 4.9% of the men and 4.1% of the women reported a same-gender sexual experience since age 18 (Laumann et al.,
1994). In the 1970 Kinsey/NORC survey, 6.7% of the men reported at
least one homosexual experience since age 20 (Rogers & Turner, 1991). In
the 1989 and 1990 NORC General Social Surveys, about the same proportions of the male respondents (4.9% and 4.8%) reported at least one
homosexual experience since age 18 (Rogers & Turner, 1991). Similarly,

in the 1988 and 1989 NORC General Social Surveys, 5.5% of the males in the combined data sets indicated at least one same-gender sexual experience since age 18 (Laumann et al., 1994). The authors of the 1994 NHSLS survey also combined their data with those from the 1988-1991 and 1993 NORC-GSS studies and found that 6.4% of the men and 3.5% of the women had at least one homosexual experience since puberty, and 4.9% of men and 4.1% of women had a homosexual experience since age 18 (Laumann et al., 1994).

In the 1988 Center for Health Affairs research conducted by Harris and Associates, 6.2% of the men and 3.6% of the women indicated at least one same-gender sexual experience in the past 5 years (Sell, Wells, & Wypij, 1995). For the NHSLS and NORC-GSS combined data set, 4.1% of the men and 2.2% of the women reported at least one homosexual experience in the preceding 5 years (Laumann et al., 1994). The proportions were less in the two European surveys mentioned above, with 1.4% of the men and 0.4% of the women in the British study (Wellings et al., 1994) and 1.1% of the men and 0.4% of the women in the French study (ACSF Investigators, 1992; Spira et al., 1993) indicating that they had at least one homosexual experience in the preceding 5 years.

Several surveys asked respondents if they had any homosexual experiences in the preceding 12 months. The proportions for men were 1.6% to 2.0% in the 1970 Kinsey-NORC study, 2.4% in the 1988 NORC-GSS study, 1.2% in the 1989 and 1990 Kinsey-NORC studies combined, and 4.6% in the 1989 National Center for Health Statistics survey conducted by the Research Triangle Institute (Rogers & Turner, 1989). The figures from the combined NHSLS and NORC-GSS data set were 2.7% for men and 1.3% for women (Laumann et al., 1994). The proportions were somewhat less in the European surveys, with 1.1% of the men and 0.4% of the women in the British study (Wellings et al., 1994) and 1.1% of the men and 0.3% of the women in the French study (ACSF Investigators, 1992; Spira et al., 1993) reporting a same-gender sexual experience in the past 12 months.

Like the original Kinsey research, these large-scale population surveys suggest that homosexual behavior is more prevalent among men than women and that the proportion of individuals who have had some same-gender sexual experience is greater than the proportion with ongoing homosexual experience after puberty and adolescence. The data from these surveys also suggest that the incidence of homosexual behavior in the general population may be less than was found in the original Kinsey research. In examining the combined GSS/NHSLS data sets, however, researchers found that 7.8% of the men living in the largest cities in the United States reported at least one same-gender sexual experience in the past year, 11.1% reported a sexual experience with another man in the past 5 years, and 14.4% reported homosexual experience since age 18 (Binson et al., 1995). This is a higher incidence of homosexual behavior than these researchers found for men living in suburban, small urban, and rural areas and is closer to the incidence of homosexual behavior suggested by the original Kinsey research.

The large-scale general sexuality surveys also clearly indicate that, although some individuals have exclusively same-gender sexual experiences, a substantial proportion of individuals have both homosexual and heterosexual experiences and relationships. That is to say, sexual orientation is not dichotomous for everyone. For example, for the combined NHSLS and NORC-GSS sample, of the 6.4% of the men and 3.5% of the women with any homosexual experience since puberty, 91% of the men and 94% of the women had sexual experiences with both women and men (Laumann et al., 1994). Similarly, for the same combined data set, of the 4.9% of the men and the 4.1% of the women with some same-gender sexual experience since age 18, 82% of the men and 90% of the women had both homosexual and heterosexual experiences (Laumann et al., 1994). Furthermore, again for the same combined data set, of the 4.1% of the men and the 2.2% of the women who reported homosexual experiences in the past 5 years, 51% of the men and 64% of the women had sexual experiences with both women and men (Laumann et al., 1994). In the British survey, 67% of the men and 83% of the women with same-gender sexual experiences in the preceding 5 years reported both homosexual and heterosexual experiences (Wellings et al., 1994).

Of the 3.2% of the men in the 1988 NORC-GSS study (Michael, Laumann, Gagnon, & Smith, 1988) and the 1.2% of the men in the 1989 and 1990 NORC-GSS studies who reported homosexual experiences in the preceding 12 months, 15% and 25% respectively had both homosexual and heterosexual experiences (Rogers & Turner, 1991). In the 1988 Center for Health Affairs study, of the 6.2% of the men and the 3.2% of the women with homosexual experiences, 87% of the men and 91% of the women had both homosexual and heterosexual experiences (Sell et al., 1995). For the combined NHSLS and NORC-GSS sample, of the 2.7% of the men and 1.3% of the women with same-gender sexual experiences in the past year, 74% of the men and 77% of the women reported both homosexual and heterosexual experiences (Laumann et al., 1994). In the

National AIDS Behavioral Survey (NABS), a third of the men who reported any sex with men in the preceding 5 years also reported sex with women during the same time period (Binson et al., 1995). In the British survey, the National Survey of Sexual Attitudes and Lifestyles, 36% of the men and 50% of the women with same-gender sexual experiences in the preceding 12 months reported both homosexual and heterosexual experiences (Wellings et al., 1994).

In the NHSLS study, researchers queried respondents as to their sexual attractions as well as their sexual behavior. Whereas 2.4% of the men and 0.3% of the women indicated that they were attracted only to persons of the same gender, 3.9% of the men and 4.1% of the women reported sexual attractions to persons of both genders, In two studies, researchers also asked respondents to indicate their sexual orientation self-identification. In the statistically representative NHSLS sample, 2.0% of the men self-identified as gay and 0.9% of the women self-identified as lesbian, while 0.8% of the men and 0.5% of the women self-identified as bisexual (Laumann et al., 1994). In the Janus study, 4% of the men self-identified as gay and 2% of the women self-identified as lesbian, while 5% of the men and 3% of the women self-identified as bisexual (Janus & Janus, 1993).

Bisexuality in Research on Homosexuality

There is an additional portion of the research literature that specifically addresses the sexual behavior and relationships of lesbians and gay men. Just as in the general survey literature, researchers have found that a substantial proportion of their study participants had either historical or concurrent sexual attractions toward and relationships with both women and men. These researchers have differed, however, in their interpretations of how the existence of historical or concurrent homosexual and heterosexual attractions and behavior relate to sexual orientation. Some have denied that individuals with concurrent or historical heterosexual and homosexual attractions and behavior could in fact be bisexual. Others have asserted that understanding such individuals' bisexual attractions, behavior, and sexual orientation self-identification would provide greater comprehension of the diversity of their study participants' sexual lives.

Hunt (1974) believed that only a very limited number of American males are bisexual, or potentially so, in their adult lives. His perspective was that "some self-styled bisexuals . . . are basically homosexual but seek to minimize their conflicts and sense of deviance by having occasional heterosexual episodes. Others have had a bisexual period, . . . though they eventually recognized that their real orientation was toward same-sex partners" (p. 324). Likewise, Saghir and Robins (1973) took the position that the previous heterosexual attractions and relationships some of their lesbian and gay respondents reported were not a sign of bisexuality. This was also the position of Spada (1979) regarding his respondents' past and current relationships with women. He noted that "it might be argued that these men are not homosexual but bisexual. . . . It is . . . significant that such a large number of men who sufficiently consider themselves gay to respond to this survey have sexual relations with women" (p. 215). In contrast, Hite (1976, 1981) and Jay and Young (1976) took a more neutral approach, presenting information about the bisexual attractions and behavior of respondents and including respondents' comments about their bisexuality. The results of the *Playboy* Readers' Sex Survey (1983) and the *Advocate* Sex Survey (Lever, 1995) contrasted respondents based on both identity and behavior.

Weinberg and Williams (1974) questioned the polarization of sexual orientation into heterosexuality and homosexuality, noting that "by defining heterosexuality as the norm, there also has been the tendency to view persons as either heterosexual or homosexual. This . . . poses the danger of ignoring the great range and heterogeneity of homosexuals" (p. 4). One fifth of their combined San Francisco and New York samples rated themselves other than exclusively or predominantly homosexual on the Kinsey scale. These authors differentiated between "nonexclusive homosexuals" and "exclusive homosexuals" in their data analysis. Compared with the more exclusively homosexual men, the bisexual men were more involved with heterosexuals, more concerned with passing as heterosexual, and less known to others as being "homosexual." They had more frequent and enjoyable sex with women and were more likely to have been heterosexually married. The authors found no support for the argument that their bisexual respondents were confused about their sexual identities.

In their research on homosexuality in women and men, Bell and Weinberg (1978) recognized that a substantial proportion of their respondents might be bisexual:

> It would not be unreasonable to suppose that a fairly strong heterosexual element is to be found in about one third of those homosexual men most likely to

participate in surveys of this kind. Even larger numbers of comparable homosexual women are apt to exhibit a "partial bisexual lifestyle." (p. 61)

Nevertheless, the authors did not summarize the responses of their bisexual and homosexual respondents separately, even though a substantial proportion of participants rated themselves in the midrange on the Kinsey scale. MacDonald (1983) criticized this approach, asserting that combining bisexual and homosexual respondents into a single group obscures information particular to both components and limits the ability of the researchers to generalize about either component from the study results. In a later study of sexual preference, Bell, Weinberg, and Hammersmith (1981) did classify respondents rating themselves in the midrange of the Kinsey scale as bisexual. On the basis of their findings, they speculated that "among the bisexuals, adult sexual preference is much less strongly tied to preadult sexual feelings" (p. 200). They concluded that "exclusive homosexuality tends to emerge from a deep-seated predisposition, while bisexuality is more subject to influence by social and sexual learning" (p. 201).

A study of lesbian and gay male psychologists also included a substantial proportion of respondents who considered themselves bisexual (Kooden et al., 1979). Although the general responses of all groups were similar, the bisexual psychologists appeared to lack the social support networks of the gay and lesbian psychologists. They were more likely to be heterosexually married and less likely to be involved in the gay movement. Like the closeted gay and lesbian psychologists, the bisexual psychologists "did not report having the positive experiences that were reported by the gay respondents who were generally open" (p. 68).

Research on the lesbian community has revealed a variety of experiences and attitudes regarding bisexuality (Golden, 1987; Ponse, 1978; Rust, 1992, 1993, 1995; D. G. Wolf, 1979). Some lesbians have never experienced heterosexual attractions or behavior, while others have been involved in sexual relationships with men. Some are accepting of women who acknowledge ongoing sexual attractions to men or who consider themselves bisexual, but many believe that such women are not "real" lesbians or have not completed the coming out process. Similar reactions toward bisexual men were found in a study of a gay male community (Warren 1974). In research on situational homosexual behavior, most individuals self-identify as homosexual or heterosexual. Some, however, consider themselves bisexual, in studies of sex in prison (Wooden &

Parker, 1982), male prostitution (Boles & Elifson, 1994; Reiss 1961), gay bars (Read, 1980), and sex in public places (Humphreys, 1970).

In summary, general population surveys and studies that have focused on homosexuality have found that many respondents have experienced both heterosexual and homosexual attractions, behavior, and relationships. At least some of these individuals must be considered bisexual, based on their past and current sexual attractions, sexual behavior, and sexual orientation self-identification. When bisexual and homosexual respondents in sexuality research have been combined for the purposes of data analysis, information about both of these groups has been obscured. When respondents have been more adequately differentiated by sexual orientation, intergroup differences as well as similarities have been reported, providing a more accurate characterization of both groups. Sexuality surveys have played a significant role over time in documenting the existence of bisexual behavior, validating the usefulness of bisexuality as a descriptive category, and contributing to the acknowledgment of bisexuality as a sexual orientation and sexual identity.

Early Research on Bisexuality

Research focused specifically on bisexuality arose, in part, as a constructive response to the tendency of much research on sexual orientation to omit or gloss over findings pertaining to bisexual respondents, particularly in studies focusing on gay men and lesbians where homosexuality was considered a unitary category. Researchers who sought a fuller understanding of the range and diversity of sexual attractions and behavior recognized the need to conduct research focused specifically on bisexuality. Early research on bisexuality addressed several questions about bisexuality as a valid sexual orientation and sexual identity that were raised by the illness model of homosexuality and the dichotomous model of sexual orientation: bisexuality and psychological adjustment, bisexual identity and sexual behavior, typologies of bisexuality, and homosexuality and bisexuality in heterosexual marriages.

Psychological Adjustment

The decision of the American Psychiatric Association to remove homosexuality as a diagnostic category was influential in the development of a more affirmative approach toward homosexuality. Nevertheless, the dichotomous model of sexual orientation remained and supported the belief that bisexuals were psychologically maladjusted. Two psychiatrists (Klein, 1978, 1993; Wolff, 1979) challenged the traditional psychiatric position that sexual relationships with both women and men are an indication of immaturity and psychopathology. Wolff (1979) supported the concept of an inherent bisexuality and believed that bisexuality is an intrinsic factor in psychosexual development (Wolff, 1971): "We certainly are bisexual creatures, and this innate disposition is reinforced by the indelible memory of childhood attachments, which know no limitation of sex" (pp. 45-46). Klein (1978) maintained that bisexuality is as normal an outcome of the developmental process as are heterosexuality or homosexuality and that awareness and expression of both heterosexual and homosexual attractions can enhance the individual's experience of intimacy and personal fulfillment.

Just as research has demonstrated that homosexuality is not associated with psychopathology, research has revealed no evidence of psychopathology or psychological maladjustment in bisexual women and men (Harris, 1977; Harwell, 1976; LaTorre & Wendenberg, 1983; Markus, 1981; Masters & Johnson, 1979; Nurius, 1983; M. W. Ross, 1983; Twitchell, 1974; Weinberg & Williams, 1974; Zinik, 1984). In fact, some research found that self-identified bisexuals were characterized by high self-esteem (Galland, 1975; Rubenstein, 1982), self-confidence and autonomy (Galland, 1975), a positive self-concept independent of social norms (Twining, 1983), assertiveness (Bode, 1976), and cognitive flexibility (Zinik, 1984).

Identity and Sexual Behavior

Theorists and researchers who saw heterosexuality and homosexuality as irreconcilable opposites have asserted that individuals who self-identify as bisexual or whose sexual attractions or behavior are not exclusively heterosexual or homosexual are in denial about their "real" gay or lesbian sexual orientation (Fast & Wells, 1975; Miller, 1979; H. L. Ross, 1971; Schäfer, 1976). In contrast, Blumstein and Schwartz (1976a, 1976b, 1977) found that a variety of sexual behaviors were associated with bisexual, lesbian, and gay identities. Although some self-identified bisexual respondents had sexual relationships with both men and women during a particular period of time, others did not. Furthermore, although many respondents who considered themselves lesbian or gay had exclusively homosexual relationships, some also had heterosexual relationships. For many individuals, gender is not necessarily a deciding factor in their choice of a sexual or relationship partner (Ross & Paul, 1992). Other research has also found a variety of sexual behaviors among self-identified gay, lesbian, bisexual, and heterosexual individuals (Doll et al., 1992; Lever, Rogers, Carson, Kanouse, & Hertz, 1992; McKirnan, Stokes, Doll, & Burzette, 1995; Reinisch, Ziemba-Davis, & Sanders, 1990; Stokes, McKirnan, & Burzette, 1993).

Sexual identity may also be influenced by factors other than current sexual behavior, such as whether a person is in a heterosexual or homosexual relationship, fear of being known as gay or bisexual, or political reasons, such as loyalty to the gay or lesbian communities (Blumstein & Schwartz, 1976a, 1976b, 1977; Golden, 1987, 1994; Rust, 1992, 1993, 1995). Some individuals move from a heterosexual identity to a bisexual identity, whereas others first consider themselves lesbian or gay before they consider themselves bisexual (Golden, 1987, 1994; Fox 1995b; Rust, 1992, 1993, 1995). These findings suggest that sexual attractions, fantasy, and behavior and self-identification may vary over time for lesbian, gay, and heterosexual individuals as well as for bisexual individuals.

Other research suggests that most self-identified bisexuals fall in the midrange of the Kinsey scale for ideal sexual behavior but tend to fall at either the heterosexual or homosexual ends of the scale for actual behavior (Fox, 1995b; George, 1993; Klein et al., 1985; Reinhardt, 1985). Actual sexual behavior appears to be constrained by the structure and dynamics of the current relationships in which individuals may be engaged. It is clear that although sexual identity does change for some bisexual men and women, identity remains constant for many individuals, whether or not their bisexual attractions are expressed in terms of sexual behavior or relationships during a particular period of time.

Typologies of Bisexuality

Several typologies of bisexuality have been elaborated, based on the extent and timing of past and present heterosexual and homosexual behavior. Klein (1978) differentiated transitional, historical, sequential, and concurrent bisexuality. For some individuals, bisexuality does represent a stage in the process of coming out as lesbian or gay (transitional bisexuality), whereas for others, a gay or lesbian identity is a step in the process of coming out bisexual. Some individuals, whose sexual lives are presently heterosexual or homosexual, have experienced both same- and opposite-gender sexual attractions or behavior in the past (historical bisexuality). Other individuals have had relationships with both women and men, but with only one person during any period of time (sequential bisexuality), whereas some have had relationships with both men and women during the same time period (concurrent bisexuality). Similar typologies have been developed by other authors (Berkey, Perelman-Hall, & Kurdek, 1990; Boulton & Coxon, 1991; Weinberg, Williams, & Pryor, 1994). Other relevant factors have also been identified, including the social context in which a person lives (heterosexual, homosexual, or both); the relationship(s) in which an individual is involved; and how open a person is with others about being bisexual (Doll et al., 1991).

Bisexuality has also been described in terms of the circumstances in which homosexual behavior takes place (M. W. Ross, 1991b). For example, a person may be hiding a homosexual orientation, exploring homosexuality, or transitioning to a gay or lesbian identity (defense bisexuality). When a society provides no alternatives to marriage, homosexual behavior may take place away from the family environment (married bisexuality). There may be an expectation of homosexual behavior for some or all members of a society, as in Melanesia (ritual bisexuality). For some people, gender is not a criterion for sexual attraction or partner selection (equal bisexuality). In some cultures, a male who takes only the insertor role in anal intercourse with another male is considered heterosexual ("Latin" bisexuality). Homosexual behavior may be circumstantial, taking place once or a few times (experimental bisexuality) or only when there are no heterosexual outlets (secondary bisexuality). Homosexual behavior also may occur as part of male or female prostitution (technical bisexuality).

Homosexuality and Bisexuality in Heterosexual Marriages

The traditional psychiatric position has been that homosexual attractions and behavior in heterosexually married individuals are an indication of psychopathology (Allen, 1961; Bieber, 1969; Hatterer, 1970; Imielinski, 1969). Other authors have also portrayed mixed-orientation marriages as problematic, with separation as the typical outcome and a necessary step for the husband in the process of coming out as a gay man (Bozett, 1982; Hill, 1987; Maddox, 1982; Malone, 1980; Miller, 1979; H. L. Ross, 1971).

Several authors focused on adjustments that gay and bisexual men and their spouses have made in order to continue their marriages (Deabill, 1987; Gochros, 1989; Latham & White, 1978; Nahas & Turley, 1979; M. W. Ross, 1983; Whitney, 1990). Other authors have identified characteristics of successful marriages of bisexual men (Brownfain, 1985; Coleman, 1981/1982a, 1985b; D. Dixon, 1985; Matteson, 1985; T. J. Wolf, 1985) and bisexual women (Coleman, 1985a; J. K. Dixon, 1985; Reinhardt, 1985). These include open communication between partners, acceptance of and discussion about the bisexual partner's homosexual feelings, commitment to making the relationship work, the spouse's maintenance of a sense of worth outside the context of the relationship, and, in some cases, agreement to some degree of open relationship. The impact of a husband's disclosure of sexual orientation on his spouse and the marital relationship also has been examined (Buxton, 1994; Gochros, 1989; Hays & Samuels, 1989).

Research on Bisexual Identity Development

The articulation of lesbian and gay identity theory set the stage for affirmative research on the development of gay and lesbian identities. Bisexual identity theory, however, has emerged out of the results of empirical research. For example, Twining (1983) identified several tasks that bisexual women face in the coming out process: self-acceptance, resolving societal homophobia, developing a support network, and deciding to whom disclosures of sexual orientation will be made. She concluded that "an initial formulation of a conceptual theory of bisexual identity development seems to call for a task model rather than a phase or stage model" (p. 158). In contrast, based on the results of their 1983, 1984/1985, and 1988 studies, Weinberg et al. (1994) outlined the stages they believed were involved in the development of bisexual identities: initial confusion, finding and applying the label, settling into the identity, and a fourth stage, continued uncertainty, which they saw as a common experience of many bisexuals. They saw bisexuality as an "add-on" to an already established heterosexual identity.

Rust (1992, 1993, 1995) and Fox (1995a, 1995b) have emphasized that multiple factors are at work in the development of bisexual identities and that dichotomous and linear conceptual approaches to sexual identity formation do not adequately describe the coming out experiences of many individuals. Gender, age, social class, and ethnicity as well as sexual and emotional attractions, fantasies, and behavior affect the experience and presentation of bisexual identities. Furthermore, although many men and women develop a bisexual identity after first considering themselves heterosexual, others arrive at a bisexual identity from an established lesbian or gay identity. This suggests that sexual identity is not as immutable for all individuals as some theorists and researchers have assumed.

The identification of patterns involved in bisexual identity development can be facilitated by examination of research findings on typical milestone events in the development of bisexual, lesbian, and gay identities. A more comprehensive picture of the coming out process is revealed by looking at both the average ages at which milestone events occur and the patterns for these same events that are suggested by gender and age differences.

Heterosexual Attractions, Behavior, and Relationships

The findings from several studies indicate that bisexual women and men have their first heterosexual attractions, on average, in their early teens, as seen in Table 7.1. This is somewhat earlier than for lesbians and gay men who have had heterosexual attractions, as seen in Table 7.2. Bisexual women have their first sexual experiences and relationships with men in their middle teens, somewhat earlier than bisexual men have their first sexual experiences and relationships with women, as seen in Table 7.1. This pattern is similar to the pattern that has been found for lesbians and gay men who have had sexual experiences with persons of the other gender, as seen in Table 7.2.

Homosexual Attractions, Behavior, and Relationships

Research findings suggest that, on average, bisexual men have their first homosexual attractions in their early to middle teens, whereas bisexual women have their first homosexual attractions in their middle to late teens, as seen in Table 7.1. On average, bisexual men have their first same-gender sexual experiences in their middle to late teens, whereas bisexual women have their first same-gender sexual experiences in their early 20s. These events tend to occur somewhat later than for gay men

Table 7.1 Average Ages at Milestone Events in Research on Bisexual Identity Development

Research	Date	N	Age	First Heterosexual: Attractions	First Heterosexual: Behavior	First Heterosexual: Relationship	First Homosexual: Attractions	First Homosexual: Behavior	First Homosexual: Relationship	Identity as: Gay	Identity as: Bisexual
Bisexual Women											
Harris	1977	10	28.0	—	21.1	—	—	22.2	—	—	25.8
Klein	1978	41	28.5	11.3	15.5	—	17.0	23.0	—	—	24.4
Kooden et al.	1979	17	—	—	—	—	16.0	22.0	24.9	27.9	—
Zinik	1984	63	31.8	10.8	16.5	—	16.9	21.6	—	—	23.7
Morse	1989	16	35.0	11.5	—	—	—	—	—	—	23.2
George	1993	121	30.6	—	—	—	—	—	—	—	25.0
Rust	1993	60	32.5	—	—	—	18.1	21.4	—	24.5	26.8
Weinberg et al.	1994	44[a]	—	11.6	14.7	—	16.9	23.5	—	—	27.0
		96[b]	—	10.9	15.1	—	18.5	20.0	—	—	—
Fox	1995b	486	30.3	11.1	15.1	18.0	15.8		22.4	22.8	22.5
Bisexual Men											
Harris	1977	15	34.9	—	20.1	—	—	14.5	—	—	27.3
Klein	1978	103	32.4	13.1	16.0	—	16.0	17.8	—	—	24.2
Kooden et al.	1979	64	—	—	—	—	12.6	13.9	19.1	22.3	—
Zinik	1984	72	36.2	11.9	—	—	16.2	—	—	—	—
Wayson	1985	21	—	—	19.8	—	—	18.6	—	—	—
Weinberg et al.	1994	49[a]	—	11.7	17.3	—	13.5	16.3	—	—	27.2
		116[b]	—	12.8	15.9	—	17.1	17.2	—	—	29.0
Fox	1995b	349	34.8	11.4	16.6	20.0	13.7	16.4	23.5	21.6	22.6

a. Results from authors' 1983 study.
b. Results from authors' 1984/1985 study.

Table 7.2 Average Ages at Milestone Events in Research on Lesbian and Gay Identity Development

Research On	Date	N	Age	First Heterosexual:			First Homosexual:			Identity as:
				Attractions	Behavior	Relationship	Attractions	Behavior	Relationship	Lesbian or Gay
Lesbians										
Kenyon	1968	123	36.4	—	—	—	16.1	21.5	—	—
Schäfer	1976	151	26.2	—	18.5	—	14.5	19.8	—	20.7
Vance	1978	43	27.7	—	15.5	—	14.2	18.5	—	—
Califia	1979	286	27.5	—	—	—	—	20.0	—	20.5
Kooden et al.	1979	63	—	—	—	—	13.8	19.9	22.8	23.2
Etorre	1980	201	30.3	—	—	—	13.1	21.8	—	22.6
Fitzpatrick	1983	112	37.4	—	—	—	13.9	23.1	—	22.0
Zinik	1984	54	29.0	13.2	—	—	14.0	—	—	—
Chapman/ Brannock	1987	197	34.0	—	16.8	—	—	20.6	—	22.5
Rust	1993	342	31.2	—	—	—	15.4	—	—	21.7
Weinberg et al.	1994	94[a]	—	14.3	16.4	—	16.4	20.5	—	22.5

Table 7.2 *Continued*

Research On	Date	N	Age	First Heterosexual:			First Homosexual:			Identity as:
				Attractions	Behavior	Relationship	Attractions	Behavior	Relationship	Lesbian or Gay
Gay Men										
Dank	1971	182	32.5	—	—	—	13.5	—	—	19.3
Dannecker/Reiche	1974	581	27.5	—	—	—	—	16.7	—	19.0
Weinberg, T. S.	1977	30	—	—	18.3	—	—	14.1	—	19.9
Lehne	1978	47	22.8	—	—	—	—	16.0	—	—
Kooden et al.	1979	138	—	—	—	—	12.8	14.9	21.9	21.1
Troiden	1979	150	30.0	—	—	—	—	14.9	23.9	21.3
McDonald	1982	199	31.0	—	—	—	13.0	15.0	21.0	19.0
Sommers	1982	97	29.5	—	—	—	10.8	—	—	18.4
Benitez	1983	178	32.0	—	18.9	20.3	12.3	19.5	23.2	20.2
Zinik	1984	61	27.5	14.3	—	—	11.4	—	—	—
Cohen-Ross	1985	93	27.9	—	14.7	—	9.0	14.4	—	16.8
Wayson	1985	58	—	—	20.6	—	—	11.0	—	—
Edgar	1987	148	35.4	—	—	—	12.1	16.9	—	—
Prine	1987	51	35.1	—	—	—	15.2	17.7	—	—
Weinberg et al.	1994	186[a]	—	14.5	17.7	—	11.5	14.7	—	21.1

a. Results from authors' 1984/1985 study.

and lesbians, as seen in Table 7.2. The earlier ages of first homosexual attractions and behavior for bisexual men compared to bisexual women are strikingly parallel to the earlier ages for gay men compared to lesbians. Bisexual men and women have their first homosexual relationships at about the same ages, in their early 20s.

Sexual Orientation Self-Identification

The results of research indicate that bisexual men and women first self-identify as bisexual on average in their early to middle 20s, as seen in Table 7.1. This is somewhat later than the ages of first homosexual self-identification of gay men and lesbians, as seen in Table 7.2. Among bisexual men and women who have considered themselves gay or lesbian, men self-identify as gay in their early 20s, somewhat earlier than women self-identify as lesbian. This parallels the earlier homosexual self-identification of gay men compared to lesbians, as seen in Table 7.2.

Self-Disclosure of Sexual Orientation

Bisexual women and men typically first disclose their sexual orientation to another person in their 20s, at about the same time they first self-identify as bisexual (Fox, 1995b; Weinberg et al., 1994). This is about the same as for lesbians (Fitzpatrick, 1983) and gay men (Benitez, 1983; Bilotta, 1987; Cody, 1988; Edgar, 1987; McDonald, 1982). Bisexual women and men are most likely to have disclosed their sexual orientation to their friends and relationship partners or a therapist and less likely to have disclosed to family members or to people at work or at school (Fox, 1995b; Weinberg et al., 1994). This is the same pattern as for lesbians (Bell & Weinberg, 1978; Chapman & Brannock, 1987; Etorre, 1980; Fitzpatrick, 1983; Hencken, 1984; Jay & Young, 1979; Kooden et al., 1979; Loftin, 1981; Weinberg et al., 1994) and gay men (Bell & Weinberg, 1978; Benitez, 1983; Cody, 1988; Cramer & Roach, 1988; Edgar, 1987; Hencken, 1984; Jay & Young, 1979; Kooden et al., 1979; Weinberg et al., 1994). The proportions of bisexuals disclosing their sexual orientation to persons other than friends and relationship partners, however, are somewhat less than for lesbians and gay men.

Gender and Age Differences in the Coming Out Process

The timing and sequence of developmental milestone events reveal different normative patterns for bisexual women and men. Most bisexual women experience their first homosexual attractions and behavior after their first heterosexual attractions and behavior. It is also more usual for bisexual women to adopt a bisexual identity sooner after their first homosexual attractions than bisexual men. In contrast, a greater proportion of bisexual men experience their first homosexual attractions and behavior before or at about the same age as their first heterosexual behavior. It is therefore more common for bisexual men to experience concurrent heterosexual and homosexual attractions and behavior at an earlier age than most bisexual women and for a longer period of time before their first bisexual self-identification. On the other hand, some bisexual women do experience their first homosexual attractions and behavior earlier than suggested in the predominant pattern, and some bisexual men do experience their first homosexual attractions and behavior after their first heterosexual attractions and behavior. These patterns are not significantly related to whether or not such individuals have previously self-identified as lesbian or gay.

There are significant differences in the ages at which these developmental milestone events occur for younger and older individuals, suggesting that the entire coming out process is occurring earlier for younger bisexuals (Fox, 1995b). This parallels a similar shift in the timing of developmental milestone events for younger and older gay men (Dank, 1971; McDonald, 1982; Troiden & Goode, 1980). These trends reflect the development of more affirmative cultural attitudes toward homosexuality and bisexuality, greater access to accurate information about sexuality and sexual orientation, and the development of visible and supportive lesbian, gay, and bisexual communities.

Coming Out Issues

Several issues that bisexual women and men typically face in coming out have been identified (Coleman, 1981/1982a, 1985a, 1985b; Firestein, 1996; Little, 1989; Lourea, 1987; Matteson, 1987; Morse, 1989; Nichols, 1988, 1989; Paul, 1983/1984, 1985; Shuster, 1987; Twining, 1983; T. J. Wolf,

1987, 1992). These include uncertainty about how to interpret concurrent sexual attractions to both women and men; alienation, feeling different from heterosexuals and from gay men and lesbians; isolation, not knowing other bisexual women or men and feeling the lack of a sense of community; self-acceptance, dealing with external and internalized homophobia and biphobia; and apprehension about the impact of disclosing bisexual attractions, behavior, and identity in existing or new relationships. A number of autobiographical and descriptive accounts provide insight into these issues by illustrating how bisexual individuals in diverse circumstances have experienced and successfully moved through the coming out process (Bisexual Anthology Collective, 1995; Bode, 1976; Falk, 1975; Garber, 1995; Geller, 1990; Hutchins & Kaahumanu, 1991; Kohn & Matusow, 1980; Norris & Read, 1985; Ochs & Deihl, 1992; Rose et al., 1996; Scott, 1978; The Off Pink Collective, 1988; Weise, 1992; D. Wolf, 1979).

An important difference historically between coming out bisexual and coming out lesbian or gay has been the relative lack of access of bisexual women and men to a community of similar others. As a result, bisexual men and women have often looked to the gay and lesbian communities for support and understanding regarding their homosexual interests and sexual minority status. Beginning in the 1970s and early 1980s, bisexual groups were organized in several urban areas (Barr, 1985; Mishaan, 1985; Rubenstein & Slater, 1985; Tucker, 1995). Since then, there has been a substantial growth in local, regional, and national bisexual groups and organizations, as reflected in the increase in the number of listings in the *Bisexual Resource Guide* (Ochs, 1995). The emergence of a more visible bisexual community indicates a major positive change in the degree to which bisexual women and men will have access to the experience of community during the coming out process and on an ongoing basis.

Current Trends and Future Directions in Research on Bisexuality

As described above, early research on bisexuality focused on issues such as psychological adjustment, identity and behavior, and homosexuality and bisexuality in the context of heterosexual marriages. More recent research has focused on bisexual identity development, as well as several other related areas, such as bisexuality and HIV/AIDS, bisexuality and ethnicity, and bisexuality and transgender status.

Bisexuality and HIV/AIDS

The primary focus of most early HIV/AIDS research and prevention efforts was on gay men and the gay male community. As the epidemic progressed, however, it became clear that there was a significant incidence of HIV infection in other populations as well, including intravenous drug users and their sexual partners, bisexual men, women of all sexual orientations, and people of color (Doll et al., 1991; Tielman, Carballo, & Hendriks, 1991b). It also became evident that sexual orientation and sexual identity categories were inadequate by themselves for understanding and accurately predicting HIV infection patterns (Doll et al., 1991; Gómez, 1995; Lever et al., 1992; Reinisch, Ziembar, Davis, & Saunders, 1990). The focus of research and prevention efforts shifted to sexual and other risk behaviors. Two behaviorally based categories emerged alongside the identity categories heterosexual, bisexual, and homosexual: MSM (men who have sex with men) and WSW (women who have sex with women). Some researchers, particularly those investigating sexual behavior cross-culturally and among ethnically diverse populations, have contributed significantly to our understanding of bisexuality by adopting a multidimensional approach and examining both the sexual behavior and the sexual identities of their respondents (Doll et al., 1992; McKirnan et al., 1995; Stokes, McKirnan, & Burzette, 1993).

Bisexuality and Ethnicity

Most of our scientific knowledge about sexual behavior and relationships, and sexual orientation and sexual identity, has been based on research which has not typically included people of color. An important impetus for the current interest in research on sexuality and ethnicity has been a recognition of the substantial impact of the HIV/AIDS epidemic on communities of color. A significant result of this research has been an increase in information about homosexuality and bisexuality among African Americans (Mays & Cochran, 1993; Peterson, 1995), Asian Americans (Chan, 1995; Matteson, 1995), Native Americans (Tafoya,

1989), and Hispanic Americans (Carballo-Diéguez, 1995; Magaña & Carrier, 1991; Morales, 1990).

Bisexuality and Transgender Status

Another area that has been neglected in mainstream sexuality research is the relationship between transgender status and sexual orientation. Psychologists' assumptions about the sexual orientation of transsexual women and men, intersexual people, cross-dressers, and others with transgendered status often have not been informed by objective empirical research grounded in the experiences of transgendered people. For example, just as attitudes of mental health professionals about bisexuality have been based on a dichotomous model of sexual orientation, attitudes about transgendered people have been based on a dichotomous model of gender. This has led psychologists to assume that the sexual identity of transsexual persons is heterosexual. Recent research (Devor, 1993) suggests that the variability in sexual behavior and sexual identity found in the general population also characterizes the transsexual population, which includes not only individuals with a heterosexual identity but individuals with homosexual and bisexual identities as well. Such findings add to our understanding of transsexual and other transgendered people and further challenge the dichotomous concepts of sexual orientation and gender that have traditionally characterized research and clinical work with sexual minorities.

Implications for Future Research on Bisexuality

Several areas in the literature on bisexuality offer promising opportunities for further research: bisexual identity development, bisexuality and relationships, biphobia, and the bisexual community. For example, although there is now substantial research on the transition from a heterosexual identity to a bisexual identity and on the transition from a heterosexual or bisexual identity to a gay or lesbian identity, little research exists on the transition from lesbian and gay identities to a bisexual identity or on identity development involving multiple sexual orientation self-identification sequences. Likewise, although extensive research has been conducted on relationships in which one partner is heterosexual and the other is bisexual, not all bisexual women and men are in relationships with heterosexuals. Research on relationships in which one partner is bisexual and the other is gay or lesbian, or both partners are bisexual, would add to our understanding of the relationships in which bisexual women and men are involved, as would research on triadic and other polyamorous relationships.

Furthermore, although substantial and valuable research has been conducted on the attitudes that heterosexuals have toward gay men and lesbians and on homophobia, there is very little research on the attitudes that heterosexuals, gay men, and lesbians have toward bisexuals or on biphobia. Finally, research on how bisexual identity development has been affected by the emergence and continued presence of a visible bisexual community would augment our understanding of changes in the coming out process that have occurred as a function of time and the development of community.

In addition, most research on gay men, lesbians, and bisexual men and women has been based on retrospective reports. As a result, in-depth longitudinal research is needed to better understand how bisexual identities develop and are maintained over time. There is also a need for further research in which sexual orientation is used as an independent variable, which would allow comparisons between lesbians, gay men, heterosexuals, and bisexuals on a variety of topics. Furthermore, the largest proportion of participants in most such research have been middle-class white women and men in their 20s and 30s. Contemporary research on HIV/AIDS and on sexuality and ethnicity have demonstrated the need for a truly multidimensional approach to research on homosexuality and bisexuality. Consequently, there is a clear need for further in-depth research on bisexual youth, older bisexuals, working-class bisexuals, transgendered bisexuals, and bisexual people of color, as well as people with bisexual behavior but other sexual orientation self-identifications, all of whom have been underrepresented or inadvertently combined with other populations in research to date.

Conclusion

The elimination of homosexuality as a clinical diagnostic category marked an important shift away from the illness model of homosexuality to a more affirmative approach to homosexuality. This served to encourage the development of theory and research on the development of positive lesbian and gay identities. At the same time, abundant research on human sexuality had clearly demonstrated that a significant proportion of individuals has experienced both heterosexual and homosexual attractions and behavior. Nevertheless, thinking about sexual orientation and sexual identity continued to be based on the assumption of monosexuality, or exclusivity of heterosexual or homosexual "object choice." Through the lens of this dichotomous model, bisexuality appeared anomalous, and individuals who claimed a bisexual identity were seen as psychologically and socially maladjusted, just as lesbians and gay men were considered maladjusted from the point of view of the illness model. Research on bisexual women and men, however, found no indication of psychopathology, just as prior research had found no evidence of psychopathology in lesbians and gay men. Over time, a multidimensional model of sexual orientation has been developed. This model views bisexuality as a valid and distinct sexual orientation and identity and that acknowledges that a number of factors in addition to sexual attractions, fantasies, and behavior are involved in the development and experience of sexual orientation and identity. These include emotional and social preferences, lifestyle, and self-identification, as well as gender, age, social class, and ethnicity.

Affirmative theoretical approaches to bisexuality and the results of research on bisexuality have challenged several traditional assumptions about sexual orientation: first, the belief that exclusive heterosexuality and homosexuality are the only normal outcomes of the process of sexual identity development; second, that heterosexuality and homosexuality are mutually exclusive; third, that gender is the primary criterion for sexual partner selection; and fourth, that sexual orientation is immutable. As a result, bisexual identity development has not been conceptualized as a linear process with a fixed outcome but, rather, as a complex and open-ended process. In fact, bisexuals, homosexuals, and heterosexuals are not three totally distinct groups. Research indicates that there is significant overlap in membership in these categories for many individuals in terms of both past and present sexual and emotional attractions and behavior. Both traditional developmental theory and lesbian and gay identity development theory have tended to ignore or dismiss this diversity within groups. Research on bisexuality has further validated the evidence from other sexuality research that indicates that for some individuals, sexual identity remains constant, whereas for others, sexual identity varies in response to changes in sexual and emotional attractions, behavior, and relationships, and the social and political contexts in which these occur.

It is clear that there are both similarities and differences in coming out bisexual and coming out gay or lesbian. Like lesbians and gay men, bisexual women and men need to acknowledge and validate their homosexual attractions and relationships to achieve positive and integrated sexual identities. Bisexual men and women, however, need to acknowledge and validate both the homosexual and the heterosexual components of their identities, regardless of the degree to which either or both of these are actualized in sexual behavior or relationships. The development of a multidimensional approach to sexual orientation has been essential in more accurately conceptualizing bisexuality. Recent theory and research on bisexuality and bisexual identities have contributed significantly to a more comprehensive understanding of sexual orientation. A continued focus on bisexuality within the larger context of sexual orientation research would further enhance our knowledge and understanding of sexual orientation and sexual identity, as well as provide a greater appreciation of the interrelatedness of lesbian, gay, and bisexual issues.

References

ACSF Investigators. (1992). AIDS and sexual behaviour in France. *Nature, 360,* 407-409.

Adam, B. D. (1985). Age, structure, and sexuality: Reflections on the anthropological evidence on homosexual relations. *Journal of Homosexuality, 11*(3/4), 19-34.

Aina, T. A. (1991). Patterns of bisexuality in Sub-Saharan Africa. In R. A. P. Tielman, M. Carballo, & A. C. Hendriks (Eds.), *Bisexuality and HIV/AIDS: A global perspective* (pp. 81-90). Buffalo, NY: Prometheus.

Alexander, F. (1933). Bisexual conflict in homosexuality. *Psychoanalytic Quarterly, 2,* 197-201.

Allen, C. (1961). When homosexuals marry. In I. Rubin (Ed.), *The third sex* (pp. 58-62). New York: New Book.

Bailey, D. S. (1975). *Homosexuality and the Western Christian tradition.* Hamden, CT: Ardeon.

Barr, G. (1985). Chicago bi-ways: An informal history. *Journal of Homosexuality, 11*(1/2), 231-234.

Bayer, R. (1981). *Homosexuality and American psychiatry: The politics of diagnosis.* New York: Basic Books.

Bell, A. P., & Weinberg, M. S. (1978). *Homosexualities: A study of diversity among men and women.* New York: Simon & Schuster.

Bell, A. P., Weinberg, M. S., & Hammersmith, S. K. (1981). *Sexual preference: Its development in men and women.* Bloomington: Indiana University Press.

Benitez, J. C. (1983). The effect of gay identity acquisition on the psychological adjustment of male homosexuals (Doctoral dissertation, Northwestern University, 1982). *Dissertation Abstracts International, 43*(10), 3350B.

Bergler, E. (1956). *Homosexuality: Disease or way of life.* New York: Collier.

Berkey, B., Perelman-Hall, T., & Kurdek, L. A. (1990). Multi- dimensional scale of sexuality. *Journal of Homosexuality, 19*(4), 67-87.

Bieber, I. (1969). The married male homosexual. *Medical Aspects of Human Sexuality, 3*(5), 76-84.

Bieber, I., Dain, H. J., Dince, P. R., Drellich, M. G., Gunlach, R. H., Kremer, M. W., Rifkin, A. H., Wilbur, C. B., & Bieber, T. B. (1962). *Homosexuality: A psychoanalytic study.* New York: Random House.

Bilotta, G. J. (1987). Gay men coming out to their families or origin: An exploratory-descriptive investigation (Doctoral dissertation, United States International University, 1987). *Dissertation Abstracts International, 48*(4), 1026A.

Binson, D., Michaels, S., Stall, R., Coates, T. J., Gagnon, J. H., & Catania, J. A. (1995). Prevalence and social distribution of men who have sex with men: United States and its urban centers. *Journal of Sex Research, 32*(3), 245-254.

Bisexual Anthology Collective. (1995). *Plural desires: Writing bisexual women's realities.* Toronto: Sister Vision: Black Women and Women of Colour Press.

Blackwood, E. (1984). Sexuality and gender in certain Native American tribes: The case of cross-gender females. *Signs: Journal of Women in Culture and Society, 10,* 27-42.

Blackwood, E. (1985). Breaking the mirror: The construction of lesbianism and the anthropological discourse on homosexuality. *Journal of Homosexuality, 11*(3/4), 1-18.

Blumstein, P., & Schwartz, P. (1976a). Bisexuality in men. *Urban Life, 5*(3), 339-358.

Blumstein, P. W., & Schwartz, P. (1976b). Bisexuality in women. *Archives of Sexual Behavior, 5*(2), 171-181.

Blumstein, P. W., & Schwartz, P. (1977). Bisexuality: Some social psychological issues. *Journal of Social Issues, 33*(2), 30-45.

Bode, J. (1976). *View from another closet: Exploring bisexuality in women.* New York: Hawthorne.

Boles, J., & Elifson, K. W. (1994). Sexual identity and HIV: The male prostitute. *Journal of Sex Research, 31*(1), 39-46.

Boswell, J. (1980). *Christianity, social tolerance, and homosexuality: Gay people in western Europe from the beginning of the Christian era to the fourteenth century.* Chicago: University of Chicago Press.

Boulton, M., & Coxon, T. (1991). Bisexuality in the United Kingdom. In R. A. P. Tielman, M. Carballo, & A. C. Hendriks (Eds.), *Bisexuality and HIV/AIDS: A global perspective* (pp. 65-72). Buffalo, NY: Prometheus.

Bozett, F. W. (1982). Heterogeneous couples in heterosexual marriages: Gay men and straight women. *Journal of Marital and Family Therapy, 8*(1), 81-89.

Brownfain, J. J. (1985). A study of the married bisexual male: Paradox and resolution. *Journal of Homosexuality, 11*(1/2), 173-188.

Buxton, A. P. (1994). *The other side of the closet: The coming out crisis for straight spouses and families.* New York: John Wiley.

Califia, P. (1979). Lesbian sexuality. *Journal of Homosexuality, 4*(3), 255-266.

Callender, C., & Kochems, L. M. (1985). Men and no-men: Male gender-mixing statuses and homosexuality. *Journal of Homosexuality, 11*(3/4), 165-178.

Cantarella, E. (1992). *Bisexuality in the ancient world* (C. O'Cuilleanain, Trans.). New Haven, CT: Yale University Press.

Carballo-Diéguez, A. (1995). The sexual identity and behavior of Puerto Rican men who have sex with men. In G. M. Herek & B. Greene (Eds.), *AIDS, identity, and community: The IV epidemic and lesbians and gay men* (pp. 105-114). Newbury Park, CA: Sage.

Carrier, J. M. (1980). Homosexual behavior in cross-cultural perspective. In J. Marmor (Ed.), *Homosexual behavior: A modern reappraisal* (pp. 100-122). New York: Basic Books.

Carrier, J. M. (1985). Mexican male bisexuality. *Journal of Homosexuality, 11*(1/2), 75-86.

Cass, V. C. (1979). Homosexual identity formation: A theoretical model. *Journal of Homosexuality, 4*(3), 219-235.

Cass, V. C. (1983/1984). Homosexual identity: A concept in need of definition. *Journal of Homosexuality, 9*(2/3), 105-126.

Cass, V. C. (1984). Homosexual identity formation: Testing a theoretical model. *Journal of Sex Research, 20*(2), 143-167.

Cass, V. C. (1990). The implications of homosexual identity formation for the Kinsey model and scale of sexual preference. In D. P. McWhirter, S. A. Sanders, & J. M. Reinisch (Eds.), *Homosexuality/heterosexuality: Concepts of sexual orientation* (pp. 239-266). New York: Oxford University Press.

Chan, C. S. (1995). Issues of sexual identity in an ethnic minority: The case of Chinese American lesbians, gay men, and bisexual people. In A. R. D'Augelli & C. J. Patterson (Eds.), *Lesbian, gay and bisexual identities over the lifespan: Psychological perspectives* (pp. 87-101). New York: Oxford University Press.

Chapman, B. E., & Brannock, J. C. (1987). Proposed model of lesbian identity development: An empirical examination. *Journal of Homosexuality, 14*(3/4), 69-80.

Chetwynd, J. (1991). Bisexuality in New Zealand. In R. A. P. Tielman, M. Carballo, & A. C. Hendriks (Eds.), *Bisexuality and HIV/AIDS: A global perspective* (pp. 131-138). Buffalo, NY: Prometheus.

Churchill, W. (1967). *Homosexual behavior among males: A cross-cultural and cross-species investigation.* New York: Hawthorn.

Cody, P. J. (1988). The personal development of gay men: A study of the relationship of length of time "out of the closet" to locus of control, self-concept, and self-actualization (Doctoral dissertation, California Institute of Integral Studies, 1988). *Dissertation Abstracts International, 49*(7), 2847B.

Cohen-Ross, J. L. (1985). An exploratory study of the retrospective role of significant others in homosexual identity development (Doctoral dissertation, California School of Professional Psychology, Los Angeles, 1984). *Dissertation Abstracts International, 46*(2), 628B.

Coleman, E. (1981/1982a). Bisexual and gay men in heterosexual marriage: Conflicts and resolutions in therapy. *Journal of Homosexuality, 7*(2/3), 93-104.

Coleman, E. (1981/1982b). Developmental stages of the coming out process. *Journal of Homosexuality, 7*(2/3), 31-44.

Coleman, E. (1985a). Bisexual women in marriages. *Journal of Homosexuality, 11*(1/2), 87-100.

Coleman, E. (1985b). Integration of male bisexuality and marriage. *Journal of Homosexuality, 11*(1/2), 189-208.

Coleman, E. (1987). Assessment of sexual orientation. *Journal of Homosexuality, 14*(1/2), 9-24.

Cramer, D. M. & Roach, A. J. (1988). Coming out to mom and dad: A study of gay males and their relationships with their parents. *Journal of Homosexuality, 15*(3/4), 79-91.

Cronin, D. M. (1974). Coming out among lesbians. In E. Goode & R. R. Troiden (Eds.), *Sexual deviance and sexual deviants* (pp. 268-277). New York: William Morrow.

Dank, B. M. (1971). Coming out in the gay world. *Psychiatry, 34*, 180-197.

Dannecker, M., & Reiche, R. (1974). *Der gewöhnliche Homosexuelle.* Frankfurt: Fisher.

Davenport, W. (1965). Sexual patterns and their regulation in a society of the Southwest Pacific. In F. A. Beach (Ed.), *Sex and behavior* (pp. 164-207). New York: John Wiley.

Davenport, W. (1977). Sex in cross-cultural perspective. In F. A. Beach (Ed.), *Human sexuality in four perspectives* (pp. 115-163). Baltimore: Johns Hopkins University Press.

Deabill, G. (1987). *An investigation of sexual behaviors in mixed sexual orientation couples: Gay husband and straight wife.* Unpublished doctoral dissertation, Institute for Advanced Study of Human Sexuality, San Francisco.

DeMonte Flores, C., & Schulte, S. J. (1975). Coming out: Similarities and differences for lesbians and gay men. *Journal of Social Issues, 34*(3), 59-72.

Devor, H. (1993). Sexual orientation identities, attractions, and practices of female-to-male transsexuals. *Journal of Sex Research, 30*(4), 303-315.

Diamond, M. (1993). Homosexuality and bisexuality in different populations. *Archives of Sexual Behavior, 22*(4), 291-310.

Dixon, D. (1985). Perceived sexual satisfaction and marital happiness of bisexual and heterosexual swinging husbands. *Journal of Homosexuality, 11*(1/2), 209-222.

Dixon, J. K. (1985). Sexuality and relationship changes in married females following the commencement of bisexual activity. *Journal of Homosexuality, 11*(1/2), 115-134.

Doll, L., Peterson, J., Magana, J. R., & Carrier, J. M. (1991). Male bisexuality and AIDS in the United States. In R. A. P. Tielman, M. Carballo, & A. C. Hendriks (Eds.), *Bisexuality and HIV/AIDS: A global perspective* (pp. 27-40). Buffalo, NY: Prometheus Books.

Dover, K. J. (1978). *Greek homosexuality.* New York: Vintage.

Downing, C. (1989). *Myths and mysteries of same-sex love.* New York: Continuum.

Edgar, T. M. (1987). The disclosure process of the stigmatized: Strategies to minimize rejection (Doctoral dissertation, Purdue University, 1986). *Dissertation Abstracts International, 47*(9), 3238A.

Eglinton, J. Z. (1964). *Greek love.* New York: Oliver Layton.

Ellis, H. (1942). *Studies in the psychology of sex (Vol. I).* New York: Random House. (Original work published in 1905)

Etorre, E. M. (1980). *Lesbians, women, and society.* London: Routledge & Kegan Paul.

Falk, R. (1975). *Women loving: A journey toward becoming an independent woman.* New York: Random House.

Fast, J., & Wells, H. (1975). *Bisexual living.* New York: Pocket Books.

Fay, R. E., Turner, C. F., Klassen, A. D., & Gagnon, J. H. (1989). Prevalence and patterns of same-gender sexual contact among men. *Science, 243,* 338-348.

Firestein, B. (1996). Development of a bisexual identity: Understanding the process (Published under pseudonym Ann Fox). In M. Adams, P. Brigham, P. Dalpes, & L. Marchesani (Eds.), *Social diversity and social justice: Gay, lesbian, and bisexual oppression* (pp. 29-33). Dubuque, IA: Kendall/Hunt.

Fitzpatrick, G. (1983). Self-disclosure of lesbianism as related to self-actualization and self-stigmatization (Doctoral dissertation, United States International University, 1982). *Dissertation Abstracts International, 43*(12), 4143B.

Ford, C. S., & Beach, F. A. (1951). *Patterns of sexual behavior.* New York: Harper & Row.

Fox, R. C. (1995a). Bisexual identities. In A. R. D'Augelli & C. J. Patterson (Eds.), *Lesbian, gay, and bisexual identities over the lifespan* (pp. 48-86). New York, Oxford University Press.

Fox, R. C. (1995b). Coming out bisexual: Identity, behavior, and sexual orientation self-disclosure. (Doctoral dissertation, California Institute of Integral Studies, 1993). *Dissertation Abstracts International, 55*(12), 5565B.

Freud, S. (1962). *Three essays on the theory of sexuality* (J. Strachey, Trans.). New York: Basic Books. (Original work published 1905)

Freud, S. (1963). *An autobiographical study* (J. Strachey, Trans.; rev. ed.). New York: Norton. (Original work published 1925)

Freud, S. (1963). Analysis terminable and interminable. In P. Rieff (Ed.), *Therapy and technique* (pp. 233-272). New York: Collier. (Original work published 1937)

Gagnon, J. M., & Simon, W. (1968). Homosexuality: The formulation of a sociological perspective. In M. Lefton, J. K. Skipper, Jr., & C. H. McGaghy (Eds.), *Approaches to deviance: Theories, concepts and research findings* (pp. 349-361). New York: Appleton-Century-Crofts.

Galland, V. R. (1975). Bisexual women (Doctoral dissertation, California School of Professional Psychology, San Francisco, 1975). *Dissertation Abstracts International, 36*(6), 3037B.

Garber, M. (1995). *Vice versa: Bisexuality and the eroticism of everyday life.* New York: Simon & Schuster.

Garcia, M. L. G., Valdespino, J., Izazola, J., Palacios, M., & Sepulveda, J. (1991). Bisexuality in Mexico: Current perspectives. In R. A. P. Tielman, M. Carballo, & A. C. Hendriks (Eds.), *Bisexuality and HIV/AIDS: A global perspective* (pp. 41- 58). Buffalo, NY: Prometheus.

Geller, T. (Ed.). (1990). *Bisexuality: A reader and sourcebook.* Ojai, CA: Times Change.

George, S. (1993). *Women and bisexuality.* London: Scarlet.

Gerard, K., & Hekma, G. (Eds.). (1989). *The pursuit of sodomy: Male homosexuality in Renaissance and Enlightenment Europe.* New York: Harrington Park.

Gochros, J. S. (1989). *When husbands come out of the closet.* New York: Harrington Park.

Golden, C. (1987). Diversity and variability in women's sexual identities. In Boston Lesbian Psychologies Collective (Ed.), *Lesbian psychologies: Explorations and challenges* (pp. 18-34). Chicago: University of Illinois Press.

Golden, C. (1994). Our politics and choices: The feminist movement and sexual orientation. In B. Greene & G. M. Herek (Eds.), *Lesbian and gay psychology: Theory, research, and clinical applications* (pp. 54-70). Thousand Oaks, CA: Sage.

Gómez, C. A. (1995). Lesbians at risk for HIV: The unresolved debate. In G. M. Herek & B. Greene (Eds.), *AIDS, identity, and community: The IV epidemic and lesbians and gay men* (pp. 19-31). Thousand Oaks, CA: Sage.

Green, R. (1972). Homosexuality as a mental illness. *International Journal of Psychiatry, 10,* 77-128.

Greenberg, D. F. (1988). *The construction of homosexuality.* Chicago: University of Chicago Press.

Harris, D. A. I. (1977). Social-psychological characteristics of ambisexuals (Doctoral dissertation, University of Tennessee, 1977). *Dissertation Abstracts International, 39*(2), 574A.

Harwell, J. L. (1976). Bisexuality: Persistent lifestyle or transitional state? (Doctoral dissertation, United States International University, 1976). *Dissertation Abstracts International, 37*(4), 2449A.

Hatterer, L. J. (1970). *Changing homosexuality in the male: Treatment for men troubled by homosexuality.* New York: Dell.

Hays, D., & Samuels, A. (1989). Heterosexual women's perceptions of their marriages to bisexual or homosexual men. *Journal of Homosexuality, 18*(1/2), 81-100.

Hencken, J. D. (1984). Sexual-orientation self-disclosure (Doctoral dissertation, University of Michigan, Ann Arbor, 1984). *Dissertation Abstracts International, 45*(7), 2310B.

Herdt, G. (1984). A comment on cultural attributes and fluidity of bisexuality. *Journal of Homosexuality, 10*(3/4), 53-62.

Herdt, G. (1990). Developmental discontinuities and sexual orientation across cultures. In D. P. McWhirter, S. A. Sanders, & J. M. Reinisch (Eds.), *Homosexuality/heterosexuality: Concepts of sexual orientation* (pp. 208-236). New York: Oxford University Press.

Hill, I. (Ed.). (1987). *The bisexual spouse: Different dimensions in human sexuality.* New York: Harper & Row.

Hinsch, B. (1990). *Passions of the cut sleeve: The male homosexual tradition in China.* Berkeley: University of California Press.

Hite, S. (1976). *The Hite report: A nationwide study of female sexuality.* New York: Dell.

Hite, S. (1981). *The Hite report on male sexuality.* New York: Knopf.

Hoffman, M. (1968). *The gay world: Male homosexuality and the social creation of evil.* New York: Basic Books.

Hooker, E. (1956). A preliminary analysis of group behavior of homosexuals. *Journal of Psychology, 42,* 217-225.

Hooker, E. (1965). Male homosexuals and their "worlds." In J. Marmor (Ed.), *Sexual inversion: The multiple roots of homosexuality* (pp. 83-107). New York: Basic Books.

Humphreys, L. (1970). *Tearoom trade: Impersonal sex in public places.* Chicago: Aldine.

Hunt, M. (1974). *Sexual behavior in the 1970s.* New York: Dell.

Hutchins, L., & Kaahumanu, L. (Eds.). (1991). *Bi any other name: Bisexual people speak out.* Boston: Alyson.

Ihara, S. (1972). *Comrade loves of the Samurai.* Rutland, VT: Tuttle.

Imielinski, K. (1969). Homosexuality in males with particular reference to marriage. *Psychotherapy and Psychosomatics, 17,* 126-132.

Janus, S. S., & Janus, C. L. (1993). *The Janus report on sexual behavior.* New York: John Wiley.

Jay, K., & Young, A. (1979). *The gay report: Lesbians and gay men speak out about sexual experiences and lifestyles.* New York: Summit Books.

Kenyon, F. E. (1968). Studies in female homosexuality IV: Social and psychiatric aspects. *British Journal of Psychiatry, 114,* 1337-1350.

Khan, M. M. R. (1974). Ego orgasm and bisexual love. *International Review of Psychoanalysis, 1,* 143-149.

Kinsey, A. C., Pomeroy, W. B., & Martin, C. E. (1948). *Sexual behavior in the human male.* Philadelphia: W. B. Saunders.

Kinsey, A. C., Pomeroy, W. B., Martin, C. E., & Gebhard, P. H. (1952). *Sexual behavior in the human female.* Philadelphia: W. B. Saunders.

Klein, F. (1978). *The bisexual option: A concept of one hundred percent intimacy.* New York: Arbor House.

Klein, F. (1990). The need to view sexual orientation as a multi-variable dynamic process: A theoretical perspective. In D. P. McWhirter, S. A. Sanders, & J. M. Reinisch (Eds.), *Homosexuality/heterosexuality: Concepts of sexual orientation* (pp. 277-282). New York: Oxford University Press.

Klein, F. (1993). *The bisexual option* (2nd ed.). New York: Harrington Park Press.

Klein, F., Sepekoff, B., & Wolf, T. J. (1985). Sexual orientation: A multi-variable dynamic process. *Journal of Homosexuality, 11*(1/2), 35-50.

Kohn, B., & Matusow, A. (1980). *Barry and Alice: Portrait of a bisexual marriage.* Englewood Cliffs, NJ: Prentice Hall.

Kooden, H. D., Morin, S. F., Riddle, D. I., Rogers, M., Sang, B. E., & Strassburger, F. (1979). *Removing the stigma: Final report of the Board of Social and Ethical Responsibility for Psychology's Task Force on the status of lesbian and gay male psychologists.* Washington, DC: American Psychological Association.

Krafft-Ebing, R. (1965). *Psychopathia sexualis: A medico-forensic study* (H. Wedeck, Trans.). New York: G. P. Putnam. (Original work published 1886)

Kubie, L. S. (1974). The drive to become both sexes. *Psychoanalytic Quarterly, 43*, 349-426.

Kumar, B. (1991). Patterns of bisexuality in India. In R. A. P. Tielman, M. Carballo, & A. C. Hendriks (Eds.), *Bisexuality and HIV/AIDS: A global perspective* (pp. 91-96). Buffalo, NY: Prometheus.

Latham, J. D., & White, G. D. (1978). Coping with homosexual expression within heterosexual marriages: Five case studies. *Journal of Sex and Marital Therapy, 4*(3), 198-212.

LaTorre, R. A., & Wendenberg, K. (1983). Psychological characteristics of bisexual, heterosexual, and homosexual women. *Journal of Homosexuality, 9*(1), 87-97.

Laumann, E. O., Gagnon, J. H., Michael, R. T., & Michaels, S. (1994). *The social organization of sexuality: Sexual practices in the United States.* Chicago: University of Chicago Press.

Lehne, G. K. (1978). Gay male fantasies and realities. *Journal of Social Issues, 34*(3), 28-37.

Lever, J. (1994, August 23). Sexual revelations: The 1994 *Advocate* survey of sexuality and relationships: The men. *The Advocate*, 16-24.

Lever, J., Rogers, W. H., Carson, S., Kanouse, D. E., & Hertz, R. (1992). Behavior patterns and sexual identity of bisexual males. *Journal of Sex Research, 29*(2), 141-168.

Limentani, A. (1976). Object choice and actual bisexuality. *International Journal of Psychoanalytic Psychotherapy, 5*, 205-218.

Little, D. R. (1989). Contemporary female bisexuality: A psychological phenomenon (Doctoral dissertation, The Union for Experimenting Colleges and Universities, 1989). *Dissertations Abstracts International, 50*(11), 5379B.

Loftin, E. C. (1981). The study of disclosing and support in a lesbian population (Doctoral dissertation, University of Texas at Austin). *Dissertation Abstracts International, 42*(3), 1348A.

Lourea, D. R. (1987). Psycho-social issues related to counseling bisexuals. *Journal of Homosexuality, 11*(1/2), 21-34.

MacDonald, A. P., Jr. (1983). A little bit of lavender goes a long way: A critique of research on sexual orientation. *Journal of Sex Research, 19*(1), 94-100.

Maddox, B. (1982). *Married and gay: An intimate look at a different relationship.* New York: Harcourt Brace Jovanovich.

Magaña, J. R., & Carrier, J. M. (1991). Mexican and Mexican American male sexual behavior and spread of AIDS in California. *Journal of Sex Research, 28*(3), 425-441.

Malone, J. (1980). *Straight women and gay men: A special relationship.* New York: Dial.

Markus, E. B. (1981). An examination of psychological adjustment and sexual preference in the female (Doctoral dissertation, University of Missouri, Kansas City, 1980). *Dissertation Abstracts International, 41*(10), 4338A.

Marmor, J. (Ed.). (1965). *Sexual inversion: The multiple roots of homosexuality.* New York: Basic Books.

Marmor, J. (1972). Homosexuality—Mental illness or moral dilemma? *International Journal of Psychiatry, 10*, 114-117.

Masters, W. H., & Johnson, V. E. (1979). *Homosexuality in perspective.* Boston: Little, Brown.

Matteson, D. R. (1985). Bisexual men in marriage: Is a positive homosexual identity and stable marriage possible? *Journal of Homosexuality, 11*(1/2), 149-172.

Matteson, D. R. (1987). Counseling bisexual men. In M. Scher, M. Stevens, G. Good, & G. A. Eichenfeld (Eds.), *Handbook of counseling and psychotherapy with men* (pp. 232-249). Newbury Park, CA: Sage.

Matteson, D. R. (1995, August). *Bisexual and homosexual behavior and HIV risk among Chinese American, Filipino American, and Korean American men.* Paper presented at the annual convention of the American Psychological Association, New York.

Mays, V. M., & Cochran, S. D. (1993). Applying social psychological models to predicting HIV-related sexual risk behaviors among African Americans. *Journal of Black Psychology, 19,* 142-151.

McDonald, G. J. (1982). Individual differences in the coming out process for gay men: Implications for theoretical models. *Journal of Homosexuality, 8*(1), 47-60.

McKirnan, D. J., Stokes, J. P., Doll, L., Burzette, R. G. (1995). Bisexually active men: Social characteristics and sexual behavior. *Journal of Sex Research, 32*(1), 65-76.

Mead, M. (1961). Cultural determinants of sexual behavior. In W. C. Young (Ed.), *Sex and internal secretions (Vol. II)* (3rd ed., pp. 1433-1479). Baltimore: Williams & Wilkins.

Mead, M. (1975, January). Bisexuality: What's it all about? *Redbook,* pp. 6-7.

Michael, R. T., Laumann, E. O., Gagnon, J. H., & Smith, T. W. (1988). Number of sex partners and potential risk of sexual exposure to Human Immunodeficiency Virus. *Morbidity and Mortality Weekly Report, 37*(37), 565-568.

Miller, B. (1979). Gay fathers and their children. *Family Coordinator, 28,* 544-552.

Mishaan, C. (1985). The bisexual scene in New York City. *Journal of Homosexuality, 11*(1/2), 223-226.

Morales, E. (1990). HIV infection and Hispanic gay and bisexual men. *Hispanic Journal of Behavioral Sciences, 12,* 212-222.

Morse, C. R. (1989). Exploring the bisexual alternative: A view from another closet (Master's thesis, University of Arizona, 1989). *Master's Abstracts, 28*(2), 320.

Murray, S. O. (1992). Homosexuality in cross-cultural perspective. In S. O. Murray (Ed.), *Introduction: Oceanic homosexualities* (pp. xiii-xi). New York: Garland.

Nahas, R., & Turley, M. (1979). *The new couple: Women and gay men.* New York: Seaview Books.

Nanda, S. (1985). The Hijras of India: Cultural and individual dimensions of an institutionalized third gender role. *Journal of Homosexuality, 11*(3/4), 55-68.

Nichols, M. (1988). Bisexuality in women: Myths, realities, and implications for therapy. In E. Cole & E. Rothblum (Eds.), *Women and sex therapy: Closing the circle of sexual knowledge* (pp. 235-252). New York: Harrington Park.

Nichols, M. (1989). Sex therapy with lesbians, gay men, and bisexuals. In S. R. Leiblum & R. C. Rosen (Eds.), *Principles and practice of sex therapy: Update for the 1990s,* (2nd ed., pp. 269-297). New York, Guilford.

Norris, S., & Read, E. (1985). *Out in the open: People talking about being gay or bisexual.* London: Pan Books.

Nurius, P. S. (1983). Mental health implications of sexual orientation. *Journal of Sex Research, 19*(2), 119-136.

Ochs, R. (Ed.). (1995). *The bisexual resource guide.* Cambridge, MA: Bisexual Resource Center.

Ochs, R., & Deihl, M. (1988). Moving beyond binary thinking. In W. Blumenfeld (Ed.), *Homophobia: How we all pay the price* (pp. 67-75). Boston: Beacon.

Oetomo, D. (1991). Patterns of bisexuality in Indonesia. In R. A. P. Tielman, M. Carballo, & A. C. Hendriks (Eds.), *Bisexuality and HIV/AIDS: A global perspective* (pp. 119-126). Buffalo, NY: Prometheus.

Off Pink Collective. (1988). *Bisexual lives.* London: Off Pink Publishing.

Opler, M. (1965). Anthropological and cross-cultural aspects of homosexuality. In J. Marmor (Ed.), *Sexual inversion: The multiple roots of homosexuality* (pp. 108-123). New York: Basic Books.

Parker, R. G. (1991). *Bodies, pleasures, and passions: Sexual culture in contemporary Brazil.* Boston: Beacon.

Parker, R. G., & Tawil, O. (1991). Bisexual behavior and HIV transmission in Latin America. In R. A. P. Tielman, M. Carballo, & A. C. Hendriks (Eds.), *Bisexuality and HIV/AIDS: A global perspective* (pp. 59-64). Buffalo, NY: Prometheus.

Paul, J. P. (1983/1984). The bisexual identity: An idea without social recognition. *Journal of Homosexuality, 9*(2/3), 45-64.

Paul, J. P. (1985). Bisexuality: Reassessing our paradigms of sexuality. *Journal of Homosexuality, 11*(1/2), 21-34.

Peterson, J. L. (1995). AIDS-related risks and same-sex behaviors among African American men. In G. M. Herek & B. Greene (Eds.), *AIDS, identity, and community: The IV epidemic and lesbians and gay men* (pp. 85-104). Thousand Oaks, CA: Sage.

Playboy readers' sex survey (Part 3). (1983, May). *Playboy Magazine*, pp. 126-128, 136, 210-220.

Ponse, B. (1978). *Identities in the lesbian world: The social construction of self.* Westport, CT: Greenwood.

Prine, K. A. (1987). Gay men: The open behavioral expression of sexual orientations and descriptions of psychological health (Doctoral dissertation, University of Cincinnati, 1987). *Dissertation Abstracts International, 48*(4), 1185B.

Rado, S. (October, 1940). A critical examination of the concept of bisexuality. *Psychosomatic Medicine, II*(4), 459-467.

Read, K. E. (1980). *Other voices: The style of a male homosexual tavern.* Novato, CA: Chandler & Sharp.

Reinhardt, R. U. (1985). Bisexual women in heterosexual relationships: A study of psychological and sociological patterns (Doctoral dissertation, The Professional School of Psychological Studies, San Diego, 1985). *Research Abstracts International, 11*(3), 67.

Reinisch, J. M., Ziemba-Davis, M., & Sanders, S. A. (1990). In B. Voeller, J. M. Reinisch, & M. Gottlieb (Eds.), *AIDS and sex: An integrated biomedical and biobehavioral approach* (pp. 37-80). New York: Oxford University Press.

Reiss, A. J. (1961). The social integration of queers and peers. *Social Problems, 9*, 102-120.

Ritvo, L. B. (1990). *Darwin's influence on Freud: A tale of two sciences.* New Haven, CT: Yale University Press.

Rogers, S. M., & Turner, C. F. (1991). Male-male sexual contact in the U.S.A.: Findings from five sample surveys, 1970-1990. *Journal of Sex Research, 28*(4), 491-519.

Roscoe, W. (1987). Bibliography of berdache and alternative gender roles among North American Indians. *Journal of Homosexuality, 14*(3/4), 81-171.

Roscoe, W. (Ed.). (1988). *Living the spirit: A gay American Indian anthology.* New York: St. Martin's.

Rose, S., Stevens, C., Parr, Z., Gollain, F., Behr, A., Cano, K. Wilson, V., Chapman, G., & Sands, D. (Eds.). (1996). *Bisexual horizons: Politics, histories, lives.* London: Lawrence & Wishart.

Ross, H. L. (1971). Modes of adjustment of married homosexuals. *Social Problems, 18*, 385-393.

Ross, M. W. (1983). *The married homosexual man: A psychological study.* London: Routledge & Kegan Paul.

Ross, M. W. (1991a). Bisexuality in Australia. In R. A. P. Tielman, M. Carballo, & A. C. Hendriks (Eds.), *Bisexuality and HIV/AIDS: A global perspective* (pp. 127-130). Buffalo, NY: Prometheus.

Ross, M. W. (1991b). A taxonomy of global behavior. In R. A. P. Tielman, M. Carballo, & A. C. Hendriks (Eds.), *Bisexuality and HIV/AIDS: A global perspective* (pp. 21-26). Buffalo, NY: Prometheus.

Ross, M. W., & Paul, J. P. (1992). Beyond gender: The basis of sexual attraction in bisexual men and women. *Psychological Reports, 71*, 1283-1290.

Ruan, Fang Fu. (1991). *Sex in China: Studies in sexology in Chinese culture.* New York: Plenum.

Rubenstein, M. (1982). *An in-depth study of bisexuality and its relationship to self-esteem.* Unpublished doctoral dissertation, Institute for Advanced Study of Human Sexuality, San Francisco.

Rubenstein, M., & Slater, C. A. (1985). A profile of the San Francisco Bisexual Center. *Journal of Homosexuality, 11*(1/2), 227-230.

Rust, P. C. (1992). The politics of sexual identity: Sexual attraction and behavior among lesbian and bisexual women. *Social Problems, 39*(4), 366-386.

Rust, P. C. (1993). "Coming out" in the age of social constructionism: Sexual identity formation among lesbian and bisexual women. *Gender and Society, 7*(1), 50-77.

Rust, P. C. (1995). *Bisexuality and the challenge to lesbian politics: Sex, loyalty and revolution.* New York: New York University Press.

Saghir, M. T., & Robins, E. (1973). *Male and female homosexuality: A comprehensive investigation.* Baltimore: Williams & Wilkins.

Sandfort, T. G. M. (1991). Bisexuality in the Netherlands: Some data from Dutch studies. In R. A. P. Tielman, M. Carballo, & A. C. Hendriks (Eds.), *Bisexuality and HIV/AIDS: A global perspective* (pp. 73-80). Buffalo, NY: Prometheus.

Schäfer, S. (1976). Sexual and social problems of lesbians. *Journal of Sex Research, 12*(1), 50-79.

Scott, J. (1978). *Wives who love women.* New York: Walker.

Sell, R. L., Wells, J. A., & Wypij, David. (1995). The prevalence of homosexual behavior and attraction in the United States, the United Kingdom and France: Results of national population-based samples. *Archives of Sexual Behavior, 24*(3), 235-248.

Sergent, B. (1984). *Homosexuality in Greek myth.* (A. Goldhammer, Trans.). Boston: Beacon.

Shively, M., & De Cecco, J. (1977). Components of sexual identity. *Journal of Homosexuality, 3*(1), 41-48.

Shively, M. G., Jones, C., & De Cecco, J. P. (1983/1984). Research on sexual orientation: Definitions and methods. *Journal of Homosexuality, 9*(2/3), 127-136.

Shuster, R. (1987). Sexuality as a continuum: The bisexual identity. In Boston Lesbian Psychologies Collective (Ed.), *Lesbian psychologies: Explorations and challenges* (pp. 56-71). Chicago: University of Illinois Press.

Sittitrai, W., Brown, T., & Virulrak, S. (1991). Patterns of bisexuality in Thailand. In R.A.P. Tielman, M. Carballo, & A. C. Hendriks (Eds.), *Bisexuality and HIV/AIDS: A global perspective* (pp. 97-118). Buffalo, NY: Prometheus.

Socarides, C. W. (1978). *Homosexuality.* New York: Jason Aronson.

Sommers, M. A. (1982). The relationship between present social support networks and current levels of interpersonal congruency of gay identity (Doctoral dissertation, California School of Professional Psychology, Los Angeles, 1982). *Dissertation Abstracts International, 43*(6), 1962B.

Sophie, J. (1985/1986). A critical examination of stage theories of lesbian identity development. *Journal of Homosexuality, 12*(2), 39-51.

Spada, J. (1979). *The Spada report: The newest survey of gay male sexuality.* New York: New American Library.

Spira, A., Bajos, N., & le Groupe ACSF. (1993). *Les comportements sexuels en France : Rapport au Ministre de la Recherche et de l'Espace.* Paris: La Documentation Française.

Stekel, W. (1946). *Bi-sexual love.* New York: Emerson Books. (Original work published 1922)

Stokes, J. P., McKirnan, D. J., & Burzette, R. G. (1993). Sexual behavior, condom use, disclosure of sexuality, and stability of sexual orientation in bisexual men. *Journal of Sex Research, 30*(3), 203-213.

Stoller, R. J. (1972). The 'bedrock' of masculinity and femininity: Bisexuality. *Archives of General Psychiatry, 26,* 207-212.

Storms, M. D. (1980). Theories of sexual orientation. *Journal of Personality and Social Psychology, 38*(5), 783-792.

Sulloway, F. J. (1979). *Freud, biologist of the mind: Beyond the psychoanalytic legend.* New York: Basic Books.

Szasz, T. S. (1965). Legal and moral aspects of homosexuality. In J. Marmor (Ed.), *Sexual inversion: The multiple roots of homosexuality* (pp. 124-139). New York: Basic Books.

Szasz, T. S. (1970). *The manufacture of madness: A comparative study of the inquisition and the mental health movement.* New York: Dell.

Tafoya, T. (1989). Pulling coyote's tale: Native American sexuality and AIDS. In V. M. Mays, G. W. Albee, & S. F. Schneider (Eds.), *Primary prevention of AIDS: Psychological approaches* (pp. 280-289). Newbury Park, CA, Sage.

Tielman, R. A. P., Carballo, M., & Hendriks, A. C. (Eds.). (1991a). *Bisexuality and HIV/AIDS: A global perspective.* Buffalo, NY: Prometheus.

Tielman, R. A. P., Carballo, M., & Hendriks, A. C. (1991b). Introduction. In R. A. P. Tielman, M. Carballo, & A. C. Hendriks (Eds.), *Bisexuality and HIV/AIDS: A global perspective* (pp. 27-40). Buffalo, NY: Prometheus.

Troiden, R. R. (1979). Becoming homosexual: A model of gay identity acquisition. *Psychiatry, 42,* 362-373.

Troiden, R. R. (1988). *Gay and lesbian identity: A sociological analysis.* Dix Hills, NY: General Hall.

Troiden, R. R., & Goode, E. (1980). Variables related to the acquisition of a gay identity. *Journal of Homosexuality, 5*(4), 383-392.

Tucker, N. (Ed.). (1995). *Bisexual politics: Theories, queries, and visions.* New York: Harrington Park.

Twining, A. (1983). Bisexual women: Identity in adult development (Doctoral dissertation, Boston University School of Education, 1983). *Dissertation Abstracts International, 44*(5), 1340A.

Twitchell, J. (1974). Sexual liberality and personality: A pilot study. In J. R. Smith & L. G. Smith (Eds.), *Beyond monogamy: Recent studies of sexual alternatives in marriage* (pp. 230-245). Baltimore: Johns Hopkins University Press.

Vance, B. K. (1977). Female homosexuality: A social psychological examination of attitudinal and etiological characteristics of different groups (Doctoral dissertation, Oklahoma State University, 1977). *Dissertation Abstracts International, 39,* 451B.

Warren, C. A. B. (1974). *Identity and community in the gay world.* New York: John Wiley.

Watanabe, T., & Iwata, J. *The love of the Samurai: A thousand years of Japanese homosexuality.* (D. R. Roberts, Trans.). London: GMP.

Wayson, P. D. (1985). Personality variables in males as they relate to differences in sexual orientation. *Journal of Homosexuality, 11*(1/2), 63-74.

Weinberg, G. (1972). *Society and the healthy homosexual.* New York: St. Martin's.

Weinberg, M. S., & Williams, C. J. (1974). *Male homosexuals: Their problems and adaptations.* New York: Penguin Books.

Weinberg, M. S., Williams, C. J., & Pryor, D. W. (1994). *Dual attraction: Understanding bisexuality.* New York: Oxford University Press.

Weinberg, T. S. (1977). Becoming homosexual: Self-discovery, self-identity, and self-maintenance (Doctoral dissertation, University of Connecticut, 1977). *Dissertation Abstracts International, 38*(1), 506A.

Weininger, O. (1903/1908). *Sex and character.* New York: Heinemann & G. P. Putnam.

Weise, E. R. (1992). *Closer to home: Bisexuality and feminism.* Seattle: Seal Press.

Wellings, K., Wadsworth, J., & Johnson, A. (1994). Sexual diversity and homosexual behaviour. In A. M. Johnson, J. Wadsworth, K. Wellings, & J. Field, *Sexual attitudes and lifestyles* (pp. 183-224). Oxford: Blackwell Scientific.

Whitehead, H. (1984). The bow and the burden strap: A new look at institutionalized homosexuality in native North America. In S. B. Ortner & H. Whitehead (Eds.), *Sexual meanings: The cultural construction of gender and sexuality* (pp. 80-115). Cambridge, UK: Cambridge University Press.

Whitney, C. (1990). *Uncommon lives: Gay men and straight women.* New York: Plume Books.

Williams, W. L. (1992). *The spirit and the flesh: Sexual diversity in American Indian culture.* Boston: Beacon.

Wolf, D. G. (1979). *The lesbian community.* Berkeley: University of California Press.

Wolf, T. J. (1985). Marriages of bisexual men. *Journal of Homosexuality, 11*(1/2), 135-148.

Wolf, T. J. (1987). Group counseling for bisexual men. *Journal for Specialists in Group Work, 11*, 162-165.

Wolf, T. J. (1992). Bisexuality: A counseling perspective. In S. H. Dworkin & F. J. Gutierrez (Eds.), *Counseling gay men and Lesbians: Journey to the end of the rainbow* (pp. 175-187). Alexandria, VA: American Association for Counseling and Development.

Wolff, C. (1971). *Love between women.* New York: St. Martin's.

Wolff, C. (1979). *Bisexuality: A study.* London: Quarter Books.

Wooden, W., & Parker, J. (1982). *Men behind bars: Sexual exploitation in prison.* New York: Plenum.

Zinik, G. A. (1984). The relationship between sexual orientation and eroticism, cognitive flexibility, and negative affect. (Doctoral dissertation, University of California, Santa Barbara, 1983). *Dissertation Abstracts International, 45*(8), 2707B.

8

Lesbians, Gays, and Family Psychology

Resources for Teaching and Practice

ROBERT-JAY GREEN

Having participated in and led various kinds of diversity training on the topics of race relations, gender, and sexual orientation (Green, 1998a, b, c), I believe that five overlapping elements are important for learning to work with a given minority group: (1) *sensitization*, developing a comfortable awareness of "not knowing every- thing" and an enthusiasm for learning more; (2) *didactic training*, acquiring information through lectures and readings; (3) *personal contact*, reducing phobic and prejudicial responses through cooperative interactions with members of the cultural group; (4) *supervised clinical experience*, acquiring intervention skills that are culturally-attuned, under the guidance of professionals who specialize in working with members of the cultural group; and (5) *seeking consultation*, developing the self-awareness and comfort to seek future case-consultation from such experts.

In this chapter, I describe resources for facilitating the first three of these training components (sensitization, didactic training, and per-

AUTHOR'S NOTE: This chapter is a revised and expanded version of Green, R.-J. (1996). Why ask, why tell? Teaching and learning about lesbians and gays in family therapy. Reprinted with permission from Vol. 35:1996, 389-400. *Family Process.* © 1996, *Family Process.*

sonal contact), with an emphasis on learning to work with lesbians/gays in couples and families. These materials originally were developed for a family psychology doctoral-level course, but the interview questions and treatment planning guidelines are geared for practicing therapists as well. Instructors can use these materials to create modules or short workshops on lesbian/gay issues in couples therapy, family therapy, cultural diversity, human sexuality, or human development. Most of the videotapes I recommend can be used in talks given to nonprofessionals. Before presenting these teaching and practice resources, however, I describe the status of lesbian/gay/bisexual issues in the field of family psychology and demonstrate why training in these issues has become so crucial.

Lesbians, Gay Men, and the Field of Family Psychology

The *official* U.S. government policy on lesbians and gays in the armed forces ("Don't ask, don't tell") now parallels what has been, historically, the *unofficial* policy in many families and in the field of family psychology: "Don't ask, don't tell, don't teach much about it, don't write about it!"

During the years 1990-1995, of the 718 articles submitted for publication to the *Journal of Marital & Family Therapy* (Sprenkle & Bailey, 1995), only 7 (or approximately 1%) were on the topic of homosexuality. A similar picture emerged in terms of manuscripts submitted to *Family Process* during this period.

Given the overall rejection rates for all types of manuscripts, the result is that only a minuscule number of articles on lesbians and gays has ever been published in these two leading family therapy journals (Laird & Green, 1996a). Not only is there a dearth of articles explicitly addressing this theme, but even books and articles on other popular subjects in the field of family psychology (for example, couples therapy, eating disorders, substance abuse, depression, stepfamilies) almost never use case examples with lesbian or gay family members.

I believe the low visibility of this topic in print has lead to the false impression that family psychologists and other family therapists rarely see lesbian and gay clients in their practices. Therefore, it is important to examine two growing myths. One is the idea that heterosexual family therapists seldom work with lesbian and gay clients. The second is the related idea that such clients almost exclusively seek the services of lesbian and gay mental health professionals.

Recently, S. K. Green and M. Bobele (1994) surveyed a random sample of clinical members (454 therapists) of the American Association for Marriage & Family Therapy (AAMFT), the vast majority of whom presumably are heterosexual. Among their current caseloads, "72% . . . of these family therapists reported that approximately one tenth of their practice involved gays and/or lesbians . . ." (p. 357). If we estimate the average family therapist's caseload at 20 clients per week, then these therapists are seeing two cases every week that involve gays or lesbians. Another 8% of the AAMFT sample reported that some proportion of their current caseload (but less than one tenth) involved lesbian and gay clients. Most likely, these findings are underestimates in that some lesbian, gay, and bisexual clients (particularly adolescents, married persons, some parents who fear loss of child custody, and elderly clients who grew up in more repressive times) never reveal their homosexual or bisexual orientations to their therapists.

Although many lesbians and gay men prefer to see openly lesbian and gay therapists, such matching does not feel essential to a plurality of these clients. In a survey of 128 lesbian or gay male individuals who were currently in couple relationships, 47% stated that a therapist's sexual orientation would *not* be a factor in their selection of whom to see for couple problems, and 40% would prefer seeing a lesbian or gay professional (Modrcin & Wyers, 1990). Among lesbians and gays who had sought therapy for couple problems in the past, 41% never knew the sexual orientations of their therapists.

Openly lesbian and gay couples seem to be more willing to participate in therapy than are heterosexual couples. In various large national surveys, about half (44% to 54%) of the lesbian respondents and about one third (27% to 32%) of gay male respondents indicate that they had sought professional help for couple problems (Bradford, Ryan, & Rothblum, 1994; Bryant & Demian, 1994; Modrcin & Wyers, 1990). When asked whether they would seek therapy in the future if they had a serious relationship difficulty, 86% of lesbians and 60% of gay men who were currently in couple relationships answered unequivocally "yes" (Modrcin & Wyers, 1990). More than half of these respondents (53%) said they would prefer couple over individual therapy.

Taken together, findings from the various surveys indicate clearly that most family therapists during their careers—whether they are heterosexual, bisexual, lesbian, or gay—will be working with substantial numbers of lesbian and gay clients. Given that most family therapists are heterosexual, one wonders why so very little has been written about cross-cultural issues for straight therapists working with lesbian and gay couples and families (for a notable exception, see Siegel & Walker, 1996). Or why so little has been written on how family therapy teachers and supervisors can prepare trainees, and themselves, for this work. Most disturbing, in light of the practice patterns detailed above, is that Doherty and Simmons (1996) recently found that almost half of all family therapists in the AAMFT reported that they do *not* feel competent treating lesbians or gay men. Clearly, there is an urgent need for more training on lesbian and gay issues in the field of family psychology and family therapy. Extrapolating from the above surveys, it seems that many professionals are working with lesbian and gay couples and families even though they do not feel competent doing so. Therefore, in what follows, I describe some resources for teaching and learning about lesbians and gays in couples and families.

Readings

Instructors and students first need a basic introduction to the lives of lesbian and gay people in families, couples, and family therapy. Until very recently, there was no adequate collection of readings in this area. In an attempt to fill this void, Joan Laird and I edited a new volume, *Lesbians and Gays in Couples and Families: A Handbook for Therapists* (Laird & Green, 1996b). This book was designed to provide family therapists with a fairly comprehensive overview of lesbian and gay therapy issues in five domains: (1) family of origin relationships; (2) couple relationships; (3) lesbian and gay parents and their children; (4) the social contexts of lesbian and gay families; and (5) their therapists. The book also contains chapters specifically focused on ethnic minority issues, including African American lesbians (Greene & Boyd-Franklin, 1996); Asian American lesbians, gays, and bisexuals (Liu & Chan, 1996); and Latino gay/bisexual men (Morales, 1996).

Because the literature on lesbian and gay issues is vast and growing rapidly, I have listed in Appendix A (by topics) some selected readings that are most up-to-date, comprehensive, and relevant to family therapists.

There also are many excellent books on coming out and parenting that can be used for bibliotherapy with lesbian and gay clients and their family members (Borhek, 1993; Clark, 1987; Fairchild & Hayward, 1989; Martin, 1993; Siegel & Lowe, 1994). An annotated bibliography of self-help readings and a list of local support groups for all family members is available from Parents, Families, and Friends of Lesbians and Gays (PFLAG, 1996). A new magazine edited by Laura Markowitz, *In the Family,* is an excellent source of personal essays on lesbian and gay family life.[1] A fun and challenging way to teach heterosexual students about lesbian and gay stereotypes is to use Rochlin's (1992) "The Heterosexual Questionnaire" (a one-page parody of myths about lesbians and gay men), having classmates pair-off and interview each other using Rochlin's questions.

Videotapes

For the majority of students—who have had little or no personal contact with lesbian and gay people—videotapes are absolutely essential for conveying the texture of family life. Although instructors can automatically assume that students are familiar with the lives of ordinary, well-functioning *heterosexual* families, the same assumption cannot be made about students' familiarity with ordinary lesbians and gays in families. As one might imagine, if students' only lifetime exposure to heterosexuals occurred through viewing tapes of dysfunctional families in treatment, then students would develop a rather negatively skewed image of the "heterosexual lifestyle."

Therefore, it is crucial for instructors to show some videos of *ordinary/nonclinical* lesbian and gay couples and families, rather than only tapes of lesbians and gays in treatment. Nontherapy videotapes that I have screened with much positive feedback from students are listed by topical area in Appendix B at the end of this chapter.

If instructors have time and resources to order only one videotape, I highly recommend the documentary *Gay Youth* (Walton, 1992) for its insightful treatment of coming-out, parental support versus rejection, peer harassment at school, and suicidality among lesbian and gay youths from various ethnic groups. Regarding youth suicide, Gibson (1993) presented harrowing evidence that lesbian and gay youths are two to three times more likely to attempt suicide than heterosexual youths and that *lesbian and gay youths comprise 30% of all completed youth suicides* (see also Savin-Williams, 1994, 1996). This elevated suicide rate is a consequence of disapproval from families, peers, and teachers, and of the youths' internalization of society's prejudice ("internalized homophobia," a form of self-hatred).

In this context, the governor of Massachusetts and the state's Board of Education endorsed an exemplary set of guidelines for *Making Schools Safe for Gay and Lesbian Youth* (Governor's Commission on Gay and Lesbian Youth, 1993). These guidelines include:

1. Developing policies to protect students from harassment, violence, and discrimination
2. Offering training to school personnel in violence and suicide prevention
3. Offering school-based support groups on lesbian and gay issues for all students and for the formation of "gay/heterosexual student alliances"
4. Providing school-based counseling for family members of lesbian and gay students

Similar programs are starting up in other localities and in some private high schools (Woog, 1995).

The videotape *Gay Youth* (Walton, 1992) does a superb job of educating professionals about the relevant issues for adolescents and young adults. Lesbian/gay-affirmative community presentations, consultation to high schools, and support groups for lesbian and gay youths and their families have the potential to save many lives. Trainees can participate as co-leaders and co-facilitators in such community outreach projects.

Personal Contact: Interviews

The research on homophobia (antigay prejudice) shows that heterosexuals who have more contact with lesbians and gay men express more positive attitudes toward these groups (Herek, 1994). For example, in research on family therapists' attitudes, less prejudice is related to more personal contact with lesbians and gays either as clients, friends, or relatives (Green & Bobele, 1994). Thus, it seems likely that greater contact between heterosexual trainees and lesbian and gay people (especially if it is positive in tone and requires a cooperative effort toward shared goals) leads to a reduction in trainees' homophobia.

The obvious implication of these findings is that training programs should increase opportunities for positive, cooperative contact between heterosexual students and lesbian and gay people both within and outside the therapy context. This requires making sure that lesbian and gay instructors and students are admitted into the program and creating a safe environment for their open participation. In the field of family therapy training, the Commission on Accreditation for Marriage & Family Therapy Education finally voted (in November 1995) to add sexual orientation to its antidiscrimination clause. Strict enforcement of this standard will help ensure that lesbian and gay students and faculty members are protected against the most blatant forms of discrimination in admissions, hiring, retention, evaluation, and promotion. However, no amount of legislation can protect lesbians and gays from the more subtle bigotry and ignorance that sometimes appear. Personal contact and education are the only routes to countering prejudicial attitudes.

As a way to increase students' comfort with and knowledge about lesbians and gays in families, I have assigned students in my classes the task of interviewing ordinary (nonclient) lesbian and gay individuals and couples from the community. The complete interviewing instructions are presented in Appendix C at the end of this chapter. Note that the interview topics and most of the questions in Appendix C can be used by experienced therapists also, as a framework for exploring the couple and family issues of lesbian and gay clients in treatment.

In terms of students' learning on both an affective and cognitive level, this interview assignment has proven to be uniformly positive and ranks as the single most enlightening and rewarding learning activity. For some heterosexual students, it is their first sustained personal contact with an openly lesbian or gay person and provides at least minimal preparation for later seeing lesbian and gay clients in therapy. Even for lesbian and gay students with years of such contact, the interviews provide an unusual opportunity to reflect on commonalities and diversity within the community.

In the San Francisco Bay Area where I teach, every student has been able to locate an interviewee on their own. In smaller or more conservative communities, it may be necessary for the instructor to visit a local lesbian and gay organization to ask for volunteer interviewees and to prepare volunteers for the possible naiveté, of the therapists-in-training.

Treatment Planning

For an in-class exercise and/or an exam on treatment planning, I have used the "Family Treatment Plan" presented in Appendix D. For this assignment, the instructor shows any of the commercial videotapes listed in Appendix B that depict couples or families undergoing intense conflict over discovery/disclosure of a family member's lesbian or gay identity. Alternatively, instructors can use videos of actual therapy sessions with lesbian and gay family members or couples. After viewing the tape, students are asked to write (in class) a treatment plan based on the case material they have just seen. This can be followed by class discussion of students' responses, or if used as an exam, the instructor can provide written comments and evaluations of each student's treatment plan. In addition, practicing professionals may use this framework for developing actual treatment plans for their cases.

Conclusion

The study of lesbian and gay couple and family relationships provides new perspectives on heterosexual family patterns and challenges the universality of many assumptions built into family systems theories. Research on this topic also highlights the need for a "multiplex gender theory" to replace dichotomous thinking about supposedly invariant male and female gender roles across all social classes and ethnic/racial groups (Green, Bettinger, & Zacks, 1996). Lesbians, gay men, and heterosexual women and men live in partially overlapping but partially separate cultures, and their gender role development often follows distinctive trajectories culminating in unique patterns of couple and family relationships. In the past, this nonconformity of lesbians and gay men has been used to pathologize them or to exclude them from consideration as bona fide family members, as if lesbians and gays live a "nonfamily lifestyle" or an "antifamily lifestyle" simply because their couple relationships do not follow the traditional gender prescriptions.

In this vein, not very long ago, I witnessed one of the leading national figures in the field of family therapy taunt the "father" in a family role-play by sarcastically and derisively asking him if he was "a queer" and then asking the adolescent son and daughter in the role-play whether they thought their father might be "a queer" because he was not "standing up" to their mother. I happened to be role-playing the part of the son, and I argued (in role) with the therapist over these remarks.

In the discussion period afterward, several audience members commented that they were quite moved that the son stood up for his father so vehemently, "modeling" for father "how to be a man." Everyone who spoke was very complimentary toward the therapist. Nobody in this audience of over 300 people commented on the therapist's implied contempt toward gay people, or his use of the word "queer" as an epithet to shame the parents into conforming to a traditional gender hierarchy.

Did anybody else perceive the antigay hostility in the therapist's behavior? Did anyone consider that the adolescent son (or the person role-playing the son) was gay? Were all 300 of these family therapists too intimidated by the leader's reputation to comment publicly on his behavior? Were they afraid of being perceived as "impolite" or labeled "queer" for even raising the issue? Did their muteness under such circumstances tacitly encourage other family therapists in the audience to make antigay comments in therapy?

Don't ask, don't tell ... In a culture with widespread antipathy toward lesbian and gay relationships, what messages do silence, "neutrality," and omission of lesbian and gay family topics convey to students in our classes, workshops, and supervision groups?

Appendix A: Some Recommended Readings on Lesbian and Gay Issues

1. Families and Couples—*Lesbians and Gays in Couples and Families: A Handbook for Therapists* (Laird & Green, 1996b); and the chapter on "Lesbian and Gay Families" in *Normal Family Processes* (2nd ed.) (Laird, 1993).
2. Lifespan Developmental Psychology—*Lesbian, Gay, and Bisexual Identities over the Lifespan: Psychological Perspectives* (D'Augelli & Patterson, 1995); *The Lives of Lesbians, Gays, and Bisexuals: Children to Adults* (Savin-Williams & Cohen, 1996).
3. Clinical, Personality, and Social Psychology—*Homosexuality: Research Implications for Public Policy* (Gonsiorek & Weinrich, 1991); and *Lesbian and Gay Psychology: Theory, Research, and Clinical Applications* (Greene & Herek, 1994).
4. Lesbians/Gays/Bisexuals of Color—*Ethnic and Cultural Diversity Among Lesbians and Gay Men* (Greene, 1997); chapters by Greene and Boyd-Franklin (1996), Liu and Chan (1996), and Morales (1996) in *Lesbians and Gays in Couples and Families: A Handbook for*

Therapists; The Spirit and the Flesh: Sexual Diversity in American Indian Culture (Williams, 1986/1992).

5. AIDS and Gay Men—*In the Midst of Winter: Counseling Families, Couples, and Individuals with AIDS Infection* (Walker, 1995).

6. Recent Empirical Research—special issues of the journals *Developmental Psychology* (Patterson, 1995); and *Journal of Consulting & Clinical Psychology* (Rothblum, 1994).

7. Cultural Anthropology—*Families We Choose: Lesbians, Gays, Kinship* (Weston, 1991); *Gay Culture in America: Essays from the Field* (Herdt, 1992); *The Spirit and the Flesh: Sexual Diversity in American Indian Culture* (Williams, 1986/1992).

Appendix B: Lesbian/Gay/Bisexual Family Topics and Related Videotapes for Teaching

For documentaries, complete ordering information appears in the reference list to this chapter. Commercial videos are listed below without reference information as these can be obtained through local video stores.

1. Lesbian and Gay Youths—*Gay youth* (Walton, 1992); *From a secret place* (Heller, 1993); *Homoteens* (Jubela, 1993).

2. Initial Coming Out and Family Conflict—*Oranges are not the only fruit; Doing time on Maple Drive; Consenting adult.*

3. Parents' Long-Term Coping With a Son or Daughter's Coming Out—*Parents come out* (Cooper, 1985); *Straight from the heart* (Mosbacher & Reid, 1994); *Coming out, coming home: Asian American and Pacific Islander family stories* (Hima, 1995); *Family values: An American tragedy* (Walton, 1996).

4. Transitions of a Heterosexually Married Couple as the Husband Comes Out—*Making love.*

5. Lesbian Couples—*Serving in silence: The Margarethe Cammermeyer story* (1995 NBC movie); *The incredibly true adventure of two girls in love.*

6. Gay Male Couples—*The wedding banquet;* segments on gay male couples in *For better or worse: Five long-term couples* (Collier, 1993).

7. Lesbian and Gay Parents—*Not all parents are straight* (White & Faro, 1986).

8. Children of Lesbian and Gay Parents—*Both of my moms' names are Judy* (Lesbian & Gay Parents Association, 1994).

9. Ethnic Minority Lesbians and Gays—*Coming out, coming home: Asian American and Pacific Islander family stories* (Hima, 1995); *Psychotherapy with gay & lesbian clients: Program 4-Diversity* (Buendía Productions, 1995); *Homoteens* (Jubela, 1993); *The wedding banquet* (interracial Chinese/White male couple, dealing with family of origin issues).

10. Older Lesbians and Gays—*Silent pioneers: Gay and lesbian elders* (Snyder, Winer, & Marks, 1984).

11. AIDS and Gay Male Couples—*Silverlake life: The view from here; Longtime companion; Philadelphia.*
12. Legal Issues for Lesbian and Gay Couples—*Lifetime commitment: A portrait of Karen Thompson* (Zeldes, 1987).

Appendix C
Family-Oriented Interviews
of Lesbians and Gay Men

Instructions

Your task is to interview a lesbian or gay male couple or an individual (over age 18) around the topic "lesbian and gay couple and family relationships." In a subsequent class meeting, you will be discussing with your classmates the results of your interview.

The interviews should last 1 to 2 hours each. Specific interview questions could cover the topics below, but you should freely edit or omit certain questions to fit the circumstances, language, and comfort level of both the person(s) you are interviewing and yourself.

Do *not* enlist interviewees from among your clients or from colleagues' clients. Choose friends, friends of friends, acquaintances, neighbors, relatives, etc. All interviewees must sign two copies of the "Consent Form to Be Interviewed for a Graduate Psychology Class," and one copy is for them to keep. You should inform the interviewee that you are doing this interview as an assignment for a lesbian/gay-affirmative graduate class on family and couple relationships. Inform them that your course instructor's name, phone number, and address appear on the consent form in case they have any questions or concerns later. You must inform the interviewees in advance that they may freely decline to participate and can decline to answer any question or topic during the interview. Also inform the interviewees that their names and other identifying information (such as occupation) will be omitted or disguised in your summary for the class discussion.

With the interviewees' permission, you may take notes during the interview so that you can recall what was said and summarize it for purposes of discussion in class. Keep in mind that you are not doing "therapy" or "formal research" in these interviews, but are simply gathering some information for a class assignment. You can ask simple clarifying questions in order to understand the overt content of the interviewee's first response to your questions, but do *not* probe for "unconscious" or unspoken feelings beyond the overt content that the interviewee spontaneously offers. Also, do *not* give interpretations, analysis, or commentary on the material. You are there to learn, not teach or do therapy. Just try to get the story from the interviewees' perspectives and in their own words.

Interview Topics and Questions

Families of Origin

1. When did you first become aware that you might be lesbian or gay?
2. How do you think this "differentness" may have affected your relationships with family members as you were growing up?
3. If you have *not* come out to certain family members, what factors led to this decision?
4. If you have come out to certain family members, describe the process, including what preceded, happened during, and has followed the disclosure up to the present time?

Lesbian and Gay Couple Relationships

1. How do you define being "a couple" (what does it mean to you that you are a "couple")?
2. What has been the history of your becoming a couple?
3. How did your becoming a couple affect your relationships with other family members, friends, the lesbian/gay community, and the straight community?
4. Using your own experience as an example, how do you think lesbian/gay couple relationships are similar to and different from heterosexual couple relationships?
5. What are the challenges that lesbian and gay couples face in a predominantly heterosexual and homophobic society, and how have you dealt with these challenges?

Lesbian and Gay Parents

1. What has been the history of your becoming a parent?
2. If your children did not always know you were lesbian or gay, how did you handle coming out to them? How have they reacted?

3. How has being a lesbian/gay parent affected your relationships with former or current partners (if any), with family members, friends, the lesbian/gay community, and the straight community?

4. Using your own experience as an example, what are the challenges that lesbian/gay *parents* face in a predominantly heterosexual and homophobic society?

5. What are the challenges that *children* of lesbian/gay parents face in a predominantly heterosexual and homophobic society?

6. How does your child relate with you (and your partner, if any) on the issue of having a lesbian/gay parent(s)?

7. How does your child deal with her/his friends, teachers, and others around the issue of your being lesbian/gay?

8. Based on your experience, how can lesbian/gay parents prepare or help children deal with these challenges?

Families of Choice

1. Who are the people in your closest social support network (including relatives, friends, coworkers, neighbors, etc.)?

2. How closely do the people in this network relate to one another?

3. Describe the activities and any "rituals" (birthdays, holidays, couple anniversaries, regular get-togethers for meals) that you participate in with your closest network members.

4. What sorts of mutual emotional support and practical assistance do you and these persons provide for each other?

5. Some lesbian and gay people consider their closest friends to be "family," and some authors have used the term "families of choice" to describe these relationships. Does this term fit your experience with your closest friends, that they have become a "family"?

Advice to Professionals

1. What do you think therapists most need to keep in mind when trying to understand and help lesbians and gay men in couples and families?

2. Are there new kinds of support groups, counseling services, or community organizations that you think need to be developed to help lesbian and gay couples and families?

Appendix D: Treatment Planning Guidelines

This exercise is based on the videotape shown in class. You should follow the outline below exactly, using the outline format to organize your answers. After the videotape is shown, you will have approximately one hour to write your answers. Print or write clearly, every other line.

A. Clinical Hypotheses (formulation)

List hypotheses that describe the possible relationship between the presenting problem(s) and characteristics of the client's significant interpersonal systems (including family, friends, community).

- Hypothesis #1: . . . .
- Hypothesis #2: . . . .
- Hypothesis #3: . . . .
- Etc.

B. Goals

What goals would you set for the client? Give behavioral examples of the kinds of things the client would be *doing or saying differently at the end of treatment* so that you would know whether each of your stated goals had been reached. Use the following format to answer this question:

- Goal statement #1: . . . .
  Behavioral examples: . . . .

- Goal statement #2: . . . .
  Behavioral examples: . . . .

- Goal statement #3: . . . .
  Behavioral examples: . . . .

C. Structure of Treatment

- Would you include other significant system members in sessions? If so, who and when? Give rationale.

- How frequently would you schedule sessions, and how long do you think therapy would last?
- Would you use any "adjunctive" treatments or referrals (e.g., hospitalization; vocational testing; medication; addiction treatment programs such as AA, NA, OA, Al-Anon; therapeutic, psychoeducational, or support groups; lesbian/gay/bisexual/ transgender community organizations; etc.)? Give rationale for each referral.

D. Therapeutic Relationship

- How would you expect this client to relate to you (e.g., cooperation, open defiance, passive resistance, excessive dependency, aggression, avoidance, denial, control, intellectualization, humor as resistance, other forms of resistance, etc.)?
- How would you expect to feel and relate to this client? How would you go about joining with this client? Use of self? Any difficulties you anticipate around taking sides in family conflicts, getting frustrated, maintaining the therapeutic frame, setting limits, forming a therapeutic alliance, "countertransference," cultural ethnocentrism.

E. Specific Interventions and Rationale

Based on the ideas presented in this course, *write exactly what you might say and/or do with this client (as if you were writing a script for a play)* to attain each of the goals you established in item B above. You may use techniques from any therapy approach if they are consistent with and would facilitate reaching your stated goals. Use the following format:

- Techniques for reaching goal #1: . . . .
- Techniques for reaching goal #2: . . . .
- Techniques for reaching goal #3: . . . .
- Etc.

Note

1. *In the Family* is published by Family Magazine, Inc., PO Box 5387, Takoma Park, MD 20913 (Tel. 301-270-4771).

References

Borhek, M. V. (1993). *Coming out to parents: A two-way survival guide for lesbians and gay men and their parents* (2nd ed.). Cleveland, OH: Pilgrim.

Bradford, J., Ryan, C., & Rothblum, E. D. (1994). National lesbian health care survey: Implications for mental health care. *Journal of Consulting & Clinical Psychology, 62,* 228-242.

Bryant, A. S., & Demian. (1994). Relationship characteristics of American gay and lesbian couples: Findings from a national survey. *Journal of Gay & Lesbian Social Services, 1,* 101-117.

Buendía Productions (1995). *Psychotherapy with gay & lesbian clients: Program 4—Diversity* [Videotape]. (Available from Buendía Productions, PO Box 1896, Santa Ana, CA 92702, Tel. 800- 513-1092)

Clark, D. K. (1987). *Loving someone gay* (2nd ed.). Berkeley, CA: Celestial Arts.

Collier, D. (Director). (1993). *For better or for worse: Five long-term couples* [Videotape]. (Available from Videofinders, Public Broadcasting Corporation, New York; Tel: 800-842-2298)

Cooper, A. (Director). (1985). *Parents come out* [Videotape]. (Available from Parents, Families, and Friends of Lesbians and Gays—PFLAG, 1101 14th St., NW, Suite 1030, Washington, DC, 20005- 3406; Tel: 202-638-4200, Fax 202-638-0243, E-mail: pflagntl@aol.com, http://www.pflag.org)

D'Augelli, A. R., & Patterson, C. J. (Eds.). (1995). *Lesbian, gay, and bisexual identities over the lifespan: Psychological perspectives.* New York: Oxford University Press.

Doherty, W. J., & Simmons, D. S. (1996). Clinical practice patterns of marriage and family therapists: A national survey of therapists and their clients. *Journal of Marital & Family Therapy, 22,* 9-25.

Fairchild, B., & Hayward, N. (1989). *Now that you know: What every parent should know about homosexuality.* San Diego, CA: Harcourt Brace Jovanovich.

Gibson, P. (1989). Gay male and lesbian youth suicide. In *Report of the Secretary's Task Force on Youth Suicide: Vol. 3. Prevention and interventions in youth suicide.* Rockville, MD: U.S. Department of Health & Human Services.

Gonsiorek, J. C., & Weinrich, J. D. (Eds.). (1991). *Homosexuality: Research implications for public policy.* Newbury Park, CA: Sage.

Governor's Commission on Gay and Lesbian Youth. (1993). *Making schools safe for gay and lesbian youth: Breaking the silence in schools and in families* (Publication No. 17296-60-500-2/93-C.R). [Available from Commonwealth of Massachusetts, State House, Room 111, Boston, MA 02133; Tel: 617-727- 3600, ext. 312]

Green, R.-J. (1998a). Race and the field of family therapy. In M. McGoldrick (Ed.), *Revisioning family therapy: Multicultural systems theory and practice* (pp. 93-110). New York: Guilford.

Green, R.-J. (1998b). Training programs: Guidelines for multicultural transformation. In M. McGoldrick (Ed.), *Revisioning family therapy: Multicultural systems theory and practice* (pp. 111-117). New York: Guilford.

Green, R.-J. (1998c). Traditional norms of masculinity. *Journal of Feminist Family Therapy, 10,* 81-83.

Green, R.-J., Bettinger, M., & Zacks, E. (1996). Are lesbian couples fused and gay male couples disengaged?: Questioning gender straightjackets. In J. Laird & R.-J. Green (Eds.), *Lesbians and gays in couples and families: A handbook for therapists* (pp. 185-230). San Francisco: Jossey-Bass.

Green, S. K., & Bobele, M. (1994). Family therapists' response to AIDS: An examination of attitudes, knowledge, and contact. *Journal of Marital & Family Therapy, 20,* 349-367.

Greene, B. (Ed.). (1997). *Ethnic and cultural diversity among lesbians and gay men.* Thousand Oaks, CA: Sage.

Greene, B., & Boyd-Franklin, N. (1996). African American lesbians: Issues in couples therapy. In J. Laird & R.-J. Green (Eds.), *Lesbians and gays in couples and families: A handbook for therapists* (pp. 251-271). San Francisco: Jossey-Bass.

Greene, B., & Herek, G. (Eds.). (1994). *Lesbian and gay psychology: Theory, research, and clinical applications.* Thousand Oaks, CA: Sage.

Heller, K. (Director). (1993). *From a secret place: America's families cope with the coming out process of gay and lesbian youth* [Videotape]. (Available from Guilford Publications, 72 Spring St., New York, NY 10012; Tel: 1-800-365-7006, Catalog #0264)

Herdt, G. (Ed.). (1992). *Gay culture in America: Essays from the field.* Boston: Beacon.

Herek, G. (1994). Assessing heterosexuals' attitudes toward lesbians and gay men: A review of empirical research with the ATLG Scale. In B. Greene & G. Herek (Eds.), *Lesbian and gay psychology: Theory, research, and clinical applications* (pp. 206-228). Thousand Oaks, CA: Sage.

Hima, B. (Director) & A/PI-PFLAG Family Project (Producer). (1995). *Coming out, coming home: Asian American and Pacific Islander family stories* [Videotape]. (Available from A/PI-PFLAG Family Project, PO Box 640223, San Francisco, CA 94164; Tel: 415-921-8859, ext. 2, E-mail: VisCamp@aol.com)

Jubela, J. (Director). (1993). *Homoteens* [Videotape]. (Available from Frameline Distribution, 346 Ninth St., San Francisco, CA 94103; Tel: 415-703-8654 or 415-703-8655, FAX 415-861-1404, E-mail: info@frameline.org, http://www.frameline.org)

Laird, J. (1993). Lesbian and gay families. In F. Walsh (Ed.), *Normal family processes* (2nd ed., pp. 282- 328). New York: Guilford.

Laird, J., & Green, R.-J. (1996a). Lesbians and gays in couple and family relationships: Central issues. In J. Laird & R.-J. Green (Eds.), *Lesbians and gays in couples and families: A handbook for therapists* (pp. 1-12). San Francisco: Jossey-Bass.

Laird, J., & Green, R.-J. (Eds.). (1996b). *Lesbians and gays in couples and families: A handbook for therapists.* San Francisco: Jossey-Bass.

Lesbian & Gay Parents Association (Producer). (1994). *Both of my mom's names are Judy* [Videotape]. (Available from Gay and Lesbian Parents Coalition International, Box 50360, Washington, DC, 20091; Tel: 202-583-8029)

Liu, P., & Chan, C. (1996). Lesbian, gay, and bisexual Asian Americans and their families. In J. Laird & R.-J. Green (Eds.), *Lesbians and gays in couples and families: A handbook for therapists* (pp. 137-152). San Francisco: Jossey-Bass.

Martin, A. (1993). *The lesbian and gay parenting handbook.* New York: HarperCollins.

Modrcin, M. J., & Wyers, N. L. (1990). Lesbian and gay couples: Where they turn when help is needed. *Journal of Gay & Lesbian Psychotherapy 1,* 89-104.

Morales, E. (1996). Gender roles among Latino gay/bisexual men: Implications for family and couple relationships. In J. Laird & R.-J. Green (Eds.), *Lesbians and gays in couples and families: A handbook for therapists* (pp. 272-297). San Francisco: Jossey-Bass.

Mosbacher, D., & Reid, F. (Directors). (1994). *Straight from the heart* [Videotape]. (Available from The Cinema Guild, 1697 Broadway, Suite 506, New York, NY, 10019-5904; Tel: 800-723-5522)

Patterson, C. J. (Ed.). (1995). Sexual orientation and human development [Special issue]. *Developmental Psychology, 31*(1).

PFLAG. (1996). *Recommended readings.* [Available free from Parents, Families, and Friends of Lesbians and Gays—PFLAG, 1101 14th St., NW, Suite 1030, Washington, DC, 20005-3406; Tel: 202-638-4200, Fax 202-638-0243, E-mail: pflagntl@aol.com, http:// www. pflag.org)

Rochlin, M. (1992). The heterosexual questionnaire. In M. S. Kimmel & M. A. Messner (Eds.), *Men's lives* (2nd ed., pp. 482-483). New York: Macmillan.

Rothblum, E. (Ed.). (1994). Mental health of lesbians and gay men [Special section]. *Journal of Consulting & Clinical Psychology, 62*(2), 211-261.

Savin-Williams, R. C. (1994). Verbal and physical abuse as stressors in the lives of lesbian, gay male, and bisexual youths: Associations with school problems, running away, substance abuse, prostitution, and suicide. *Journal of Consulting & Clinical Psychology, 62,* 261-269.

Savin-Williams, R. C. (1996). Self-labeling and disclosure among gay, lesbian, and bisexual youths. In J. Laird & R.-J. Green (Eds.), *Lesbians and gays in couples and families: A handbook for therapists* (pp. 153-182). San Francisco: Jossey-Bass.

Savin-Williams, R. C., & Cohen, K. M. (Eds.). (1996). *The lives of lesbians, gays, and bisexuals: Children to adults.* Fort Worth, TX: Harcourt Brace.

Siegel, S., & Lowe, E., Jr. (1994). *Uncharted lives: Understanding the life passages of gay men.* New York: Dutton.

Siegel, S., & Walker, G. (1996). Connections: Conversation between a straight therapist and a gay therapist. In J. Laird & R.-J. Green (Eds.), *Lesbians and gays in couples and families: A handbook for therapists* (pp. 28-68). San Francisco: Jossey-Bass.

Snyder, P., Winer, L., & Marks, H. (Directors/Producers). (1984). *Silent pioneers: Gay and lesbian elders* [Videotape]. (Available from The Filmmakers Library, 124 East 40th St., Suite 901, New York, NY 10016; Tel: 212-808-4980)

Sprenkle, D., & Bailey, C. E. (1995, October). *Journal of Marriage and Family Therapy Advisory Editor Newsletter, 6*(1).

Walker, G. (1995). *In the midst of winter: Counseling families, couples, and individuals with AIDS infection.* New York: Norton.

Walton, P. (Producer/Director). (1992). *Gay youth* [Videotape]. (Available for purchase by individuals and high schools from Pam Walton Productions, PO Box 391025, Mountain View, CA 94039; Tel. 415- 960-3414) (Available for rental or purchase by colleges and libraries from The Filmmakers Library, 124 East 40th St., Suite 901, New York, NY 10016; Tel: 212-808-4980)

Walton, P. (Producer/Director). (1996). *Family values: An American tragedy* [Videotape]. (Available from Pam Walton Productions, PO Box 391025, Mountain View, CA 94039; Tel: 415-960-3414)

Weston, K. (1991). *Families we choose: Lesbians, gays, kinship.* New York: Columbia University Press.

White, K, & Faro, A. (Producers). (1986). *Not all parents are straight* [Videotape]. (Available from The Cinema Guild, 1697 Broadway, Suite 506, New York, NY, 10019-5904; Tel: 800-723-5522)

Williams, W. L. (1992). *The spirit and the flesh: Sexual diversity in American Indian culture.* Boston: Beacon. (Original work published 1986)

Woog, D. (1995). *School's out: The impact of gay and lesbian issues on America's schools.* Boston: Alyson.

Zeldes, K. (Director), & Media Action (Producer). (1987). *Lifetime commitment: A portrait of Karen Thompson* [Videotape]. (Available from Women Make Movies, Inc., Distribution Service, 462 Broadway, Suite 500D, New York, NY 10013; Tel: 212-925-0606)

9

Lesbian, Gay, and Bisexual Adolescent Development

Dancing With Your Feet Tied Together

JOYCE HUNTER

GERALD P. MALLON

It is no longer fair to say that the mental health literature about lesbian, gay, and bisexual youth is sparse (Malyon, 1981; Needham, 1977; Remafedi, 1987a, 1987b) as the literature in recent years has grown exponentially (D'Augelli, 1996; DeCresenzo, 1994; Schneider, 1997). Published work however has focused almost exclusively on gay male youth. This leaves a paucity of material that addresses lesbian youth. There is also a conspicuous absence of any thorough discussions of bisexuality in adolescents. Research that focuses on the needs of youth of color, who are lesbian, gay, or bisexual is also absent from the literature.

This chapter addresses developmental issues facing lesbian, gay, and bisexual youth. It is based on our clinical work with these young people who are predominately youth of color and who have experienced multiple levels of societal oppressions. Using case examples, we discuss coming out as a parallel process to adolescent development, examining sexual orientation as one of the salient domains of personal identity.

Overview of Adolescent Development

The developmental period of adolescence is characterized by substantial physical growth, change, and sociocultural challenge. This period is replete with many demands for all youth. Most young people meet these challenges successfully. Physical changes are most prominent. These changes in both young males and females are distinguished by development of body hair and changes in voice, as well as newly acquired facial hair for boys and the beginning of menstruation in girls. This period also marks the beginning of sexual maturity and the establishment of a sense of autonomy. Adolescence is marked by the crucial developmental tasks that must be mastered before going on to the next stage of development (Erikson, 1959). Major tasks are the development of a sense of self and identity formation. With achievement in these areas comes emotional and cognitive development. With these changes, adolescence is unquestionably a critical span of time, which involves the negotiation of unique biological, psychological, and social demands (Hamburg, 1974). While this is a difficult period for all adolescents, it can be particularly difficult for youth who self-identify as lesbian, gay, or bisexual. What interferes most with the development of the lesbian, gay, or bisexual young person is that they often experience intense social isolation.

Heterosexual Assumptions

A widespread assumption has been held by many researchers and practitioners that all adolescents are heterosexual. For adolescents who are lesbian, gay, and bisexual, this assumption represents a major life stressor. The idea that an adolescent could identify as a lesbian, gay, or bisexual individual is inconceivable to many. Many researchers and sex educators take the position that adolescent homosexuality is just a passing phase. Savin-Williams suggests that position may reflect "uncertainty and confusion over the distinctions between sexual behavior and identity" (1995, p. 166). Although Blos (1979), Erikson (1959), Marcia (1980), and Newman and Newman's (1987) concepts of sex-role identification are concerned only with heterosexual development and presume heterosexual identity as an eventual outcome, they have also acknowledged that children and adolescents at times engage in a range same-sex sexual behaviors. Similarly, Malyon (1981) points out that same-sex sexual behavior alone does not predispose one toward a homosexual orientation.

Because heterosexist assumptions dominate the environment of the lesbian, gay, or bisexual adolescent and the majority of the construction of adolescent theory-building, it appears there is no acceptable way to achieve adulthood as defined by traditional theories and environmental expectations. Although lesbian, gay, and bisexual adolescents face all the familiar stressors of adolescence, they also face challenges that are unique to their status as stigmatized individuals in society. As such, adaptations are necessary to achieve a "goodness of fit" between the person and the environment. It is this dilemma that serves as the theoretical framework for understanding lesbian, gay, and bisexual adolescents in a developmental context.

Personal Identity Development

Many child psychologists and social scientists working with youth believe that the major psychosocial task of adolescence is the formation of a personal identity. The development of a satisfying sexual identity is a significant aspect of the adolescent maturation process. Kroger notes that a "sense of sexual identity, facilitated through finding meaningful forms of sexual expression and sex role behavior, provide a cornerstone for future styles of adult intimacy and generativity" (1993, p. 3).

There is almost no research that speaks to the sexual orientation domain of personal identity development (Hunter, 1996). Personal identity differs from social identity. Personal identity is associated with intrapsychic processes, whereas social identity refers to the roles expected by society (Hetrick & Martin, 1984). There is a closer integration between the personal and social identities for heterosexual people than for lesbians and gay men. The stigma attached to homosexuality often creates a conflict between the two identities (Hunter & Schaecher, 1995).

For lesbian, gay, and bisexual adolescents who are exploring their identity, two parallel processes are taking place at the same time—growing up and coming out (Schneider, 1989).

Coming Out Process

Coming out is a developmental process through which gay and lesbian people recognize their sexual orientation and incorporate this knowledge into their personal and social lives (Monteflores & Schultz, 1978). Several researchers and practitioners (Cass, 1979; Coleman, 1987 ; Kinsey, Pomeroy & Martin, 1948; Kinsey, Pomeroy, Martin & Gebhard, 1953; Minton & McDonald, 1984; Troiden, 1993) have conceptualized coming out within a developmental framework that unfolds in stages. In a recent work, Mallon (1998b) discusses one four-stage model, incorporating and elaborating on other previous models, as proposed by Troiden (1993). Troiden identifies the first stage as *sensitization*, which is characterized by a general feeling of being marginal and different from others. This stage is followed by *identity confusion*, in which individuals think that they might be gay or lesbian but are unable to decide. In the third stage, *identity assumption*, individuals can begin to identify themselves as gay or lesbian. The final stage, *commitment*, culminates in the development of positive feelings about being gay or lesbian as individuals begin to incorporate this identity into other social and personal arenas. Although stage models are useful in theoretically understanding a process, in fact, this process, like most other life processes, infrequently progresses in an orderly or invariable manner.

The importance of the coming out process is paramount in developing an understanding of gay and lesbian adolescents because as self-acceptance increases, so does the internal "goodness of fit" process that enhances one's capacity for disclosure to others (Olson & King, 1995).

Gay Youth Case Example

Hector is a 16-year-old, Latino male youth who lives at home with his parents and two younger sisters. As the oldest child and only son, Hector is frequently called upon to assume parental responsibilities for his younger sisters. His mother is employed in a local clothing store in their neighborhood; his father works for the telephone company. Both parents are very proud of their family, but especially of Hector who is an honor student and a "good son."

Hector has felt "different" from other boys since he was about 6 or 7, but during the past two or three years, Hector has realized that he is attracted to boys, not girls. He dated a couple of girls, but remarks, "Something was missing, we just didn't click." Unsure of how he identifies, Hector began questioning his sexual orientation. The thought that he might be gay did occur to him, but the thought itself terrifies him. He doesn't know any openly gay people, and he knows that he is not like the gay people that he sees in movies like *The Birdcage*. He is very careful about monitoring his behavior and feels as if he is always on guard.

Sometimes the pressure gets to him and he feels overwhelmed and depressed—"I couldn't be gay—it would be such a disappointment to my father, I am the only son in our family, it's up to me to carry on the family name and my mother is always talking about when she has grandchildren." He feels pressured about being the perfect son, unclear about his feelings for girls or boys, while attempting to grow up without the benefit of gay role models.

As illustrated by the case example above, growing up with the awareness that you are gay presents many challenges for an adolescent. Although there are many issues that could be identified from an analysis of the vignette above, two salient socialization features are illuminated for discussion herein: (1) the family issues that gay and lesbian youth must address and (2) the process of being socialized to hide for gay and lesbian adolescents.

Family Issues

All gay and lesbian young people grow up within a family context, which in most cases is usually heterosexual and heterocentric. Viewed within an ecological framework, growing up gay or lesbian in a heterosexual family is by its very nature a transactional process where the young person correctly perceives that there is not a "good fit" unless the family is not homophobic. Having to keep sexual identity and affectional preferences a secret creates stress that is a result not of the individual's homosexuality but of society's heterocentrism. Growing up in a system where one cannot be or say who one really is, even to family members, requires being in a constant state of vigilance. It also means that life becomes a pervasively hostile environment that one must negotiate. Added to this dilemma are traditional societal norms with respect to gender and culture that may also impinge upon the gay or lesbian young person's development, with negative consequences.

Most families convey strong heterosexual messages. Those messages include the value that heterosexual relationships are the only valid and appropriate outcomes of psychosexual development. Families provide many opportunities for their children to receive positive reinforcement, approval, and validation for their heterosexual orientation. Heterosexual children rarely have their identity itself challenged as unacceptable. As adolescence approaches, most parents encourage dating opposite-gendered individuals, marriage, and eventually, children. It is one thing for an adolescent to rebel against his or her parents, it is understood and accepted to some degree in most cultures, but what young lesbian, gay, or bisexual youth fear most is that their families will reject their personhood in ways that will result in the destruction of their entire relationship with them. This fear, real or imagined, can prevent lesbian, gay, or bisexual young persons from fully developing their identity. Some families, particularly families with strong religious convictions, may openly condemn homosexuality, unaware that their own child may be lesbian, gay, or bisexual. Although some families might not openly denounce homosexuality, "the absence of discussion sends a negative message" (Browning, 1987, p. 48).

The fact that most families are heterosexually oriented means that it is generally not possible for a family to socialize their gay or lesbian family member to what life will mean for them as a homosexually oriented individual. Within this context, it is not possible for heterosexually oriented families to provide role modeling opportunities for gay or lesbian young people who recognize their difference within their own family. As such, gay and lesbian young people developmentally need to leave their family system to seek counsel from others who are like them.

Unlike their heterosexual counterparts, most gay and lesbian adolescents do not have opportunities to learn about their emerging sexual identity in sex education classes in their school (Mallon, 1996, 1997a). Most sex education curriculums have either limited information about lesbian, gay, and bisexual sexual development, or completely ignore these populations. Armed with very little accurate information about their emerging sexual identity, these young people frequently rely on an abundance of myths, stereotypes, and misinformation about lesbian, gay, and bisexual people as their only knowledge base (Gonsiorek, 1988). Although increasingly there are more visible gay and lesbian adult role models, historically, young lesbian, gay, and bisexual young people have not had the benefit of visible lesbian and gay adult role models in their lives. Without adult gay and lesbian role models, the negative stereotypes and attitudes toward homosexuality frequently espoused by significant adults and peers in the environment were often the only sources of information for the lesbian, gay, or bisexual teenager. Internalization of these negative messages and stereotypes leads to a weakening of self-esteem, self-pride, and pride in one's group. When young people accept and believe the negative stereotypes of lesbians and gay men, they are expressing the phenomenon of internalized homophobia (Malyon, 1981). Internalized homophobia can lead to a sense of internalized oppression (Pharr, 1988, p. 60) and a process that Martin labeled socialized to hide (1982, p. 59).

Unlike the function they often perform for heterosexual youngsters, family and other social systems (i.e., school, community, church) do not facilitate the socialization of gay and lesbian youngsters. Most opportunities for socialization presume the heterosexuality of the youth involved. Because of the absence of these opportunities for lesbian and gay youth, they become socialized to hide (Martin, 1982).

Hiding

Hiding one's orientation, which is one of several choices discussed by Martin (1982; Mallon 1998a), is the choice that most gay young people initially select. It is a choice that can lead to dysfunction and distortion of relationships, which in turn leads to social, emotional, and cognitive isolation (Hetrick & Martin, 1987). Feelings of extreme sadness and loneliness are also preeminent during this period. Lesbian, gay, or bisexual adolescents have expressed feeling a lack of authenticity, or feeling as if they are living a lie, feeling that others would not accept them if they knew the truth about their sexual orientation. Hiding can become a destructive falsehood for the lesbian, gay, or bisexual young person. Martin (1982) called this "a process of deception at all levels . . . a strategy of deception [that] distorts almost all relationships the adolescent may attempt to develop or maintain and creates a sense of isolation" (p. 58).

One of the major aspects of this sense of isolation is the ever present need to self-monitor. Gay and lesbian adolescents who hide are experts at monitoring their conscious and automatic behaviors. Feeling that you must constantly watch the way you talk, stand, carry your books, hold your hands, or dress can become unbearably stressful. Many gay and lesbian teenagers hide their feelings from others in order to "fit in" and conform to the environment's expectations for them. In a recent work, Mallon (1998b) illustrated one client's feelings about hiding:

> Hiding was so exhausting. I always had to watch myself. I always had to make sure that I was not acting too butch or dressing too much like a dyke. I always felt like I was trying to be someone who I wasn't, always trying to fit in where I

knew I didn't fit. It was really hard. I really felt all alone, I thought I was the only person in the world who felt this way. But then I finally came out and decided that I didn't have to hide anymore or keep myself in check. I just accepted the fact that I was a dyke. I was tired of hiding it and I got to a point where I didn't care who knew. (p. 119)

Many school-age and preadolescent children may be successful in hiding their sexual orientation from significant adults. However, the need to obscure one's homosexual orientation during adolescence, a developmental period when you are expected to develop romantic attachments and date opposite-gendered individuals, may make the management of one's hidden identity more perplexing and more stressful.

Although most gay and lesbian adolescents emerge from adolescence as healthy and resilient adults, the stress of hiding one's sexual orientation and living an inauthentic existence may also have negative outcomes. Some gay or lesbian adolescents may choose to anesthetize their painful feelings by abusing chemical substances, developing eating disorders, engaging in unsafe, anonymous, or promiscuous sexual behaviors, physically harming themselves, or becoming clinically depressed as maladaptive means for dealing with the isolation that comes with hiding. Others might overcompensate for their hiding by overexcelling in sports, academics, extracurricular organizations, or church activities. Although the latter endeavors are generally regarded as positive, when they interfere with traditional adolescent functioning (i.e., dating, socializing with peers, and typical adolescent rebellion) they become maladaptive means for coping with a stressful life situation.

Several years or more may elapse before the lesbian, gay, or bisexual youth resolves confusion (Schneider & Tremble, 1985) and adopts a lesbian, gay, or bisexual identity (Sullivan & Schneider, 1987). For some, this will not occur until they reach adulthood; others still may spend a lifetime hiding or may require a further expanse of time to integrate sexual feelings into a positive self-identity.

Lesbian Youth

Lesbian Youth Case Example

Monique is a 16-year-old, self-identified lesbian who called to speak with someone who could give her information about the "gay lifestyle" and to speak to someone who was supportive. She spoke about how difficult it was for her to make friends. Monique lives at home with her mother, grandmother, sister, and brother. She is attending high school in an urban area. What she wanted most was information.

Monique also talked about being afraid to be open with anyone because she was afraid that they might tell others in school, or worse yet, that someone in her family might find out. She spoke about being lonely, but she did not know how to make friends. "I was just too scared," she said. She kept talking about how she felt different from her family and friends. She also disclosed that she was African American and that her family was "into the church." Now she had to manage another identity in addition to her racial/cultural and religious identities. Her primary presenting issue was loneliness. She wanted to meet other gay girls her own age.

Developmental Considerations for Young Women

Teenaged lesbians are in a transition between their socially defined roles as women and their stigmatized identities as lesbians. Young women who identify as lesbian, like their female heterosexual counterparts, must master various developmental tasks as they mature. Building a sense of identity, self-esteem, and social skills; creating and maintaining friendships; and managing social and sexual roles (Hunter, 1995) are among those tasks. We must examine both the cultural context and expectations that young women wrestle with in general, as well as the oppression of lesbians within the culture. Women's sexuality has traditionally been defined in male terms and included restrictions of lifestyle choices for all women. Challenging sanctions against independence for all women, and lesbian women in particular, is a necessary part of providing safe environments for those who do not conform to cultural and sexual "scripts" (Browning, 1984).

With the arrival of menstruation comes the awaking of burgeoning sexuality. During this period of their young lives, exploration and experimentation is considered normal. During their journey through adolescence, lesbian youth will be presented with many challenges. Dating and the development of romantic attachments is one such challenge. Dating in adolescence is a rehearsal for young adulthood. For example, in most Western cultures, girls do not usually initiate the process of asking a potential dating partner for a date. What role models do young lesbians have for initiating the dating process with other young women? And, conversely, how does a lesbian-identified young woman turn down the dating advances of a young man who might be attracted to her? For a young woman who realizes that she has a same-sex attraction, many questions are raised, such as "Where are other young people like me, and how do I meet them?" and "What is lesbian sex?" Friendships, dating, and sexual behavior all need to be discussed within the context of being female.

Sexual behavior is culturally defined. What is the sexual script for lesbians? If the sexual scripts we have now are culturally defined as limited by heterosexual expectations, then this sexual scripting will attempt to influence both sexual behavior and identity. Anyone who steps outside the culturally defined script will be denounced and/or denied. Some parents have a difficult time with the idea that they might have a lesbian daughter. In fact, some young women have reported that their parents would prefer to deal with their daughter's unwanted pregnancy than with the knowledge that she is a lesbian.

Teenage lesbians are in the midst of a period of transition between what they were taught about their identity as women and what their place in the world as women should be as well as the emerging awareness of their sexual orientation (Hunter, 1995). The isolation that these young people experience is both emotional and social. For many, the fear of rejection from family, peer, and social networks results in youth hiding their sexual orientation from others. While hiding is a coping strategy, it distorts the developmental process. As noted above, the tasks of adolescence include the management of sexual roles and the development of romantic relationships. We must ask how a person can do this if they are forced to hide significant aspects of their person. How honest can the relationships with family, friends, and peers be? The young person is constantly making up stories, changing pronouns, or not sharing their lives with others. The need to constantly distort and change one's self-presentation interferes with development. The consequence is the development of an inauthentic sense of self, which can be characterized as a Posttraumatic Stress Disorder-like syndrome. This syndrome is characterized by the individual's proclivity to shut down and compartmentalize behaviors and actions.

In terms of social roles, lesbians really have more in common with women than with gay men. However, at a time when many of their heterosexual sisters are receiving acceptance and support from families, friends, teachers, and peers regarding their sexual and emotional feelings, as well as their emerging sexual identity, many young lesbians feel they must hide their attraction to other women (Hunter, 1995). Lesbians are women who step outside of socially constructed gender roles. Television, movies, and other media also teaches us socially expected gender roles. Most girls are still taught that their sexual desires should emerge and be expressed only in the context of heterosexual marriage.

Bisexual Adolescents

The literature on bisexual adolescents is limited (Savin-Williams, 1995), but in brief, there appear to be two types of bisexual adolescents. One type consists of those who identify as bisexual but who are actually in a transition toward a gay/lesbian or heterosexual identity. The other type consists of those who are attracted to both genders equally. There has been considerable dialogue and debate about the developmental status of bisexual adolescents. Based on our clinical work with young people, bisexuality is often a transitional period toward an identity that is later acknowledged as gay, lesbian, or heterosexual.

Bisexual Youth Case Example

Eric is an 18-year-old adolescent who has dated both girls and boys. He is ambivalent about his sexual orientation and currently identifies himself as bisexual. Eric has always felt "different" and many of his peers have assumed that he is gay, but he feels more comfortable identifying as bisexual. He feels that he is not accepted by nongay peers because he is bisexual; neither is he fully accepted by the gay or lesbian community because they feel he is a "fence sitter." He feels pressured from all sides. While he attends a youth group that is open to all youth, he is frequently conflicted about his feelings.

As illustrated by the above vignette, bisexual youth have their own set of issues to address. The impact of "biphobia" from heterosexual, gay male, and lesbian communities can be stressful. A major complication for a bisexual youth, as cited by Savin-Williams (1995), is how to comprehend his or her sexual feelings and desires, whether they are relating to a member of the same or other sex.

For bisexual adolescents, because of the stigma attached to the orientation and the fear about coming out as gay, one will find much more heterosexual experimentation. In many families, heterosexuality remains the preferred sexual orientation, as represented by the following example. In one of our groups, a young person said that his father would tolerate it more if he got a young woman pregnant than if he had a "faggot" for a son. Thus the pressure to chose an orientation is a paramount concern for youths who identify as bisexual.

Youth of Color

In Western society, different groups of people are defined by race, religion, or ethnicity. These racial, ethnic, and religious groups define themselves by their common ancestry and experiences. In the United States, many of these groups are referred to as ethnic minority groups and are identified as victims of long-standing racism. Because of this discrimination, they have often had to develop strategies to survive societal oppression. A person's cultural/racial group (social environment of community and family) becomes very important as a support system in a hostile environment. It is in this environment that the individual develops a sense of identity (Adams & Schlesinger, 1988).

People of color who are lesbian, gay, or bisexual confront a tricultural experience. They experience membership in their ethnic or racial community and in the larger society. They are not born into the lesbian and gay community. They usually become aware of their difference in sexual orientation during adolescence. Not only must they address the stigma within their own cultural/racial community but they must also find a supportive lesbian/gay community to which they can relate. The lesbian and gay community is often a microcosm of the larger society, and as such, lesbian and gay youth of color will encounter racism there, just as it exists in the dominant culture. To sustain oneself in three distinct communities requires an enormous effort and may also be quite stressful (Chan, 1989; Hunter & Schaecher, 1995; Morales, 1989).

Conclusion

For lesbian, gay, and bisexual people, adolescence and early adulthood are the most significant years for exploring their identities. By the time adolescents reach adulthood, identity consolidation should have taken place. As noted earlier in this chapter, however, due to the impact of

heterosexism and stigma, the normative expectation of identity exploration and development, usually associated with adolescence, is much more
difficult for the lesbian, gay, or bisexual young person in developing a
positive lesbian or gay identity. As a consequence of social stigma, lesbian,
gay, and bisexual youth must make continuous adjustments and adapt to
an environment almost completely devoid of the necessary components
that one would need to grow into a healthy, productive adult.

The most effective means for working with the gay and lesbian adolescent is to assist them in developing strategies to enhance their lesbian,
gay, and bisexual identity. Efficacy in clinical practice with lesbian, gay,
and bisexual youths requires that providers first become comfortable
and then acquire a comprehensive base of knowledge about lesbian, gay,
and bisexual sexual orientations. Part of that knowledge base includes
acknowledging the extent to which heterosexist society has created a
hostile environment for lesbian, gay, and bisexual people and an awareness of the psychological challenges associated with that ubiquitous
hostility and degradation.

Those who work with gay and lesbian adolescents must be open to developing individualized treatment plans, using a variety of approaches
designed to address the unique needs of each client. In attempting to
help lesbian, gay, and bisexual adolescents find a "fit" that both affirms
their lives and promotes health, social workers and other professionals
must be willing to move beyond the stereotypes and mythology that surround lesbian, gay, and bisexual orientations.

Helping young people grow into healthy, well-adjusted adults is one
of the primary goals of good practice. The primary role of the professional in this process is to assist in promoting a "good fit" between the
young person and their environment. Most young people have affirming environments to assist and support them on this journey. Lesbian,
gay, and bisexual young people often experience greater levels of estrangement from their environment and in some cases are completely rejected. They therefore need other caring adults in their lives to help them
make this journey successfully.

Implications for Clinical Practice

Because of the stigma that a lesbian, gay, or bisexual identity holds for
most people, these young people will hide their sexual orientation and

sexual feelings, compounding and distorting their own developmental processes. We make the following recommendations for those practitioners who are interested in working with lesbian, gay, and bisexual youths.

1. Lesbian, gay, and bisexual young people need service providers and others working with youth who are nonjudgmental and who can assist them in dealing with the stigma and discrimination that they experience, as well as other problems which may or may not have to do with one's sexual orientation. Providers should augment social services for lesbian, gay, and bisexual young people by providing them with accurate and relevant information about their emerging identity. Literature written by gay and lesbian young people for gay and lesbian young people are most helpful (Due, 1995; Heron, 1994; Kay, Estepa, & Desetta, 1996; Miranda, 1996; Monette, 1992; Valenzuela, 1996). Videotapes and guest speakers should also be utilized. This information should assist the lesbian or gay oriented young person in abolishing myths and stereotypes, correcting misconceptions, and combating the cognitive isolation they experience. This information can also help educate straight teens about their gay and lesbian peers (Greene, 1996).

The development of lesbian, gay, and heterosexual alliances, particularly in the school system, should be supported.

2. Providers should not pretend to have all the answers. They may need to become familiar with existing lesbian, gay, and bisexual affirmative mental health literature that addresses the needs of lesbian, gay, and bisexual youth from a provider's perspective. The reader is referred to Cates (1987), DeCrescenzo (1994), Mallon (1992, 1994, 1997b), Morrow (1993), and Needham (1977), for a more comprehensive discussion.

3. Practicing professionals must not fall into the trap of attempting to identify lesbian, gay, and bisexual clients. Instead, professionals must focus their energy on creating lesbian and gay affirming environments that respect the developmental process and where it is safe for all young people to be themselves. Practitioners working with this population must also remember to accept the client as a total person. Too often, the knowledge that a young person is lesbian, gay, or bisexual obscures everything else about them, rather than acknowledge their sexual orientation as one of many important facets of their identity.

4. Help the client to understand and clarify their feelings about their sexual orientation. Allow the client to talk about their feelings, their frus-

trations, and their successes. A basic helping professional principle states that practitioners should meet the client where they are. Let the client know that it is acceptable to be bisexual, gay, lesbian, or confused about their identity. The clinician must also help the client to understand that it is acceptable to choose not to be sexually involved or enter a relationship before they feel ready to do so. Of course, it should be clear to the client that it is equally acceptable for the client to change one's mind about one's sexual orientation from time to time. The role of the clinician is to facilitate the process of the client's self-exploration, not to insist that the lesbian, gay, or bisexual youth either "grow out of it," at one extreme, or, at the other extreme, immediately disclose to family and friends.

5. Clinicians must also be able to provide or be able to refer youngsters to nonsexual, healthy peer support groups within their local communities or schools. Social interaction between other lesbian, gay, and bisexual youth will help to alleviate the extreme social isolation and loneliness that most gay and lesbian adolescents experience and that leaves them at risk.

6. Clinicians must assist clients in developing other appropriate contacts within the gay and lesbian community toward the end of developing a social support and peer network. Providers should know these resources and be able to refer clients to them.

7. Providers must assist the client in developing effective interpersonal coping mechanisms to address the negative effects of societal stigmatization. Assisting young people in exploring and developing mechanisms to deal with conflict, relationships, depression, safer sex, and peer pressures are crucial to this task.

8. It is important to be aware of the signs of stress and emotional distress, especially with respect to suicidal ideation and excessive alcohol and substance abuse. Practitioners must be familiar with the resources clients can be referred to where help addressing these issues is available.

9. Practitioners must help the client to address a wide variety of family issues and be prepared to help families as well. Whenever possible, young people should be encouraged to reunite or reconcile with their families. If it is not possible to do this, then it is important to help the young person find a supportive, gay-affirming, out-of-home placement and encourage them to develop life skills to enable them to live independently. Providers should proceed very cautiously when assisting the lesbian, gay, or bisexual youngster who wants to disclose their sexual

orientation to their families. They must understand the risks involved as no one can predict in advance how any particular family will respond.

10. Assist in training other professionals, by providing them with accurate and adequate information about lesbian, gay, and bisexual adolescent issues. Help other professionals to view homosexuality from a nonjudgmental, nonpejorative perspective.

11. Be prepared to be an advocate for the youngster who is having trouble at school, in their own family, or in the group home. Protection of the gay and lesbian youth from homophobic practices is an important task for the clinician.

12. Respect confidentiality at all times. The relationship between client and clinician must be based on trust, understanding, and respect.

References

Adams, A. C., & Schlesinger, E. G. (1988). Group approach to training ethnic-sensitive practitioners. In C. Jacobs & D. D. Bowles (Eds.), *Ethnicity & race: Critical concepts in social work* (pp. 204-216). Silver Springs, MD: National Association of Social Workers Press

Blos, P. (1979). *The adolescent passage: Developmental issues.* New York: International Universities Press.

Browning, C. (1984). Changing theories of lesbianism: Challenging the stereotypes. In T. Darty & S. Potter (Eds.), *Women-identified women* (pp. 11-30). Palo Alto, CA: Mayfield.

Browning, C. (1987). Therapeutic issues and intervention strategies with young adult lesbian clients: A developmental approach. *Journal of Homosexuality, 13*(4), 45-53.

Cass, V. (1979). Homosexual identity formation: A theoretical model. *Journal of Homosexuality, 4,* 219-235.

Cates, J. A. (1987). Adolescent sexuality: Gay and lesbian issues. *Child Welfare League of America, 66,* 353-363.

Chan, C. (1989). Issues of identity development among Asian American lesbians and gay men. *Journal of Counseling and Development, 68*(1), 16-20.

Coleman, E. (1987). Assessment of sexual orientation. *Journal of Homosexuality, 14,* 9-24.

D'Augelli, A. R. (1996). Lesbian, gay, and bisexual development during adolescence and young adulthood. In R. P. Cabaj & T. S. Stein (Eds.), *Textbook of homosexuality and mental health* (pp. 267-288). Washington, DC: American Psychiatric Press.

DeCrescenzo, T. (Ed.). (1994). *Helping gay and lesbian youth: New policies, new programs, new practices.* New York: Haworth.

Due, L. (1995). *Joining the tribe: Growing up gay and lesbian in the 90s.* New York: Anchor Books.

Erikson, E. H. (1959). Identity and the life-cycle. *Psychological Issues, 1,* 1-171.

Gonsiorek, J. C. (1988). Mental health issues of gay and lesbian adolescents. *Journal of Adolescent Health Care, 9*(2), 114-122.

Greene, Z. (1996). Straight, but not narrow-minded. In P. Kay, A. Estepa, & A. Desetta (Eds.), *Out with it: Gay and straight teens write about homosexuality* (pp. 12-14). New York: Youth Communications.

Hamburg, B. A. (1974). Early adolescence: A specific and stressful stage of the life cycle. In G. V. Coelho, D. A. Hamburg, & J. E. Adams (Eds.), *Coping and adaptation* (pp. 101-124). New York: Basic Books.

Heron, A., (Ed.). (1994). *Two teenagers in 20.* Boston: Alyson.

Hetrick, E., & Martin, A. D. (1984). Ego-dystonic homosexuality: A developmental view. In E. Hetrick & T. Stein (Eds.), *Innovations in psychotherapy with homosexuals,* (pp. 2-21). Washington, DC: American Psychiatric Association.

Hetrick, E., & Martin, A. D. (1987). Developmental issues and their resolution for gay and lesbian adolescents. *Journal of Homosexuality, 13*(4), 25-43.

Hunter, J. (1995). At the crossroads: Lesbian youth. In K. Jay (Ed.), *Dyke life* (pp. 50-60). New York: Basic Books.

Hunter, J. (1996). *Emerging from the shadows: Gay lesbian and bisexual adolescents. Personal identity achievement, coming out and sexual risk behaviors.* Unpublished doctoral dissertation, City University of New York.

Hunter, J., & Schaecher, R. (1995). Gay and lesbian adolescents. In R. L. Edwards (Ed.), *Encyclopedia of social work* (pp. 1055-1063). Washington, DC: National Association of Social Workers.

Kay, P., Estepa, A., & Desetta, A. (Eds.). (1996). *Out with it: Gay and straight teens write about homosexuality.* New York: Youth Communications.

Kinsey, A. C., Pomeroy, W. B., & Martin, C. E. (1948). *Sexual behavior in the human male.* Philadelphia: W. B. Saunders.

Kinsey, A. C., Pomeroy, W. B., Martin, C. E., & Gebhard, P. W. (1953). *Sexual behavior in the human female.* Philadelphia: W. B. Saunders.

Kroger, J. (1993). Ego identity: An overview. In J. Kroger (Ed.), *Discussion on ego identity* (pp. 3-4). London: Erlbaum.

Mallon, G. P. (1992). Gay and no place to go: Serving the needs of gay and lesbian youth in out-of-home care settings. *Child Welfare, 71*(6), 547-557.

Mallon, G. P. (1994). Counseling strategies with gay and lesbian youth. In T. DeCrescenzo (Ed.), *Helping gay and lesbian youth: New policies, new programs, new practices* (pp. 75-91). New York: Haworth.

Mallon, G. P. (1996). It's like opening Pandora's box: Addressing the needs of gay and lesbian students and families in educational systems. In L. M. Bullock, R. A. Gable, & J. R. Rigky (Eds.), *Understanding individual differences: Highlights from the National symposium on what educators should know about adolescents who are gay, lesbian, or bisexual* (pp. 1-6). Reston, VA: Council for Children with Behavioral Disorders.

Mallon, G. P. (1997a). When schools are not safe places: Gay, lesbian, bisexual, and trans-gendered young people in educational settings. *Reaching Today's Youth, 2*(1), 41-45.

Mallon, G. P. (1997). Toward a competent child welfare service delivery system for gay and lesbian adolescents and their families. *Journal of Multicultural Social Work, 5*(3/4), 177-194.

Mallon, G. P. (1998a). *We don't exactly get the welcome wagon: The experiences of gay and lesbian adolescents in child welfare systems.* New York: Columbia University Press.

Mallon, G. P. (1998b). Gay, lesbian and bisexual childhood and adolescent *development*: An ecological perspective. In G. Appleby & J. Anastas (Eds.), *Not just a passing phase: Social work with gay, lesbian and bisexual persons.* New York: Columbia University Press.

Malyon, A. K. (1981). The homosexual adolescent: Developmental issues and social bias. *Child Welfare League of America, 60*(5), 321-330.

Marcia, J. E. (1980). Identity in adolescence. In J. Adelson (Ed.), *Handbook of adolescent psychiatry* (pp. 159-187). New York: John Wiley.

Martin, A. D. (1982). Learning to hide: The socialization of the gay adolescent. In S. C. Feinstein, J. G. Looney, A. Schartzberg, & A. Sorosky (Eds.), *Adolescent psychiatry: Developmental and clinical studies* (Vol. 10, pp. 52-65). Chicago: University of Chicago Press.

Minton, H. L., & Mc Donald, G. J. (1984). Homosexual identity formation as a developmental process. In J. P. De Cecco & M. G. Shively (Eds.), *Origins of sexuality and homosexuality,* (pp. 91-104). New York: Harrington Park Press.

Miranda, D. (1996). I hated myself. In P. Kay, A. Estepa, & A. Desetta (Eds.), *Out with it: Gay and straight teens write about homosexuality* (pp. 34-39). New York: Youth Communications.

Monette, P. (1992). *Becoming a man: Half a life story.* New York: Harcourt Brace Jovanovich.

Monteflores, C., de, & Schultz, S. J. (1978). Coming out: Similarities and differences for lesbians and gay men. *Journal of Social Issues, 34,* 59-72.

Morales, E. S. (1989). Ethnic minority families and minority gays and lesbians. In *Marriage and Family Review,* 14, 217-239.

Morrow, D. F. (1993). Social work with gay and lesbian adolescents. In *Social Work, 38*(6), 655-660.

Needham, R. (1977). Casework intervention with a homosexual adolescent. *Social Casework, 58,* 387-394.

Newman, B. M., & Newman, P. R. (1987). *Development through life: A psychosocial approach* (4th ed.). Belmont, CA: Dorsey Press.

Olson, E. D., & King, C. A. (1995). Gay and lesbian self-identification: A response to Rotherram-Borus and Fernandez. *Suicide and Life-Threatening Behavior, 25,* 35-39.

Pharr, S. (1988). *Homophobia: A weapon of sexism.* Little Rock, AK: Chardon Press.

Remafedi, G. (1987a). Male homosexuality: The adolescent's perspective. *Pediatrics, 79,* 326-330.

Remafedi, G. (1987b). Adolescent homosexuality: Psychosocial and implications. *Pediatrics, 79,* 331-337.

Savin-Williams, R. C. (1995). Lesbian, gay male, and bisexual adolescents. In A. R. D'Augelli & C. J. Patterson (Eds.), *Lesbian, gay and bisexual identities over the lifespan: Psychological perspectives* (pp. 165-189). New York: Oxford University Press.

Scheider, M. (1989). Sappho was a right-on adolescent: Growing up lesbian. In G. Herdt (Ed.), *Gay and lesbian youth* (pp. 111-130). New York: Haworth.

Schneider, M. (Ed.). (1997). *Pride & prejudice: Working with lesbian, gay, and bisexual youth.* Toronto, ON: Central Toronto Youth Services.

Schneider, M., & Tremble, B. (1985). Gay or straight? Working with the confused adolescent. *Journal of Homosexuality, 4*(1/2), 71-82.

Sullivan, T., & Schneider, M. (1987). Development and identity issues in adolescent homosexuality. *Child and Adolescent Social Work, 4*(1), 13-24.

Troiden, R. R. (1993). The formation of homosexual identities. In L. D. Garnets & D. G. Kimmel (Eds.), *Psychological perspectives on lesbian and gay male experiences* (pp. 191-217). New York: Columbia University Press.

Valenzuela, W. (1996). A school where I can be myself. In P. Kay, A. Estepa, & A. Desetta (Eds.), *Out with it: Gay and straight teens write about homosexuality* (pp. 45-46). New York: Youth Communications.

10

Therapeutic Responses to Sexual Orientation

Psychology's Evolution

DOUGLAS C. HALDEMAN

The science informing clinical practice in psychology has undergone a number of changes with respect to standard treatments for various mental disorders. In no case have these changes been more dramatic than in the domain of sexual orientation. Once assumed to be a mental disorder, same-sex sexual orientation is now viewed as a normal variant of the human experience and is not, in and of itself, grounds for inferring developmental arrest or pathological status. As a result, the treatments once considered appropriate for sexual orientation are categorically questionable since the diagnostic entity itself no longer exists.

The present discussion traces the journey out of pathology for same-sex sexual orientation, focusing primarily on the therapeutic implications thereof. It is common knowledge that the organized mental health professions have dismissed pathological theories of homosexuality as scientifically indefensible. However, we still live in a world that stigmatizes same-sex sexual orientation. As a result, some individuals seek professional support coping with deeply conflicted feelings about their sexual orientation. Furthermore, we know that lesbians, gay men, and bisexual men and women utilize psychotherapy in greater proportions than do their heterosexual counterparts (Morgan, 1992; Nystrom, 1997).

At the same time, many graduate training programs in psychology may provide distorted information, or no information at all, about sexual orientation. The present discussion is intended to provide guidance to the practitioner seeking to work responsibly with clients who are confused or uncomfortable with their sexual orientation. This discussion is also directed toward those training all clinicians, not simply those who have identified sexual orientation as a specialty area of interest.

Sexual Orientation Conversion Therapy

When homosexuality was assumed to be a mental disorder, some form of sexual orientation conversion therapy was thought to be the treatment of choice. These treatments encompassed a considerable variety of style and level of invasiveness, ranging from classic psychoanalytically based "talk therapies" to behavioral interventions (including masturbatory reconditioning, excessive bicycle riding, or rest) to electroshock treatments, emetic drugs, and surgery. Murphy (1992) describes the use of such methods in detail. In all cases, these treatments were designed to reorient to heterosexuality the sexual orientation of homosexual males. Stein (1996) considers this to be the result of a generally greater emphasis on men in the psychological literature coupled with "a stronger and frequently more virulent reaction to homosexuality in men than to homosexuality in women in our society" (p. 525).

Abandoning the illness model of homosexuality, however, has not extinguished the conversion therapy movement. "Ex-gay" groups, largely proliferated under the auspices of fundamentalist Christian churches who view homosexuality as biblically proscribed, are the most visible purveyors of such treatments. Typically, such groups are somewhat circumspect about their actual methods, but they are thought to consist primarily of prayer and other religious interventions. Several of these groups, and the activities of their leaders, have been reviewed elsewhere (Haldeman, 1996). The perspective of most pastoral counselors reflects a valuing of scriptural interpretation as superior to science. For example, Dallas (1996), in advocating treatment for homosexuality, regardless of scientific evidence which would not justify viewing it as a mental illness, exhorts counselors not to "compromise revealed (biblical) truth" (p. 369). He cites several unproven theories and long-challenged studies as the empirical basis for his antigay position.

The trend for professional organizations to disavow antigay perspectives over the past 20 years has led to a backlash of sorts. The National Association for the Research and Therapy of Homosexuality (NARTH) has emerged as a multidisciplinary organization dedicated to promoting the illness model of homosexuality. NARTH officers typically suggest that gay-affirmative policies are the result of professional organizations having been strong-armed by the powerful "gay lobby," and in so doing characterize gay-affirmative professionals as interested in stifling free speech. Nonetheless, NARTH's officers make it clear that they may remove a member whose writings or public remarks vary from the position that homosexuality is a treatable mental illness (Drescher, 1997). The organization's cofounders are Charles Socarides, a psychoanalyst whose antigay bias is legendary, and Joseph Nicolosi, a psychologist whose view of homosexuality as a developmental arrest is a curious mix of psychoanalytic thought and spirituality. The title of Nicolosi's 1991 work, *Reparative Therapy for Male Homosexuality,* makes clear his bias that same-sex sexual orientation is a broken condition in need of repair. He claims that the abnormalities of homosexuality are represented by the homosexual's shunning of the "male-female polarity" in favor of the "attempt to fulfill a deficit in wholeness of one's original gender" (Nicolosi, 1991, pp. 109-110). An extensive critique of Nicolosi's hypotheses is offered by Drescher (1998).

Sexual orientation conversion therapy has always rested on the unfounded assumption that same-sex sexual orientation is a disorder. Attempts to cure homosexuality were not critically evaluated until it became clear that there was reason to question whether or not homosexuality was a mental illness. The reader is referred to Gonsiorek (1991) for an extensive review of the literature in this area and a more comprehensive discussion. The lack of support for an illness model is twofold. First, those studies that support a pathological perspective of homosexuality and bisexuality commonly suffer from an unclear definition of terms, including inadequately articulated classification criteria by which subjects are considered homosexual, heterosexual, or bisexual. The studies also demonstrate, in varying degrees, inappropriate comparison of groups, discrepant sampling procedures, and questionable outcome measures. Most often, homosexual clinical samples are compared against heterosexual nonclinical samples. Second, when nonclinical homosexual and heterosexual samples are compared, there is no difference found in a number of variables related to psychological adjustment. These factors led to the declassification of homosexuality as a mental illness by the American Psychiatric Association in 1973 and by the American Psychological Association in 1975.

The empirical methods that have been used to demonstrate that sexual orientation can be changed suffer from flaws similar to those described in studies purporting to prove that homosexual orientation is a mental illness. A variety of conversion therapy methodologies have been examined (Haldeman, 1991, 1994). These studies have serious flaws in their selection criteria, subject classification, assessment, and outcome measures. Haldeman (1991, 1994) discusses in detail a number of conversion therapy studies, none of which suggests that sexual orientation is amenable to redirection or significant influence from psychological interventions.

Quite apart from the question of whether or not sexual orientation can be changed is the question of whether or not it *should* be changed. Conversion therapists would argue that the individual needs to be free to select treatment options based upon his or her own life experience; and if seeking sexual orientation change is what is chosen, then the profession has a responsibility to provide such treatments. But what is the origin of such a request, and does it really reflect "free" will? No parallel process of sexual orientation dissatisfaction has been reported in heterosexuals, likely due to the fact that they enjoy social sanction and privilege. Can individuals who have spent their lives burdened by the judgment of a disapproving family, a shame-inducing church, and a hostile society be seen as acting out of their "free will" when they seek the services of a conversion therapist? Martin (1984) states that "a clinician's implicit acceptance of the homosexual orientation as the cause of ego-dystonic reactions, and the concomitant agreement to attempt sexual orientation change, exacerbates the ego-dystonic reactions and reinforces and confirms the internalized homophobia that lies at their root" (p. 46).

Davison (1991) objects to conversion therapies on the grounds that they reinforce antigay prejudice and stigma. He asks, "How can therapists honestly speak of nonprejudice when they participate in therapy regimens that by their very existence, and regardless of their efficacy, would seem to condone the current societal prejudice and perhaps also impede social change?" (p. 141). This point is echoed by Begelman (1975), who states that "[conversion therapies], by their very existence, constitute a significant causal element in reinforcing the social doctrine that homosexuality is bad; therapists . . . further strengthen the prejudice that homosexuality is a 'problem behavior,' since treatment may be offered for it" (p. 180).

The concerns about conversion therapies, then, encompass practical and ethical issues. With respect to the former, there is no empirically valid study that suggests that sexual orientation is amenable to change or modification through any type of psychological intervention. There is no precedent for offering treatments for those conditions that are established purely as an artifact of social or religious construction. Stein (1996) likens conversion therapy to the former Chinese practice of foot-binding for females. An important corollary to this phenomenon is the fact that conversion therapy exists as part of a constellation of factors including social prejudice and stigma, discrimination, and antigay violence that lead some individuals to become dissatisfied with their sexual orientation. Such treatments and their practitioners exist as a significant element in the set of factors that creates a market for their services. Above all, sexual orientation conversion therapies are rooted in a pathological view of homosexuality that psychology has firmly rejected.

Policy Development

The removal of homosexuality from the *DSM* was an important initial step in furthering scientific understanding about homosexuality. It did not, however, neutralize generalized social antigay stigma or correct all misperceptions about sexual orientation, even among practitioners. Garnets, Hancock, Cochran, Goodchilds, and Peplau (1991), in their report of a survey of psychologists, found a wide range of variability in knowledge and prejudice regarding homosexuality. These biases and lack of information have a potentially harmful effect on psychotherapeutic treatment of lesbian, gay, and bisexual individuals. In an effort to clarify appropriate therapeutic responses to patients' concerns about sexual orientation and to provide guidance to practitioners, lesbian, gay, and bisexual groups within organized psychology commenced work on policy and practice guideline development.

The first such group to draft a policy in this area was the Committee on Lesbian, Gay and Bisexual Concerns of the Washington State Psychological Association. Responding to the fact that sexual orientation conversion therapy was still being conducted by psychologists in

Washington State, the Committee drafted a policy statement that was ultimately adopted by the WSPA Executive Committee in March 1991. The policy reads, in part,

> Psychologists do not provide or sanction cures for that which has been judged not to be an illness. Individuals seeking to change their sexual orientation do so as the result of internalized stigma and homophobia, given the consistent scientific demonstration that there is nothing about homosexuality per se that undermines psychological adjustment. It is therefore our objective as psychologists to educate and change the intolerant social context, not the individual who is victimized by it. Conversion treatments, by their very existence, exacerbate the homophobia which psychology seeks to combat. (Washington State Psychological Association, 1991)

This policy was an attempt to educate the practice community and the public about some of the issues that influence individuals seeking to change their sexual orientation. The ethical implications of conversion therapy, rather than the scientific limitations thereof, were the focal point of this policy statement. It made the point that providing a treatment for a nonpathological condition, particularly when individuals are likely to seek such treatment as a function of socially mediated stigma, serves to exacerbate the very social condition that psychology seeks to combat. The question of efficacy with regard to conversion treatments was omitted from the policy, given that there is no reputable science in this area. On the proconversion therapy side, anecdotal evidence of "cures" abound. None of these has ever been empirically substantiated, however, which is crucial given the enormous social demand characteristics associated with having successfully "changed" one's sexual orientation. The previously cited reviews simply make clear the significant methodological flaws in all heretofore published studies of conversion treatments.

The opposite side of the argument, however, does not offer compelling evidence against conversion treatments. Practitioners treating individuals who have undergone some form of conversion therapy have anecdotally reported a wide range of effects in their patients (Haldeman, 1994). Some patients, particularly those who have undergone an aversive conversion therapy process, report significant posttraumatic emotional and physiological sequelae from the treatments, such as chronic depression, anxiety, intimacy-avoidance, and sexual dysfunction. Some patients report that the treatments were ineffective, but without residual negative effect, and still others report that a failed attempt at conversion therapy actually helped them to accept and solidify a positive gay identity. This is not to cast in a neutral light the potential for psychological harm due to a failed effort at sexual orientation. There are indeed anecdotal reports that document the harm done by conversion treatments, but there are no controlled studies. The difficulty of obtaining a random sample of individuals who have gone through conversion therapy would be extraordinary; therefore there can be no open solicitation for patients, either "cured" or traumatized, which would not be susceptible to extreme response bias. It is this dilemma that led one scholar to refer to attempts to quantify both the success and failures of conversion therapy as "dueling bad science."

This absence of compelling documentation of the harm done by conversion treatments led the APA in 1995 to oppose consideration of an outright ban on conversion therapies. A resolution drafted for APA's Council of Representatives, which would have dissuaded psychologists from engaging in conversion therapies, based upon ethical grounds, was not considered for discussion largely due to restraint of trade issues. There is no precedent for prohibiting any kind of therapy based upon either lack of efficacy or social stigma. Perhaps the situation would be different with considerable empirical evidence that conversion therapy is harmful, but as it is now, the association is disinclined to set any kind of precedent that would interfere with practitioner and patient autonomy.

A coalition of groups from within APA's Public Interest, Practice, and Science constituencies then crafted a resolution that would address the issues of psychotherapy with lesbian, gay, and bisexual clients in a nonrestrictive manner. The resolution, titled "Appropriate Therapeutic Responses to Sexual Orientation," was approved in a near-unanimous vote by the APA's Council of Representatives at its August 1997 meeting (APA, 1997). This resolution does not outlaw any type of therapeutic practice but holds all practitioners responsible for the inclusion in their work with lesbian, gay, and bisexual clients of a number of ethical principles directly relating to sexual orientation.

The reinforcement of ethical principles relevant to practice with sexual minority clients has been considered one of the primary means of eliminating heterosexism and bias in treatment with these populations. Brown (1996) argues, "The expression of . . . bias in the context of mental health practice must be defined as a gross deviation from the norms of good care, not simply a matter of personal beliefs" (p. 49).

The ethical principles cited in the 1997 resolution are briefly described in this section; the practice and training implications thereof follow in the next. The resolution also states that portrayals of lesbians, gay men, and bisexual individuals as mentally ill are to be rejected because such characterizations are inconsistent with scientific understanding, and supports the dissemination of accurate information about sexual orientation in order to counteract myths, stereotypes, and misinformation.

The resolution acknowledges the influences of social prejudice and misinformation as motivating factors in causing many lesbian, gay, bisexual, and questioning individuals to seek conversion treatments. It notes that children and youth are particularly vulnerable to social peer pressure and, at the same time, lack adequate legal protection from coercive treatments. Further, the resolution observes that conversion therapies are promoted by mental health professionals adhering to a pathology-based view of same-sex sexual orientation and that these treatments are under extensive scrutiny and debate from the standpoints of ethics, efficacy, and potential for benefit and harm.

Of the ethical considerations raised by the resolution, first and foremost is that the practitioner is constrained against knowingly engaging in discriminatory practices, specifically discrimination based upon sexual orientation. Automatic devaluing of lesbian, gay, or bisexual sexual orientation, inappropriate attribution of a patient's problems to her/his sexual orientation, disseminating inaccurate information about sexual orientation, advocating views that suggest an egregious ignorance about lesbian, gay, and bisexual individuals, their lives, and relationships, or permitting the therapeutic interaction to become contaminated with the practitioner's personal prejudices. These all exemplify potentially discriminatory practices. Corollary to the last of these is the practitioner's responsibility to respect the rights of others to hold different opinions. Ethical practice requires that the practitioner respect the opinions and feelings of the client, regardless of whether she/he personally agrees with them or not. This does not mean, of course, that the practitioner is obliged to offer treatment which is inconsistent with her/his own beliefs or scope of practice. It does mean that the experience of the patient is not to be demeaned, negated, or trivialized because it does not match the experience of the practitioner. The practitioner is bound to respect the self-determination of the patient. Treatment should be designed in a manner that supports the patient's autonomy, not as an agenda imposed by a therapist with preconceptions.

The final ethical caveat related to discriminatory practice involves the practitioner's responsibility to eliminate bias that is based on cultural and other differences due to sexual orientation. As with all clients, practitioners working with lesbian, gay, and bisexual individuals should not rely on their patients to educate them about the social, cultural, and individual aspects of sexual orientation that may be relevant to a particular case. Responsible psychologists seek consultation and/or make appropriate referrals, depending upon the psychologist's level of familiarity and scope of practice when dealing with a particular population.

The other major ethical domain relevant to treatment with lesbian, gay, and bisexual clients has to do with the way in which the treatment is described to the patient. Significant information relative to the procedure(s) to be used must be relayed to the patient in a way that is commensurate with her/his capacity to understand it. This practice would automatically jeopardize a parent's ability to bring an adolescent to conversion treatment, since it would require the adolescent's consent. This scenario is familiar to numerous lesbians and gay men, who have reported that their first experiences in therapy were at the behest of parents wanting them to "become straight." Psychologists may not make false or deceptive statements concerning the scientific or clinical basis for their services, which seriously limits the degree to which conversion therapists may rely on scientific credibility to justify their treatments, or the theoretical formulations upon which they are based. The APA resolution has undercut conversion therapy's scientific legitimacy by removing its foundation. As one conversionist responded, "It is like making a restaurant put a sign in the window saying, 'This food might make you sick'."

Predictably, reaction to the APA's resolution from the conversion therapy contingent, specifically NARTH and the Christian fundamentalist "ex-gay" groups, was negative. NARTH leaders branded the resolution "an attempt to brainwash the public by denying that homosexuality is a purple menace that is threatening the proper design of gender distinctions in society" ("In Brief, " 1997, p. 17). In truth, of course, psychology does not see same-sex sexual orientation as a menace of any color; it has simply removed its tacit support of those who do. Further, psychological science does not subscribe to a unitary vision of what would constitute a "proper design of gender distinctions." Conversion therapists are still free to practice their trade, but they now bear the burden of proof respective to their methods. The hypotheses that serve as the basis for their methods now stand without support from organized psychology.

The fundamentalist groups that sponsor religious "ex-gay" programs were similarly outraged by APA's resolution. One religious leader called it a "death sentence" for those wishing to change their sexual orientation. This reaction came in contrast to previous statements on the matter, in which it seemed to be of little concern to religious organizations what a secular professional group might resolve. According to many pastoral counselors, the laws of scripture, however variously they may be interpreted, supersede the policies of secular groups, scientific or otherwise. In any case, the APA's policy is not intended to impinge upon anyone's free exercise of religion. Rather, it serves to underscore the basic principle that clinical and religious practices should be kept separate.

Gay rights advocacy organizations were generally supportive of the resolution, most notably the Human Rights Campaign and the National Youth Advocacy Coalition. The National Lesbian and Gay Task Force, however, took issue with the fact that the practice of conversion therapy was not banned outright, and it criticized the resolution for not going far enough.

Clinical and Training Implications

As a policy, the APA resolution does not offer specific guidance to practitioners and trainers. Nevertheless, because of the resolution's numerous references to ethical behavior and appropriate theoretical foundations of clinical work with lesbian, gay, and bisexual clients, there are implications for clinical work and training that should be considered. The following is an elaboration of the above-mentioned ethical aspects of the resolution, with case vignettes to illustrate key points. It should be noted that these illustrations are presented to suggest considerations for practice, inform consultation, and stimulate classroom discussion. They are not to be interpreted as a cookbook, nor are they codified as formal guidelines. Rather, they are suggestive of a general framework for consideration in clinical practice and training with lesbian, gay, and bisexual clients. Further, the content of these vignettes represents but a fraction of the nature and scope of cases to be encountered in clinical work with sexual minority individuals.

The first general area of ethical concern relative to practice with sexual minority individuals has to do with discriminatory practice. As previously noted, the APA resolution cites the Code of Ethics injunction against discriminatory practices applied to sexual minority individuals. There are numerous clinical applications to this concept. To illustrate some of these applications, let us consider the following case vignette:

> Mr. J, a 30-year-old African American man, is a corporate executive. He has never had a long-term relationship with a woman but has made several attempts, since he has been hopeful of having a family. He reports that he has always had strong sexual fantasies about other men but has never acted upon them. Mr. J indicates that he is becoming increasingly lonely but finds it hard to imagine having a relationship with another man; additionally, he fears his inexperience with the gay community and the potential risk of HIV infection would be obstacles should he come out. Furthermore, Mr. J comes from a close-knit, conservative family, is very religious, and feels that living as a gay man is incompatible with both his family and his life goals. He seeks guidance from the therapist relative to his sexual orientation.

A case such as this shows some of the basic issues of responsible clinical practice with sexual minority clients. First, the therapist is cautioned to carefully scrutinize her/his own agenda. Hearing the story of Mr. J, some might be tempted to automatically assume that he is not gay or that his same-sex attraction is the root of his problems. Such a knee-jerk reaction should be avoided at all costs because it incorrectly assumes a pathological effect of same-sex feelings and discounts the strong possibility that this client may have been traumatized by his social environment, not his sexual orientation. Similarly, a temptation to advocate a gay-affirmative stance is equally problematic because it has yet to be determined that the client is ready to claim a gay identity, and furthermore has yet to decide that he wants to do anything different in his life. What is called for here is a thoughtful investigation of the factors affecting Mr. J. First, his sexual orientation itself must be assessed. This involves not just a history of sexual behavior, since for many gay and lesbian individuals, behavior itself may be misleading. The individual's fantasy life, including autoerotic activities and affectional attractions, needs to be explored in order to assist the individual in understanding her/his sexual orientation.

A host of other sociocultural factors are evident in the story of Mr. J. How has his view of himself been influenced by his family, culture, and church? Does his wish to have a traditional heterosexual family stem from social expectation rather than from genuine desire, and if so, what are the implications of this? If he were to self-identify as gay and come out, what losses would he potentially face? And how would he cope with his anxieties about life as a gay man—from social, sexual, and racial perspectives? Caucasians in such a situation have significant challenges when they come out; for people of color, the difficulties can be exponentially greater due to racism. And how are Mr. J's spiritual concerns, which he says are important, to be integrated into his life, whatever solution he finds to the question of his sexual orientation?

The foregoing suggests the basic tenet of psychotherapy with lesbian, gay, and bisexual individuals: that issues of sexual identity invariably exist in a crucible forged by personal, familial and social factors. The therapist's primary task with such individuals is to suspend all assumptions and to lead an exploration with often difficult questions. Most assuredly, there are no easy answers to questions such as Mr. J's. Nevertheless, the therapist is obliged to carefully examine her/his own assumptions about sexual orientation and not impose a directive of orientation change on an individual whose problems may ultimately result from the introjection of antigay social stigma.

The therapist's capacity for introspection is particularly critical when she/he is faced with a client who holds opinions, or has thoughts and feelings, that differ from the therapist's. The following example is one that comes up frequently in training settings:

> Ann is an intern who is doing an internship at a community mental health agency in a small town. She hopes to specialize in working with children and adolescents. A 16-year-old female client with whom she has been working tells her of a strong attraction she is experiencing toward another girl in her school. The client goes on to say that this is not the first such attraction she has experienced, and she wonders if it might mean that she is gay. The intern belongs to a church which views homosexuality as a sin, and she cannot explore this issue with her young client in a value-neutral manner. The intern seeks guidance from her supervisor.

This situation is particularly common for therapists-in-training, some of whom may have yet to determine what their own internal limitations may be relative to the provision of services to different populations. The rule, however, is relatively straightforward: Professional ethics supersede personal beliefs, whatever they may be. There are no justifications for therapeutic neutrality to be compromised for personal feelings, even strongly held religious convictions. If the therapist or intern is unable, because of personal beliefs, to help a client explore issues around her/his sexual orientation in a value-neutral manner, then it is the responsibility of the clinician to refer.

A case opposite in content but similar in principle might be the individual who presents seeking to change his sexual orientation. Thorough investigation of the underlying reasons does nothing to change the person's intentions, and it reveals that the strength of religious convictions and primacy of identification with the church are in fact as strong as the individual's experience of sexual orientation. The rigidity of this stance may be difficult for some gay-affirmative practitioners; further, it may cause speculation about repression, which may well be accurate. However, our responsibility is to assist people in their life journeys to the extent that we are able; it is not to instruct them in how to live their lives. People whose deeply held religious beliefs make reconciling their same-sex sexual orientation impossible are probably better off seeking counsel in their religious institutions.

A corollary to the principle that we respect the different thoughts and feelings of others is that we acknowledge the client's right to self-determination. Often, heterosexually-married lesbians or gay men will present to treatment seeking support in leaving their marriages. This case is a slightly different spin on a familiar clinical issue:

> Mr. D is a 40-year-old mid-level manager for a small company. He has been married for 10 years and has three young children, with a fourth on the way. He acknowledges that his relationship with his wife has always been unfulfilling, largely because he considers himself to be homosexual. Mr. D has attended a local support group for heterosexually-married gay men, but has no interest in leaving the marriage or coming out, given his strong commitment to the family. Mr. D seeks consultation and guidance around this difficult choice.

In a case such as this, one wonders what the ultimate effect of Mr. D's choice is on his wife and children. Does the fact of his stated homosexual orientation impact his capacity to function as a parent or husband? While it may be quite likely that, at the very least, Mr. D's wife experiences a distant quality to the marital relationship, it is nonetheless important for the therapist to honor, not attempt to dismantle, the paradox that Mr. D has created in his life. On the one hand, it might occur to the therapist to challenge Mr. D's assertion that he is indeed homosexual, because he is heterosexually married and soon to be the father of four. In and of itself, however, heterosexual marriage is not a meaningful criterion by which to assess sexual orientation; for numerous reasons, many homosexually oriented people marry heterosexually. On the other hand, it is not the business of the therapist in this case to challenge Mr. D's choice, as if to encourage him to embrace his "true," homosexual self. Problematic though this choice may be, particularly for Mr. D's wife, this is a case where the client's right to self-determination must be honored. Therefore, the therapist is available to process the complexities of living with this choice and recognizes that Mr. D may come to make a different choice in the future, or he may not. But in any event, the choice is his.

Often, therapists may be unfamiliar both personally and clinically with issues of sexual orientation, given the relative paucity of training in this area in graduate psychology programs (Pilkington & Carter, 1996). Nevertheless, as consumers of psychotherapy in proportionally greater numbers than heterosexuals, it is likely that most practitioners will see lesbian, gay, and bisexual clients at some point in their practices. Advanced expertise on the issues faced by many lesbian, gay, or bisexual clients cannot be expected of the generalist; however, understanding of basic principles is a prerequisite for competent practice. One area that is particularly distorted by misinformation in clinical issues presented by sexual minority clients is that of relationships. The following case example illustrates two very basic and important points about relationships:

> Ms. H and Ms. T, both in their mid-40s, come for relationship counseling. They live in a small town and present with needs for conflict resolution and general communication styles. The couple seems unable to make joint decisions, even relatively minor ones, such as whether to spend the holidays together or with their respective families of origin. Further, they have been subjected to harassment and verbal abuse in their small town. They are fearful that the name-calling and vandalism to their home may escalate to physical attacks. Ms. T has two children, ages 7 and 12, from a previous marriage.

Fundamentally, the therapist must confer legitimacy upon this family. To attribute the couple's problems to their sexual orientation verges on malpractice. As such, it is entirely plausible that the couple may need modeling for good communication and conflict resolution, understanding that they have grown up in a society that provides them no models for how to interact. It is also likely that some interventions relative to issues of the combined family, as well as the unique concerns faced by children and adolescents with lesbian and gay parents, will need to be considered. Further, they may need support for whatever ways they choose to establish the primacy of their relationship, such as the act of creating their own holiday traditions. But most important, the potential effect of the hostile social environment on the psychological functioning of this family must be considered. Lesbian and gay couples, unlike heterosexuals, cannot take for granted the support of society and its institutions. In many cases, such couples are faced with social isolation at best or outright physical attack at worst, particularly those in rural areas who are not insulated by a gay community. The natural responses to such environmental stress, which may be cumulative and life-long, must never be misinterpreted as somehow the result of same-sex sexual orientation. The legitimacy of same-sex relationships along with the capacity for healthy family lives, including the potential to be healthy, loving, parents, must be assumed by the practitioner. At the same time, the potentially injurious impact of living in a homophobic world must be considered.

> Jason is a 17-year-old high school student who has been referred to the school psychologist by his parents. Of particular concern is what appears to be Jason's gender atypical behavior; he is often socially isolated, or in the company of a few female friends. He has been beaten up numerous times. Jason's parents are fearful that he may become gay if he does not participate in a therapy program to change his feelings. The school psychologist is asked to make an assessment and a referral. Though Jason is reluctant to speak openly, he does admit that sometimes he thinks he may be gay, although he is uncertain about his feelings.

Concerned as the family may be, Jason is the school psychologist's first priority. His hesitancy to talk may be more than just adolescent reticence; he has clearly been victimized in violent ways by peers and may likely feel quite self-protective around his family, given their agenda. The school psychologist in this situation is not required to make up Jason's mind for him about his sexual orientation but, rather, to provide a place—perhaps the only place—where Jason may explore freely his feelings relative to sexual orientation. More than anything, Jason needs validation; to be told that he is experiencing a "transitory phase," or to be advised to seek conversion therapy when the idea does not originate with him, is unhelpful and inappropriate.

The notion of making a referral to a conversion therapist, should that be Jason's wish, is in and of itself problematic. First, like all practitioners, conversion therapists are ethically required to state honestly the theoretical basis for the treatment offered, to describe the treatment itself, and to offer a clear sense of reasonable expectations for treatment outcomes. The theoretical premise of all conversion therapies has been rejected; in the ethical interest of full disclosure, this must be reported to the prospective patient. The treatments and their outcomes may not be misrepresented; therefore, claims of successful "cures" must be tempered with the qualifiers that such outcomes are not empirically validated. Further, conversion therapists themselves acknowledge that their interventions are more likely to result in increased heteroerotic competence than an actual shift in sexual orientation itself; this, too, needs to be part of fully informed consent to treatment. Minors such as Jason are not legally able to consent to conversion treatments. This is of particular significance due to the anecdotal reports of adolescents being subjected to aversive procedures to change sexual orientation, under the diagnostic guise of some variety of personality disorder. Last, referral to any specialist implies that the practitioner has a scope of practice that is founded in formal training and/or continuing education. Organized psychology sanctions no such curricula with regard to sexual orientation conversion therapy, thus rendering improbable the legitimate referral to such practitioners.

A comprehensive understanding of clinical issues relevant to lesbian, gay, and bisexual clients could seem out of reach to the practitioner unfamiliar with these populations. Nevertheless, some familiarity with the aforementioned basic issues, while not a substitute for clinical training, will serve as a good start for the clinician seeking to serve lesbian, gay, and bisexual clients in a competent fashion. Consultative assistance for therapists is available through the APA's Society for the Psychological Study of Lesbian, Gay, and Bisexual Issues or the APA's Office of Lesbian, Gay, and Bisexual Concerns.

Summary: Future Directions

The case vignettes illustrate several basic principles relative to work with sexual minority clients. First and foremost, same-sex sexual orientation itself should never be pathologized nor interpreted as the basis for an individual or couple's problems. The therapist must consciously confront whatever biases she/he may hold relative to same-sex sexual orientation so that they do not contaminate the therapeutic process or lead the therapist to develop an a priori agenda relative to the goals of treatment. When discomfort with sexual orientation is at issue, it is especially important that the therapist conduct a careful inquiry that includes the historical and existential implications of this discomfort rather than impose a personal agenda on an individual who is likely already burdened with confusion and guilt. Heterosexual therapists need to be particularly sensitive to the potential impact of familial, social, and institutional antigay prejudice on the individual's psychological functioning. Normative responses to social stressors and victimization are sometimes mimetic of intrinsic emotional problems. Additionally, all therapists need to be aware of the potential impact of multiple minority status faced by lesbian, gay, and bisexual people of color. Gay, lesbian, and bisexual individuals may indeed be in a statistical minority, but that does not disqualify them from being excellent partners and parents, nor does it diminish their capacity for healthy, loving family relationships.

In adopting its 1997 policy on "Appropriate Therapeutic Responses to Sexual Orientation," the APA has taken a major step forward, from clarifying its position on the psychological nature of sexual orientation to developing an ethical framework within which competent practice with lesbian, gay, and bisexual clients occurs. The next step is a formal, detailed set of practice guidelines, which would provide practitioners and educators with specific recommendations and their relevant bases in the literature. Such guidelines are currently in development as a joint project between APA's Division 44 and the Committee on Lesbian, Gay, and Bisexual Concerns.

The development of policies and guidelines to assist practitioners and trainers in their work with lesbian, gay, and bisexual clients serves more than the obvious practical needs. This evolution of psychology's position on the treatment of lesbian, gay, and bisexual individuals makes a strong public statement about the way in which psychological science views same-sex sexual orientation. By bringing the substantial knowledge base of psychology into the public arena, we can keep the promise we made so long ago: "to take the lead in removing the stigma long associated with homosexual orientation" (Conger, 1975, p. 633). In this way, sexual minorities living in areas where antigay legislative efforts are fueled by erroneous arguments that sexual orientation is "freely chosen," thus legitimizing denying civil rights to sexual minorities, are assisted by psychology's public declarations of what science reveals. Thus, psychology's policies about sexual orientation benefit all lesbian, gay, and bisexual individuals, client and nonclient alike.

References

American Psychological Association (1997). *Appropriate therapeutic responses to sexual orientation.* Unpublished policy statement.

Begelman, D. A. (1975). Ethical and legal issues of behavior modification. In M. Hersen, R. Eisler, & P. M. Miller (Eds.), *Progress in behavior modification* (pp. 175-188). San Diego, CA: Academic Press.

Brown, L. S. (1996). Preventing heterosexism and bias in psychotherapy and counseling. In E. Rothblum & L. Bond (Eds.), *Preventing heterosexism and homophobia* (pp. 36-58). Thousand Oaks, CA: Sage.

Conger, J. J. (1975). Proceedings of the American Psychological Association, Incorporated, for the year 1974: Minutes of the annual meeting of the Council of Representatives. *American Psychologist, 30,* 620-651.

Dallas, J. (1996). In defense of clinical treatment for homosexuality. *Journal of Psychology and Christianity, 15*(4), 369-372.

Davison, G. C. (1991). Constructionism and morality in therapy for homosexuality. In J. C. Gonsiorek and J. D. Weinrich (Eds.), *Homosexuality: Research implications for public policy* (pp. 137-148). Newbury Park, CA: Sage.

Drescher, J. (1997). I'm your handyman: A history of reparative therapies. *Journal of Homosexuality, 30*(1), 19-47.

Garnets, L. D., Hancock, K. A., Cochran, S. D., Goodchilds, J., & Peplau, L. A. (1991). Issues in psychotherapy with lesbians and gay men: A survey of psychologists. *American Psychologist, 46,* 964-972.

Gonsiorek, J. (1991). The empirical basis for the demise of the illness model of homosexuality. In J. Gonsiorek & J. Weinrich (Eds.), *Homosexuality: Research implications for public policy* (pp. 115-136). Newbury Park, CA: Sage.

Haldeman, D. C. (1991). Sexual orientation conversion therapy: A scientific examination. In J. Gonsiorek & J. Weinrich (Eds.), *Homosexuality: Research implications for public policy* (pp. 149-160). Newbury Park, CA: Sage.

Haldeman, D. C. (1994). The practice and ethics of sexual orientation conversion therapy. *Journal of Consulting and Clinical Psychology, 62*(2), 221-227.

Haldeman, D. C. (1996). Spirituality and religion in the lives of lesbians and gay men. In T. Stein & R. Cabaj (Eds.), *Textbook of homosexuality and mental health* (pp. 881-896). Washington, DC: American Psychiatric Press.

In brief. (1997, August 22). *The Advocate,* p. 17.

Martin, A. (1984). The emperor's new clothes: Modern attempts to change sexual orientation. In E. S. Hetrick & T. S. Stein (Eds.), *Innovations in psychotherapy with homosexuals* (pp. 24-57). Washington, DC: American Psychiatric Press.

Morgan, K. (1992). Caucasian lesbians' use of psychotherapy. *Psychology of Women Quarterly, 16,* 127-130.

Murphy, T. (1992). Redirecting sexual orientation: Techniques and justifications. *Journal of Sex Research, 29,* 501-523.

Nicolosi, J. (1991). *Reparative therapy of male homosexuality: A new clinical approach.* Northvale, NJ: Jason Aronson.

Nystrom, N. (1997, February). *Mental health experiences of gay men and lesbians.* Paper presented at the annual meeting of the American Association for the Advancement of Science, Seattle, WA.

Pilkington, N., & Cantor, J. (1996). Perceptions of heterosexual bias in professional psychology programs: A survey of graduate students. *Professional Psychology: Research and Practice, 27*(6), 604-612.

Stein, T. A (1996). Critique of approaches to changing sexual orientation. In T. Stein & R. Cabaj (Eds.), *Textbook of homosexuality and mental health* (pp. 525-537). Washington, DC: American Psychiatric Press.

Washington State Psychological Association. (1991, March). *Policy statement on sexual orientation conversion therapy.* Unpublished document.

11

Lesbian, Gay, and Bisexual People of Color

A Challenge to Representative Sampling in Empirical Research

GLADYS L. CROOM

Facilitating the participation and inclusion of underrepresented group members in research samples continues to be a challenge even as we approach the new millennium. Empirical studies containing lesbian, gay, bisexual, and transgendered (LGBT) people from limited segments of the white community have been more forthcoming in contemporary research efforts. However, people of color are rarely included in these efforts (Bradford, Ryan, & Rothblum, 1994; Gonsiorek, 1991). This chapter examines some of the historical problems encountered when attempts have been made to include persons of color in empirical research efforts. It also examines challenges, concerns, and the implications of failed attempts to include LGBT people of color in those endeavors.

Theoretical models for conceptualizing "homosexual" identity formation or sexual orientation have been proposed by researchers from the lesbian, gay, and bisexual (LGB) communities (Cass, 1979, 1984; MaCarn & Fassinger, 1996; Sophie, 1985, 1986; Troiden, 1989) and for people of color (Chan, 1989; Morales, 1983, 1990). These models, and the models proposed by others for people of color, consistently underscore the presence of an intrapsychic conflict resulting from the need to negotiate race and the effect of racism on their identity, the need to resolve the conflict, and identity shifts surrounding issues of sexual orientation, and/or sexual orientation and ethnicity, along a developmental continuum. Most LGB persons move through this developmental process without the need to negotiate race and racism's effects on the synthesis of a positive LGB identity, as well as a positive ethnic identity (Chan, 1989; Greene, 1997; Greene & Boyd-Franklin, 1996; Morales, 1990). However, these salient realities and dynamics affect LGB people of color differently than white LGB people because they have multiple identities that are associated with negative stereotypes and are stigmatized. The challenges associated with these multiple identities influence how, when, and where members attempt to negotiate the world psychologically.

In a study on Latina lesbians, Espin (1987) wrote, "When confronted with the choice of being among Latins without coming out, or living among lesbians who are not Latin or who are unfamiliar with the Latin culture, eleven of the women (interviewed) said they had chosen or would choose the second alternative" (p. 47). Loiacano (1989) observed that "black American gay men and lesbians have the challenge of integrating at least two central identities that can be highly charged in our society— being black and gay or lesbian. This particular challenge is likely to be similar for other people of color and is not faced by white Americans. These and other similar issues warrant further research" (p. 24). Chan (1989) adds that "because identity development is a fluid, ever changing process, an individual may choose to identify and identify more closely with being lesbian or gay or Asian American at different times depending on need and situational factors" (p. 383). These writers acknowledge the existence of multiple identities of gay, lesbian, and bisexual people of color, particularly when minority status, disadvantage, and stigma are associated with ethnic group membership.

It is fair to say that LGB people of color have multiple allegiances and identities, and the expression of different aspects of their identities is something that they must constantly negotiate. As a result they must often hide or conceal their sexual orientations from their ethnic communities. They may also have to limit, ignore, or minimize the ethnic parts of themselves when interacting with the larger gay community, as they confront the racism within that community (Greene, 1994; Mays & Cochran, 1988). LGB people of color must negotiate the realities of racial and ethnic discrimination as well as homophobia. This complicates the process of identity development because it is done in a climate that is pervasively hostile to these individuals. Managing multiple identities in a hostile climate requires both flexibility and fluidity. LGB people of color must routinely move within and between different cultures. For many LGB people of color, the need to move between and within different cultures can leave them feeling as if they are caught between mutually exclusive worlds. This is particularly painful when each culture or community may be antagonistic to other aspects of the person's identity. The LGB person of color may be left with a sense of having no one place to call home, where both their ethnicity and sexual orientation can be treated with respect and accepted. It is in this nexus of feeling caught between worlds that do not appear to intersect that a sense of conflicting allegiances may develop among LGB people of color. Individuals may feel as if they must establish a primary identity and/or a primary identification with one group, and relinquish others. Those feelings may be reinforced by family members or ethnic peers who openly demand that the individual "choose sides" or declare one identity or peer group to be more important than the other. However, individuals who feel compelled to make such choices may also feel conflicted about which group or identity to claim and which to relinquish. An outcome that does not result in the integration of all aspects of a person's identity into an integrated whole is not only painful for the individual but lacks authenticity and is problematic psychologically.

The different values that society has ascribed to the varied aspects of LGB people of color and their identities, the degree to which they are internalized or not, the conscious and unconscious decisions made regarding what part of themselves to present, and how they feel about themselves are all important areas of exploration in psychology. In fact, their exploration is required if we are to discern the reality of the lives of lesbians and gay men in ways that reflect the realistic diversity of this large heterogeneous group. These variables must be included in any research endeavor. Without them, the failure to appropriately contextualize the lives of the population or phenomena being studied leads to results and generalizations that are of questionable validity. The presence of these unique challenges and life experiences, the ways they alter the lives of LGB people of color for better or worse (that is not shared by their white counterparts) would certainly influence measurement outcomes in empirical research (Gerrard, 1995; Loiacano, 1989; Morales, 1990). We know that sexuality is contextual and its meaning, expression, and salience varies from culture to culture. We have learned from HIV research with people of color that the way information about sexuality is presented and by whom may greatly determine whether or not people use that information or even believe it. This has been critical in the work that addresses safe-sex techniques, their communication, and their role in HIV infection prevention. Without gathering empirical data on LGB people of color, we are at a loss to make reliable scientific statements about them or about the broader population of lesbians and gay men in which they are embedded.

Facilitating the participation and inclusion of underrepresented group members in research samples continues to be a challenge in empirical psychological research. When LGBT people of color are included, sample sizes are too often too small to be statistically rigorous, relevant, or generalizable. Hence, they are not indicative of behavior beyond the group sampled. In some cases, they are subsumed within the larger group being studied. This does not allow readers to discern how the LGBT persons of color, who are subjects, respond to those measurements as ethnic groups. These subgroups of people of color typically remain absent from empirical research as hidden, invisible members whose presence is assumed or ignored but whose voices are rarely heard.

The omission of members of LGBT ethnic groups from the psychological literature may not be intentional but certainly reflects the historically difficult relationships and the dynamics of power between the dominant community of white Americans and people of color. The practice of omitting LGBT members of ethnic minority groups in the manner previously described fosters a range of assumptions about people of color and white Americans that are of questionable validity. The omission of ethnic minority group members may in part be a result of the assumption that only people of color have ethnic and cultural characteristics that are important to identify or that influence their behavior. Research scientists who believe this may view the presence of people of color in research samples to be unnecessary unless the research focuses specifically on ethnic characteristics. The continued practice of omission reinforces this and other questionable assumptions. One example is reflected in the assumption that not only are white people devoid of cultural distinctions but that the behavior, values, and attitudes attributed to them are normative. This leads to the assumption that the behaviors and values attributed to white Americans as a group should serve (and has served) as the behavioral standard to which people of color should be compared. Not surprisingly, when people of color are measured against this presumed standard, they rarely compare favorably. It is important to understand the arbitrary nature of the standards that are applied when the aforementioned assumptions are made and to appreciate the many ways that they distort our understanding of human behavior.

Ostensibly, the goal of behavioral research is to learn as much as the state of the art allows about how people behave, what determinants influence their behavior, the means by which behavior is influenced and the significance of the influence, how people understand their behavior, and how they attempt to negotiate practical and psychological challenges to optimize their functioning. As clinicians we are confronted with the need to discern the factors that interfere with optimal functioning as well as the factors that facilitate it. This information is essential in our efforts to help individuals who do not function optimally and who seek psychological services to assist them in doing so.

Historical Research With Ethnic Populations

Concerns have been raised about the role of white cross-cultural researchers in the development of historical data about ethnic populations. Neighbors, Jackson, Campbell, and Williams (1989) discuss how racial factors influence psychiatric diagnosis. Often, diagnostic errors occur in clinical practice because of a lack of awareness and/or sensitivity to cultural distinctions and differences that are affecting behavior. Without this sensitivity it may be difficult for a clinician to determine the variability of presenting symptoms and complaints in different ethnic groups. This would make the diagnostic process more difficult as well. Graham (1992), in her examination of the trends in published research, observed that many empirical studies on black Americans lacked methodological rigor. The journal articles surveyed in Graham's study did not measure the socioeconomic status (SES) of the subjects and lacked careful controls on the ethnicity of the experimenter. Furthermore, much of the research does not include African American research scientists and data collectors at all. The preponderance of data collected in empirical studies on African Americans were obtained by white researchers with no consideration or discussion of the effect of the experimenter's ethnicity on the results. Moreover, Graham (1992) observed that there is a diminishing pool of African American psychologists and that this small pool will ultimately diminish the pool of potential African American research scientists who are capable of and/or interested in participating in empirical research efforts.

Other studies (Helms, 1993; Mio & Iwamasa, 1993; Pedersen, 1993; Ponterotto, 1993; Sue, D. W. & Sue, D. 1972) examined ethnic minority research scientists' feelings about white cross-cultural research scientists. Historically, research efforts by members of ethnic minority groups have not been published to the degree that their white counterparts have in major journals (Graham, 1992; Ponterotto, 1988). Concurrently, white research scientists have often been the sole beneficiaries of research efforts "obtaining grants, promotion, and tenure" without contributing to the betterment of the ethnic group under study (Gerrard, 1995; Sue, 1993). Ethnic minority subjects reported feeling that their uniqueness was deemed unimportant or less desirable when they participated in research efforts (Pedersen, 1993). A variety of explanations are offered for the tendency to stigmatize the characteristics of ethnic minority participants. One explanation is that it may be, and has historically been, used to manipulate and control them. The ultimate goal of this manipulation is to make them feel that they should want to assimilate into the dominant culture (Pedersen, 1993, 1998). Mio et al. (1993) noted the tendency of white research scientists to conduct research without caring for or understanding the people studied in ways that often left ethnic minority subjects feeling "raped" by the process. Furthermore, due to the historical and contemporary manner that research efforts are conducted by white cross-cultural research scientists, both ethnic minority subjects, potential ethnic minority subjects, and ethnic minority research scientists generally remain suspicious of white researchers' continued research efforts (Gerrard, 1995; Graham, 1992; Mays & Cochran, 1988; Pedersen, 1993).

One of the problems that accompanies white cross-cultural research is the research scientists' own lack of awareness of his or her own self as a cultural/ethnic entity. As the presence of white skin is valued, rewarded, and therefore privileged in the United States, differences between members of white ethnic groups are minimized and their ethnic heritage, values, beliefs, and experiences of ethnic prejudice are rendered invisible (Dworkin, 1997; Fygetakis, 1997). This may be reflected in the tendency of many white Americans to see themselves as simply "Americans." Many white Americans felt compelled to relinquish their own ethnic identity to assimilate into the dominant culture and to escape ethnic discrimination themselves. They may be reluctant to revisit the unpleasant feelings associated with their own ethnic struggles. These feelings, a lack of familiarity with the populations being studied, and other factors may be evoked when similar issues in members of ethnic minority groups are addressed. Hence, this process may generate general feelings of discomfort for all parties concerned. Many white cross-cultural research scientists have difficulty confronting and/or acknowledging the discomfort they experience working with ethnic minority populations. Mio and Iwamasa (1993) write that white cross-cultural research scientists also have difficulty working as equal partners in research with ethnic minority research scientists. Ethnic minority members may have been identified by ethnic minority group members as experts on multicultural issues and concerns (Mio & Iwamasa, 1993). Some white cross-cultural research scientists may fear rejection or intellectual dismissal from ethnic minority colleagues when their weaknesses in these areas are exposed (Ponterotto, 1993). They may be unfamiliar with being in a position where they are not the presumed authority on all matters. They may also fear angry confrontations and challenges from members of ethnic minority groups in subject pools (Ponterotto, 1993). However, the presence and expression of such fears and concerns can be informative and instructive. It can be viewed as an opportunity for white cross-cultural research scientists to acquire feedback about the way their ideas, beliefs, and approaches to members of ethnic minority groups affect members of those groups and perhaps warrant scrutiny. These feelings among subjects and research scientists may interfere with conducting the very research that is being attempted. Similarly, the ideas, beliefs, and approaches taken by ethnic minority cross-cultural research scientists will also affect the process. Hence, white cross-cultural research scientists must be willing to examine their feelings, perceptions, and misperceptions about ethnic minority populations. Self-examination by white cross-cultural research scientists involves a willingness to experience some level of discomfort as they attempt to open themselves to the experience of ethnic minority people and white cross-cultural researchers' beliefs, ideas, thoughts, and misperceptions about them. Although this process of self-examination may heighten white cross-cultural researchers' awareness of the ways they have behaved and regarded ethnic minority people, the process will not necessarily result in the elimination of ingrained beliefs, misperceptions, attitudes, and behaviors toward ethnic minority people in the future. Including ethnic minority research scientists as equal partners in research efforts can temper and/or eliminate the potential for white cross-cultural researcher biases to interfere in research endeavors. By engaging in authentic, not tokenistic collaborative efforts, they can learn from their ethnic minority colleagues and maintain or develop a more open discourse (Mio & Iwamasa, 1993; Pedersen, 1993).

Nikki Gerrard (1995) addressed many of these issues when she reported on her experience as a white feminist researcher confronted with reactions from the women of color she attempted to include in her research. She observed,

> Part of addressing racism is to hear the stories of women who have been the targets of it. The research in which I was involved was an endeavor to render visible the stories of women of color who had been clients in mental health systems. (p. 56) . . . As I examined my own feelings I realized that I had reacted to her (a black feminist therapist) as I do to anyone who leaves me feeling dismissed and powerless. I realized that this probably was part of how it would feel to be black: to have whites reject, dismiss, and disempower me without any knowledge of who I am as a person. (p. 58)

Although discouraged and hurt in this process, she continued to reflect on her experience and reported that some of her intended subjects had been hurt by "research abuse." She describes research abuse as

> the practice of researchers parachuting into peoples lives, interfering, raising painful old feelings, and then vanishing, leaving the participants to deal with unresolved feelings alone and isolated. (p. 62)

The challenges inherent in conducting research with representative ethnic minority groups sampled become even more complex when one attempts to examine other groups who are also marginalized and therefore may be hidden and/or invisible. These omissions can have serious implications. For example, subgroups of Asian Americans have been observed to have lower rates of cancer, diabetes, and hypertension than white Americans, whereas African Americans have a higher rate than either group populations (Anderson & Cohen, 1989). Groups comprising aged ethnic minority group members are rarely included in populations sampled. This occurs despite data that suggests that there is an interaction between aging and ethnicity. This is evident when examining life expectancies, differential disease rates, physiological characteristics, ethnic variations in responses to psychotropic drugs, as well as within race variability of occurrence of disease rates (Anderson & Cohen, 1989; Jacobsen, 1994). Hence, the failure to include hidden populations can affect the efficacy of chosen treatment approaches as well as how symptoms are viewed. The omission of these populations in research can also leave us with inaccurate information about measurement levels used to denote the presence of disease thresholds. These omissions influence the assessment of clinical trials. For example, when clinical trials of new drug therapies are performed that exclude or have inadequate representation from ethnic minority populations, such trials may yield erroneous data on the efficacy as well as the risks and dangers of those drug therapies. Moreover, the exclusion of ethnic minority or subgroups of ethnic minority populations from research samples and/or clinical trials influence whether or not established norms indicate the presence or absence of physical disease and/or mental health in these individual groups.

Barriers to Empirical Research With LGBT People of Color

Locating persons belonging to hidden or invisible populations can pose many realistic obstacles to research scientists. However, many of those obstacles can be overcome. Often, research scientists do not have access to randomized samples, and they must employ other techniques. One technique is the snowball method. When this method is used, subjects are gathered through outreach to friends and organizations known to provide refuge and protection to the population being studied. This often yields significant numbers of subjects. Other methods used to locate subjects involve soliciting through magazines catering to LGBT persons and conferences as well as social events held and attended primarily by LGBT persons. However, although these methods yield some participation, they consist of or are overrepresented by middle- class ethnic minority group members. Members of these groups or middle-class members may be selectively informed about such events. They may attend organizational meetings and may be attending or have graduated from college or graduate school. They generally do not include people who may avoid what they perceive to be classist/racist/sexist institutions and establishments, whether in fact those venues are or not. This is one example of how they are hidden. Hence, outreach to any of the aforementioned establishments will not usually include grassroots group members or people who are not aware of the existence of such venues. They also do not generally include those who avoid frequenting such places if they fear disclosure of their sexual orientation and the attendant loss of support from their ethnic communities or loss of employment. There are also small groups of LGB persons in many parts of the United States who privately socialize in each others' homes rather than in public bars and clubs. They represent another hidden population of LGB people. Furthermore, there are many who belong to clubs or organizations, whose members are lesbian or gay but who do not openly identify themselves as such.

Hence, the exclusion of more representative LGBT ethnic minority subjects limits the information we gather on the development of self-esteem, disclosure, the impact of diversity on and within ethnic minority group members, parenting, and so forth. It is important to consider the implications of our ignorance about the loss of such support on the subsequent development of a person with a healthy, positive sense of self, capable of acting authentically in their ethnic communities as well as in the LGBT community.

Mentoring

Finding persons who are open to conducting research with LGBT persons of color may be particularly difficult and challenging. Some LGBT researchers, whether they are white or members of ethnic minority groups, may avoid revealing their sexual orientation. This is particularly true for those who are not "out" at work, to family, friends, or their communities. Often, ethnic minority faculty members will not openly support the conduct of research on LGBT persons and may avoid being associated with such research. Others who are not LGBT may fear that their colleagues will presume that only LGBT people would be interested in such research and erroneously label them. They may have realistic fears about being doubly vulnerable as ethnic minority faculty members who are associated with stigmatized research or research that their university or departments deem a low priority or of less value. They may also fear spending time on research that is assigned a low priority in the discipline as it may be more difficult to publish in mainstream venues. The failure to publish sufficiently in refereed venues is a frequent obstacle to obtaining tenure in academic institutions, and it has had disproportionately negative effects on ethnic minority faculty members. Other reasons for avoiding or failing to support research in this area for ethnic minority group faculty members may also be attributed to their personal religious beliefs, expressed sense of morality, their own heterosexism, and/or homophobia. They may also harbor realistic fears of a loss of support from their ethnic minority colleagues and their communities as well. Many scientists who may lack expertise in this area of the literature may hesitate to embark on such efforts out of fear that they may not be competent to do so. This concern is at times warranted. Still, others may be unwilling to become more knowledgeable about and/or open about exploring data involving LGBT members of their ethnic group. There are also many research scientists who have distinctly different research interests who do not wish to expand their foci.

White cross-cultural faculty members and research scientists might be willing to assist students with research efforts, but as discussed previously, there have been numerous historical concerns and about being associated with these efforts. Undoubtedly, some ethnic minority research scientists or faculty members may not see themselves as ethnic persons. Their need to distance themselves from group membership may prevent them from appreciating many of the challenges, concerns, and fears that people of color have about being research participants. By and large, white cross-cultural faculty members and research scientists have not always demonstrated an appropriate sensitivity to the way people of color feel when they are being examined. Such researchers may be unaware of negative experiences that ethnic minority group members have had in these situations, or for that matter their anger about how they, or people they know, have been treated. White cross-cultural researchers are frequently unaware that ethnic minority subjects report feeling judged less desirable than white subjects on some dimension or dimensions (Mio & Iwamasa, 1993; Pedersen, 1993; Sue, 1993). White cross-cultural research scientists may not understand how ethnic minority group members feel when asked to reflect on painful aspects of their experiences as people of color. Recalling one's life in the context of a racist, heterosexist, and sexist environment can stir up painful memories and feelings. Many research scientists may be unaware that their questions may require a reliving of many events both recent and distant. Even when struggles associated with these memories were successfully negotiated or managed, they may nonetheless be painful to revisit. Frequently, when the data collection is complete, subjects are summarily dismissed. Their feelings and/or their distress may not be attended to despite the ethical mandate to do so. The experience leaves many subjects feeling used, abused, and dismissed when the research scientists' needs are met. Furthermore, results obtained from research may not be shared with participants or shared in ways that they can understand. This adds to the feeling of being used and disconnected from the outcome.

Materials

Many tests and assessment instruments used for research have been normed on white populations. These instruments have frequently failed to include normative data on ethnically diverse populations. Although some of these standardized instruments may be appropriate for ethnic minority groups, their absence from the norming process raises questions about the standards used in the interpretation and analysis of test responses. The cultural beliefs, characteristics, and values associated with distinct ethnic groups may also impinge on measurement outcomes. For example, how a person experiences family members, family structure, dynamics, roles, and involvement varies across racial and ethnic groups. In some ethnic groups, their cultural practices may dictate that the members prioritize the needs of the group over the needs of an individual or self. Hence, an instrument measuring locus of control may yield results indicative of the cultural values of ethnic minority subjects rather than the locus of control per se. It may suggest the presence of less independent locus of control because the instrument does not address or include cultural values and practices of ethnic minority groups. Furthermore, results may become more difficult to interpret if the subjects are LGBT people of color who are members of different groups or who may be members of more than one minority group. Results may confirm the presence of a locus of control, but the degree to which the trait is present as measured by an instrument may be skewed. The results may more accurately reflect how the individual self-actualizes given his or her multiple status and cultural values. Similarly, instruments designed and normed on specific ethnic minority groups may only be used with accuracy with ethnic members of those specific groups included in the standardization samples. When sexual orientation and/or ethnicity is added as a variable not represented in the sample, the findings may be questionable.

Other Concerns

Frequently when people of color are represented in research samples, results are not tabulated for each ethnic minority group represented. The results therefore do not reveal which ethnic group is represented nor do they reflect how ethnic minority subjects from different ethnic minority groups performed on the traits being studied. Hence, an opportunity to learn where ethnic minority groups differ from one another, how they are similar, and how they make psychological sense of those experiences is missed.

When data are obtained and tabulated, research scientists often make generalizations about groups not included in their samples. This violates the basic methodological principles that govern the generalizability of findings. Tentative speculations about the degree to which findings may be generalized to other groups can be made but must be clearly represented as speculative rather than substantive. The failure to clearly state these limitations in research findings, or to allow the reader to assume otherwise is unethical. With this exception, generalizations should only be applied to the group the sample represents. Hence, if all the subjects were white, results are only generalizable to that population. This assumes that the sample is large enough to warrant any generalizations at all. If the research included a very small sample of people of color from a specific ethnic group, homogeneous ethnic LGBT persons, and/or heterogeneous LGBT people of color, statements regarding the generalization of findings to other LGBT people of color should not be made.

Overcoming Obstacles to Diverse Sampling: Preliminary Suggestions

It is my conviction that, ideally, research scientists and teams conducting research on LGBT persons of color should be representative of the group being studied. Research efforts by white cross-cultural research scientists who are culturally sensitive and aware of the unique challenges confronting LGBT people of color and who are aware of their own perceptions, feelings and misperceptions about LGBT people of color should be supported. However, such research should be conducted by research teams that include a person or people with research expertise, who is a member of the ethnic minority group being studied. The ethnic minority team member or members should be a full partner(s) in the research effort, not simply a consultant(s) with no real authority or input into the project. The latter does not generally assist in this process. Furthermore, the absence of partnership can give the impression that the person of color is merely a token whose presence is intended to convey inclusion in the design and implementation of a study, that is not in fact inclusive.

The use of control groups is problematic for hidden, invisible, and some underrepresented populations. The use of white subjects as control groups is often inappropriate. Using white American subjects as the standard that other groups are or should be compared to negates the attributes, values, and standards of ethnic minority group members. Because LGBT ethnic minority members are not a typical population, research institutions should be open to alternative methodologies when conducting research with these and other underrepresented populations.

Random sampling of LGBT people of color is usually impossible because it is a small, isolated, and often invisible group that is often inaccessible to research scientists. Therefore, the scientist must use a number of techniques and exercise their creativity in attempts to recruit subjects who will ultimately participate.

It is essential in any of these endeavors to approach subjects with respect. By lending their time and assisting us in this work, they are doing us a favor, not the corollary. Some participants may be more inclined to engage in open-ended interviews, whereas others may prefer to complete questionnaires or take standardized tests. There are participants who will be willing to come together during group sessions, some of whom may actually relish opportunities to tell their stories to an interested listener or listeners. Still other participants may prefer to take forms with them, complete them in private, and return them by mail or some other method.

Providing participants with opportunities to debrief is essential, and the absence of these opportunities is considered unethical. It is my personal conviction that when research projects produce financial profits for the institution sponsoring the research for the research scientist(s), or if the scientist is paid for the data, a donation to an organization that can benefit the population being studied should be made. A major obstacle encountered in recruiting subjects from many underserved populations is not merely their justifiable suspiciousness of research efforts coordinated by dominant culture institutions. Neither is their concern about the use of data to further stigmatize them the sole obstacle. Often, they fail to see how, in any way, such efforts actually benefit them. They may have participated in such efforts before or know of people who have. Participants may have given their time and effort and never heard from the research team after the data was collected. With no feedback about the usefulness of their contribution, or in some cases even a thank-you, they may see no reason to participate again.

Research scientists may ask friends and/or colleagues to use their own mailing lists of organizations and LGBT people of color and ask their friends to do the same. The scientists should obtain a letter of introduction from friends and/or colleagues explaining who they are, that their efforts are supported by friends, colleagues, or relevant organizations of the subjects being recruited, and that the friends, not the scientist, are mailing out the enclosed contents to prospective participants. Place the friend's and/or colleague's letter and a self-addressed stamped postcard (to allow the prospective participant to indicate their wish to participate in the research by mailing back the card with their mailing address, etc.) in envelopes that are adequately posted. The letter should include information about how the identities of participants will remain confidential, what the study entails, who will benefit from the data and the outcome, and how they will benefit. The letter should provide details about why you would like to have these participants represented in the data, whether or not results will be made available to them, and when the results will be available. It may be helpful to include the rationale or reason for your interest in the area. The letter of introduction should list the names of any person of color and /or LGBT scientists of color involved in the research project and information about their credentials and expertise. It should also include a telephone number where subjects can contact you should they have questions or want to process their thoughts and feelings during any stage of the research. Of course, the letter should inform them that they can withdraw at any time.

This process can be duplicated somewhat when approaching other sources. Advertisements can be placed in LGBT news magazines. Phone calls can be made to local LGBT organizations (LGBT churches, bookstores, bars, music festivals, conferences, social organizations) to ask for support/participation. Gonsiorek (1991) and Bradford et al. (1994) discuss the methodological limitations of such samples. Personal legwork is essential. It is important to personally go to bars, conferences, and other LGBT events and introduce yourself and your research. Letters can also be sent to organizations requesting an opportunity to meet with them or their representatives to solicit participation from their membership and/or to be allowed to send information for them to disseminate.

Psychology and social science programs must include courses about LGBT persons as a routine feature of their curriculums. It has been scarcely 20 years since the American Psychiatric Association removed "homosexuality" from its diagnostic nomenclature. Despite this and other trends that encourage de-pathologizing LGB sexual orientations, misinformation about LGB persons continues to abound, even within the scientific community. Some of that misinformation may be fueled by the lack of diversity in research samples and the tendency to view the lesbian and gay community as if it were a monolithic entity. Hence, there is a great deal more to be learned about the distinctiveness and similarities between and among lesbians and gay men who are members of ethnic minority groups, as well as white lesbians and gay men who are members of ethnic minority groups themselves. Training programs should openly encourage more research not only with the broader gay and lesbian community but with its members of color as well. This must take place in the context of support for students and research scientists in these endeavors as they may be more costly and time consuming than research with members of majority groups. This may be addressed in part by making certain that relevant journals, books, and other publications, that are not routinely available, are made available in university libraries. When it becomes impossible to make these resources available in libraries, academic departments may be required to take the responsibility for ordering them and making them available to students. Films and videotaped material may be purchased to augment material found in the psychological literature. Forging alliances between the academic community, the lesbian and gay community, and communities of people of color is important. Members of organizations based in those respective communities should be invited to participate on panels in conferences within the university community as part of the training programs' educational process. In the long run, such efforts may serve to decrease the perceived and often realistic distance between those communities and foster working alliances on projects that can be mutually beneficial. Overall, it is less likely that members of those communities will experience the prospect of participating in research endeavors as occasions to be exploited and discarded for someone else's benefit if they are embraced, respected, and encouraged to give input.

Empirical research course content can include examples of data samples from LGBT populations from both ethnic minority groups and the larger LGBT population. Faculty members of these programs must be encouraged to expand their own skills and knowledge base in this area or they will be unable to appropriately teach research skills or supervise research in this area. Additionally, training programs should provide incentives for scientists who have the requisite research expertise and/or membership in the populations being studied to become advisors to students. This may be done in the form of course reductions, salary increments, or other means of compensating them for the additional time and work involved in a process that may include more responsibility as chairs and committee members on dissertations and clinical research projects. Furthermore, funding agencies must prioritize the work of LGB scientists who are people of color. Without adequate funding this work will not take place and groups that are currently underrepresented will continue to be so.

Finally, good research designs are necessary for all populations. Moreover, given that LGBT and ethnic minorities have been pathologized historically in empirical research and in the psychological literature, it is especially important to provide accurate information to correct those distortions. We are challenged to develop a new and accurate database to supplant preexisting information of questionable validity.

References

Anderson, N. B., & Cohen, H. J. (1989). Health status of aged minorities directions for clinical research. *Journal of Gerontology: Medical Sciences, 44*(1), m1-m2.

Bradford, J., Ryan, C., & Rothblum, E. D. (1994). National lesbian health care survey implications for mental health care. *Journal of Consulting and Clinical Psychology, 62*(2), 228-242.

Cass, V. (1979). Homosexual identity formation: A theoretical model. *Journal of Homosexuality, 4,* 219-235.

Cass, V. (1984). Homosexual identity formation: Testing a theoretical model. *Journal of Sex Research, 9,* 143-167.

Chan, C. S. (1989). Issues of identity development among Asian-American lesbians and gay men. *Journal of Counseling and Development, 68,* 16-20.

Dworkin, S. (1997). Lesbian and Jewish: Complex and invisible. In B. Greene (Ed.), *Ethnic and cultural diversity among lesbians and gay men* (pp. 63-87). Thousand Oaks, CA: Sage.

Espin, O. M. (1987). Issues of identity in the psychology of Latina lesbians. In Boston Lesbian Psychologies Collective (Eds.), *Lesbian psychologies* (pp. 35-55). Urbana: University of Illinois Press.

Fygetakis, L. (1997). Greek American Lesbians: Identity odysseys of honorable good girls. In B. Greene (Ed.), *Ethnic and cultural diversity among lesbians and gay men* (pp. 152-190). Thousand Oaks, CA: Sage.

Gerrard, N. (1995). Some painful experiences of a white therapist doing research with women of colour. In J. Adleman & G. Enguidanos (Eds.), *Racism in the lives of women: Testimony, theory, and guides to practice* (pp. 53-63). New York: Harrington Park.

Gonsiorek, J. (1991). The empirical basis for the demise of the illness model of homosexuality. In J. Gonsiorek & J. Weinrich (Eds.), *Homosexuality: Research implications for public policy* (pp. 115-136). Minneapolis, MN: Walk-In Counseling Center.

Graham, S. (1992). Most of the subjects were white and middle class: Trends in published research on African Americans in selected APA journals 1970-1989. *American Psychologist, 47, 3,* 629-639.

Greene, B. (1994). Lesbian women of color: Triple jeopardy. In L. Comas-Diaz & B. Greene (Eds.), *Women of color: Integrating ethnic and gender identities in psychotherapy* (pp. 389-427). New York: Guilford.

Greene, B. (1997). Ethnic minority lesbians and gay men mental health and treatment issues. In B. Greene (Ed.), *Psychological perspectives on lesbian and gay issues: Ethnic and cultural diversity among lesbians and gay men,* (Vol. 3, pp. 216-239). Thousands Oaks, CA: Sage.

Greene, B., & Boyd-Franklin, N. (1996). African American lesbian couples: Ethnocultural considerations in psychotherapy. *Women & Therapy, 19, 3,* 49-60.

Helms, J. E. (1993). I also said "white racial identity influences white researchers." *Counseling Psychologist, 21, 2,* 240-243.

Jacobsen, F. (1994). Psychopharmacology and women of color. In L. Comas-Diaz & B. Greene (Eds.), *Women of color: Integrating ethnic and gender identities in psychotherapy* (pp. 319-338). New York: Guilford.

Loiacano, D. K. (1989). Gay identity issues among black Americans: Racism, homophobia, and the need for validation. *Journal of Counseling & Development, 68,* 21-25.

MaCarn, S. R., & Fassinger, R. E. (1996). Revisioning sexual minority identity formation: A new model of lesbian identity and its implications for counseling and research. *Counseling Psychologist, 24, 3,* 508-534

Mays, V. M., & Cochran, S. D. (1988). The black women's relationship project: A national survey of Black lesbians. In M. Shernoff & W. A. Scott (Eds.), *A sourcebook of gay/lesbian health care* (pp. 55-62). Washington, DC: National Gay and Lesbian Health Foundation.

Mio, J. S., & Iwamasa, G. (1993). To do, or not to do: That is the question for white cross-cultural researchers. *Counseling Psychologist, 21, 2,* 197-212.

Morales, E. S. (1983). *Third world gays and lesbians: A process of multiple identities.* Paper presented at the Ninety-first Annual Convention of American Psychological Association. Anaheim, California.

Morales, E. (1990). Ethnic minority families and minority gays and lesbians. In F. Bozett & M. Sussman (Eds.), *Homosexuality and family relations* (pp. 217-239). New York: Harrington Park.

Neighbors, H. W., Jackson, J. S., Campbell, L., & Williams, D. (1989). The influence of racial factors on psychiatric diagnosis: A review and suggestions for research. *Community Mental Health Journal, 25,* 4, 301-311.

Pedersen, P. (1993). The mulitcultural dilemma of white cross-cultural researchers. *Counseling Psychologist, 21,* 2, 229-232.

Ponterotto, J. G. (1988). Racial/ethnic minority research in the Journal of Counseling Psychology: A content analysis and methodological critique. *Journal of Counseling Psychology, 35,* 4, 410-418.

Ponterotto, J. G. (1993). White racial identity and the counseling professional. *Counseling Psychologist, 21,* 2, 213-217

Sophie, J. (1985). Internalized homophobia and lesbian identity. In J. C. Gonsiorek (Ed.), *A guide to psychotherapy with gay and lesbian clients* (pp. 53-65). New York: Harrington Park.

Sophie, J. (1985-1986). A critical examination of stage theories of lesbian identity development. *Journal of Homosexuality, 12,* 39-51.

Sue, D. W. (1993). Confronting ourselves: The white and racial/ethnic-minority researcher. *Counseling Psychologist, 21,* 2, 244-249

Sue, D. W., & Sue, D. (1972). Ethnic minorities: Resistance to being researched. *Professional Psychology, 2,* 11-17.

Troiden, R. R. (1989). The formation of homosexual identities. *Journal of Homosexuality, 17,* 43-73.

12

The Lesbian and Gay Workplace

An Employee's Guide to Advancing Equity

SUSAN GORE

G ay men and lesbians are coming out all over America, and the impact on the workplace is transformative. Executives, coworkers, human resource professionals, and lesbian, gay, bisexual, and transgendered (LGBT) employees themselves, are confronted with unanswered questions about what it means to acknowledge the existence of nonheterosexuals throughout the business world. The questions are not new. Employment of known gay men became a national issue in 1943 with implementation of the military's policy of exclusion during the second World War (Shilts, 1990). Thirty years later, IBM became the first major U.S. corporation to add sexual orientation to its nondiscrimination policy in 1974, followed soon after by AT&T in 1975.

Since then, the number of employers with gay-inclusive nondiscrimination policies has ballooned to more than 1,600 today, including more than half of the *Fortune* 500, 1,100 other corporations, 200 governmental entities, and 300 educational and nonprofit organizations. Domestic partner benefit (DPB) policies take nondiscrimination a step further by extending access to corporate benefits such as medical care, family leave, and/or pension benefits to the "spouse equivalents" of gay and, frequently, unmarried heterosexual employees. More than 350 employers, ranging from banks to multinational corporations to city and state governments now offer DPBs.

Nonetheless, employers often profess ignorance when it comes to understanding how to address or achieve LGBT workplace equity. This chapter is designed to highlight strategies found to be useful in overcoming that ignorance and the fear most Americans have in relation to LGBT issues, with the goal of promoting workplace equity for all employees.

The LGBT Workplace Survey

Parts of this chapter reflect responses to a survey of LGBT workplace issues created by the author. Of the 202 survey respondents to date, 40% are female and 60% are male, with one self-identified male-to-female transgendered person. Of the respondents, 33% identify as lesbian, 54% as gay male, 7% as bisexual, and 5% as heterosexual. A total of 58% reported working for a corporation, while 24% claimed academic ties. The remaining 19% did not specify their type of employment. Employer size varied widely both within and across the types of employment reported. When asked "Are you 'out' or known to be a LGBT ally?" less than 4% responded "Not at all." More than 28% chose "If someone doesn't know, they haven't met me," and the remainder said they were out to some degree.

Limitations of the survey include the relatively small number of survey respondents and the absence of random sampling techniques used in recruiting responses. Unless otherwise noted, however, highlighted responses reflect trends (or the lack of unanimity) that are consistent across the entire sample. All comments are quoted with permission. Data collection is an ongoing process.

Educating Ourselves

Conventional wisdom suggests that a company's CEO is the best place to start educating about workplace equity for LGBT employees.

More often, the most important educational process takes place within ourselves, as we address internalized homophobia or heterosexism.

Heterosexism

Heterosexism describes the American cultural assumption that everyone is, should be, and really would prefer to be heterosexual. This bias is reflected in virtually all existing institutions, including those that attempt to level the playing field through nondiscrimination employment policies and domestic partner benefits. *These policies would not be necessary in the absence of heterosexism.*

Heterosexism is like other forms of social disadvantage designed to enforce "traditional" cultural values that include negative stereotypes of homosexuality, as well as other "isms" held by Americans. Even the healthiest gay person carries residues of the following influences into adulthood and the workplace:

- **Isolation**—Almost all lesbians, gay men, and bisexual people grow up in families that assume all of its members are heterosexual and which share negative stereotypes and judgments about homosexuality. We are taught about our "deviance" by the people we depend on most during our formative years for acceptance and support.
- **Invisibility**—Because LGBT people as a group are not "obviously" different by skin color, gender, and so on, we may conceal our sexual orientation, either by lying overtly or by failing to correct the presumption of our heterosexuality. Hiding requires ongoing vigilance, however, and can have a high social, psychological, and career cost.
- **Moral, legal, psychological, and religious stigmas**—Despite the American Psychiatric Association's removal of homosexuality from the *Diagnostic and Statistical Manual of Mental Disorders* (APA, 1980), homosexuality is still treated as sinful, psychologically sick, sexually obsessed, criminal, and fatally unhealthy by most institutions and by vocal segments of the population. These institutionally supported stigmas are used to justify discrimination against LGBT people in employment as well as in other personal matters.
- **Silence**—Institutional stigmas make open discussions about homosexuality taboo. The majority of schools, corporations, professional organizations, and researchers still avoid the topic for fear of losing credibility or funding. As a result, misinformation and fear of discovery dominate the experience of anyone beginning to question their presumed heterosexual orientation.

- **Confusion of behavior and identity**—Many people perceive homosexuality to be a behavior rather than an identity. Confusion of behavior with identity also results in the factually inaccurate linkage of homosexuality with child molestation, which is an overwhelmingly heterosexual male behavior.
- **Connection with sexuality**—Open, honest discussion of sexuality or sexual orientation of any kind is difficult in U.S. society. One result is the distortion of sexuality into a commodity (as in advertising), grist for lewd jokes, and the justification for negative stereotypes and discrimination against people who are LGBT.
- **Question of origin and cure**—Questions about what causes a person to be lesbian, gay, bisexual, or transgendered are not directed at heterosexuality. The implied assumption is that if we can identify the cause(s) of homosexuality, we can "cure" it. In the absence of clear medical origins, religious factions claim (sinful) choice.
- **Coming out process**—Because no one is identified as gay or transgendered at birth, LGBT people discover their identities over time, in contradiction to the explicit and implicit teachings of family and other social institutions. In addition to coming to terms with one's own sexual orientation, those who identify as lesbian, gay, bisexual, or transgendered also must decide how much of themselves to make known to others in each new situation.
- **Impact of AIDS**—Like it or not, the AIDS epidemic was the catalyst for attention to "gay issues" in the workplace and throughout society. It is hard to imagine a more highly charged entry into the nation's consciousness. The association of a deadly disease, sexually transmitted, and concentrated among gay men elicited intense reactions in Judeo-Christian middle American culture. Lesbians were affected by the negative stereotypes as well, despite evidence that lesbians are at the lowest risk of AIDS of any sexually active demographic group.

Educated, successful white men who also happened to be gay had never experienced the level of social rejection visited upon them in the company of AIDS. Sick or well, they could not help but perceive their expendability. Having "nothing to lose" because of a terminal diagnosis brought many the courage to advocate for fair treatment. Need for medical benefits and ongoing income was another powerful motivation. It is not possible to quantify the impact of AIDS in the workplace directly. Fundamental to the proliferation of nondiscrimination and domestic partner benefits policies, however, is a shift from the closet to workplace visibility among gay men, lesbians, and our allies.

Risks and Rewards of Coming Out

The risks of coming out in the workplace as LGBT people are well-documented. Our nation's largest employer, the U.S. military, *requires* employees known or suspected to be gay to be discharged regardless of job performance. To date, courts have found this practice to be legal. In addition to risks, potential "rewards" of being out in the workplace include:

- **Increased productivity**—It is hard to focus on your job if you are constantly monitoring conversations or fear being "outed." Shedding pretenses about your personal life frees up the energy needed to work effectively and creatively at the tasks at hand.

- **Improved work relationships**—Research on high-performing teams consistently points to trust, open communications, and mutual respect as critical elements in their success (Bartlett & Ghoshal, 1995; Handy, 1995; Starcevick & Stowell, 1990). Sharing information about life outside work sends several positive messages: you are comfortable with yourself and don't feel compelled to hide a significant part of your life; you trust your coworkers to place more importance on your skills and workplace behavior than on stereotypes and misinformation about "gays"; you are willing to be real with them and expect the same in return. Being out also allows people to see how similar gay and nongay daily routines really are, contrary to stereotype.

- **Job opportunities**—The gay grapevine, like the "old boys' network," has always existed. In 1993, Joe McCormick institutionalized this resource when he opened an executive recruiting firm strictly to place gay and lesbian candidates, most of whom were coming from the military. Today, Joe McCormack and Associates employs four recruiters who billed more than $300,000 in 1996 for placing job candidates. Approximately 15% of McCormack's business now comes from nongay organizations that see value in a diversity-affirmative search firm (McCormack, 1997).

- **Legal standing**—By adding sexual orientation to their nondiscrimination statements and/or offering domestic partner benefits, corporations and governmental entities are formally acknowledging gay employees' rights. It is hard to claim discrimination or to access DPBs, however, from the closet.

- **Fairer compensation**—The U.S. Chamber of Commerce estimates that employee benefits represent 40% in additional value to the average American's salary package. Access to DPBs is a matter of equitable compensation, whether or not an individual employee utilizes specific benefits. LGBT employees who cannot claim DPBs are being significantly undercompensated relative to their married heterosexual coworkers.

- **Self-worth**—The insidious effects of constantly lying about your life are grossly underestimated, perhaps because they, like sexual orientation, are largely invisible. The importance of personal integrity is reflected in several comments from the LGBT workplace survey:

    I am lesbian; I cannot and will not live a lie. When I first came out so visibly, I worried about all this stuff . . . . But it never materialized and, if anything, I've been promoted and treated very well by everyone, including management. I think management is happy to have a happy, productive, contributing dyke in a position of some management power. (Being out is the) sine qua non for me to maintain integrity and have credibility. I have middle-class privilege, so I look upon being out as a duty, not a risk.

Race, Class, and Gender in the LGBT Community

Although we are a minority, being gay does not ensure empathy with the challenges faced by other minorities. Growing up, all of us were taught the values and biases common to our social group of origin. Black, Hispanic, Asian, and other people of color who are gay frequently have different cultural experiences than European American gays. The cost-benefit analysis may well be different for women than for men or for people in different industries or job levels. Although workplace risks for transgender individuals often parallel those experienced by gay men, lesbians, and bisexual people, they also differ significantly.

Consciousness of diversity, avoiding stereotypes, and breaking well-learned habits requires energy and may be ridiculed as "politically correct." It is our diversity across race, class, gender, job classification, and all other attributes, however, that is *potentially* our greatest strength.

Who's Doing What About Gay Workplace Issues?

Ten years ago the notion that gay-inclusive policies could produce added value in the workplace simply did not exist. McNaught (1993) outlines succinctly what gay employees want:

1. A specific employment policy that prohibits discrimination based on sexual orientation.
2. Creation of a safe work environment that is free of heterosexist, homophobic, and AIDS-phobic behaviors.

3. Company-wide education about gay issues in the workplace and about AIDS.
4. Equitable benefits programs that recognize the domestic partners of gay, lesbian, and bisexual employees.
5. Support of a gay/lesbian/bisexual employee support group.
6. Freedom for all employees to participate fully in all aspects of corporate life.
7. Public support of gay issues.

It is estimated that every week another corporation adds sexual orientation to its personnel policies. After the fact, most would say it is a good business decision. First, however, there has to be awareness that "gay" issues are business issues.

Only once have I personally observed a CEO initiate inclusion of LGBT issues in corporate policies and training. Ironically, he was straight; he was thinking of a gay cofounder of the company. Even *more* ironically, the gay cofounder thought it was "okay" to change the corporation's policy but that diversity training specific to sexual orientation was unnecessary because everybody treated him fine.

In October 1996, the Society of Human Resource Management surveyed 3,000 randomly selected individuals from among its 79,000 professional and student members to determine the prevalence of DPB policies (SHRM, 1997). Of the 777 survey responses received, 9 out of 10 respondents said their organizations do not provide DPB. Lack of employee interest was cited as the dominant reason for this absence (56%), followed by concern over increased health care costs (30%), and moral objections (21%).

In contrast, of the 53 organizations offering DPBs, 77% named "work/life needs of employees" as the primary reason. More than half had extended their policy within the previous 2 years, while 34% had offered DPBs for 5 years or more. Among the DPB group, 85% reported their health care costs had remained "about the same." In fact, other surveys of health care costs related to DPB's show slight increases or decreases (1% to 3% either way) corporate wide, due to the likelihood that LGBT employees are younger and less likely to add coverage for the most expensive categories of dependents, a nonworking spouse and children (Becker, 1994).

Size, Geography, Industry Sector

High-tech, multinational *Fortune* 500 companies are among the most visible providers of inclusive nondiscrimination or DPB. Eight of the top 10 North American corporations, ranked in terms of sales, have one or both policies. The sheer number of employees affected highlights the importance of large corporations' support for workplace equity. In terms of social impact, however, the passage of nondiscrimination or DPB policies in cities, counties, and states may be greater. Iowa City, Iowa does not leap to mind as a hotbed of radicalism, yet gay and lesbian employees there enjoy both protection against discrimination and DPBs. Ten states now outlaw employment discrimination based on sexual orientation. Minnesota includes transgender identity in its nondiscrimination statute. Waldron (1996) observes that more than one third of all Americans live in states where discrimination against gays and lesbians in private employment is illegal and violates state law. Employers of every size, industry sector, and geographic reach are potential candidates for advancing workplace equity; the existence of individuals who are willing and able to step forward is the common thread. Individuals are unlikely to succeed in isolation, however. Finding or creating a group of like-minded individuals who can envision a fairer workplace is a critical next step in the process.

Employee Resource Groups

The first groups established to promote LGBT workplace equity were called employee support groups (ESGs). They existed primarily as a buffer against the isolation experienced by LGBT employees. Today, most LGBT affinity groups identify themselves as employee resource groups (ERGs) to emphasize their role as a *resource* in promoting the corporation's overall business objectives. American Airlines' ERG, GLEAM, actively participates in the development of incentive programs targeting the gay consumer market, for example, as do many other employee resource groups in their respective fields. In general, ERGs serve some or all of the following functions:

- **Personal support**—LGBT employees may feel isolated or have experienced difficulties in the workplace due to their sexual orientation or gender identity; some simply may want to meet others with presumably similar interests.

- **Safety in numbers**—Being part of a group enables individuals to take actions that may be too risky if taken alone, (e.g., coming out in the workplace or pointing out a heterosexist practice such as "family only" social events).

- **Diverse perspectives**—Groups expand the range of potential solutions available in a problem-solving situation such as strategizing to gain a non-discrimination policy. A group also provides more contacts, or points of access, in the process of seeking support for fairer treatment of LGBT employees.

- **Financial resources**—Group dues or individual contributions can be useful in producing literature or events designed to communicate the importance of workplace equity. Some groups pay for member training or participation in conferences on workplace issues (e.g., Creating Change, Out and Equal, PROGRESS Leadership Summit).

- **Division of responsibilities**—Advantages of dividing responsibilities among a group's members include avoidance of burn out, effective utilization of a variety of talents and democratization of the process of changing the organizational culture.

- **Credibility**—A group that is seen as legitimately representing LGBT employees' interests is far more credible than an individual in most organizational settings. A group also provides a focal point for contact between LGBT employees and management, both for input from the group and for accountability to the employer.

- **Allied support**—An LGBT ERG can join forces with other affinity groups to promote attention to more broadly defined "diversity" goals. Advocating promotion of qualified women, black, Latino, and other minority group members, for example, is one way to increase the support of allies, as well as the support of LGBT members in each of those groups, for policies that include LGBT employees.

- **Organizational culture change**—Organizations change at a glacial rate, extending beyond the tenure and resources of any single employee. Achieving the critical mass necessary for an expanded view of workplace equity is, by definition, a group process, even as the transition occurs one person as at time.

Typical ERGs From the LGBT Workplace Survey

Just over 51% of respondents to the LGBT workplace survey reported that their workplace has an ERG for LGBT employees. While a disproportionate number of survey respondents were from AT&T (18 of 109), the "typical" ERG revealed by the survey generally reflects the functional description previously outlined. Almost 90% of the ERG members reported that their group was begun by an individual or small group initiative rather than resulting from "an incident" or "proposed by management." Most groups are locally based, relying on local dues and a variety of other funding mechanisms, including employer funding "on request." ERG funds pay for internal communication, group meetings, publicity (e.g., external mailings), publications, and conference attendance by members, in that order.

Tools for Increasing LGBT Workplace Equity

Businesses exist to make a profit. Efforts to promote workplace equity must address the "business case" or payoff for creating inclusive employment policies and a workplace that supports "all employees to participate fully in all aspects of corporate life."

The Business Case for Gay-Inclusive Employment Policies

- **Attracting the "best and brightest" employees**—Becoming the "employer of choice" in any industry is easy to recognize as a competitive advantage. A superior work environment, pay, and benefits are time-honored means to attract talent. As more companies institute nondiscrimination and DPB policies, those without them will be at a disadvantage among most prospective gay employees.
- **Retaining good employees**—Losing employees because they take a "better offer" is an expensive organizational problem. Hard costs typically include finding another qualified employee, relocation, training, and lost productivity. Intangible costs such as loss of continuity add significantly to this figure. Employees who feel valued as individuals as well as for their work-related skills are less likely to leave satisfying employment.
- **Increased productivity**—Avoiding "personal" conversations or lying about social activities requires constant vigilance that detracts from the energy available for work-related tasks. Not being able to seek out or expect support in times of personal crisis is another debilitating effect of life in the closet. Heterosexuals generally just don't think about the effects of enforced silence on LGBT coworkers. The significant difference is that heterosexuals who choose not to disclose information about their personal

lives are exercising their right to privacy, not attempting to avoid potential harm for being open.

- **Targeting desirable consumer markets**—Not all gay people are affluent, discriminating consumers, but an identifiable target market within the gay community does exist. According to a 1994 survey by Overlooked Opinions, that market is valued at $500 billion. American Airlines, American Express Financial Services, AOL, Ikea, Subaru and the "spirits" (beer, wine, liquor) industry are notable examples of corporations that have profited from targeting the gay consumer market.

- **Litigation avoidance**—Litigation is an expensive proposition, both for employers accused of abuses and for their accusers. Ironically, having gay-inclusive personnel policies may support a corporation's defense against "hostile environment" claims because they evidence recognition of LGBT employees' right to nondiscrimination.

- **Corporate values**—Treating LGBT employees equitably with full access to the opportunities and benefits available to all other employees is ethical, and the "right" thing to do. Many executives seem to think ethical arguments are contradictory to good business reasoning, however. Using the business case to demonstrate the costs of unequal treatment and the benefits of inclusive policies generally is necessary to begin a dialogue on workplace equity for LGBT employees.

Setting ERG Goals

Employee resource group goal-setting to achieve workplace equity exists on three primary levels: (1) what the employer would prefer, (2) what is perceived as possible by ERG members, and (3) what is required to change the organizational culture.

- **Employer preferences**—Organizations want neat, immediate answers to employee issues, especially when the questions are uncomfortable or potentially volatile. That bias drives the preference for adding the words "sexual orientation" to existing nondiscrimination policies with a minimum of public acknowledgment, one-day "training" sessions on sexual orientation or rejection of DPBs without examination of employees' needs and concerns regarding LGBT workplace equity.

- **LGBT employee goals**—Like employers, many employees are most comfortable with neat, immediate "solutions" to LGBT workplace concerns. Internalized heterosexism and lack of perceived self-interest in advocating for *any* sort of workplace changes produce divisions among LGBT employees. Nondiscrimination policy expansion, DPBs, or obtaining recognition as an ERG may feel like all that is possible at a particular point in time. ERGs that limit their mission to official recognition or gaining policy changes often succeed, only to find little has changed in terms of their inclusion as a valued organizational team member. In fact, policy changes typically generate vocal opposition and, with it, pressure for LGBT employees to return to the closet of invisibility.

- **Organizational change goals**—Virtually all organizations claim the "people piece" of their mission is for employees to be valued for their personal and professional attributes and supported to participate fully in all aspects of corporate life. Integrating LGBT workplace concerns into these statements requires a significant shift for most organizational cultures. Cultural change, in turn, requires commitment to an ongoing vision of workplace equity, and to long-term strategies for achieving it. These strategies vary from organization to organization, as well as over time. A vision of organizational culture change calls for progress in achieving workplace equity for LGBT employees as a continuing priority and process with identifiable results.

No matter how small an ERG may be or how limited its apparent resources, it is imperative to articulate its goals at the employer, employee, and organizational levels, to make them explicit and to agree on them as a group. The process will reveal group strengths and weaknesses that will influence future functioning significantly. Successful ERGs have specific benchmarks at each goal level and move among them flexibly, based on current needs and opportunities.

- **Organizational culture**—Successful ERGs translate the business case for inclusive workplace policies into terms that reflect their specific organizational culture. Assessing the culture's overall openness to diverse perspectives and change is critical. Questions to ask in examining potential support for LGBT equity focus on two issues:
  1. Do other "diversity" employee resource groups or affinity groups exist, e.g., focusing on the concerns of women or people of color? If not, why not? If yes, how are they structured? Are the groups active or are they "window dressing"? What resources (e.g., use of facilities, financial support) are provided by the employer?
  2. How does management relate to existing ERGs? Is there a diversity council or other means for group input to be conveyed to upper management? Does management respond? Is participation as a diversity council representative considered a "plus" in the career advancement column or is it a "kiss of death"?
- **Potential allies**—Any assessment of the organizational culture needs to include the consideration of allies. Heterosexual allies exert a disproportionate positive influence in the process of gaining recognition for LGBT equity because self-interest is not perceived to motivate them, even though

a fair workplace benefits all employees. In addition, heterosexual allies may be privy to information unlikely to be shared with "gay activist" employees. Human resources (HR) personnel are a primary target in the search for allies. They are critical gatekeepers of information on benefits and, frequently, the interpretation of benefits policies. It is important to distinguish between HR people and their roles, however. No matter how sympathetic or *unsympathetic* someone may be personally, HR professionals are primarily accountable to uphold the policies and management philosophy of their, and your employer. Other allies may include LGBT employees who choose not to be visibly involved in promoting workplace change. There are likely to be gay members of other ERGs (e.g., women, people of color, disabled, nationality-based) who may prefer to focus primarily on that aspect of their identity but who can be valuable as bridges between groups.

All employees who uphold fairness as a fundamental workplace value are potential allies. Enlist every ally's help in assessing likely responses to formation of a gay ERG or efforts to change organizational policies by other ERGs and/or the employer. Remember, too, not everyone will be an ally, gay or nongay. Treating different perspectives with respect and moving on is far more productive than being distracted by pursuing an unattainable goal of unanimous support for LGBT workplace equity.

- **Existing policies**—Existing organizational policies provide the foundation for effective ERG action; study them closely. Almost all organizations have an Equal Employment Opportunity (EEO) and/or Affirmative Action (AA) policy, in addition to an organizational nondiscrimination statement. At a minimum EEO, AA, and nondiscrimination policies list federally recognized or "protected" categories of employees. Based on federal law, it currently is illegal to discriminate in hiring or other work-related dimensions on the basis of race, gender, age, disability, Vietnam veteran status, religious affiliation, and national origin. Organizations often include other categories in their nondiscrimination statements, such as ethnicity and marital/parental status. As noted previously, sexual orientation is known to be part of more than 1,600 nondiscrimination policies.

The addition of sexual orientation to an organization's EEO, AA, or nondiscrimination policy is significant. It represents a written commitment to enforcing a standard of conduct at an organization-wide level. Once a written policy exists, there is recourse against different interpretations of what is "fair" or "acceptable practice" in relation to sexual orientation and hiring, training, promotion and a whole range of employment-related activities.

When examining organizational employment policies, it is important to look beyond the local level. Organizations often have policies that affect employees in various geographic locations differently. For example, Electronic Data Systems (EDS) announced DPBs for gay and lesbian employees on October 16, 1997. Founded by Ross Perot in 1962, EDS has a strongly conservative image as a "Christian values-based" organization, especially among employees who have worked there for more than 20 years. The announcement of DPBs at EDS, however, contained a surprising acknowledgment that the company already provided such access in ten countries where DPBs are legally mandated. Existing benefit policies also clearly are relevant in the pursuit of DPBs. A scan of any corporate benefits policy will show access to these benefits is weighted significantly in favor of legally married couples. Spouses and dependent children routinely are included in married employees' coverage, usually without additional employee contributions toward cost. Other nonbiological relatives (e.g., ex-spouses, adopted children) may be covered as well. This differential treatment of "married" versus "single" employees arises from the historical myth of single-earner heterosexual families, with mom and the children at home. These policies treat all employees classified as "single" and "child-free" unequally. Inequity specific to LGBT employees derives from the fact that same-gender life partners cannot legally marry. This legal inequity has been reinforced most recently by the federal Defense of Marriage Act (DOMA). Adoption also provides children access to their parents' employment benefits. In almost all states, however, gay coparents cannot jointly adopt or adopt each other's children, as heterosexual adoptive, foster, and step-parents may.[1]

Hard data on the cost of nondiscrimination policies and employee benefits and DPBs derived from sources within and outside the organization can be invaluable in promoting a balanced view of their impact. In the Society for Human Resource Management (1997) survey, 85% of the employers offering DPBs reported their health care costs had "remained about the same." Other studies show an approximate 1% to 3% shift up or down in benefit costs (Becker, 1994).

- **Competitors' policies**—Another incentive for organizations is to compare their policies with competitors'. Organizations frequently make these comparisons to evaluate, or benchmark, their relative performance in sales volume or services provided, organizational growth, and employee retention, to name a few common areas. Benchmarking nondiscrimination and DBP policies provides additional valuable information through their linkage to the business case for being "gay friendly."

For example, in 1995, Texas Instrument's ERG was actively pursuing inclusion of sexual orientation in the company's nondiscrimination statement. Among the resources TI's ERG provided to company executives was a comparison of TI policies with those of its top nine competitors. Seven of these competitors have inclusive nondiscrimination statements. TI added sexual orientation to its nondiscrimination policy in August 1996.

On-Line Resources

The Internet is, possibly, the single most powerful source of information on LGBT workplace concerns. Both the Human Rights Campaign (HRC) and National Gay and Lesbian Task Force (NGLTF) maintain websites that provide frequently updated answers to the question of "Who has nondiscrimination and/or DPB policies?" Subscription-based electronic mailing lists are another way to find out "who's doing what" among employers, especially if the company is not well-known. Interactivity is the highlight of these lists.

Off-Line Resources

Annual conferences such as Out & Equal and the PROGRESS Leadership summit are places where people get together to focus on LGBT workplace issues. More general conferences also include workplace issues (e.g., NGLTF's Creating Change Conference), and an increasing number of ERGs and professional groups host their own meetings. The main benefits of such gatherings are opportunities to ask questions of leaders in specific content areas as well as exposure to the "bigger picture." It is also tremendously energizing to be part of the majority in a work-related setting and to be able to let your guard down and laugh.

Workplace Awareness Activities

Increasing workplace awareness takes place on many levels, from one-to-one conversations to organization-wide programs. Some examples of how ERGs can promote attention to the presence of LGBT coworkers and their concerns include:

- **Participation in events**—Many organizations hold annual picnics, volunteer days, "diversity" days, or monthly celebrations recognizing various minority groups. Choosing activities valued by the organizational culture, starting small, constantly educating allies and gatekeepers, and boundless persistence are critical to the process of gaining greater visibility for LGBT employees and their concerns.
- **Speakers**—Organizations like outside experts, sometimes. ERG meetings offer the most readily available forum for a presentation on LGBT workplace issues. Diversity-themed events may provide another venue for speakers. ERG interest also may help an organization avoid inviting an uninformed or gay-negative speaker.
- **Consultants**—Most consultants are uncomfortable with issues related to sexual orientation and do not routinely address LGBT equity in their consultations or workshops. ERGs can play an important role in increasing organizational awareness simply by asking for their concerns to be addressed. Providing feedback to workshop presenters and to the departments responsible for hiring consultants is another approach, as is suggesting qualified presenters or consultants.
- **Institutionalization**—Throughout this chapter emphasis has been placed on integrating awareness of LGBT workplace issues into the organizational culture. "Official" recognition of an ERG for gay employees (and allies) and inclusion of a representative for LGBT employees on an organization's diversity council or its equivalent are two ways to institutionalize attention to workplace equity. Obtaining financial support for LGBT activities in and outside the workplace *on an ongoing basis* is another.

The inclusion of sexual orientation in organizational policies, "diversity" programming, management practices, and budget decisions pushes responsibility for sustained awareness beyond gay or allied activists. As silence is replaced with knowledge, a critical mass of advocates for workplace equity will be reached. Only then will grassroots efforts and corporate policies come together in an institutional culture that treats LGBT people fairly and supports all employees in contributing fully to the organization's success.

Summary

As "gay issues" have gained visibility throughout American society, workplaces have become a central focus of efforts to advance LGBT equity. More than 1,600 corporations, governmental entities, and educational, religious, and nonprofit employers have instituted nondiscrimination and/or domestic partner benefits (DPB) policies that include same-gender employees. Nonetheless, most employers and employees remain fearful and uninformed about how to address LGBT issues in the workplace. Heterosexism, the assumption that everyone is, should be or would rather be heterosexual, is the root cause of this fear and ignorance.

Although high-tech, multinational corporations are perceived as typical "enlightened" workplaces, a review of employers with inclusive nondiscrimination and DPB policies shows tremendous variety. Results from a survey on LGBT workplace equity highlight the necessity of individual initiative and organizational support in promoting a more gay-friendly work environment. Increasing awareness of LGBT workplace issues is like coming out, a process, not an event. Making the case that sexual orientation is a business issue is a critical step in generating dialogue around fair treatment of LGBT employees. Assessing the organization's culture for its openness to "diversity" and change, identifying and cultivating allies, evaluating employer and competitor policies, increasing organization-wide awareness of LGBT coworkers' existence, and understanding of their concerns and institutionalizing support are further key elements in the pursuit of LGBT equity. A sample workshop and additional resources are provided toward expanding efforts to achieve LGBT workplace equity. Who shall do this important work? To paraphrase Margaret Mead, "Never doubt that a small group of thoughtful employees committed to LGBT equity can change the workplace—and the world. Indeed, it's the only thing that ever has."

Note

1. On December 17, 1997, New Jersey became the first state to allow same-gender partners to adopt children jointly on the same basis as heterosexually married couples.

Appendix: Sexual Orientation as a Business Issue

A Sample One-Day Workshop

I. Introduction and Overview of the Session
- facilitators introduction
- session agenda
- goals and agreements
- pretest: Attitudes Toward Lesbians and Gay Men
- group introductions

II. Dimensions of Diversity
- the power of perception
- examining stereotypes

III. Why Sexual Orientation Is a Business Issue
- linkages among the "isms"
- demographic changes in the workforce
- worker productivity and "employer of choice" issues
- nondiscrimination and domestic partner benefit policies
- legislation pertaining to LGBT workplace equity

IV. Handling Diversity in the Workplace
- common concerns
- business case illustrations
- role-playing work situations

V. Action Planning for Increased Awareness
- individual strategies
- organizational strategies

VI. Wrap-Up
- unanswered questions
- workshop evaluation
- closing exercise

Notes on Presenting "Sexual Orientation as a Business Issue"

My bias as an educator is that learning requires personal engagement as well as factual information. Nowhere is that combination more important than when educating about LGBT topics, toward which most people have deep-seated, unexamined ne}upported to voice their beliefs and to ask questions without fear of retribution.

One-and-one-half and two-day versions of this outline delve further into nondiscrimination and DBP policies, alliance-building, and strategies for organizational change. Workshops utilize two facilitators, usually a male-female pair, who may be selected to reflect additional attributes such as age, race, or nationality identified as relevant to the target audience. Liberal use of humor and personal stories helps reduce the tension LGBT workplace issues invariably generates.

Introduction/Overview

The day starts with a pretest, which is readministered at the end of the session. This instrument is used as much to stimulate thought about previously unexamined beliefs about LGBT people as an attitude survey.

Session goals and agreements emphasize the importance placed on open dialogue. Group member introductions provide an early opportunity to test individuals' willingness to risk disclosure of personal information. Participants are given a list of "primary" and "secondary" dimensions of diversity and asked to describe two "that have shaped who you are today." This exercise takes approximately an hour for 20 to 25 participants.

Dimensions of Diversity

Following group introductions, a brief exercise establishes the elusive nature of fact and the power of perception on one's interpretation of information. Attention to similarities among stereotypes and their consequences for a variety of nondominant social groups seeks to facilitate conscious linkages between heterosexism and more familiar "isms" such as racism, sexism, and ageism.

Why Sexual Orientation Is a Business Issue

The "business case" follows, focusing on the cost of heterosexism and the benefits of inclusive employment practices. Discussion of nondiscrimination policies as well as relevant legislation sets the stage for focusing on group members' concerns about LGBT workplace equity.

Handling Diversity

Lunch may be used as "decompression" time or as an opportunity for small group discussion. For example, participants at each table may be asked to identify one concern they have about increasing visibility of LGBT employees or issues in the workplace. This discussion typically provides an energetic segue into afternoon activities. Following lunch, volunteers are secured to role-play various work-related situations involving LGBT employees. Workshop evaluations consistently highlight individual differences in whether participants love or hate this element of the program.

Action Planning

Development of individual and organization strategies for increasing awareness of LGBT workplace concerns challenges participants to commit to ongoing action. One technique for reminding participants of their commitments is to have them enclose a written goal in a self-addressed envelope, which is mailed back to them in approximately 3 weeks.

The final portion of a day-long session is devoted to group questions, completion of the "Attitudes" survey again and workshop evaluations. The continuing work of organizational change depends on those who remain. A closing exercise is included to add to the sense of cohesion and accomplishment promoted throughout the day.

References

American Psychiatric Association (1980). *Diagnostic and statistical manual of mental disorders* (3rd ed.). Washington, DC: Author.

Bartlett, C. A., & Ghoshal, S. (1995, May-June). Changing the role of top management: Beyond systems to people. *Harvard Business Review, 132-142.*

Becker, L. (1994, November 30). Recognition of domestic partnerships by governmental entities and private employers. *National Journal of Sexual Orientation Law, 1,* 1. Available http:\\www.cs.cmu.edu\afs\cs\user\scotts\bulgarians\njsol\dp'recog.txt

Handy, C.(1995, May-June). Trust and the virtual organization. *Harvard Business Review,* 40-50.

McCormack, J. (1997, November 10). Personal communication.

McNaught, B. (1993). *Gay issues in the workplace.* New York: St. Martin's.

Shilts, R. (1993). *Conduct unbecoming: Gays and lesbians in the U.S. Military.* New York: St. Martin's.

Society for Human Resource Management (1997, January). *Domestic partner benefits minisurvey* (pp. 5-6). Alexandria, VA: Author.

Starcevick, M. M., & Stowell, S. J. (1990). Teamwork: We have met the enemy and they are us. Salt Lake City, UT: Center for Management and Organizational Effectiveness.

Waldron, J. (1996). Statutory protection for gays and lesbians in private employment. *Harvard Law Review, 109*(7), 1626.

Appendix I: American Psychological Association Policy Statements on Lesbian, Gay, and Bisexual Concerns

Lesbian, Gay, and Bisexual Concerns Office

Public Interest Directorate

750 First Street, NE

Washington, DC 20002-4242

Discrimination Against Homosexuals

[Adopted by the American Psychological Association Council of Representatives on January 24-26, 1975]

1. The American Psychological Association supports the action taken on December 15, 1973, by the American Psychiatric Association, removing homosexuality from that Association's official list of mental disorders. The American Psychological Association therefore adopts the following resolution:

Homosexuality per se implies no impairment in judgment, stability, reliability, or general social and vocational capabilities; Further, the American Psychological Association urges all mental health professionals to take the lead in removing the stigma of mental illness that has long been associated with homosexual orientations.

2. Regarding discrimination against homosexuals, the American Psychological Association adopts the following resolution concerning their civil and legal rights:

The American Psychological Association deplores all public and private discrimination in such areas as employment, housing, public accommodation, and licensing against those who engage in or have engaged in homosexual activities and declares that no burden of proof of such judgment, capacity, or reliability shall be placed upon these individuals greater than that imposed on any other persons. Further, the American Psychological Association supports and urges the enactment of civil rights legislation at the local and state and federal level that would offer citizens who engage in acts of homosexuality the same protections now guaranteed to others on the basis of race, creed, color, etc. Further, the American Psychological Association supports and urges the repeal of all discriminatory legislation singling out homosexual acts by consenting adults in private (Conger, 1975, p. 633).

Conger, J. J. (1975) Proceedings of the American Psychological Association, Incorporated, for the year 1974: Minutes of the annual meeting of the Council of Representatives. *American Psychologist, 30,* 620-651.

Child Custody or Placement

[Adopted by the American Psychological Association Council of Representatives on September 2 & 5, 1976.]

The sex, gender identity, or sexual orientation of natural, or prospective adoptive or foster parents should not be the sole or primary variable considered in custody or placement cases (Conger, 1977, p. 432).

Conger, J. J. (1977). Proceedings of the American Psychological Association, Incorporated, for the year 1976: Minutes of the annual meeting of the Council of Representatives. *American Psychologist, 32,* 408-438.

Employment Rights of Gay Teachers

[Adopted by the American Psychological Association Council of Representatives on January 23-25, 1981]

WHEREAS, the American Psychological Association deplores all public and private discrimination in such areas as employment, housing, public accommodation, and licensing against those who engage in or have engaged in homosexual activities and declares that no burden of proof of such judgment, capacity, or reliability shall be placed upon these individuals greater than that imposed on any other person;

BE IT RESOLVED that the American Psychological Association protests personnel actions against any teacher solely because of sexual orientation or affectional preference (Abeles, 1981, p. 581).

Abeles, N. (1981). Proceedings of the American Psychological Association, Incorporated, for the year 1980: Minutes of the annual meetings of the Council of Representatives. *American Psychologist, 36,* 552-586.

Use of Diagnoses "Homosexuality" and "Ego-dystonic Homosexuality"

[Adopted by the American Psychological Association Council of Representatives on August 27 & 30, 1987]

WHEREAS, the American Psychological Association has been on record since 1975 that "homosexuality per se implies no impairment in judgment, stability, reliability, or general social and vocational capabilities"; and

WHEREAS, it appears that the ICD-9-CM is widely used either by mandate or choice by many psychologists nationwide in connection with third-party reimbursement, institutional-based service delivery, and research; and

WHEREAS, the next revision of the ICD is not anticipated to be completed until 1992 and may, according to current proposals, then contain the "ego-dystonic homosexuality" diagnosis which APA also opposes; and

WHEREAS, the Council of Representatives already has urged APA members not to use the proposed DSM-III-R diagnoses of Periluteal Phase Disorder, Self-Defeating Personality Disorder, and Sadistic Personality Disorder because they lack adequate scientific basis and are potentially dangerous to women;

BE IT RESOLVED that the American Psychological Association urge its members not to use the "302.0 Homosexuality" diagnosis in the current ICD-9-CM or the "302.00 Ego-dystonic Homosexuality" diagnosis in the current DSM-III or future editions of either document (Fox, 1988, p. 528).

Fox, R. E. (1988). Proceedings of the American Psychological Association, Incorporated, for the year 1987: Minutes of the annual meeting of the Council of Representatives. *American Psychologist, 43*, 527-528.

Hate Crimes

[Adopted by the American Psychological Association Council of Representatives on February 5-7, 1988]

WHEREAS, the experience of criminal and violent victimization has profound psychological consequences; and

WHEREAS, the frequency and severity of crimes and violence manifesting prejudice have been documented; and

WHEREAS, the American Psychological Association opposes prejudice and discrimination based upon race, ethnicity, religion, sexual orientation, gender, or physical condition.

THEREFORE BE IT RESOLVED that the American Psychological Association condemns harassment, violence, and crime motivated by such prejudice;

BE IT FURTHER RESOLVED that the American Psychological Association encourages researchers, clinicians, teachers, and policymakers to help reduce and eliminate hate crimes and bias-related violence and to alleviate their effects upon the victims, particularly those victims who are children, youth, and elderly;

BE IT FURTHER RESOLVED that the American Psychological Association supports government's collection and publication of statistics on hate crimes and bias-related violence, provision of services for victims and their loved ones, and interventions to reduce and eliminate such crimes and violence, and policies that perpetuate them (Fox, 1988, p. 528).

Fox, R. E. (1988). Proceedings of the American Psychological Association, Incorporated, for the year 1987: Minutes of the annual meeting of the Council of Representatives. *American Psychologist, 43,* 527-528.

Sodomy Laws and APA Convention

[Adopted by the American Psychological Association Council of Representatives on August 11 & 14, 1988]

APA reaffirms its opposition to laws criminalizing consensual adult sexual behavior in private and directs the Board of Convention Affairs to consider the presence of such laws as a factor in the selection of future convention sites and in programming (Fox, 1989, p. 1026).

Fox, R. E. (1989). Proceedings of the American Psychological Association, Incorporated, for the year 1988: Minutes of the annual meeting of the Council of Representatives. *American Psychologist, 44,* 1026.

U.S. Department of Defense Policy on Sexual Orientation and Advertising in APA Publications

[Adopted by the American Psychological Association Council of Representatives, August 18, 1991]

WHEREAS, the American Psychological Association (APA) deplores discrimination on the basis of sexual orientation; and

WHEREAS, APA will not let its publication, as advertising media, be used by others in support of discriminatory employment practices;

WHEREAS, the U.S. Department of Defense (DoD) maintains a policy that homosexual orientation is "incompatible with military service"; and

WHEREAS, the DoD will not knowingly admit bisexual, lesbian or gay individuals to military service, including research and clinical internship programs in psychology; and

WHEREAS, an average of 1,500 men and women are unfairly discharged from military service each year because their sexual orientation becomes known;

THEREFORE BE IT RESOLVED that the APA opposes the DoD policy which finds homosexual orientation "incompatible with military service"; and

BE IT FURTHER RESOLVED that APA take a leadership role among national organizations in seeking to change this discriminatory DoD policy; and

BE IT FURTHER RESOLVED that APA will not permit its publications, as advertising media, to be used by the DoD after December 31, 1992, unless the DoD policy that homosexual orientation "is incompatible with military service" has been rescinded by that date. (Fox, 1992, p. 927).

Fox, R. E. (1992). Proceedings of the American Psychological Association, Incorporated, for the year 1991: Minutes of the annual meeting of the Council of Representatives. *American Psychologist, 47*, 927.

Resolution on Lesbian, Gay, and Bisexual Youths in the Schools

[Adopted by the American Psychological Association Council of Representatives on February 28, 1993]

WHEREAS, society's attitudes, behaviors, and tendency to render lesbian, gay and bisexual persons invisible permeate all societal institutions including the family and school system (Gonsiorek, 1988; Hetrick & Martin, 1988; Ponse, 1978; Uribe & Harbeck, 1992);

WHEREAS, it is a presumption that all persons, including those who are lesbian, gay, or bisexual, have the right to equal opportunity within all public educational institutions;

WHEREAS, current literature suggests that some youths are aware of their status as lesbian, gay, or bisexual persons by early adolescence (Remafedi, 1987; Savin-Williams, 1990; Slater, 1988; Troiden, 1988);

WHEREAS, many lesbian, gay, and bisexual youths and youths perceived to belong to these groups face harassment and physical violence in school environments (Freiberg, 1987; Hetrick & Martin, 1988; Remafedi, 1987; Schaecher, 1988; Uribe & Harbeck, 1992; Whitlock, 1988);

WHEREAS, many lesbian, gay, and bisexual youths are at risk for lowered self-esteem and for engaging in self-injurious behaviors, including suicide (Gibson, 1989; Gonsiorek, 1988; Harry, 1989; Hetrick & Martin, 1988; Savin-Williams, 1990);

WHEREAS, gay male and bisexual youths are at an increased risk of HIV infection (Savin-Williams, 1992);

WHEREAS, lesbian, gay, and bisexual youths of color have additional challenges to their self-esteem as a result of the negative consequences of discrimination based on both sexual orientation and ethnic/racial minority status (Garnets & Kimmel, 1991);

WHEREAS, lesbian, gay, and bisexual youths with physical or mental disabilities are at increased risk due to the negative consequence of societal prejudice toward persons with mental or physical disabilities (Pendler & Hingsburger, 1991; Hingsburger & Griffiths, 1986);

WHEREAS, lesbian, gay, and bisexual youths who are poor or working class may face additional risks (Gordon, Schroeder, & Abramo, 1990);

WHEREAS, psychologists affect policies and practices within educational environments;

WHEREAS, psychology promotes the individual's development of personal identity including the sexual orientation of all individuals;

THEREFORE BE IT RESOLVED that the American Psychological Association and the National Association of School Psychologists shall take a leadership role in promoting societal and familial attitudes and behaviors that affirm the dignity and rights, within educational environments, of all lesbian, gay, and bisexual youths, including those with physical or mental disabilities and from all ethnic/racial backgrounds and classes;

THEREFORE BE IT RESOLVED that the American Psychological Association and the National Association of School Psychologists support providing a safe and secure educational atmosphere in which all youths, including lesbian, gay, and bisexual youths, may obtain an education free from discrimination, harassment, violence, and abuse, and which promotes an understanding and acceptance of self;

THEREFORE BE IT RESOLVED that American Psychological Association and the National Association of School Psychologists encourage psychologists to develop and evaluate interventions that foster nondiscriminatory environments, lower risk for HIV infection, and decrease self-injurious behaviors in lesbian, gay, and bisexual youths;

THEREFORE BE IT RESOLVED that the American Psychological Association and the National Association of School Psychologists shall advocate efforts to ensure the funding of basic and applied research on and scientific evaluations of interventions and programs designed to address the issues of lesbian, gay, and bisexual youths in the schools, and programs for HIV prevention targeted at gay and bisexual youths;

THEREFORE BE IT RESOLVED that the American Psychological Association and the National Association of School Psychologists shall work with other organizations in efforts to accomplish these ends (DeLeon, 1993, p. 782).

DeLeon, H. (1993). Proceedings of the American Psychological Association, Incorporated, for the year 1992; Minutes of the annual meeting of the Council of Representatives August 13 and 16, 1992, and February 26-28, 1993, Washington, DC. *American Psychologist, 48,* 782.

Freiberg, P. (1987, September). Sex education and the gay issue: What are they teaching about us in the schools? *The Advocate,* pp. 42-48.

Garnets, L., & Kimmel, D., (1991). Lesbian and gay male dimensions in the psychological study of human diversity. In J. Goodchilds (Ed.), *Psychological perspectives on human diversity in America* (pp. 156-160). Washington, DC: American Psychological Association.

Gonsiorek, J. C., (1988). Mental health issues of gay and lesbian adolescents. *Journal of Adolescent Heath Care, 9,* 114-122.

Gordon, B. N., Schroeder, C. S., & Abramo, J. M., (1990). Age and social class differences in children's knowledge of sexuality. *Journal of Clinical Child Psychology, 19*(1), 33-43.

Gibson, P. (1989). Gay male and lesbian youth suicide. In M. Feinleib (Ed.), *Report of the secretary's task force on youth suicide* (Vol. 3, pp. 110-142). Washington, DC: Department of Health and Human Services.

Harry, J. (1989). Sexual identity issues. In M. Feinleib (Ed.), *Report of the secretary's task force on youth suicide* (Vol. 2, pp. 131-142). Washington, DC: Department of Health and Human Services.

Hetrick, E. S., & Martin, A. D. (1988). Developmental issues and their resolution for gay and lesbian adolescents. In E. Coleman (Ed.), *Integrated identity for gay men and lesbians: Psychotherapeutic approaches for emotional well-being* (pp. 25-43). Binghamton, NY: Harrington Park Press.

Hingsburger, D., & Griffiths, D. (1986). Dealing with sexuality in a community residential service. *Psychiatric Aspects of Mental Retardation Reviews, 5*(12), 63-67.

Pendler, B., & Hingsburger, D. (1991). Sexuality: Dealing with parents. Special Issue: Sexuality and developmental disability. *Sexuality and Disability, 9*(2), 123-130.

Ponse, B. (1978). *Identities in the lesbian world: The social construction of the self.* Westport, CT: Greenwood.

Remafedi, G. (1987). Adolescent homosexuality: Psychosocial and medical implications. *Pediatrics, 79,* 331-337.

Savin-Williams, R. C. (1990). *Gay and lesbian youth: Expressions of identity.* New York: Hemisphere.

Schaecher, R. (1988, Winter). Stresses on lesbian and gay adolescents. *Independent Schools,* pp. 29-35.

Slater, B. R. (1988). Essential issues in working with lesbian and gay male youths. *Professional Psychology: Research and Practice, 19,* 226-235.

Troiden, R. R. (1988). *Gay and lesbian identity: A scoiological study.* Dix Hills, NY: General Hall.

Uribe, V., & Harbeck, K. M. (1992). Addressing the needs of lesbian, gay and bisexual youth: The origins of PROJECT 10 and school-based intervention. In K. Harbeck (Ed.), *Coming out of the classroom closet: Gay and lesbian students, teachers and curriculum* (pp. 9-28). Binghamton, NY: Harrington Park Press.

Whitlock, K. (Ed.). (1988). *Bridges of respect: Creating support for lesbian and gay youth.* Philadelphia: American Friends Service Committee.

Resolution on State Initiatives and Referenda

[Adopted by the American Psychological Association Council of Representatives on August 22, 1993]

WHEREAS, referenda to limit anti-discrimination legislation as it applies to lesbian, gay, and bisexual persons have been proposed in several states and passed in one;

WHEREAS, the American Psychological Association has repeatedly stated its position that lesbian, gay, and bisexual orientation should not be the basis for discrimination;

WHEREAS, the American Psychological Association deplores the use of scientifically unsound research to support discrimination against lesbian, gay, and bisexual persons;

THEREFORE BE IT RESOLVED that the American Psychological Association opposes the implementation of any state constitutional amendment or statute that prohibits anti-discrimination legislation for lesbian, gay, and bisexual persons because there is no basis for such discrimination and such discrimination is detrimental to mental health and the public good;

BE IT FURTHER RESOLVED that the Council of Representatives of the American Psychological Association directs the chief executive officer to undertake immediate initiative to disseminate scientific information on sexual orientation to the state psychological associations and provide support in their advocacy efforts in the prevention of or challenge to state legislation that prohibits antidiscrimination for lesbian, gay, or bisexual persons;

BE IT FURTHER RESOLVED that the CEO of the American Psychological Association take immediate steps to disseminate scientific information on sexual orientation to policymakers and to the public and to provide consultation to parties involved in constitutional challenges to legislation that prohibits antidiscrimination for lesbian, gay, and bisexual persons in those states in which such constitutional challenges are occurring;

BE IT FURTHER RESOLVED that the CEO of the American Psychological Association will consult with the relevant state psychological association and will immediately consider a motion at the next Board of Directors meeting and the Council of Representatives meeting to neither sponsor meetings nor authorize participation of its representatives in meetings in any state in which a constitutional amendment or statute that prohibits antidiscrimination legislation for lesbian, gay, or bisexual persons has the force of law except when the purpose of the meeting is to work publicly to overturn the law in conjunction with state and local organizations. (DeLeon, 1994, p. 628)

DeLeon, Patrick, H. (1994). Proceedings of the American Psychological Association, Incorporated, for the year 1993; Minutes of the annual meeting of the Council of Representatives August 19 and 22, 1993, Toronto, Ontario, Canada, and February 25 and 27, 1994, Washington, DC. *American Psychologist, 49*, 628.

Resolution on Appropriate Therapeutic Responses to Sexual Orientation

[Adopted by the American Psychological Association Council of Representatives, August 14, 1997]

WHEREAS, societal ignorance and prejudice about same gender sexual orientation put some gay, lesbian, bisexual, and questioning individuals at risk for presenting for "conversion" treatment due to family or social coercion and/or lack of information (Haldeman, 1994);

WHEREAS, children and youth experience significant pressure to conform with sexual norms, particularly from their peers;

WHEREAS, children and youths often lack adequate legal protection from coercive treatment;

WHEREAS, some mental health professionals advocate treatments of lesbian, gay, and bisexual people based on the premise that homosexuality is a mental disorder (e.g., Socarides et al., 1997);

WHEREAS, the ethics, efficacy, benefits, and potential for harm of therapies that seek to reduce or eliminate same-gender sexual orientation are under extensive debate in the professional literature and the popular media (Davison, 1991; Haldeman, 1994; *Wall Street Journal*, 1997);

THEREFORE BE IT RESOLVED that APA affirms the following principles with regard to treatments to alter sexual orientation:

- that homosexuality is not a mental disorder (American Psychiatric Association, 1973); and

- that psychologists "do not knowingly participate in or condone unfair discriminatory practices" (*Ethical Principles of Psychologists and Code of Conduct*, American Psychological Association, 1992, Principle D, p. 1600); and

- that "in their work-related activities, psychologists do not engage in unfair discrimination based on . . . sexual orientation" (*Ethical Principles of Psychologists and Code of Conduct*, American Psychological Association, 1992, Standard 1.10, p. 1601); and

- that "in their work-related activities, psychologists respect the rights of others to hold values, attitudes, and opinions that differ from their own." (*Ethical Principles of Psychologists and Code of Conduct*, American Psychological Association, 1992, Standard 1.09; p. 1601); and

- that "psychologists . . . respect the rights of individuals to privacy, confidentiality, self-determination and autonomy" (*Ethical Principles of Psychologists and Code of Conduct*, American Psychological Association, 1992, Principle D, p. 1599); and

- that "psychologists are aware of cultural, individual and role differences, including those due to . . . sexual orientation" and "try to eliminate the effect on their work of biases based on [such] factors" *Ethical Principles of Psychologists and Code of Conduct*, American Psychological Association, 1992, Principle D, pp. 1599-1600); and

- that "where differences of . . . sexual orientation . . . significantly affect psychologist's work concerning particular individuals or groups, psychologists obtain the training, experience, consultation, or supervision necessary to ensure the competence of their services, or they make appropriate referrals" (*Ethical Principles of Psychologists and Code of Conduct*, American Psychological Association, 1992, Standard 1.08, p. 1601); and

that "psychologists do not make false or deceptive statements concerning . . . the scientific or clinical basis for . . . their services," (*Ethical Principles of Psychologists and Code of Conduct*, American Psychological Association, 1992, Standard 3.03(a), p. 1604); and

that "psychologists attempt to identify situations in which particular interventions . . . may not be applicable . . . because of factors such as . . . sexual orientation" (*Ethical Principles of Psychologists and Code of Conduct*, American Psychological Association, 1992, Standard 2.04 (c), p. 1603); and

that "psychologists obtain appropriate informed consent to therapy or related procedures" [which] "generally implies that the [client or patient] (1) has the capacity to consent, (2) has been informed of significant information concerning the procedure, (3) has freely and without undue influence expressed consent, and (4) consent has been appropriately documented" (*Ethical Principles of Psychologists and Code of Conduct*, American Psychological Association, Standard 4.02(a), 1992, p. 1605); and

"when persons are legally incapable of giving informed consent, psychologists obtain informed permission from a legally authorized person, if such substitute consent is permitted by law" (*Ethical Principles of Psychologists and Code of Conduct*, American Psychological Association, 1992, Standard 4.02(b), p. 1605); and

that "psychologists (1) inform those persons who are legally incapable of giving informed consent about the proposed interventions in a manner commensurate with the persons' psychological capacities, (2) seek their assent to those interventions, and (3) consider such persons' preferences and best interests" (*Ethical Principles of Psychologists and Code of Conduct*, American Psychological Association, 1992, Standard 4.02(c), p. 1605); and

that the American Psychological Association "urges all mental health professionals to take the lead in removing the stigma of mental illness that has long been associated with homosexual orientation" (Conger, 1975, p. 633); and

THEREFORE BE IT FURTHER RESOLVED that the American Psychological Association opposes portrayals of lesbian, gay, and bisexual youths and adults as mentally ill due to their sexual orientation and supports the dissemination of accurate information about sexual orientation, and mental health, and appropriate interventions in order to counteract bias that is based in ignorance or unfounded beliefs about sexual orientation.

American Psychiatric Association. (1973). Position statement on homosexuality and civil rights. *American Journal of Psychiatry, 131*(4), 497.

American Psychological Association. (1992). Ethical principles of psychologists and code of conduct. *American Psychologist, 47*(12), 1597-1611.

Conger, J. J. (1975). Proceedings of the American Psychological Association, Incorporated, for the year 1974: Minutes of the annual meeting of the Council of Representatives. *American Psychologist, 30,* 620-651.

Davison, G. C., (1991). Constructionism and morality in therapy for homosexuality. In J. C. Gonsiorek and J. D. Weinrich (Eds.), *Homosexuality: Research implications for public policy* (pp. 137-148). Newbury Park, CA: Sage.

Haldeman, D. C. (1994). The practice and ethics of sexual orientation conversion therapy. *Journal of Consulting and Clinical Psychology, 62*(2), 221-227.

Socarides, C., Kaufman, B., Nicolosi, J., Satinover, J., & Fitzgibbons, R. (1997, January 9). Don't forsake homosexuals who want help. *Wall Street Journal,* p. A12.

Wall Street Journal. (1997, January 23). Letters to the editor. *Wall Street Journal,* p. A17.

Resolution on Legal Benefits for Same-Sex Couples

[Adopted by the American Psychological Association Council of Representatives August 16, 1998. As of this date, August 28, 1998, the text has not been reviewed and approved by the APA Recording Secretary.]

WHEREAS there is evidence that homosexuality per se implies no impairment in judgement, stability, reliability, or general social and vocational capabilities (Conger, 1975) for individuals;

WHEREAS legislation, other public policy, and private policy on issues related to same sex couples is currently under development in many places in North America (e.g., Canadian Psychological Association, 1996);

WHEREAS the scientific literature has found no significant difference between different-sex couples and same-sex couples that justify discrimination (Kurdek, 1994;1983; Peplau, 1991);

WHEREAS scientific research has not found significant psychological or emotional differences between the children raised in different-sex versus same-sex households (Patterson, 1994);

WHEREAS APA has, as a long established policy, deplored "all public and private discrimination against gay men and lesbians in such areas as employment, housing, administration, and licensing . . ." and has consistently urged "the repeal of all discriminatory legislation against lesbians and gay men" (Conger, 1975);

WHEREAS denying the legal benefits that the license of marriage offers to same-sex households (including, but not limited to, property rights, health care decision-making, estate planning, tax consequences, spousal privileges in medical emergency situations and co-parental adoption of children) is justified as fair and equal treatment;

WHEREAS the absence of access to these benefits constitutes a significant psychosocial stressor for lesbians, gay men, and their families;

WHEREAS APA provides benefits to its members' and employees' domestic partners equivalent to those provided to members' and employees' spouses;

WHEREAS psychological knowledge can be used to inform the current public and legal debate on "same-sex marriage" (e.g., Baehr v. Levin);

THEREFORE BE IT RESOLVED that APA supports the provision to same-sex couples of the legal benefits that typically accrue as a result of marriage to same-sex couples who desire and seek the legal benefits; and

THEREFORE BE IT FURTHER RESOLVED that APA shall provide relevant psychological knowledge to inform the public discussion in this area and assist state psychological associations and divisions in offering such information as needed.

Canadian Psychological Association. (1996). *Policy statement on equality for lesbians, gay men, and their relationships and families.* [Available from the Canadian Psychological Association.]

Conger, J.J. (1975). Proceedings of the American Psychological Association, Incorporated, for the year 1974: Minutes of the Annual Meeting of the Council of Representatives. *American Psychologist, 30,* 620-651.

Kurdek, L.A. (1993). The nature and correlates of relationship quality in gay, lesbian, and heterosexual cohabiting couples: A test of the individual difference, interdependence, and discrepancy models. In B. Greene & G.M. Herek (Eds.), *Lesbian and gay psychology: Theory, research, and clinical issues* (pp. 133-155). Thousand Oaks, CA: Sage.

Patterson, C.J. (1993). Children of the lesbian baby boom: Behavioral adjustment, self-concepts, and sex role theory. In B. Greene & G.M. Herek (Eds.), *Lesbian and gay psychology: Theory, research, and clinical issues* (pp. 156-175). Thousand Oaks, CA: Sage.

Peplau. A.L. (1991). Lesbian and gay relationships. In J. C. Gonsiorek and J. D. Weinrich (Eds.), *Homosexuality: Research implications for public policy* (pp. 177-196). Newbury Park, CA: Sage.

Appendix II: Lesbian, Gay, and Bisexual Concerns at the American Psychological Association

CLINTON W. ANDERSON

Available Resources

Lesbian, Gay, and Bisexual Concerns Office

American Psychological Association
750 First Street, NE
Washington, DC 20002-4242
(202) 336-6041; FAX: (202) 336-6040
e-mail: publicinterest@email.apa.org

Lesbian, gay, and bisexual concerns at the American Psychological Association (APA) are handled by the Lesbian, Gay, and Bisexual Concerns Office which is housed within the Public Interest Directorate. The major functions of the APA Lesbian, Gay, and Bisexual Concerns Office are:

- to support the APA Committee on Lesbian, Gay, and Bisexual Concerns,
- to advocate policy,
- to disseminate psychological knowledge,
- to provide consultation and referral, and
- to represent the APA.

The office publishes an annual summary of its activities: *Lesbian, Gay, and Bisexual Concerns at APA.*

APA on the World Wide Web

Some of the resource documents produced by the APA are available from APA's site on the World Wide Web at http://www.apa.org. To access the resources of the Lesbian, Gay, and Bisexual Concerns Office, use the address http://www.apa.org/lgbc/. For those documents currently available on the World Wide Web, the URL is provided below.

APA Policy Statements on Lesbian and Gay Issues

(http://www.apa.org/pi/lgbc/policies.html)

APA's policy advocacy is based on the resolutions that have been adopted by APA's Council of Representatives. The Council of Representatives has adopted policies on the following lesbian, gay, and bisexual concerns:

- discrimination against homosexuals;
- child custody and placement;
- employment rights of gay teachers;
- use of diagnoses "homosexuality" and "Ego-dystonic homosexuality";
- hate crimes;
- sodomy laws and APA convention;
- U.S. Department of Defense policy on sexual orientation and advertising in APA publications;
- lesbian, gay, and bisexual youths in the schools;
- constitutional amendments and statutes prohibiting civil rights protections for lesbians, gay men, and bisexual people; and
- appropriate therapeutic responses to sexual orientation.

The full text of the APA policy resolutions is provided in the following section.

In addition to the policy resolutions on lesbian, gay, and bisexual concerns, sexual orientation is included in nondiscrimination statements in the APA's by-laws, equal employment opportunity statement, the *Ethical Principles of Psychologists and Code of Conduct,* the *Guidelines and Principles for Accreditation of Programs in Professional Psychology,* and the APA advertising policy. APA also provides benefits for the registered domestic partners of its staff and members equivalent to those provided for spouses.

The Committee on Lesbian, Gay, and Bisexual Concerns

The Committee on Lesbian, Gay, and Bisexual Concerns (CLGBC) (established 1980) provides policy development and advisory oversight for lesbian, gay, and bisexual concerns at APA. CLGBC is a six-person committee and reports through the Board for the Advancement of Psychology in the Public Interest (BAPPI) to the board of directors and council of representatives. The committee's mission is to:

- study and evaluate on an ongoing basis how the issues and concerns of lesbian, gay male, and bisexual psychologists can best be dealt with;
- encourage objective and unbiased research in areas relevant to lesbian, gay male, and bisexual adults and youths, and the social impact of such research;
- examine the consequences of inaccurate information and stereotypes about lesbian, gay male, and bisexual adults and youths in clinical practice;
- develop educational materials for distribution to psychologists and others; and
- make recommendations regarding the integration of these issues into the APA's activities to further the cause of civil and legal rights of lesbian, gay male, and bisexual psychologists within the profession.

Information about the activities of CLGBC is available in its *Annual Report* published in January of each year.

Additional Resources

Answers to Your Questions About Sexual Orientation and Homosexuality

(http://www.apa.org/pubinfo/answers.html)—A four-page public information brochure about sexual orientation and homosexuality.

Lesbian and Gay Parenting: A Resource for Psychologists

(http://www.apa.org/pi/answers.html)—Includes a summary of research findings on lesbian mothers, gay fathers, and their children; an annotated bibliography of the published psychological literature; and additional resources relevant to lesbian and gay parenting, 1995, 40 pages.

- **Amicus Brief . . .** in the case of Colorado vs. Evans, before the Supreme Court of the United States, 1995, 27 pages. (http://www.apa.org/pi/romer.html)
- **Amicus Brief . . .** in the case of Bottoms vs. Bottoms, before the Supreme Court of Virginia, 1994, 34 pages. (http://www.apa.org/pi/lgbc/campbell.html)

- **Amicus Brief . . .** in the case of Campbell vs. Sundquist before the Court of Appeals of Tennessee, 1995, 44 pages. (http://www.apa.org/pi/lgbc/campbell.html)
- **Graduate Faculty In Psychology Interested in Lesbian, Gay, and Bisexual Issues**

(http://www.apa.org/pi/lgbc/lgbcsurvey/)—Results of a survey of graduate programs in psychology. Questions asked about lesbian, gay, and bisexual concerns in courses, research, and professional training.

Avoiding Heterosexual Bias in Language

Reprint: Committee on Lesbian and Gay Concerns. (1991). Avoiding heterosexual bias in language. *American Psychologist, 46*(9), 973-974.

Avoiding Heterosexual Bias in Psychological Research

Reprint: Herek, G. M., Kimmel, D. C., Amaro, H., & Melton, G. B. (1991). Avoiding heterosexual bias in psychological research. *American Psychologist, 46*(9), 957-963.

Psychotherapy With Lesbians and Gay Men: A Survey of Psychologists

Reprint: Garnets, L., Hancock, K. A., Cochran, S. D., Goodchilds, J., & Peplau, L. A. (1991). Issues in psychotherapy with lesbians and gay men: A survey of psychologists. *American Psychologist, 46*(9), 964-974.

Additionally, as the occasion arises, APA publishes other resource documents on particular topics (e.g., legislative testimony, briefing papers, etc). When resources are sought on a particular topic that is currently being debated in public policy or media contexts, it is worthwhile to inquire whether APA has published something relevant.

Index

Abeles, N., 304
Ableism, 39
Abramo, J. M., 308
Acocell, J. R., 81, 82
ACSF Investigators, 173, 174
Adam, B. D., 168, 169, 170
Adams, A. C., 237
Adjustment difficulties:
    in transgendered psychotherapy clients, 151
Adolescent development, 227
    and LGB youth, 227
    heterosexual assumptions and, 227-228
African Americans:
    diminishing psychologist pool, 267-268
    discrimination against, 9
    resilience of, 7-8
    transsexualism among female, 149
    treating LGB, 254-255
    See also People of color, LGB
Age, LGB research omission of, 13-16
Ageism, 39
Aging as LGB issue, 66
Aina, T. A., 171
Alexander, F., 163
Allen, C., 182
Allen, M. S., 61
Allison, D., 22, 23
Alloy, L. B., 81, 82
Alquijay, M., 107
Alternative families, 115
American Airlines:
    GLEAM (ERG), 289
    targeting gay consumer market, 292

American Association for Marriage &
    Family Therapy (AAMFT), 209, 210
American Baptists Concerned, 97
American Broadcasting Company, 34
American Psychiatric Association, 132,
    138, 142, 143, 152, 247, 284, 311
American Psychological Association
    (APA), 91, 95, 247, 250, 311, 312
    Committee on Lesbian, Gay, and Bisexual Concerns, 260, 315-316
    Convention of August 1996, 46
    conversion therapy policy/stance, 150,
        250-253, 254, 260
    Council of Representatives, 250, 315
    Division 44, 260
    LGB concerns at, 314-317
    Office of Lesbian, Gay, and Bisexual
        Concerns, 259, 314
    policy statements on LGB concerns,
        303-313, 315
    Public Interest, Practice, and Science
        constituencies, 250
    Society for the Psychological Study of
        Lesbian, Gay, and Bisexual issues,
        46, 259
    World Wide Web resources, 314-315,
        316
    See also Diagnostic and Statistical Manual
        of Mental Disorders (DSM)
Americans with Disabilities Act, removal
    of transgendered people from, 135
Ames, L. J., 12, 13
Anderson, B. F., 154, 156
Anderson, N. B., 270, 271

Androgynes, 141
Androgynists, 141, 153
Anti-gay attitudes, 75
    factors in formation of, 63
    See also Homophobic
Anti-Semitism, 35
Appathurai, C., 27
Ariel, J., 113, 114
Asch, A., 17, 29, 30, 31, 32
Ashbrook, P., 92
Assessment of Sexual Orientation, 167
AT&T, 282, 291
Atkins, D., 91, 92

Bailey, C. E., 208
Bailey, D. S., 168
Bajos, N., 173, 174
Barr, G., 190
Bartlett, C. A., 286
Basow, S., 98, 99, 107, 111, 123
Beach, F. A., 168, 170
Becker, L., 288, 295
Begelman, D. A., 247
Behavior genetics, 62
Bell, A. P., 177, 178, 188
Bem, D. J., 61
Bem, S., 97, 98
Bem, S. L., 61
Benitez, J. C., 187, 188
Benjamin, H., 132, 142
Bepko, C., 108
Bergler, E., 163
Berkey, B., 182
Berrill, K., 103
Berzon, B., 103, 110
Bettinger, M., 108, 109, 214
Bieber, I., 75, 163, 164, 182
Bieber, T. B., 75, 163, 164
Bigender, 140
Bilotta, G. J., 188
Binson, D., 175, 176
Biphobia, 236
    dealing with, 190
    dealing with internalized, 190
Bisexual adolescents, 118, 226, 227, 236-237
    family issues, 231
    heterosexual assumptions and, 227-228

    heterosexual experimentation among,
        236
    personal identity development, 228
    social identity development, 228
    stigmatization of, 228
    types, 236
    See also Bisexual identity development
        research; Coming out process
Bisexual Anthology Collective, 190
Bisexual community, 190
Bisexual groups, 190
Bisexual identity development research,
    183-190
    age differences in coming out process,
        189
    coming out issues, 189-190
    first disclosure of sexual orientation,
        188
    first heterosexual attractions, 184, 185-
        187
    first heterosexual experiences, 184,
        185-187
    first heterosexual relationships, 184,
        185-187
    first homosexual attractions, 184, 185-
        187
    first homosexual experiences, 184, 185-
        187
    first homosexual relationships, 188,
        185-187
    first identification as bisexual, 188
    gender differences in coming out pro-
        cess, 189
Bisexuality, 61, 93
    affirmative approach toward, 161-162
    as explanation for homosexuality, 162
    as homosexuality, 163-164
    as sexual identity, 166
    as valid sexual orientation, 165, 166
    definition of, 162
    in Classical Greece, 168, 169
    in Classical Rome, 168, 169
    in couples, 109
    in heterosexual marriages, 182-183
    in historical and cross-cultural inquiry,
        168-172
    in lesbian and gay identity theory, 164-
        166, 166, 183

in psychoanalytic theory, 162-164
omission of in LGB research, 16-17
rejection of as descriptive category, 163
See also Bisexuality, sexual orientation
    theory and; Bisexuality, typologies
    of; Bisexuality research, cross-
    cultural; Bisexuality research, early;
    Homosexuality research, bisexuality
    in; Sexuality research (U.S.), bisexu-
    ality in
Bisexuality, sexual orientation theory and,
    166-168
Bisexuality, typologies of, 181-182
    concurrent, 181, 281
    defense, 182
    equal, 182
    experimental, 182
    historical, 181, 182
    "Latin," 182
    married, 182
    ritual, 182
    secondary, 182
    sequential, 181, 182
    technical, 182
    transitional, 181
Bisexuality research, cross-cultural:
    Africa, 169
    Australia, 169, 171
    Caribbean, 169
    China, 169
    Indonesia, 171
    Japan, 169
    Latin American cultures, 169-170, 171
    Mediterranean cultures, 169
    Melanesia, 169, 171
    New Zealand, 171
    Thailand, 171
    Netherlands, 171
    United Kingdom, 171
Bisexuality research, current trends in,
    190-192
    ethnicity, 191-192, 193
    HIV/AIDS, 191, 193
    transgender status, 192
Bisexuality research, early, 179-183, 190
    on bisexual identity and sexual behav-
        ior, 179, 180-181

on homosexuality and bisexuality in
    heterosexual marriage, 179, 182, 183
on psychological adjustment, 179-180
on typologies of bisexuality, 179, 181-
    182
Bisexuality research, future of, 192-193
Bisexuals, 2
    female, 183
    identity and sexual behavior, 180-181
    positive characteristics of, 180
    See also Bisexual adolescents; Bisexual-
        ity; Bisexuality, typologies of
Blackwood, E., 168, 169, 170
Blanchard, R., 142
Blos, P., 227
Blumenfeld, W., 94, 96, 98, 111
Blumenstein, P., 108
Blumstein, P., 180, 181
Blumstein, P. W., 180, 181
Board for the Advancement of Psychol-
    ogy in the Public Interest (BAPPI),
    315
Bobele, M., 209, 212
Bockting, W. O., 153
Bode, J., 180, 190
Body dysmorphic disorder, 151, 152
Bohan, J., 12, 16
Boles, J., 179
Bolin, A., 140, 141
Bootzin, R. R., 81, 82
Borhek, M. V., 211
Bornstein, K., 136
Boswell, J., 168
Boswell, J. E., 75, 86
Bottoms v. Bottoms, 316
Boulton, M., 171, 182
Boyd-Franklin, N., 27, 34, 210, 215, 264
Bozett, F. W., 182
Bradford, J., 16, 20, 209, 263, 278
Bradley, S., 134
Brannock, J. C., 165, 186, 188
Brinkin, L., 135, 140, 141, 145
Brooks, W. K., 75
Brown, A., 79
Brown, L., 103, 109, 110, 111, 112, 118, 119,
    120, 122, 123
Brown, L. S., 37, 250
Brown, M., 133, 135, 137, 140, 141, 144,
    145, 146, 147, 148, 151, 152, 153, 157
Brown, T., 171

Brownfain, J. J., 183
Browning, C., 85, 86, 231, 234
Bryant, A. S., 209
Buendía Productions, 216
Buhrke, R., 91, 119
Bullock, B., 143
Burch, B., 99, 108
Burke, P., 134
Burzette, R. G., 181, 191
Butler, J., 99
Buxton, A. P., 183

Cabaj, R., 118, 119, 121, 122
Califia, P., 132, 133, 134, 137, 139, 141, 153, 155, 186
Callender, C., 169
Campbell, L., 267
Campbell, S., 108, 110
Campbell v. Sundquist, 316
Cantarella, E., 168, 169
Cantor, J., 91, 92
Caplan, P., 133
Carballo, M., 171, 191
Carballo-Dieguez, A., 192
Carrier, J. M., 168, 170, 171, 181, 182, 191, 192
Carson, S., 177, 181, 191
Cass, V., 106, 107, 115, 229, 263
Cass, V. C., 164, 165
Cassie, N., 105
Catania, J. A., 175, 176
Cates, J. A., 239
Chan, C., 20, 27, 100, 101, 102, 107, 108, 210, 215, 237
Chan, C. S., 191, 263, 264
Chan, Y., 102
Chapman, B. E., 165, 186, 188
Chase, Cheryl, 147
Chetwynd, J., 171
Chukchee shamans, 169
Chumship, 63
Churchill, W., 168
Clark, D. K., 211
Classism, 39, 149
    in psychological practice, 11
    in psychological theory, 11
Clunis, D., 108
Coates, T. J., 175, 176
Cochran, S., 27, 91, 101, 105, 110, 120, 123
Cochran, S. D., 191, 248, 264, 268

Cody, P. J., 188
Cohen, H. J., 270, 271
Cohen, K., 115, 116, 117, 118
Cohen, K. M., 67, 215
Cohen-Ross, J. L., 187
Cole, M., 82
Cole, S. R., 82
Coleman, E., 93, 116, 120, 121, 153, 164, 165, 167, 183, 189, 229
Collier, D., 216
Colorado v. Evans, 316
Comer, R. J., 83
Coming out, 65, 105-108, 144, 164, 165
    as bisexual, 145
    as gay, 145
    as lesbian, 145
    as transgendered person, 144, 145
    as transsexuals, 145
    class and, 107
    culture and, 107-108
    ethnicity and, 107-108
    gender differences in, 107
    stage theory of, 164-165
    within-group differences and, 108
    See also Coming out process; Identity foreclosure
Coming out in workplace, rewards of, 286-287
    fairer compensation, 286-287
    improved work relationships, 286
    increased productivity, 286
    legal standing, 286
    job opportunities, 286
    self-worth, 287
Coming out process, 228-230, 285
    example of, 229-230
    first stage, 164, 229
    fourth stage, 165, 229
    second stage, 164-165, 229
    third stage, 165, 229
    See also Coming out
Commission on Accreditation for Marriage & Family Therapy Education, 213
Comstock, G. D., 77
Conger, J. J., 76, 260, 304
"Conspiratorial invisibility," 35
Conversion therapists, 247, 248-250, 252-253, 259
    referrals to, 259

See also Conversion therapy
Conversion therapy, 2, 93, 150, 245-253
   behavioral interventions, 245
   drugs, 245
   effectiveness of, 247, 249
   effects of, 249-250
   electroshock treatments, 245
   ethical considerations, 251-252
   ethical implications, 249
   homophobia and, 249
   objections to, 247-248
   policy development about, 248-253
   psychoanalytic talk therapy, 245
   surgery, 245
   underlying assumption for, 246
   See also Ex-gay groups
Conversion therapy movement, 245-246
   fundamentalist Christian churches and,
      245, 252, 253
Coombs, M., 136, 137, 144
Cooper, A., 216
Cotton, B., 13, 14
Countertransference, 120, 122, 154
Coxon, T., 171, 182
Creating Change, 290
Cronin, D. M., 164
Cross-blaming, 36
Cross-dressers, 140-141, 142-143
   bisexual, 141
   gay, 141, 142
   heterosexual, 141, 143
   lesbian, 141, 142-143
   See also Cross-dressing; Transvestites
Cross-dressing, 140-141, 143
   therapist acceptance of, 156
   See also Cross-dressers; Transvestites
Crumpacker, L., 77, 85
Custody issues, gay/lesbian adults and,
   66

Dain, H. J., 163, 164
Dallas, J., 245
Dank, B. M., 164, 186, 189
Dannecker, M., 187
D'Augelli, A., 116, 118
D'Augelli, A. R., 67, 215, 226
Davenport, W., 168, 169, 171
Davidson, D., 86
Davis, L., 32

Davison, G., 92
Deabill, G., 183
Deaux, K., 12
De Cecco, J., 167
De Cecco, J. P., 167
DeCrescenzo, T., 226, 239
Defense of Marriage Act (DOMA), 295
Deihl, M., 190
DeLeon, H., 308, 310
Demian, 209
Denmark, F. L., 75, 77
Depression:
   in transgendered psychotherapy cli-
      ents, 151
Desetta, A., 239
Developmental psychology:
   Bem's theory of sexual orientation, 61
   Freudian theory of sexual orientation,
      61
   Sullivan's lust dynamism theory, 61, 63
   See also Teaching developmental psy-
      chology, sexual orientation as
      subject in
Devor, H., 192
*Diagnostic and Statistical Manual of Mental
   Disorders* (DSM)
   declassification of homosexuality as
      mental disorder, 75-76, 82, 86, 91,
      132, 144, 161, 164, 179-180, 193, 245,
      247, 248, 278, 284
   definition of mental disorder, 143
   IV, 138, 142, 143
   III, 132, 138
   III-R, 142
Dignity, 97
DiLapi, E. M., 78
Dince, P. R., 163, 164
Dinno, A. B., 146, 148
Discrimination, 39, 101
   against African Americans, 9
   against gay men, 9
   against lesbians, 9
   against transgendered people, 134-135,
      145, 152, 157
   ethnic, 264
   reactions to perception of, 65
   reactions to reality of, 65
   See also Social discrimination
Dissociation, 7
Divorce, gay/lesbian adults and, 66

Dixon, D., 183
Dixon, J. K., 183
Doctor, R. F., 142
Doherty, W. J., 210
Doll, L., 171, 181, 182, 191
Domestic partnerships, 65
"Don't ask, don't tell" policy, 208, 215
Dover, K. J., 168, 169
Downing, C., 168
Drag, 99
Drag queens, 135
Drellich, M. G., 163, 164
Drescher, J., 246
Due, L., 239
Dworkin, S., 27, 100, 118, 122, 268

Edgar, T. M., 187, 188
Eglinton, J. Z., 168, 169
Ego-dystonic homosexuality, 138, 247
Ehrenberg, M., 14, 15, 16
Ekins, R., 142
Electronic Data Systems (EDS), 295
Elifson, K. W., 179
Ellis, H., 162, 163
Employee resource groups (ERGs), 289-
    291, 297
  characteristics of successful, 293-294
  functions served by, 290
  goal-setting, 292-296
  typical, 290-291
  See also specific names of companies
Erikson, E. H., 227
Espin, O., 27, 37, 100, 101, 102
Espin, O. M., 264
Essed, P., 3
Estepa, A., 239
Ethnic groups, white, 10
Ethnicity/cultural distinctiveness:
  omission of in LGB research, 24-29
  See also Research sampling issues,
    LGBT people of color and
Ethnic populations, historical research
    with, 267-271
Etorre, E. M., 186, 188
Evans, N., 116, 118
Ex-gay groups, 245, 252, 253
Eyler, A. E., 137

Fairchild, B., 211
Falk, R., 190
Family of origin issues, LGB, 66, 110-113,
    230-232
  coming out, 110
  LGB partner's treatment, 112
  pre-coming out coping strategies, 111
  revelation crisis, 111-112
  within-family stigmatization, 112-113
  See also Alternative families
Family psychologists, lesbian/gay-related
    resources for, 214-215
  interviews, 212-213, 217-219
  readings, 210-211, 215-216, 278
  treatment planning, 214, 220-221
  videotapes, 211-212, 216-217, 278
  See also Family psychology, les-
    bian/gays and; Therapists, gender
Family psychology, lesbian/gays and,
    208-210
  myths, 208-209
  See also Family psychologists, les-
    bian/gay-related resources for
Faro, A., 216
Fassinger, R. E., 263
Fast, J., 180
Fay, R. E., 173
Fear, existing biases and, 3
Feinberg, L., 133, 147
Feminist psychology, 3-4
Ferguson, S. A., 19
Fine, M., 17, 29, 30, 32
Firestein, B., 119, 189
Fitzgibbons, R., 311
Fitzpatrick, G., 186, 188
Fivush, R., 98
Fontaine, C., 84
Ford, C. S., 168, 170
Forisha, B. L., 136
Fox, R. C., 61, 181, 183, 185, 188, 189
Fox, R. E., 305, 306, 307
Franklin, A. J., 34
Freiberg, P., 307
Freud, S., 75, 162, 163
Fygetakis, L., 24, 25, 26, 107, 268

Gagnon, J. H., 173, 174, 175, 176
Gagnon, J. M., 164
Galland, V. R., 180

Games, R., 111
Garber, M., 190
Garcia, M. L. G., 171
Garnets, L., 91, 101, 103, 104, 105, 110, 120, 123, 307
Garnets, L. D., 67, 75, 76, 248
Gartrell, N., 121, 122
Gates, H. L., Jr., 20, 21, 35, 36
Gatz, M., 13, 14
Gay community, invisible subculture of, 8
Gay consumer market, corporations targeting, 292
Gay male adolescents, 226, 227
    clinical depression among, 233
    eating disorders among, 233
    family issues, 230-232
    heterosexual assumptions and, 227-228
    hiding sexual orientation, 232-233
    nonsocialization of, 232
    overcompensation by, 233
    personal identity development, 228
    self-harming, 233
    social identity development, 228
    stigmatization of, 228
    substance abuse among, 233
    unsafe sexual behavior among, 233
    See also Coming out process
Gay men, 2, 11, 39, 40
    discrimination against, 9
    massive coming out of, 282
    negative stereotypes of, 10
    of color, 10
    resilience of, 7
    See also Gay male adolescents
Gebhard, P. H., 166, 172
Gebhard, P. W., 229
Geller, T., 190
George, S., 181, 185
Gender:
    as biological construct, 136
    as sociocultural construct, 136, 137
    See also Sex and gender
Gender assignment, 141
Gender-bending, 99
Gender categories:
    and "fitting in," 12
Gender dysphoria, 138, 139-140, 152, 154
    as socially constructed, 138
    in adolescent transsexuals, 147
Gender freedom, 137

Gender identity, 137-138, 156
    expressions of, 137
    versus sexual orientation, 137
Gender identity disorder (GID), 132, 134, 138, 139, 143, 152
    treating toddlers for, 134
    treating children for, 134
    treatment defenses, 134
    See also Gender nonconformity
Gender identity issues:
    in early adolescence, 64
    in early childhood, 62
    in late adolescence, 65
    versus sexual orientation issues, 65
    See also Coming out; Identity foreclosure
Gender nonconformity, 97-98, 99, 139, 152
    continued designation of, 132
    in early childhood, 62
    pathological views of, 131
Gender role expectations, flexibility in, 135-136
Gender role issues, adolescent, 64
Gender roles, 98-99
    as culturally embedded, 11-12
Genital ambiguity:
    in infancy/early childhood, 62
Genital reassignment surgery (GRS), 135, 141, 144, 149, 150
    postponement of, 148
    therapist as gatekeeper to, 154
    understanding process of, 153
Gerard, K., 168
Gerrard, N., 33, 34, 265, 268, 270
Ghoshal, S., 286
Gibson, P., 116, 211, 307
Glenn, A., 105, 119
Gochros, J. S., 183
Gock, T. S., 27
Golden, C., 178, 181
Golombok, S., 98
Gomez, C. A., 191
Gonsiorek, J., 20, 24, 33, 92, 99, 100, 102, 105, 106, 107, 115, 116, 117, 118, 122, 123, 246, 263, 278
Gonsiorek, J. C., 75, 76, 215, 231, 307
Gonzalez, F., 102
Goodchilds, J., 91, 101, 105, 110, 120, 123, 248
Goode, E., 189

Goodwin, B. J., 79
Gordon, B. N., 308
Governor's Commission on Gay and Lesbian Youth, 212
Graham, S., 267, 268
Gramick, J., 107
Green, G., 108
Green, J., 135, 140, 141, 145
Green, R., 108, 109, 115, 142, 145, 164
Green, R.-J., 207, 208, 210, 214, 215
Green, S. K., 209, 212
Greenberg, D. F., 169, 170
Greene, B., 4, 13, 20, 25, 26, 27, 39, 40, 41, 84, 94, 100, 101, 102, 107, 111, 122, 153, 210, 215, 264
Greene, Z., 239
Griffin, C. W., 86
Griffiths, D., 308
Grover, K. P., 151
Gunlach, R. H., 163, 164
Gutierrez, F., 100

Haldeman, D., 92, 96
Haldeman, D. C., 245, 247, 249, 311
Hall, B. A., 79
Hall, R., 4, 13
Hamburg, B. A., 227
Hammersmith, S. K., 178
Hammond, B. E., 142, 143, 144
Hancock, K., 91, 99, 101, 105, 108, 110, 120, 123
Hancock, K. A., 248
Handy, C., 286
Harbeck, K. M., 85, 307
Harris, D. A. I., 180, 185
Harris and Associates, 174
Hartigan, J., 19, 21
Harwell, J. L., 180
Hatterer, L. J., 164, 182
Hays, D., 183
Hayward, N., 211
Hekma, G., 168
Heller, K., 216
Helms, J. E., 268
Helms, Jesse, 135
Hencken, J. D., 188
Hendriks, A. C., 171, 191
Herdt, G., 133, 168, 169, 171, 216
Herek, G., 102, 103, 104, 212, 215
Herek, G. M., 75, 77
Hermaphrodites, 141. See also Intersex people

Heron, A., 239
Hertz, R., 177, 181, 191
Herzog, H. A., 76, 85
Heterocentrism, 230
Heterosexism, 2, 10, 12-13, 39-40, 104-105, 238, 250, 273, 284-285, 298
    conflated aspects of, 2-4
    formation of, 63
    in psychological practice, 11
    in psychological theory, 11
    in teaching psychology, 74-75, 77
    See also Psychology textbooks, homosexuality in; Teaching psychology, confronting heterosexism in
Heterosexual bias, avoiding:
    in language, 317
    in psychological research, 317
Hetrick, E., 111, 228, 232
Hetrick, E. S., 307
Hickok, K., 78
Hijra, 133
Hill, I., 182
Hill, M., 100, 101, 102
Hima, B., 216
Hingsburger, D., 308
Hinsch, B., 169
Hite, S., 177
Hoffman, M., 164
Holland, D., 151
Homophobia, 8, 35, 86, 212, 264, 273
    and transgendered people, 134
    dealing with, 190
    family, 230
    formation of, 63
    instructor dealing with own, 84
    internalized, 190, 212, 232, 247
    See also Conversion therapy
Homosexual behavior:
    in gay bars, 179
    in prisons, 178
    in public places, 179
    male prostitution, 179
    situational, 178-179
Homosexuality, 168-170
    as diagnostic category, 164
    bisexuality and, 162, 163-164
    history of, 168
    illness model of, 164
    in Africa, 169, 170
    in anthropological literature, 168
    in Australia, 169, 170

in Caribbean, 169
in China, 169, 170
in Classical Greece, 168, 169
in Classical Rome, 168, 169
in heterosexual marriages, 182-183
in Japan, 169
in Melanesia, 169, 170, 171
pathology models of, 1
sociopolitical history of, 144
See also Homosexual behavior; Homosexuality, teaching about
Homosexuality, teaching about, 83-85
consequences of, 85-86
experiential strategies, 85
instructor "coming out," 85
instructor homophobia, 84
suggested topics, 84
use of neutral examples, 84
See also Psychology textbooks, homosexuality in; Teaching psychology, confronting heterosexism in
Homosexuality research, bisexuality in, 176-179. *See also* Sexual research (U.S.), bisexuality in
Hooker, E., 1, 75, 76, 164
Human Rights Campaign (HRC), 253, 296
Humphreys, L., 179
Hunt, M., 176
Hunter, J., 228, 234, 235, 236, 237
Hutchins, L., 190

IBM, 282
Icard, L., 100
Identity foreclosure, 106
bisexual self-identification as, 165
reasons for, 106
Ihara, S., 169
Imielinski, K., 182
Internalized prejudice, 102-103
assessment of, 103
Intersex people, 133, 139, 141, 147, 153. *See also* Hermaphodites
Invisibility syndrome, 34-35
Isay, R., 118, 120, 121
ISNA, 147
Isreal, G. E., 137, 138, 139, 140, 141, 142, 151, 152, 153, 154, 156
Iwamasa, G., 268, 269, 270, 273
Iwata, J., 169
Izazola, J., 171

Jackson, J. S., 267
Jackson-Lowman, H., 79
Jacobsen, F., 271
Janus, C. L., 173, 176
Janus, S. S., 173, 176
Jay, K., 177, 188
Johnson, A., 173, 174, 175, 176
Johnson, M. J., 151
Johnson, V. E., 180
Jones, B., 100, 101, 102
Jones, C., 167
Jones, F., 5, 6, 7, 8, 9, 10, 27
Journals, 278
LGB topics in, 57-58
Jubela, J., 216
Judicial system:
nonprotection of rights of LGB people, 75

Kaahumanu, L., 190
Kain, C. D., 151
Kanel, K., 151
Kanouse, D. E., 177, 181, 191
Kaschak, E., 11, 12
Katz, J., 133
Kaufman, B., 311
Kay, P., 239
Kenyon, F. E., 186
Kessler, S., 136
Khan, M., 163
Khayatt, M. D., 85
Kimmel, D., 307
Kimmel, D. C., 63, 65, 67, 75, 76
King, C. A., 229
King, D., 142
King, N., 76, 78, 82
King, T. C., 19
Kinsey, A. C., 166, 172, 229
Kirk, M., 12, 35
Kirk, S., 145, 153
Kirk, S. A., 76
Kite, M., 12
Kitzinger, C., 138
Klassen, A. D., 173
Klein, F., 93, 167, 180, 181, 185
Klein Sexual Orientation Grid (KSOG), 167
Klinger, R., 103, 104
Kochems, L. M., 169
Kohn, B., 190
Kooden, H. D., 178, 185, 186, 187, 188
Koryak shamans, 169

Kozlowski, J., 105
Krafft-Ebing, R., 162
Kremer, M. W., 163, 164
Krestan, J., 108
Kroger, J., 228
Kubie, L. S., 163
Kumar, B., 171
Kurdek, L., 99, 108, 109, 115
Kurdek, L. A., 182
Kutchins, H., 76

Laird, J., 115, 208, 210, 215
Lamborn, H., 148
Lance, L. M., 85
lang, k.d., 133
Latham, J. D., 183
LaTorre, R. A., 180
Laumann, E. O., 173, 174, 175, 176
Lee, K., 102
le Groupe ACSF, 173, 174
Lehne, G. K., 187
Lesbian, Gay, Bisexual, and Transgen-
    dered (LGBT) Psychology, ix, 1, 4.
    See also LGB research; Teaching LGB
    psychology
Lesbian adolescents, 226, 227, 233-234
    clinical depression among, 233
    developmental considerations for, 234-
        236
    eating disorders among, 233
    heterosexual assumptions and, 227-228
    hiding sexual orientation, 232-233
    nonsocialization of, 232
    overcompensation by, 233
    personal identity development, 228
    posttraumatic stress disorder-like syn-
        drome in, 235
    self-harming, 233
    social identity development, 228
    stigmatization of, 228
    substance abuse among, 233
    unsafe sexual behavior among, 233
    See also Coming out process
Lesbian & Gay Parents Association, 216
Lesbian community, invisible subculture
    of, 8
Lesbians, 2, 11, 39, 40
    bisexual behavior among, 178
    discrimination against, 9
    massive coming out of, 282
    negative stereotypes of, 10

resilience of, 7
    See also Lesbian adolescents
Les Comportements Sexuals en France,
    173, 174
Leslie, D., 36
Levado, Rabbi Yaakov, 26
Lever, J., 177, 181, 191
Levy, B., 103, 104
LGB adolescents, 226, 237-238
    defensive strategies, 116
    educational information needed by, 64
    emotional distress/depression/anxiety,
        116
    family relationships, 117, 118, 230-232
    guidelines for working with, 238-241
    heterosexual experimentation by, 64
    homelessness, 118
    identity development of, 115, 228, 238
    internalized societal condemnation, 116
    lack of role models, 117
    parental abuse of, 117
    "passing" as heterosexual, 117
    peer alienation, 117, 118
    prostitution, 118
    social stigmatization, 118, 228
    substance abuse, 116, 118
    suicide risk, 116, 211-212
    victimization of, 116
    See also Bisexual adolescents; Coming
        out; Coming out process; Gay male
        adolescents; Lesbian adolescents;
        LGB adolescents of color
LGB adolescents of color, 226, 237
LGB journals, 54
LGB parents/parenting, 113-115
    adoption, 113, 114
    and contact with heterosexual society,
        113
    artificial insemination, 113, 114
    decisions, 65
    effect on children, 62, 113
    foster parenting, 113
    legal rights/status, 114
    lesbian baby boom, 113
    parental separation, 114
    resources, 316
    surrogate mothers, 114
LGB people, 1
    behavior/identity confusion, 285
    connection with sexuality, 285
    impact of AIDS on, 285

inaccurate assumptions about, 12-13
invisibility of, 284
isolation of, 284
origin of, 285
silence of, 284
stigma against, 284
See also Bisexual men; Bisexual women;
    Coming out; Coming out process;
    Gay men; Lesbians; LGB adoles-
    cents; LGB parents/parenting;
    Workplace issues, LGB
LGB psychologists, 91
    boundaries, 122-123
    dual roles versus overlapping roles, 123
    gender of, 121
    gender role attributions of, 121
    guidelines for working with adolescent
        clients, 238-241
    sexual orientation of, 120-121
    therapy issues, 118-123
    See also Psychotherapy training and
        practice, issues in
LGB research, 40-41
    omission of age as issue in, 13-16
    omission of bisexuality in, 16-17
    omission of ethnicity/cultural distinct-
        iveness in, 24-29
    omission of LGB physically challenged
        people in, 29-33
    omission of socioeconomic issues in,
        17-23
    problems in conducting, 33-34
    sampling biases, 33
LGBT community:
    class in, 287
    gender in, 287
    race in, 287
Limentani, A., 163
Linton, S., 30, 32, 33
Little, D. R., 189
Liu, P., 100, 102
Liu, R., 210, 215
Loiacano, D., 100
Loiacano, D. K., 264, 265
Lopez, S. R., 151
Lorde, A., 41
Lothstein, L. M., 149, 150
Lourea, D. R., 189
Lowe, E., Jr., 211
Lutherans Concerned, 97

MaCarn, S. R., 263
MacDonald, A., 111
MacDonald, A. P., Jr., 188, 189
MacNeill, L., 36
Maddox, B., 182
Madsen, H., 12, 35
Magana, J. R., 171, 181, 182, 191, 192
Mahu people, 169
Mallon, G. P., 229, 231, 232, 239
Malyon, A., 115
Malyon, A. K., 226, 227, 232
Manalasan, M., 102
Marcia, J. E., 227
Markowitz, L., 103
Markowski, K., 105
Marks, H., 216
Markus, E. B., 180
Marmor, J., 164
Martin, A., 111, 211, 247
Martin, A. D., 228, 232, 307
Martin, C. E., 166, 172, 229
Masters, W. H., 180
Masturbation, 64
Masud, R., 163
Matteson, D., 99, 120, 123
Matteson, D. R., 183, 189, 191
Mattison, A., 108
Matusow, A., 190
Mays, V., 27
Mays, V. M., 191, 264, 268
McCord, D. M., 76, 85
McCormack and Associates, Joe, 286
McDonald, G., 78
McDonald, G. J., 178, 187, 229
McKenna, W., 136
McKirnan, D. J., 181, 191
McNaught, B., 287
McWhirter, D., 108
Mead, M., 168, 170
Mellins, C. A., 151
Merriam-Webster's Collegiate Dictionary, 18
Metropolitan Community Church, 97
Michael, R. T., 173, 174, 175, 176
Michaels, S., 173, 174, 175, 176
Miller, B., 180, 182
Minton, H. L., 229
Mio, J. S., 268, 269, 270, 273
Miranda, D., 239
Mishaan, C., 190
Modrcin, M. J., 209
Monette, P., 239
Money, J., 61, 136, 142
Monteflores, C. de, 164, 229

Morales, E., 27, 100, 102, 192, 210, 215, 263, 264, 265
Morales, E. S., 237, 263
Morgan, K., 244
Morgan, K. S., 76
Morin, S. F., 178, 185, 186, 187, 188
Morrow, D. F., 239
Morse, C. R., 185, 189
Mosbacher, D., 216
Multiple identities, managing, 264-265
Murphy, B., 92, 119
Murphy, T., 245
Murray, S. O., 169, 170
Myers, D. G., 81, 82

Nahas, R., 183
Nakajima, G., 102
Nanda, S., 169
National Association for the Research and Therapy of Homosexuality (NARTH), 246, 252
National Gay and Lesbian Task Force (NGLTF), 296
    Creating Change Conference, 296
National Lesbian & Gay Health Foundation, 116
National Lesbian & Gay Task Force Policy Institute, 102, 253
National Youth Advocacy Coalition, 253
Native Americans:
    Two-Spirit people, 133, 169
Needham, R., 226, 239
Neighbors, H. W., 267
Nerison, R. M., 76
Newitz, A., 18, 21, 24
Newman, B. M., 227
Newman, P. R., 227
Newton, D. E., 78, 83
Nichols, M., 189
Nicolosi, J., 246, 311
Nixon administration, 135
Norris, S., 190
Nurius, P. S., 180
Nystrom, N., 91, 244

Oasis/Integrity, 97
Ochs, R., 190
Oetomo, D., 171
Off Pink Collective, 190
O'Hare, W., 18, 19

Olson, E. D., 229
Opler, M., 168
Oppression, multiple sources of, 100-102.
    See also Discrimination
Oppression-privilege spectrum, therapists locating selves on, 36-39
Out and Equal, 290, 296
"Outed," being, 286
Overlooked Opinions survey, 292

Palacios, M., 171
Parker, J., 179
Parker, R. G., 170, 171
Paroski, R., 117, 118
Patterson, C., 113
Patterson, C. J., 67, 215, 216
Paul, J. P., 181, 189
Pearlman, S., 99
Pedersen, P., 268, 270, 273
Pela, R. L., 134, 141
Pendler, B., 308
People of color, LGB
    resilience of, 7-8
    See also African Americans; Research sampling issues, LGBT people of color and; Transgendered people of color
Peplau, L., 91, 99, 101, 105, 108, 110, 120, 123
Peplau, L. A., 83, 248
Perelman-Hall, T., 182
Perlman, G., 121
Perot, Ross, 295
Personal identity development, 228
    versus social identity development, 228
Peterson, J., 171, 181, 182, 191
Peterson, J. L., 191
PFLAG, 211
Pharr, S., 232
Physically challenged people, 10
    omission of in LGB research, 29-33
    resilience of, 7, 8
Pies, C., 114
Pilkington, N., 91, 92
Pollack, R., 154
Pomeroy, W. B., 166, 172, 229
Ponse, B., 178, 307
Ponterotto, J. G., 268, 269
Poor people, 11
    resilience of, 7
Posttraumatic stress, symptoms of

in transgendered psychotherapy clients, 151
Potgieter, C., 27
Prine, K. A., 187
PROGRESS leadership summit, 290, 296
Pryor, D. W., 182, 183, 185, 186, 187, 188
Psychoanalytic theory
  bisexuality in, 162-164
Psychological independence, 7, 9
Psychological integrity, 7, 9
Psychology, heterosexist bias in, 75-76
Psychology textbooks, homosexuality in, 78-83, 86
  content of coverage, 80, 82
  context of coverage, 80, 81-82
  definitions for homosexual, 81
  definitions for sexual orientation, 81
  fair coverage, 79, 82
  ghettoization of topic, 78
  glossary definitions, 80
  good coverage, 79-80, 83
  poor coverage, 79, 82
  quality of coverage, 80, 82-83
  quantity of coverage, 80, 81
Psychotherapy, evolution of sexual orientation, 244-245
  clinical/training implications, 253-259
  future directions in, 259-261
  policy development, 248-253
  See also Conversion therapy
Psychotherapy training and practice, issues in, 91-92
  alternative families, 115
  "coming out," 105-108
  didactic training, 207
  family of origin, 110-113
  gender, 97-100
  heterosexism, 102-105
  LGB parenting, 113-115
  multiple sources of oppression, 100-102
  personal contact, 207-208
  relationships, 108-110
  religion, 94-97
  seeking consultation, 207
  sensitization, 207
  sexual orientation, 92-94, 119
  supervised clinical experience, 207
  youth, 115-118
  See also LGB psychotherapists; Family psychology, lesbians/gays and
Puberty, homosexual orientation and, 64

Racism, 10, 35-36, 39, 149
  in psychological practice, 11
  in psychological theory, 11
  internalized, 8
Rado, S., 163
Ramsey, G., 140, 145, 146, 148, 153, 155
Raymond, D., 94, 96, 98, 111
Read, E., 190
Read, K. E., 179
Reiche, R., 187
Reid, B. V., 136, 137
Reid, F., 216
Reinhardt, R. U., 181, 183
Reinisch, J. M., 181, 191
Reiss, A. J., 179
Relationships, same-sex, 108-110
  bisexual, 109
  gender role socialization and, 109
  income and power issues, 108
  psychotherapists' demeaning/devaluing of, 110
  relationship satisfaction predictors, 108
  sexual exclusivity, 108
  sexual frequency, 108
  social stigmatization, 109
  versus heterosexual relationships, 108
Religion:
  coming out and, 106
  psychotherapy training and practice and, 94-97
Religious institutions:
  condemnation of lesbians/gays, 75, 94-97
  protesting teaching about homosexuality, 86
Religious organizations welcoming LGB people, 86, 97
Remafedi, G., 116, 118, 226, 307
Research. *See* Ethnic populations, historical research with; Research sampling issues, LGBT people of color and
Research abuse, 270
Research sampling issues, LGBT people of color and, 263-267
  barriers, 271-272
  data tabulation, 275
  hidden populations, 272
  mentoring, 272-274
  overcoming obstacles, 275-279
  personal legwork, 278

snowball method, 271
soliciting subjects at conferences, 271
soliciting subjects through targeted
    magazines, 271, 278
tests/assessment instruments, 274-275
Research Triangle Institute, 174
Resilience, psychological
    in socially disadvantaged groups, 4-11
    of African Americans, 7
    See also Strayhorn, Billy
Rhue, S., 27
Rhyne, M. C., 151
Riddle, D. I., 178, 185, 186, 187, 188
Rifkin, A. H., 163, 164
Ritvo, L. B., 162
Rivera, R. R., 75
Roback, H., 149
Roberto, L. G., 142
Robins, E., 164, 177
Rochlin, M., 211
Rodman, Dennis, 133
Rogers, M., 178, 185, 186, 187, 188
Rogers, S. M., 173, 174, 175
Rogers, W. H., 177, 181, 191
Romantic attractions, 137-138
Roscoe, W., 133, 169
Rose, S., 190
Rosenblum, K. E., 17
Ross, H. L., 180, 182
Ross, M. W., 171, 180, 181, 182, 183
Rothblatt, M., 145, 153
Rothblum, E., 20, 216
Rothblum, E. D., 209, 263, 278
Rothenberg, P., 19, 37
Rounsley, C. A., 133, 135, 137, 140, 141,
    144, 145, 146, 147, 148, 151, 152, 153,
    157
Ruan, Fang Fu, 169
Rubenstein, M., 180, 190
Rubenstein, W., 113, 114
Rubin, Z., 83
Rudolph, J., 99, 100, 102, 106, 107, 115, 123
RuPaul, 133
Russell, R., 105, 119
Russo, V., 85
Rust, P., 100, 101, 102, 111
Rust, P. C., 178, 181, 183, 185, 186
Ryan, C., 16, 20, 209, 263, 278

Saghir, M. T., 164, 177
Salovey, P., 83

Same-sex marriages, 67, 144
Samuels, A., 183
Sanchez-Hucles, J., 39, 40, 41
Sandell, J., 22, 23
Sanders, S. A., 181, 191
Sandfort, T. G. M., 171
Sang, B. E., 178, 185, 186, 187, 188
Satinover, J., 311
Savin-Williams, R. C., 67, 100, 115, 116,
    117, 118, 212, 215, 227, 236, 307
Schaecher, R., 228, 237, 307
Schafer, S., 180, 186
Schaie, K. W., 13
Scheer, J., 32
Schlesinger, E. G., 237
Schmitt, J., 108, 109
Schneider, M., 27, 226, 228, 233
Schott, R. L., 142
Schroeder, C. S., 308
Schultz, S. J., 164, 229
Schwartz, P., 108, 180, 181
Schwartz, R., 121
Scott, J., 190
Segregated communities, evolution of al-
    ternative self-images in, 8
Sell, R. L., 174, 175
Sepekoff, B., 93, 167
Sepulveda, J., 171
Sergent, B., 168, 169
Sex:
    as biological construct, 136-137
    See also Sex and gender
Sex and gender:
    essentialist binary view, 136, 137, 157
    social constructionist view, 136
Sexism, 10, 39, 149
    in psychological practice, 11
    in psychological theory, 11
Sexual behavior:
    as culturally defined, 235
Sexual/erotic arousal responses, learning:
    gender difference in, 64
Sexual experimentation, 64
Sexuality:
    as contextual, 265
Sexuality research (U.S.), bisexuality in,
    171, 172-179
    Center for Health Studies (CHPS) re-
        search, 174, 175
    general surveys of sexual behavior,
        172-179
    Janus study, 173, 176

Kinsey study, 172-173, 174, 175
National AIDS Behavioral Survey (NABS), 176
National Health and Social Life Survey (NHSLS), 173, 174, 175, 176
National Opinion Research Corporation (NORC) surveys, 173, 174, 175
National Survey of Sexual Attitudes and Lifestyles, 173
Sexual orientation, 67, 98-99, 137, 156
  as business issue, 299-301
  as social construct, 138
  criteria for defining, 167
  culture and, 94, 100-102
  early adolescent issues in, 64
  psychotherapists' knowledge of, 92-94
  versus gender identity issues, 137, 153
Sexual orientation, dichotomous model of, 166, 168, 180, 194
  reexamination of, 161
Sexual orientation, multidimensional model of, 162, 166, 168, 193, 194-195
Sexual orientation theory, bisexuality and, 166-168
Shidlo, A., 102
Shilts, R., 282
Shively, M., 167
Shively, M. G., 167
Shuster, R., 189
Siegel, R. J., 3, 36
Siegel, S., 210, 211
Simmons, D. S., 210
Simon, W., 164
Simoni, J. M., 75
Sittitrai, W., 171
Slater, B., 118
Slater, B. R., 307
Slater, C. A., 190
Smith, A., 27
Smith, T. W., 175
Snyder, P., 216
Socarides, C., 311
Socarides, C. W., 75, 164
Socarides, Charles, 246
Social discrimination:
  in early childhood, 62
Social identity development:
  versus personal identity development, 228
Society for Human Resource Management, 288, 295

Society of Human Resource Management, 288
Solomon, S., 29
Sommers, M. A., 187
Sophie, J., 165, 263
Spada, J., 177
Spira, A., 173, 174
Sprenkle, D., 208
Stall, R., 175, 176
Standards of Care for Gender Dysphoric Persons, 150
Starcevick, M. M., 286
Stearns, S., 113, 114
Stein, T., 103, 104, 118, 119, 120, 121
Stein, T. A., 245, 248
Stekel, W., 163
Stevens, C., et al., 190
Stokes, J. P., 181, 191
Stoller, R. J., 163
Stonewall Rebellion, 134-135
Storms, M. D., 61, 167
Stowell, S. J., 286
Strassburger, E., 178, 185, 186, 187, 188
Strayhorn, Billy, 5-6
Strommen, E., 103, 111, 112
Sue, D., 82
Sue, D. W., 268, 273
Sue, S., 82
Sullivan, H. S., 61
Sullivan, T., 233
Sulloway, F. J., 162
Swartz, L. H., 145
Szasz, T. S., 164

Tafoya, T., 27, 133, 191
Tarver II, D. E., 137, 138, 139, 140, 141, 142, 151, 152, 153, 154, 156
Tavris, C., 83
Tawil, O., 171
Teaching developmental psychology, sexual orientation as subject in, 59-61, 66-67
  adulthood/aging bibliographic sources, 69
  adulthood topics, 65-66
  aging as topic, 66
  children/youth bibliographic sources, 67-68
  couple relationship bibliographic sources, 70-71
  early adolescence topics, 63-64

general bibliographic sources, 67, 72
infancy/early childhood topics, 62
late adolescence topics, 65
middle childhood topics, 63
parenting bibliographic sources, 71-72
using videotapes, 63
See also Developmental psychology
Teaching LGB psychology, 54
  activities/assignments, 46, 51-52, 55-57
  affirmative model, 76
  class composition, 46, 49-50
  confronting heterosexism in, 76-77
  course content, 46, 48-49
  course structure/goals, 46, 47-48
  inclusive curriculum rationale, 77
  instructors' issues/experience, 46, 53-54
  student assessment, 46, 52
  See also Homosexuality, teaching about; LGB journals; Psychology textbooks, homosexuality in
Texas Instruments (TI), ERG of, 296
Textbooks. See Psychology textbooks, homosexuality in
Therapists, gender:
  as GRS gatekeepers, 154
  as healers, 154
  capacity for introspection, 255
  challenging own biases, 151, 155, 157, 255-256, 260
  discriminatory practice, 254-255
  ethical considerations, 254-259
  gender security of, 155
  professional ethics, 255-256
  referral to other therapist, 256
  training, 155-156
  transgendered, 155
  treating heterosexually married LGB people, 256-257
  treating minority LGB people, 254-255, 260
  treating minors, 258-259
  treating same-sex couples, 257
  trust between clients and, 153-154
  understanding LGB relationships, 257
  See also Conversion therapy; Family psychologists, lesbian/gay-related resources for; Transgendered counseling/psychotherapy clients

Tielman, R. A. P., 171, 191
Townsend, M., 91, 92
Transference, 121
Transgender:
  classifying, 142-145
  defining, 139-141
Transgendered children. See Transsexual children
Transgendered counseling/psychotherapy clients, 150-155
  common mental health issues in, 151-152
  culturally sensitive treatment for, 151, 157
  gender dysphoria/gender identity disorder versus nonconforming gender identity and, 152
  gender identity issues, 150, 153
  group therapy for, 151
  GRS issues, 150
  psychological problems, 150
  routine life problems, 150, 151
  severe psychopathology in, 151-152
  sexual orientation issues, 153
  support groups for, 151
  therapist's trusting relationship with, 153-154
  traditional psychotherapeutic approaches for, 150
  treating oppression of, 152-153
  See also Adjustment difficulties; Depression; Posttraumatic stress, symptoms of; Therapists, gender
Transgendered people, 11, 133, 134, 156, 157
  civil rights protection for, 135
  "closeted," 135
  coming out as, 144
  discrimination against, 134, 145, 152, 157
  hostility against, 145
  low self-esteem, 145
  oppression of, 145, 157
  psychological issues, 145-149
  See also Androgynists; Intersex people; Transgendered counseling/psychotherapy clients; Transgendered people of color; Transgenderists; Transsexual adolescents; Transsex-

ual children; Transsexuals;
   Transvestites
Transgendered people of color, 148-149
   classism and, 149
   discrimination against, 149
   FTM, 149
   racism and, 149
   sexism and, 149
   transphobia and, 149
Transgenderism, 142
   history of, 133
   homosexuality and, 144
   possible causes of, 142
   prevalence of, 135
   sociopolitical history of, 144
   unresolved, 152
Transgender issues, 131-132
   in employment, 135
   in legislation, 135
   in social services, 135
   political agendas and, 135
Transgenderists, 139, 140, 141, 153
Transphobia, 133, 149
Transsexual adolescents, 147-148, 157
   as runaways, 148
   body dissociation, 147
   body image, 147
   family abuse of, 148
   family ostracization of, 148
   gender dysphoria in, 147
   homeless, 148
   parental pressure to conform, 147
   school dropping out by, 148
   self-mutilation among, 148
   sexual orientation confusion, 147-148
   social isolation of, 147
   substance abuse among, 148
   suicide risk among, 148
Transsexual children, 146-147, 157
   cross-gender play by, 146
   daydreaming and, 147
   desire to please parents, 146
   revealing gender choice, 146
   secrecy and, 147
   victimization of, 147
Transsexualism, 98
Transsexuals, 11, 139, 140, 141, 142, 144
   FTM, 140, 145

gay, 145
lesbian, 145
MTF, 140, 145
negative reactions toward, 145
postponing GRS, 148
role-playing by, 148
stress-related medical conditions of,
   148
treatment for, 142
See also Transsexual adolescents; Trans-
   sexual children
Transvestic fetishism, 132, 142, 143
Transvestites, 139, 140-141, 142. *See also*
   Cross-dressers; Cross-dressing;
   Transvestic fetishism
Travis, T-M. C., 17
Tremble, B., 27, 233
Troiden, R., 115
Troiden, R. R., 164, 165, 187, 189, 229, 263,
   307
Trujillo, C., 27, 102
Tucker, N., 190
Tully, B., 132, 142
Turley, M., 183
Turner, C. F., 173, 174, 175
Twining, A., 180, 183, 189
Twitchell, J., 180

U.S. Chamber of Commerce, 286
Unger, R., 136
United Church of Christ, 97
Uribe, V., 307

Valdespino, J., 171
Valenzuela, W., 239
Vance, B. K., 186
Vander Haegen, E. M., 77, 85
Veniegas, R., 108, 110
Victimization of LGBT people, 102-104,
   147
   harassment, 102
   moral condemnation, 102
   murder, 103
   physical assault, 102, 103, 116, 147, 158
   police harassment/abuse, 103
   property damage, 103
   response to, 104

sexual abuse, 147
threats of violence, 102, 103
verbal abuse, 103, 116, 147
Virulrak, S., 171
Vitale, A., 154, 155, 156
Vulnerability, psychological:
social adversity and, 5

Wachtel, P., 3, 11
Wade, C., 83
Wadsworth, J., 173, 174, 175, 176
Waldron, J., 289
Walker, G., 210, 216
Walker, P. A., 150
Walton, P., 211, 212, 216
Warren, C. A. B., 178
Washington State Psychological Association, 249
Committee on Lesbian, Gay and Bisexual Concerns, 248-249
Watanabe, T., 169
Watter, D. N., 77, 83
Wayson, P. D., 185, 187
Weber, A. L., 85
Weinberg, G., 164
Weinberg, M. S., 177, 178, 180, 182, 183, 185, 186, 187, 188
Weinberg, T. S., 187
Weiner, I. B., 63
Weininger, O., 162
Weinrich, J., 27, 75, 76, 85, 215
Weise, E., 103
Weise, E. R., 190
Wellings, K., 173, 174, 175, 176
Wells, H., 180
Wells, J. A., 174, 175
Wendenberg, K., 180
Weston, K., 216
White, G. D., 183
White, K., 216
White, M., 96
Whitehead, H., 169
Whitehead, T. L., 136, 137
Whitlock, K., 78, 307
Whitney, C., 183
Wilbur, C. B., 163, 164
Wildman, S., 37
Williams, C. J., 177, 180, 182, 183, 185, 186, 187, 188

Williams, D., 267
Williams, W., 133
Williams, W. L., 27, 216
Wilson, K. K., 132, 134, 138, 142, 143, 144, 152
Winegarten, B., 105
Winer, L., 216
Wirth, A. G., 86
Wirth, M. J., 86 Wolf, D. G., 178, 190
Wolf, T., 93
Wolf, T. J., 167, 183, 189
Wolff, C., 180
Women's Educational Media, 63
Wooden, W., 178
Woog, D., 212
Workplace issues, LGB, 282-283, 298
Affirmative Action (AA) policy, 294
awareness activities, 297
business advocacy for gay-inclusive employment policies, 291-292
domestic partner benefit (DPB) policies, 282-283, 284, 286, 287, 288, 289, 291, 292, 295, 298
employer ignorance on LGB equity, 283
Equal Employment Opportunity (EEO), 294
gay employees' wants, 287-288
gay-inclusive nondiscrimination policies, 282, 284, 287, 289, 291-292, 294, 298
increasing workplace equity, 291-292
in high-tech *Fortune* companies, 289
in Iowa City (IA), 289
in Minnesota, 289
military, 282, 286
off-line resources for, 296
on-line resources for, 296
sample workshop, 299-301
self-education on LGB issues, 283-285
sexual orientation in personnel policies, 288
See also names of specific corporations;
Coming out in workplace, rewards of; Employee resource groups (ERGs)
Wray, M., 18, 21, 24
Wright, K., 137
Wyche, K. F., 18, 19
Wyers, N. L., 209

Wypij, D., 174, 175

Yoder, J., 105
Young, A., 177, 188

Zacks, E., 108, 109, 214
Zeldes, K., 217
Ziemba-Davis, M., 181, 191
Zimmerman, B., 78
Zinik, G. A., 180, 185, 186, 187
Zucker, K., 134

About the Editors

Beverly Greene, PhD, ABPP, is Professor of Psychology at St. John's University, and a certified clinical psychologist in private practice in New York City. A Diplomate in Clinical Psychology from the American Board of Professional Psychology, she is a Fellow of the American Psychological Association and the Academy of Clinical Psychology. A recipient of a 1994 Distinguished Humanitarian Award from the American Association of Applied and Preventive Psychology, the Association for Women in Psychology's 1991 Women of Color Psychologies Publication Award, she received the 1992 Award for Distinguished Professional Contributions to Ethnic Minority Issues from Division 44 citing her development of lesbian affirmative theoretical perspectives and clinical applications with African American women. She is a recipient of 1995 and 1996 Psychotherapy With Women Research Awards from the Division of the Psychology of Women of APA; a 1995 Distinguished Publication Award and 1995 Women of Color Psychologies Publication Award from the Association for Women in Psychology for her coedited book, *Women of Color: Integrating Ethnic and Gender Identities in Psychotherapy;* and the 1996 Outstanding Achievement Award from the American Psychological Association's Committee on Lesbian, Gay and Bisexual Concerns.

She is a member of the editorial boards of numerous scholarly journals and has served as an Associate Editor of the journal *Violence Against Women.* She is an active contributor to a range of professional books and journals on topics including psychotherapy with African Americans, the effects of multiple identities in the psychologies of women of color, and the integration of training on cultural diversity in the delivery of clinical psychological services. She is coauthor of the undergraduate text, *Abnormal Psychology in a Changing World,* and coeditor of *Psychotherapy with African American Women: Psychodynamic Perspectives.*

Gladys L. Croom, PsyD, is a certified clinical psychologist and sole proprietor of Delwe Psychological Services in Homewood, Illinois. She is the Director of the Center for Intercultural Clinical Psychology at the Chicago School of Professional Psychology. She received her Doctorate in Psychology from the Illinois School of Professional Psychology with a specialization in Health Psychology (1993) and is a member of the American Psychological Association (Divisions 9 44, and Family Psychology), the Association for Women in Psychology, the Association for the Advancement of Behavior Therapy, and the National Association of Forensic Counselors.

She is an active presenter at professional conferences and in service training. She has developed research on relationship expectations and self actualizing tendencies of African American lesbian and bisexual women, psychological effects of racism and homophobia, developing cultural competence in delivering psychological services to diverse populations, and psychotherapy with lesbians and gay men. Other research includes assessing the effects of interventions on school aged children living in high risk areas for exposure to PTSD triggers, and the effects of violence on children. Under the name "Jera," she is a writer/performer, and the author of "If you see yourself, say Amen," a performance piece divided into 5 poems that offers a woman-centered look at the struggles and conflicts in lesbian relationships.

A recipient of the Jacob Markovitz Memorial Scholarship, and the Award for Outstanding Doctoral Graduate of the Year from the Illinois School of Professional Psychology, she is also the recipient of the 1991 National Council of Professional Schools of Psychology Award for her outstanding contributions to the study of racial/ethnic diversity.

About the Contributors

Clinton W. Anderson, MA holds a master's degree in psychology from Harvard University. He has served as the American Psychological Association's (APA) Lesbian, Gay, and Bisexual Concerns Officer since 1987 and staffs the APA Committee on Lesbian, Gay, and Bisexual Concerns. As LGB Concerns Officer he provides information, referral, and consultation on lesbian, gay, and bisexual issues to APA members, public policymakers, policy advocates, and the public. He also provides policy analysis, supports APA policy development, and advocates APA policy.

Christine Browning, PhD received her doctorate in clinical psychology from the University of Maine at Orono in 1984. She is currently a senior staff psychologist at the University of California, Irvine Counseling Center and in private practice. At UC-Irvine, she directs the Peer Counseling Program for Lesbian, Gay, and Bisexual Issues and is a lecturer in women's studies where she has taught undergraduate classes on lesbian, gay, and bisexual psychology. She has served in a variety of capacities within Division 44 including President (1997-1998). She has also served on the APA Committee of Lesbian, Gay, and Bisexual Issues and the APA Committee on Women. She has presented to numerous professional organizations and campus groups on lesbian, gay, and bisexual psychology and published in the area of lesbian psychology and women's issues.

Ronald C. Fox, PhD is a psychotherapist and clinical supervisor in private practice in San Francisco. He received his doctorate in clinical psychology from the California Institute of Integral Studies. He has presented scholarly papers, workshops, and in-service trainings on sexual orientation and sexual identity issues at graduate schools, community mental health agencies, and at professional and LGB community conferences. He is the author of a large-scale study of bisexual identity development and several chapters on bisexual issues in LGB psychology books. He is currently working on edited volumes on contemporary research on bisexuality and on affirmative psychotherapy with bisexual women and bisexual men. He has served as an elected Member-at-Large of the APA Division 44 Executive Committee, co-chair of the Committee on Bisexual Issues in Psychology, and a member of the Joint Task Force on Guidelines for Psychotherapy with LGB clients.

Kathy A. Gainor, PhD is Assistant Professor of Psychology at Montclair State University in Montclair, New Jersey. She has served as a counseling psychologist at the Rutgers College Counseling Center at Rutgers, The State University of New Jersey in New Brunswick. She received her doctorate in counseling psychology from Michigan State University. Her publications and research interests include social cognitive factors affecting academic and career development in black students, racial identity development, psychotherapy with black women, cross-cultural supervision, and integrating cultural diversity in training and practice. She provides consultation and training on counseling gay, lesbian, bisexual, and transgendered youth and college students.

Susan Gore, PhD is the principal of The Mentor Group, a consulting firm providing workforce diversity, communications, and mentoring program assistance to corporate and nonprofit clients. She received her doctorate in social psychology from Vanderbilt University and taught in the United States and Europe. She has served as executive director of the National Women's Studies Association and has worked in corporate marketing positions with GTE, the Paul Revere Companies, and as the first Director of Institutional Marketing for Working Assets. She established The Mentor Group in 1991 to devote her full attention to organizational consulting. She also is a frequently invited speaker on issues such as mentoring, gender and sexual orientation as a business issue. She is the author of a forthcoming book on gay issues in the workplace.

Robert-Jay Green, PhD is Professor and Director of Family/Child Psychology Training at the California School of Professional Psychology,

San Francisco Bay Campus. Among his writings are two books, *Lesbians and Gays in Couples and Families: A Handbook for Therapists* (edited with Joan Laird, 1996); and *Family Therapy: Major Contributions* (edited with James L. Framo, 1981). He is a Fellow and Vice President for Public Interest and Diversity of Division 43 (Family Psychology) of the American Psychological Association (APA) and a Fellow of the American Association for Marriage and Family Therapy (AAMFT). He currently serves on the editorial advisory boards of *Family Process, Journal of Marital & Family Therapy,* and *Journal of Feminist Family Therapy.*

Douglas C. Haldeman, PhD is a counseling psychologist in independent practice in Seattle. He is Clinical Professor of Psychology at the University of Washington, and past chair of the American Psychological Association's Committee on Lesbian, Gay, and Bisexual Concerns. He has published and lectured extensively on clinical practice and training issues for those working with lesbian, gay, and bisexual clients and is one of the authors of APA's policy on "Appropriate Therapeutic Responses to Sexual Orientation." He is past president of the Society for the Psychological Study of Lesbian, Gay, and Bisexual Issues.

Kristin A. Hancock, PhD is Professor of Psychology at John F. Kennedy University's Graduate School of Professional Psychology in Orinda, California and a clinical psychologist in private practice. She is past chair of the Association of Lesbian and Gay Psychologists, past chair of the American Psychological Association's Committee on Lesbian and Gay Concerns, Committee on Women, and past president of Division 44. A Fellow of the American Psychological Association, she has received both the Distinguished Service and Professional Contribution Awards from Division 44 and the Outstanding Contribution Award from the Committee on Lesbian and Gay Concerns. She is currently serving as Co-Chair of a Division 44/Committee on Lesbian, Gay, and Bisexual Concerns Joint Task Force on Guidelines for Psychotherapy with Gay, Lesbian, and Bisexual Clients. Her work has focused on the education and training of psychotherapists in gay, lesbian, and bisexual issues.

Joyce Hunter, DSW is Director, Community Liaison Program, and Research Scientist at the HIV Center for Clinical and Behavioral Studies/New York State Psychiatric Institute, where she is currently examining a prevention/intervention program for youth, "Working It

Out," based on a video of scenes from the lives of lesbian/gay youth. She is also Assistant Professor at the Deparment of Psychiatry, College of Physicians and Surgeons, Columbia University. She is consulting editor of the *Encyclopedia of AIDS*, serves on the editorial board of *Journal of Gay & Lesbian Social Services*, is co-founder of the Harvey Milk High School, and has written numerous journal articles.

Craig Kain, PhD received his doctorate in counseling psychology from the University of Southern California in 1990. He is currently a consultant and clinician in private practice in Long Beach, California. He is past chair of the graduate program in psychology at Antioch University Los Angeles and is the author of *Positive: HIV Affirmative Counseling* (1996). He has been active in Division 44 in many capacities including newsletter editor and co-chair of the Public Policy Task Force. Currently, he is working as a consultant to promote graduate education on HIV/AIDS for the APA Office of Psychology Education (HOPE) program. He is a frequent presenter on the pedagogy of lesbian, gay, and bisexual courses.

Douglas C. Kimmel, PhD is Professor Emeritus of Psychology at City College, City University of New York where he had been on the faculty since 1970. He is author of *Adulthood and Aging: An Interdisciplinary Developmental View* (3rd ed., 1990; Japanese translaton, 1994); coauthor with Irving B. Weiner of *Adolescence: A Developmental Transition* (2nd ed., 1995); and coeditor with Linda D. Garnets of *Psychological Perspectives on Lesbian and Gay Male Experiences* (1993). He was a Fulbright Lecture Professor in Japan (1994-1995). His work in lesbian and gay psychology include: chair of the Association of Lesbian and Gay Psychologists (1977), chair of APA's Committee on Lesbian and Gay Concerns (1983), president of the Society for the Psychological Study of Lesbian and Gay Issues (Division 44) of the American Psychological Association (1986-1987), and APA Council Representative for Division 44 (1992-1994). His research on older gay men began in 1976, and he was a cofounder of SAGE (Senior Action in a Gay Environment) in New York City in 1977.

Gerald P. Mallon, DSW is Assistant Professor at the Hunter College School of Social Work. He also serves as director of Green Chimneys Children's Services Residential Program for gay/bi/transgendered youth. His current research focuses on child welfare practice with gay and lesbian children, youth, and families. He is also the author of *Foundations of Social Work Practice with Lesbian and Gay Persons* and *We Don't Exactly Get the Welcome Wagon: The Experiences of Gay and Lesbian Adolescents in Child Welfare Systems.*

Jane M. Simoni, PhD is a clinical psychologist who received her doctorate from the University of California, Los Angeles, in 1993. She interned at UCLA's Neuropsychiatric Institute and Hospital and was a National Cancer Institute Fellow at the Institute for Prevention Research, University of Southern California School of Medicine. As an Aaron Diamond Postdoctoral Fellow at the Columbia University School of Social Work, she conducted a longitudinal study of coping and psychological adaptation among women living with HIV/AIDS. Currently, she is an Assistant Professor at Ferkauf Graduate School of Psychology, Yeshiva University, Bronx, New York. Funded by the National Institute of Mental Health, she is currently evaluating the efficacy of a peer support intervention to enhance adherence to medication regimens among men and women with HIV/AIDS. She has published extensively and presented nationally and internationally on her research and clinical interests, which incorporate aspects of clinical, community, health, and counseling psychology. Her main research focus is identifying how cultural strengths and social support mediate psychological well-being and resilience among stigmatized groups such as gays and lesbians, ethnic minorities, and people living with HIV/AIDS.